SCOTTISH LITERATURE INTERNATIONAL

The Crooked Dividend

Essays on Muriel Spark

Edited by
GERARD CARRUTHERS
and HELEN STODDART

Editorial Assistant: STEVEN HARVIE

Occasional Papers: Number 24
Association for Scottish Literature

Published by
Scottish Literature International
Scottish Literature
7 University Gardens
University of Glasgow
Glasgow G12 8QH

Scottish Literature International is an imprint of
the Association for Scottish Literature

www.asls.org.uk

ASL is a registered charity no. SC006535

First published 2022

© ASL and the individual contributors

All rights reserved. No part of this book may be
reproduced, stored in a retrieval system, or
transmitted in any form or means, electronic,
mechanical, photocopying, recording or otherwise,
without the prior permission of the
Association for Scottish Literature.

A CIP catalogue for this title
is available from the British Library

ISBN 978-1-908980-33-5

Contents

Acknowledgements   vii

Introduction: Critical Concerns for Muriel Spark   ix
    Gerard Carruthers

I: SPARK, BIOGRAPHY, AND FEMALE EXPERIENCE

One   'I knew what was what': Correspondence and the Meta-Archival in the Muriel Spark Archive   1
    Colin McIlroy

Two   Muriel Spark's Waywardness   25
    Carole Jones

Three   Spark's Spinsters: Bedsits and Boarding Houses in the Novels of Muriel Spark   44
    Susannah Thompson

Four   Between Desire and Control: The Fashioned Image in Muriel Spark's Life and Fiction   63
    Monica Germanà

Five   'Unfortunately you have left out all the love poems': Spark in Love   88
    Willy Maley and Dini Power

II: WRITING MATERIALS

Six   Muriel Spark and J. M. Barrie   103
    Cairns Craig

Seven   All the Abbess's Nuns: Muriel Spark and the Idioms of Watergate   126
    Colin Kidd

Eight	'Making patterns with facts': Unmaking History in *The Prime of Miss Jean Brodie* **Catriona M. M. Macdonald**	144
Nine	Muriel Spark and the 'Hired Grammarians' **Helen Stoddart**	161
Ten	Already and Not Yet Written: Unfinished Acts of Writing in the Novels of Muriel Spark **Mark Currie**	180
Eleven	Muriel Spark's Windows and the Architecture of Surveillance **Amy Woodbury Tease**	204
Twelve	Art and Industry Must Walk Hand in Hand: Muriel Spark and Twentieth-Century Design Ideology **Fiona Jardine**	223
Thirteen	The Publishing Scene in *A Far Cry from Kensington* **Ernest Schonfield**	247
Fourteen	Dramatic Contexts and Metatheatricality in Muriel Spark's Writing for Performance **Ian Brown**	264

Notes on Contributors — 289

Index — 293

The various energies, archival and critical, that inform this collection are intimately connected to the acquisition and development of the Muriel Spark archive at the National Library of Scotland, and were crucially propelled early on by Kenneth Dunn and Sally Harrower to both of whom this volume is dedicated.

Acknowledgements

Some of the essays in this volume began life as papers delivered at the Muriel Spark Centenary Symposium, 1 and 2 February 2018 at the University of Glasgow. Others did not, and are written especially for this volume. The editors gratefully acknowledge the support of the School of Critical Studies and the University of Glasgow towards the 2018 symposium, as well as that of the National Library of Scotland, most especially Robin Smith (Associate Director of Collections), Kenneth Dunn (Head of Archives and Manuscript Collections), and Dr Colin McIlroy (Curator of Modern Literary Manuscripts). We are grateful also to the assiduous work of Steven Harvie acting as editorial assistant and in compiling the index. Both editors would also like to thank the kind staff of the McFarlin Library, University of Tulsa, for facilitating their research trips there to work on the wonderful Spark manuscript collection. Professor Ian Brown (Publications Convener), Duncan Jones (Director) and the Publications Board of the Association for Scottish Literature commissioned this book and brought it to publication. We are grateful for their kind professionalism. We most gratefully acknowledge also the assistance of Penelope Jardine in the completion of this volume.

Quoted with permission are the letter to Muriel Spark by John Updike. Copyright © 2021, John Updike (2021), and the two letters to Muriel Spark by Evelyn Waugh. Copyright © 2021, Evelyn Waugh (2021), used by permission of The Wylie Agency (UK) Limited. We gratefully acknowledge the kind assistance of the Wylie Agency here.

Quoted by permission are extracts from materials held in the Muriel Spark Archive at the National Library of Scotland: from 'Author's note' dated New York November 1962; from letter to Ivan von Auw dated 3 November 1962; from letter to literary agent, John Smith, 16 November 1962. © Copyright Administration Limited. We gratefully acknowledge the kind assistance of David Higham Associates here.

Introduction: Critical Concerns for Muriel Spark

GERARD CARRUTHERS

In the writing of Muriel Spark (1918–2006), persistent and never entirely settled critical concerns emerge. Readers, students and scholars have repeatedly returned to two areas, each of which is reflected in the broad division of this volume: first, into questions of biography and female experience and secondly, around issues of textuality, materiality and creative writing. In both terrains Spark's numerous memorable female characters and the author's own colourful cultural career can be discerned and dissected. Spark's novels, short stories, poetry and drama are closely interlinked in their reflection on, for instance, the vocation of the female artist, as well as the minutiae of Spark's own practice as a published writer for more than sixty years. Many of her fictional protagonists and narrative scenarios centre on publishing, communication and the media. Her striking formal fictional practices reveal, to some extent, her interest in the endeavours of the French *nouveau roman* at the mid-point of the twentieth century, but also reflect the lasting climate of post-modernity in the early twenty-first century. Spark's fictional apparatuses are invariably bound up with her role as a satirist, often acerbic, sometimes characterised by commentators as a cool or even chillingly mocking one. Yet these formal mechanics also collide and collaborate with the identification of Spark as a religious, specifically Roman Catholic, writer and sit to some degree in tension with her long-standing interest in the Romantic idea of the artist – the exuberant, lyrically-voiced visionary. Free artistic agency (the ur-quality of Romanticism), the parameters of the religious cosmos and, related to both of these things, wilfulness and morality in quotidian life are all concerns elegantly, and also problematically, bound up in the package of Spark's fiction.[1] The essays that follow unravel the still surprising Sparkian package in a wide variety of ways and speak both to long-established critical interests as well as to more recent critical emphases.

Spark's own reading practices as a critic, editor and life-writer repay close, extended study. Her *Child of Light: A Reassessment of Mary Wollstonecraft Shelley* (1951), *John Masefield* (1953) and *Emily Brontë: Her life and work* (1953), the latter written with Derek Stanford, are all highly readable and full of aperçus. Although the first and last of these studies are the most revealing when read alongside her own fiction, each one remains highly accessible and illuminating, even sixty years after publication. Not a feminist in any self-declared or programmatic sense, Spark's work on Shelley and Brontë was none the less an important part of an accelerating criticism of women's writing in the second half of the twentieth century. As Martin Stannard points out, Spark is at the vanguard of restoring Mary Shelley to serious critical attention; moreover, the 'Gothic surrealism' of which Spark sees Shelley as a progenitor is also continuously active as a developing *modus operandi* in Spark's own novels, for instance in *The Comforters* (1957), *Not to Disturb* (1971) and also in *The Prime of Miss Jean Brodie* (1961).[2] *Jean Brodie* is less explicitly Gothic, supernatural or surreal than these other two novels, but still contains implicit Gothic moments, for instance when Jean Brodie describes her dead lover Hugh Carruthers, ostensibly among the fallen in the Great War, as both a singer (like one of her present-day lovers, Gordon Lowther) and a painter (like another, Teddy Lloyd). In other words, Hugh, like Frankenstein's creature, is constructed by Brodie from the body parts of others. This wry reversal of *Frankenstein*, the dead made from the living as opposed to the other way around, also exemplifies the kind of compressed wit (referential and at the same time formally deep and expansive) by which Spark is often identified as a poet in a novelist's skin. Willy Maley and Dini Power take a rare critical look at Spark's love poetry and highlight a distinctive skill. As they observe, however, across 'her writing Spark tends to depict love and lovers with deep cynicism'. It may be the case that the much more oblique and generally more 'private' form of prose fiction suited Spark temperamentally, especially at a time in the mid-twentieth century where the raw sensuality of the work of Dylan Thomas or the signature quality of the Confessional poets did not suit her own more reserved personality. Maley and Power in their treatment are suggestive about the private Spark personality as they detect a certain occlusion in Spark's poems, even while these relate to outward anniversary celebrations, which can credibly be seen to have autobiographical relevance.³

As her response to biographical writing about her demonstrates, Spark was far from comfortable with such public examination. Her 'official' biography appeared in 2009, three years after her death. Martin Stannard had been her choice of biographer and produced a book that is excellent for both its stylishness and thorough research, qualities that Spark herself exemplified across most of her writing. Rather curiously in the end, Spark fell out with Stannard for reasons that are far from entirely clear. Here, history repeats itself because Spark had previously excoriated her erstwhile close friend and collaborator Derek Stanford (1918–2008), both in her own alternatingly arch, unbuttoned and obtuse autobiography (a quality signalled in its underwhelming title), *Curriculum Vitae* (1992), and in her novel *A Far Cry from Kensington* (1988), where Stanford's proxy in the character of Hector Bartlett is lashed as a '*pisseur de copie*'.⁴ Stanford demonstrated an entitled opportunism in publishing a biographical memoir of Spark in his *Inside the Forties* (1977) and in his *Muriel Spark* (1963), the latter being the first extensive critical study of the author who was by then an international name following the success of *Jean Brodie*. The culture of literary London in the 1940s and 1950s in which Spark and Stanford were well-connected 'minor' figures remains ripe for a critical reappraisal. Spark's part in the post-war London literary scene, as documented in her autobiography, Stanford's memoirs and refracted in *A Far Cry from Kensington*, as well as in another deliciously barbed 'historical novel' by Spark, *Loitering with Intent* (1981), would make an excellent starting point in such a project. A particularly telling vignette in such a study would be Spark's work as Secretary of the Poetry Society and editor of the organisation's journal, *The Poetry Review*, from 1947–49. Here she came into conflict with, indeed in Spark's own term she was 'harassed' by, Dr Marie Stopes (1880–1958), a Vice-President of the society and famous as a pioneer of birth control.⁵ Indeed, the evidence of her impertinent enquiries to Spark about her past private life somewhat contradicts Stopes' reputation as being in the vanguard of feminism. Perhaps the funniest moment in all of *Curriculum Vitae* is when Spark lets rip on Stopes with a stylish, full-frontal, Jean Brodie-esque vindictiveness:

> Up to his death three years earlier she had been living with Lord Alfred Douglas, the fatal lover of Oscar Wilde, an arrangement which I imagine would satisfy any woman's craving for birth control. I met her at one of our meetings and knew she disliked me intensely on sight. I was young and pretty and she had totally succumbed to the law of gravity without attempting to do a thing about it.[6]

Ernest Schonfield, in 'The Publishing Scene in *A Far Cry from Kensington*', highlights the typical Sparkian focus on entertainingly vicious human behaviour as he offers a reading of the 'literary field' which Spark assembles in that novel from her experience in the 1940s and 1950s. He foregrounds issues of professional power, class and gender, of 'art' (theoretically more idealistic) and 'craft' (negotiating cultural, institutional attitudes as well as individual egos). This is the daunting, but quotidian terrain that the central protagonist Nancy Hawkins must traverse to have a career in the publishing industry. There is, as elsewhere in Spark's oeuvre, a sharp anthropological fascination, even if the narrative itself resists drawing sociological conclusions. *A Far Cry from Kensington* is simultaneously lyrical and an essay in petty, ridiculous human behaviour; in Schonfield's reading, Spark's oblique reflections on the making of a 'good book' or novel emerge precisely from such seemingly oxymoronic elements. If resistant towards her biographers and evasive, playfully or otherwise, in *Curriculum Vitae*, Spark often has her novels point towards these qualities which reveal her own hallmark interests as a writer. Amy Woodbury Tease, in 'Muriel Spark's Windows and the Architecture of Surveillance', reminds us of Spark's career with British Intelligence during the Second World War. The strategic spreading of misinformation in which she was therein involved has obvious purchase across Spark's fiction, including the misapprehension that truth has a ready clarity in the first place. The propaganda of totalitarian movements, the Second World War, and the Cold War by the early 1960s informed this novelistic scepticism about straightforward truths. Much more work remains to be done on Spark's depiction of twentieth-century paranoia. Our human perspectives, as Spark repeatedly signals, are deceptively (often self-deceivingly) constructed. Woodbury Tease notes that in *The Girls of Slender Means* (1963), a novel set in a blitzed London during the Second World War, 'Windows secure the fantasy of stability and coherence for the girls of slender means as they are continuously replaced with new glass.' Vehicles of vision are fragile and easily undermined, as Spark the black propagandist is acutely aware.

One might suspect that Spark believes biographical (and even autobiographical) portraits are ultimately and hopelessly deceptive, personal and subjective (all the more so for affecting objectivity) and part of a routine failure in the human sensibility. At its worst, such portraits are depicted as nefariousness, especially when they involve concocting stories about fellow human beings. The book that is centred at the heart of Spark's canon, its author's most lustrous story, is *The Prime of Miss Jean Brodie*. The novel has a genuine fame and enduring popularity internationally, yet it features a jarring, if also intriguing, duplicity. The text is to a large extent an exuberant portrait of a single woman, an artist manqué, operating in difficult historical, sociological times, but the treatment of the eponymous Jean Brodie is precisely un-indulgent in the cruel flashes forward that reveal – sooner than the reader ought to want – her coming to grief professionally and also her, as yet, distant death from cancer. This 'experimental' plotting-technique jars, even undercuts, the attractive wilfulness of her character which emerges through the gradual unfolding of her adventures. Those adventures, however, are cruelly telescoped by the reader's awareness of the failed parameters of Brodie's designs and of her life in general. This allows a measure of pathos, of basic sympathy for Brodie as a human being, but the overall decentring of the central character in the novel through narrative prolepsis makes for an unsettling reading experience within the terms of realist fiction. Whether despite its being or because it is a text that combines a considerable and lovingly realistic canvas of 1930s Edinburgh with an alienating fictiveness, *Jean Brodie* was the book that made Muriel Spark an internationally known name. It was propelled in the first instance by its appearance in the *New*

Yorker (14 October 1961). This impeccably bourgeois magazine carefully cultivated Spark's writing. Though it rejected her early submissions, it continuously encouraged her so that in her life-time Spark appeared in seventeen issues over forty-three years from 1960 until 2003. *Jean Brodie* clearly made its author a darling of the publication, to be afforded much future space. Consequently, the other two big pieces she contributed were the serialisation of some parts of *The Mandelbaum Gate* from May to August 1965 and the publication, like *Jean Brodie* complete in one issue, of *The Driver's Seat* in May 1970. All three of these novels feature, each in its own way, highly cosmopolitan (or at least would-be cosmopolitan) female central protagonists. For a period during the 1960s Spark had the use of an office in the magazine's premises; a full critical account of this relationship focusing on the dynamic of the cultural politics and ethos of the *New Yorker* in Spark's writerly career remains to be written.[7]

Spark's cultural cosmopolitanism is remarkable; across her career she lived in Scotland, Africa and three particularly great centres of cultural style: London, New York and, in later years, Italy. In the early years of her association with the *New Yorker*, Spark developed a close working relationship with her editor at the magazine, Rachel MacKenzie, a great believer in Spark's talent, but whose alteration of the text for the first appearance of *Jean Brodie* in print made for a much more indirect version than that of the first book edition.[8] Helen Stoddart, in her essay, 'Muriel Spark and the "Hired Grammarians"', highlights the minutiae of this situation in discussing the excisions and unhelpfully regularised punctuation and syntax of the *New Yorker* version. Although there is now a rich body of literary criticism of Spark's work, what is still missing is more extensive and serious investigation of Spark's manuscripts, publishing history and print editions including fully annotated scholarly editions of her fiction. Colin McIlroy, in his essay '"I knew what was what": Correspondence in the Muriel Spark Archive', reflects on his experience as Spark Curator at the National Library of Scotland (NLS) and the knowledge this has afforded him of this vast archive.[9] This Spark archive comprises 'around three hundred and sixty boxes totalling over one hundred and seventy feet or fifty-two metres of shelf-space [and] is the largest modern literary archive of any single author held at the National

Library of Scotland'. It contains invaluable materials, comprising literary correspondence, much biographical material and items from Spark's personal book collection, such as her copy of John Henry Newman's *Apologia Pro Vita Sua*. Much work remains to be done on the exact influence of Newman on Spark and her adoption of Roman Catholicism.[10] Intriguingly, McIlroy takes us to his conclusion that Spark's intensive attention to archiving leads to a situation where, 'If meta-fiction is the practice of writing fiction that foregrounds its very fictionality – or in other words, writing fiction about writing fiction – then Muriel Spark is a meta-archival writer.' The archive, then, is itself another self-reflexive statement by Spark about her synthesising, creative, sensibility. McIlroy's suggestive approach here is currently being explored further in an AHRC-funded PhD project supervised between the NLS and the University of Glasgow.[11] More generally, the archival material of the *New Yorker* and at the University of Tulsa ('Muriel Spark Papers 1957–88') as well as in the NLS, now comprises a formidable set of materials that ought to allow Spark scholarship to go forward in many directions as we move beyond the centenary of the author's birth.[12]

Spark's reputation in Scotland as an international writer has of course registered, but her 'Scottishness', whatever that precisely might mean, has been called into question. In a remarkable outburst her fellow novelist Robin Jenkins (1912–2005) contended that it would be 'very difficult to get any real Scottish person accepting [Muriel Spark] as a Scottish writer'.[13] One wonders about logic and motivation here from the mouth of a fellow novelist who often writes about Scotland but also ranges further afield in his settings to include Catalonia and Afghanistan. Jenkins, by and large, follows in the wake of the nationalist literary revival of Scotland at whose centre stood Hugh MacDiarmid (1892–1978). Even if Spark had remained in Scotland as part of the boozy, masculinist literary scene MacDiarmid and others encouraged in the mid-twentieth century, her sensibilities were undoubtedly at odds with the main mover of the Scots language revival from the 1920s on. Spark expressed the view that she saw 'no point in offering Scots dialects (which in any case are not regionally consistent) to the intelligent reader [...] in Essex, or Worcestershire [...] in the United States of Australia' and which these readers 'cannot understand'.[14] In 2003 Spark described

MacDiarmid as 'treasonous' after the publication of some rediscovered poems where the latter described the English as Scotland's 'only enemies' and claimed he could 'hardly care' about the Nazi bombing of London.[15] We might here remember that Muriel Spark worked for British Intelligence during the Second World War, which further highlights her stark difference in mentality from MacDiarmid. Of Jewish heritage, a woman converting to Catholicism and living for much of her life abroad while writing, more often than not, about places other than Scotland, it is easy to see why Spark's Scottish identity might not be readily accepted from a nationalist point of view. Spark may well be British, may well be described as a European writer in her cosmopolitan range, yet her work is also often freighted with Scottish material. Her debut novel, *The Comforters*, features Georgina Hogg, a reference to James Hogg, whose *Private Memoirs and Confessions of a Justified Sinner* (1824) is such an important book for Spark in helping her to imagine religious and moral hypocrisy in her fiction and is also a clear influence for *The Prime of Miss Jean Brodie*. *The Ballad of Peckham Rye* (1960) also features an important culture-clash where a Scottish protagonist, Dougal Douglas, modelled to a large extent on traditions of Scottish folklore and balladry, is inflicted on modern-day, secular, materialist London. Towards the end of her career, Spark's *Symposium* (1990) is likewise informed by Scottish supernatural traditions.[16] Cairns Craig re-examines the inspiration of J. M. Barrie in Spark's *The Hothouse by the East River* (1973), as well as elsewhere in her fiction. He finds Barrie, and especially *Peter Pan*, is an explicit and implicit presence in Spark's work, and is yet another writer which the modern Scottish 'canon' has found it difficult to absorb. Barrie provides her with a realm of the fantastic supernatural that countermands a too realistic tradition in the novel which became (from her point of view) all too minutely psychological through the twentieth century. Barrie's influence, as well as other longstanding Scottish literary traditions then, run deep in Spark.

Her most obviously Scottish book, *Jean Brodie*, saw Spark installed as an internationally famous writer as well as within the first rank of British fiction writers. It led to her participation with six other novelists in a famous set of interviews with Frank Kermode under the title of 'The House of

Fiction' in the *Partisan Review* (Spring, 1963).[17] These other writers were Ivy Compton-Burnett, Graham Greene, Iris Murdoch, C. P. Snow, John Wain and Angus Wilson, a disparate but illustrious group of prize-winning writers, all of whom were part of the literary intellectual cream of early 1960s writing. We see the *Jean Brodie* effect again in its author's appearance in the first short monographs about her by Karl Malkoff for the 'Columbia Essays on Modern Writers' series in 1968 (where Spark was the only Scot in a most distinguished list of English, Irish and European writers) and by Patricia Stubbs for the 'Writers and Their Work' series by Longman for the British Council in 1973 (Spark, along with Compton Mackenzie, the only twentieth-century Scottish writer in the series).[18] Both of these critical works clearly see *Jean Brodie* sitting at the centre of Spark's achievement. The novel reverberated also in its spinning out into other genres: the stage version of 1966 was adapted by the American playwright and screenwriter Jay Presson Allen who drove it as a project for theatre. It premiered at Wyndham's Theatre in London, starred Vanessa Redgrave, and was a massive hit, transferring to New York in 1968 for another successful year-long run starring Zoë Caldwell. The stage version has been revived periodically due to the enduring appeal of both the novel and film (which is frequently broadcast on television channels across the English-speaking world). Allen also wrote the screenplay for the 1969 film version of *Jean Brodie*, starring Maggie Smith, which inspired a highly successful Scottish Television series in 1978 starring Geraldine McEwan. The television adaptation was heavily reliant on Allen's adaptive writing but drew on several other writers also, who added scenes and dialogue quite distant from Spark's original novelistic conception, using supplementary detail from the politics of the inter-war period.[19] Overall, a veritable constellation of theatrical and filmic talent, along with Spark's original scenario, has made *Jean Brodie* the monster-success of the Spark canon.[20]

The film version of *The Prime of Miss Jean Brodie* makes no attempt to simulate the proleptic trickery or the wayward narrative voice of Spark's novel. It presents more or less a straightforward realist filmic treatment of the novel, replete with poignant historical period-charm and the successful television version likewise grounds the text as a piece of historical fiction.

It acknowledges the Catholicism of Brodie's lover, Teddy Lloyd, but dispenses with the deeper influence of Lloyd's religion upon Brodie's star pupil Sandy Stranger, who goes on to become a nun, celebrated for her psychological treatise, 'The Transfiguration of the Commonplace'. Although early twenty-first-century readers may be more interested in the novel as an allegorical critique of Fascism, *Jean Brodie* is also a deeply Catholic, anagogic novel which is implicitly about the agency of God and freewill, with a certain satirical sideswipe at Calvinism and its doctrine of predestination. Sandy sees Brodie as mimicking the God of Calvin, observing that her teacher assumes herself above the normal moral code and attempts to write the future narratives of her chosen girls' lives. The religious perspective, largely oblique in the novel, essentially disappears in the film version. *Jean Brodie* was the zenith of Spark's early-period novels, which were valued for their Catholic spiritual outlook by the likes of Graham Greene and Evelyn Waugh. Waugh had been a huge fan of both *The Comforters* and *Memento Mori* (1959), with their religiously signposted titles, as well as of *The Bachelors* (1960), with its strong, although often satirical, theme of priestly intercession.[21] Greene, a fan of Spark's short stories from the mid-1950s, became a staunch supporter materially as well as morally.[22] One way of placing Spark is as one of the three great British Catholic fiction writers of the twentieth century (post-Chesterton), along with Waugh and Greene. The tension between the 'immaterial' context (at its most general, God) to Spark's fiction and the materialism of her formal interest is one that is not easily resolved, and is perhaps not meant to be. Peter Kemp, who ironically fought in the Spanish Civil War on the side of Franco, produced a superbly nuanced critical study, *Muriel Spark* (1974), for the British Council series, 'Novelists and Their World'. For Kemp, the disjunction between Spark's form and her treatment of humanity produces a thrilling, chilling reading experience so that, 'the form of her books is deeply satisfying [and] there is as counterpoint to this, the disturbing tenor of her content.'[23] Kemp's summation opens up the nice subtlety that it is Spark's human characterisation that is ultimately discomfiting while her deliberately jarring formal manipulation represents a kind of balm on the presentation of frequently awful human behaviour. Certainly, this is an appealing and typical twist in Spark's work where the prospect of literary trickery is potentially more upsetting than the depiction of immoral action.

*

For the present writer, the best book on Spark's work remains Ruth Whittaker's *The Faith and Fiction of Muriel Spark* (1982) which sums up Spark's modus operandi with typical aplomb, claiming of its subject that she:

> adopted twentieth-century technology, as it were, to deal with eternal truths; and, having suited her techniques to a sceptical and materialistic age, seeks to persuade us that angels and demons are neither metaphoric nor outdated conceits, but exist here and now in convents, classrooms and on the factory floor. In doing this she has remained peculiarly independent of pressures from both realism and the experimentalism of postmodernist fiction.[24]

Spark's 'independence' from realism at points extends to not 'caring' for her characters, such as the notorious example Whittaker cites of the characters killed, struck by lightning, and rendered with stark reduction in a subordinate clause in *Not to Disturb*.[25] Likewise the proleptic flash-forward technique in *Jean Brodie* and other novels performs similar, syntactical dismissals of characters whose lives cannot be allowed to unfold for the reader in 'realistic', chronological fashion. Equally, Spark's usage of postmodernist 'technology', circumscribed by an implied supernatural cosmos, means that Spark is not easily corralled within the materialist circumscriptions upon which late twentieth-century literary theory was centred. In this secular age, Spark's religious mentality has probably not enjoyed the sustained attention it deserves, although a fruitful recent channel is forged in this respect in Cairns Craig's *Muriel Spark, Existentialism and the Art of Death* (2020), which pays serious attention once again to the terrain most firmly established by Whittaker in analysing the choices made by Spark's characters in the context of the human understanding of free-will and morality.[26] In considering Spark in a context of 'Christian Existentialism', Craig makes an important contribution to a recent re-burgeoning of Spark criticism that adopts a strong theological focus.[27]

A ground-breaking attempt to foreground Spark in secular, materialist terms is found in the collection, *Theorising Muriel Spark: Gender, Race, Deconstruction* (2002), and indeed this volume laid the groundwork for a number of the critical concerns revisited in the present volume.[28] Spark's precise detailing of the material world, for all that her fiction might warn against the danger of such attention, is highlighted by Fiona Jardine in 'Art and Industry Must Walk Hand in Hand: Muriel Spark and Twentieth-Century Design Ideology'. Here she explains that 'there is much to be gained from comparing Spark's vocabulary and literary style to texts found in magazines, adverts and similar non-literary sources of the period'. Architecture, popular culture, advertising, and class all provide access to a less than coherent world, a palimpsest of past and present. In the context of this oddly jumbled world, Jardine suggests that for Spark 'all writing is prosthetic', a justified parody of an oddly layered reality inhabited by modernity's systems of mass communication. Carole Jones, in 'Muriel Spark's Waywardness', argues that Spark is alive to lazy binaries and, indeed, makes creative capital from the constructed and contrapuntal. Jones identifies in Spark's fiction, so replete with many 'wayward' female protagonists, a more general 'waywardness, a knowing engagement with the disjunction between how things are and how they could otherwise be [...] and Spark's writing inhabits that space'. That choice of liminality, both in Spark's own writing and the waywardness of so many of her female characters, forms the basis for a fresh feminist reading of the 'oddness' of Spark's fiction. Jones sums up a radical dimension of Spark's writing which often embodies a 'poetics of waywardness' wherein her 'texts [...] act out rather than psychologise the pathologies of femininity'. Jones also suggests that in the period in the writer's career that so many critics find the most intriguing, from *The Public Image* to *The Hothouse by the East River*, or between 1968 and 1973, her 'texts suggest that as the counter-cultural "sexual revolution" of that period proceeded so did Spark's scepticism increase regarding the tenets of freedom made possible in extant feminine identities'. Similarly, in 'Spark's Spinsters: Bedsits and Boarding Houses in the Novels of Muriel Spark', Susannah

Thompson discusses the boarding houses and similar locations that feature in Spark's depictions of 'spinsterhood' as liminal spaces, socially stigmatised as markers of incompleteness. For Spark such awkward, lonely spaces give rise to 'waywardness' or 'oddity' as well and this 'odd capacity for vision'[29] on Spark's part again leads us to identify a version of 'Romantic' vision. In Thompson's reading, we are taken to the centre of Spark's liberated female power: 'For Muriel Spark, writing furiously in her lodging rooms in the late 1950s, the position of the unmarried woman was the beginning of some of her most celebrated and memorable works, works which brought spinsters off the shelf'. Thematically, Spark's one foray into drama, *Doctors of Philosophy* (1962), certainly speaks generally to the context of second wave feminism featuring, as it does, female academics reflecting on the course of their careers and the barriers to these. In the present volume, Ian Brown, in 'Metatheatricality and Dramatic Contexts in Muriel Spark's Writing for Performance', re-reads Spark's play, pinpointing 'a zany quality, which, with its prominent female characters (all men reduced to being called "Charlie") combines elements of comedy of manners, West End boulevard theatre, absurdist philosophy and Monty Python'. Spark's signature qualities of generic self-reflexiveness and witty dialogue, both bitingly and laconically funny, are all in evidence in *Doctors of Philosophy*, along with that familiar Sparkian collision of the 'surreal' and the 'mundane'. Brown reminds us also of the powerful radio plays written by Spark, suggesting that it is time Spark's dramatic writing, as well as her poetry, had more critical attention paid to it. Brown also provides a revelatory account of Spark's personal relationship with radio and theatre, and the practicalities of theatrical production, in London in the late 1950s and early 1960s, and with this a much fuller picture of Spark as a member of that contemporary London literary scene.[30]

Another materialism of sorts, which is certainly present but not necessarily easy to assess in Spark's work, is the matter of history. As Catriona Macdonald argues in '"Making patterns with facts": Unmaking History in *The Prime of Miss Jean Brodie*', the novel is full of 'de-historicisation'. The beginning of Chapter 3 of *The Prime of Miss Jean Brodie* illustrates this point well, with its disorientating yet still humorous shifts in the narrative voice.

The chapter begins, 'The days passed and the wind blew from the Forth'.[31] Ostensibly the narration moves from this dreamy, romantic narrator to a more historically precise voice that tells us about the state of middle-class women in inter-war Edinburgh. A quite precise historical sociology emerges as we are told of these women:

> They went to lectures, tried living on honey and nuts, took lessons in German and then went walking in Germany; they bought caravans and went off with them into the hills among the lochs; they played the guitar; they supported all the new little theatre companies; they took lodgings in the slums and, distributing pots of paint, taught their neighbours the arts of simple interior decoration; they preached the inventions of Marie Stopes; they attended the meetings of the Oxford Group and put Spiritualism to their hawk-eyed test. Some assisted in the Scottish Nationalist Movement; others, like Miss Brodie, called themselves Europeans and Edinburgh a European capital, the city of Hume and Boswell.[32]

Here we might be left to ask: is it the women who are being described in their flaky indeterminacy or is it the novel's narrative voice, so capriciously unconventional throughout the book, that is so? Judgement of any kind from anyone is suspect amid the welter of the world's activities and this epistemological reality extends even to include Sandy's adolescent identification of Brodie with the God of Calvin, which might not be so solid in its melodramatic apprehension as might first appear. Catriona Macdonald identifies this deep rendition by Spark of subjective apprehension as inhering within the central character's all-enveloping wilfulness. As she says, 'throughout the novel things temporal and matters contextual appear at times interchangeable with character, and Brodie's "prime" – as the explanation for everything – negates the need for causality'. Though David Hume and James Boswell might now have become converged in popular versions of the Scottish Enlightenment, Boswell the diarist, the recorder of quotidian factuality, significantly diverges from Hume the archsceptic whose scepticism extends to doubting the common-sense observation of temporal cause and effect. So, Spark's final sentence referring to 'the city of Hume and Boswell' in fact suggests a fissure rather than closure, an openness that extends throughout the novel and which signals the ultimate limitations of perspective for author, characters and readers.

Real social history is no doubt registered to some extent in *Jean Brodie*'s sketch of certain British women of the time, but as well as this factual capturing of their disparate, common political, cultural and social interests, with typical Sparkian zeugma, something else is going on which renders the text even more fork-tongued. There is, we are told, a 'legion' of these women, a theological subtext from the synoptic Gospels and their telling of the story of the Gadarene swine. Jesus interrogates the demon about its identity and the demon answers 'My name is Legion; for we are many'. The polyphonous theme of deceitful fact and character in the novel, the potentially serpentine nature of the world, is registered yet again in terms that are explicitly Christian. Social and political issues remain a compelling interest in contemporary Spark criticism, but the author's formal signalling of indeterminate reality throughout her oeuvre also countermands ideological and materialistic readings. As Judy Sproxton finds when she mounts an enquiry meant to elicit some sociological certainty in *The Women of Muriel Spark* (1992), Spark ultimately presents 'a fragmentary and bafflingly mysterious life [that] will awake in the reader an admission that we see through a glass darkly'.[33] Spark's 'through the glass darkly' focus is exemplified in many moments within her fiction including in *The Girls of Slender Means* which features a scene depicting the mass joy in London in 1945 on Victory in Europe day. Amid this crowded celebration about to enjoy the appearance of a triumphant Royal Family on the balcony of Buckingham Palace, a murderer plunges a knife into a young woman; public positivity and a huge and historic community event is undercut by individual nefariousness. Spark has specialised in her fiction in essaying both group and individual behaviour and neither offers much in the way of optimism that the world is overwhelmingly moral. Indeed, the fragile consensus within social activity is often and all too easily undermined by personal wrongdoing. This contention leads us back to what is a rather old-fashioned writerly categorisation of Spark the moralist.

Allegory is conventionally a vehicle with a moral tenor, and *Jean Brodie*, as has been noted, looks somewhat like an allegory on political totalitarianism, although the religious element, even for those who wish to prioritise the book as a study in fanaticism, obtrudes not entirely helpfully. Religion and politics collide yet again in a text featuring an even more extreme character-version of Brodie in Alexandra, the convent superior in *The Abbess of Crewe* (1974), whose love of the poetic is used with an authoritarian hand to condition reality within her religious demesne. It has often been noted but seldom particularly explored, that this novel is Spark's most closely worked allegory, satirising the murky and comical corruption of Richard Nixon and his cronies amid the 'Watergate' scandal of the early 1970s. Colin Kidd helpfully assembles these allegorical particulars, pointing out their comic effect and suggesting that in this novel, 'arguably, Spark's real subject is style'. One can see why Nixon, as licentious with the truth as Jean Brodie in his creation of a self-contained version of the world in which, in the end, he personally enjoyed a very debatable grasp on truth, would attract Spark's attention. Kidd considers that *The Abbess of Crewe* might be 'in some remote sense a Catholic parable', but refuses to reach this definitive conclusion. In keeping with the endlessly, mirrored, echoing effect that other critics have found in Spark's fiction, Kidd detects in both the forms and themes of *The Abbess of Crewe* a self-reflexive echo chamber or hall of mirrors.

Spark's most experimentally self-reflexive period is represented by the sequence of novels that ends with *The Abbess of Crewe*, where the characters live lives enclosed, not so much by the convent, as by farcical allegory and by their own slavery to a system, even one that is outwardly, but not inwardly spiritual. Three novels of similarly claustrophobic formality precede that text. In *The Driver's Seat* (1970) the female central protagonist is a kind of Jean Brodie stripped back to robotic form, famously taking a formal joke from the novel itself, a 'whydunnit' rather than a 'whodunnit' in its proleptic treatment of a murder – or is it a suicide? Lise might be read as her author's ultimate moral and formal cipher, or as a judgement on the extreme effects of patriarchy. Spark herself believed this book to be her crowning achievement and one of the clearest analyses of it is provided by one of the world's best crime writers, Ian Rankin, who points out the ways in which a reader must re-read it to appreciate its chilling parameters.³⁴ *Not to Disturb* features a Gothic plot full of inevitability or a set of retrodden clichés, as it were, surreally re-energised to signal moral decadence. *The Hothouse by the East River* has central characters that are ghosts who continue to inhabit Manhattan, their choking egos refusing to admit their own deaths (and one character impossibly conceived by ghosts) as the novel riffs on J. M. Barrie's *Peter Pan*. If this claustrophobic terrain is a Spark stock-in-trade, there is also much ventilation across her oeuvre as pointed out by Mark Currie in 'Already and Not Yet Written: Unfinished Acts of Writing in the Novels of Muriel Spark'. Currie examines the 'unfinished narratives' that feature throughout Spark's fiction and the ways in which authorial authority is repeatedly destabilised. He returns us to that Sparkian collision of the freely real and the artificial. For him, Spark emerges as a writer deeply curious and reflective about her own productions whose 'dramatisations of [the] relation between contingency and writing, or between freedom and the graphic surface of a novel, belong to this species of curiosity about the book as an object'. Spark's curiosity about the book as a form and fiction as a genre, pertains throughout her career. Her witty, ironic, experimental, moral, religious and social fiction remains more than usually critically indeterminate in any definitive sense. This is the 'crooked dividend' of Muriel Spark's fiction.³⁵

Endnotes

1. For an illuminating account of Spark's post-Romantic sensibility see, Colin William McIlroy, *Muriel Spark and the Romantic ideal*. Unpublished PhD thesis (2015), University of Glasgow. theses.gla.ac.uk/6439/
2. Martin Stannard, *Muriel Spark: The Biography* (London: Weidenfeld and Nicolson, 2009), pp. 115–18; p. 117.
3. My overall speculation, however, about autobiographical relevance is just that: speculation. Spark is simply a better writer of fiction than of poetry. Her rather discontinuous published output of some seventy poems are often witty, tell entertaining narrative stories about others and quite often reflect on the process of creativity. They probably show the influence of T. S. Eliot and W. H. Auden above all others. In a late work that clearly delighted Spark, *All the Poems of Muriel Spark* (New York: New Directions, 2004), her poems are collected. In the Foreword we have something like a *cri de coeur*, perhaps, where not for the first time Spark self-identifies:

    > Although most of my life has been devoted to fiction, I have always thought of myself as a poet. I do not write 'poetic' prose, but feel that my outlook on life and my perceptions of events are those of a poet. Whether in prose or verse, all creative writing is mysteriously connected with music and I always hope this factor is apparent throughout my work. (p. xii).

    If her prose is not 'poetic' it contains a myriad of rhetorical tricks at the linguistic as well as at the formal level, including just about every species of metaphor it is possible to find. A 'literary linguistic' study of Spark's fiction would make for an excellent project. What she means above by the connection with music is anyone's guess, but one can see Spark enjoying critics trying to engage with her typically gnomic statement.

    A most useful gathering of statements by Spark about her life and art is to be found along with a compendium of well-chosen secondary criticism in Joseph K. Hynes (ed.), *Critical Essays on Muriel Spark* (New York: G. K. Hall; Toronto: Maxwell Macmillan Canada; New York: Maxwell Macmillan International, 1992). One of the most revealing interviews with Spark is to be found in Robert Hosmer, 'An Interview with Muriel Spark' in *Salmagundi* 146/147 (Spring–Summer 2005), pp. 127–58; Hosmer, one of Spark's most perceptive critics, also edits a commendably diverse range of critical perspectives in *Hidden Possibilities: Essays in Honour of Muriel Spark* (Indiana: University of Notre Dame Press, 2014).
4. Although it should be noted that the name of the '*pisseur de copie*' is taken from someone else who annoyed Spark, an American poetaster, Alice Hunt Bartlett (see *Curriculum Vitae*, pp. 169–70).
5. *Curriculum Vitae*, p. 174.
6. Ibid.
7. See, for instance, Macy Halford, 'Muriel Mysteries', *New Yorker*, 26 April 2010: www.newyorker.com/books/page-turner/muriel-mysteries
8. For more detail of the Spark-Mackenzie relationship and that of the novelist with the magazine generally, see Lisa Harrison, '"The Magazine that is considered the best in the world": Muriel Spark and the *New Yorker*' in David Herman (ed.), *Muriel Spark: Twenty-First-Century Perspectives* (Baltimore: The Johns Hopkins Press, 2010), pp. 39–62.

9   During 2017–2018 Dr McIlroy curated an excellent exhibition at the NLS, 'The International Style of Muriel Spark' (www.nls.uk/exhibitions/muriel-spark), the materials of which have influenced a number of the essays in this collection beyond the Curator's own essay-contribution.
10 An excellent starting point is made here by Benilde Montgomery in 'Spark and Newman: Jean Brodie Reconsidered' in *Twentieth Century Literature* 43.1 (Spring 1997), pp. 94–106.
11 For Steven Harvie's doctoral project, see www.gla.ac.uk/schools/critical/postgrad/currentpgs/stevenharvie/
12 For the University of Tulsa materials, see utulsa.as.atlas-sys.com/repositories/2/resources/425
13 Robin Jenkins, 'A Truthful Scot' [interview], *In Scotland* 1 (Autumn 1999), p. 12–22.
14 Quoted in Alan Taylor, *Appointment in Arezzo: A friendship with Muriel Spark* (Edinburgh: Polygon, 2017), p. 53.
15 'Spark: MacDiarmid's Poetry was Treason', *Sunday Times*, 13 April 2003. www.thetimes.co.uk/article/spark-macdiarmids-poetry-was-treason-gfbhfzvvhzg
16 For a consideration of Spark's 'Scottishness' see Gerard Carruthers, '"Fully to Savour Her Position": Muriel Spark and Scottish Identity' in *Modern Fiction Studies* 54.3 (Fall 2008), pp. 487–504. Spark has been written about from very different ends of the Scottish critical establishment. Alan Bold, a disciple of Hugh MacDiarmid, writes his thematically incisive *Muriel Spark* (London and New York: Methuen, 1986) for the 'Contemporary Writers' series (another index of Spark's reputation, as the first Scot into this series). The British Unionist Allan Massie (another fine novelist whose cultural and political credentials do not always find him a ready reception in Scotland) writes with great sympathy for Spark's stylistic panache in his *Muriel Spark* (Ramsay Head Press: Edinburgh, 1979) a volume in the publisher's series of 'New Assessments' of Scottish writers. Massie and Bold equally contribute to foregrounding Spark's Scottish cultural freight in a way that was largely absent from previous treatments. The latter includes the former's 'Calvinism and Catholicism in Muriel Spark' in Bold (ed.) *Muriel Spark: An Odd Capacity for Vision* (London: Vision, 1984), pp. 94–107; other essays in that volume are also important in signalling Spark's Scottish heritage. Another place of acceptance for Spark within the Scottish canon is her treatment in another series in the volume, Michael Gardiner and Willy Maley (eds.) *The Edinburgh Companion to Muriel Spark* (Edinburgh: Edinburgh University Press, 2010).
17 Frank Kermode, 'House of Fiction' in *Partisan Review* 30.1 (Spring 1963), pp. 61–82.
18 Karl Malkoff, *Muriel Spark* (New York: Columbia University Press, 1968); Patricia Stubbs, *Muriel Spark* (Harlow, Essex: Longman, 1973). Brian Cheyette's *Muriel Spark* (Northcote: Tavistock, 2000), with its very deft arrangement of critical concerns pursued through Spark's fiction, is a contribution to the updated 'Writers and Their Work' series.
19 Collaterally, Tomás Monterrey in a path-breaking essay on Spark in European reception and translation in 'The Reception of Muriel Spark in Spain' (*Scottish Literary Review*, 11.1, Spring/Summer 2019, pp. 85–102) offers intriguing insight into the appearance of translations of *Jean Brodie* and other Spark fictions in Spain under the dictator Franco and beyond.
20 Interestingly, other Spark films, *The Driver's Seat* (1974) starring Elizabeth Taylor (1932–2011) and *The Abbess of Crewe* under the title *Nasty Habits* (1977) and starring

Glenda Jackson (b. 1936) enjoyed neither the popular nor critical success of the film of *Jean Brodie*. Much more celebrated as a screen adaptation has been the television series of *Memento Mori* (1992), featuring a stellar cast of actors including Maggie Smith. The time is ripe for proper critical work on Spark adaptation in film and television as well as, perhaps, on radio. There have also been mis-firings too, such as the aborted project to film, *The Takeover* (1976), Spark's sprawling satire on types of European decadence. See *The New York Times* (20 May 1979), where Victoria Glendinning interviews Spark: movies2.nytimes.com/books/01/03/11/specials/spark-talk1.html
21 See Martin Stannard, *Muriel Spark: The Biography* (London: Weidenfeld and Nicolson, 2009), pp. 176–79, p. 209 & p. 233.
22 Stannard, pp. 162–63.
23 Peter Kemp, *Muriel Spark* (London: Elek Books, 1974), p. 16.
24 Ruth Whittaker, *The Faith and Fiction of Muriel Spark* (Basingstoke: Palgrave Macmillan, 1982), p. 2. Although it might be said that angels appear comparatively rarely in Spark's fiction such as in her first published short story, 'The Seraph and the Zambesi' (1951) and here and elsewhere when good does appear it has a somewhat ambiguous effect such as in another short story 'The Black Madonna' (1958) where divine agency, if that is what it is, is rather sinister. Good, of course, in its rather undramatic propensity is more difficult interestingly to narrate than evil. Devils, or at least the devil manqué, such as Dougal Douglas in *The Ballad of Peckham Rye*, or even the 'witch' Jean Brodie are dramatised more readily.
25 Ibid., p. 120.
26 Cairns Craig's, *Muriel Spark, Existentialism and the Art of Death* (Edinburgh: Edinburgh University Press, 2020).
27 See, *inter alia*, Thomas F. Haddox, 'Religion for "Really Intelligent People": the Rhetoric of Muriel Spark's *Reality and Dreams*', in *Religion & Literature* 41.3 (Autumn 2009), pp. 43–66; Martin Stannard, 'Nativities: Muriel Spark, Baudelaire, and the Quest for Religious Faith', in *Review of English Studies* 55.218 (2004), pp. 91–105. Stephanie Jones, 'The "difficult" relationship: Christine Brooke-Rose, Catholicism and Muriel Spark', in *Textual Practice* (2018), 32.2, pp. 245–63.
28 Martin McQuillan (ed.), *Theorising Muriel Spark: Gender, Race, Deconstruction* (Basingstoke: Palgrave Macmillan, 2002).
29 The phrase well-spotted by Alan Bold for the title of his collection of critical essays on Spark appears in Spark's poem, 'Elementary' (c. 1951).
30 Spark's formal range is completed by her children's short stories. Her one book for children is *The Very Fine Clock* (1968), but two other children's stories written around the same time were published latterly by Penelope Jardine in a limited edition for adult book-collectors, *The French Window* and *The Small Telephone* (1993).
31 Muriel Spark, *The Prime of Miss Jean Brodie* (London: Penguin Classics, 2000), p. 42.
32 Ibid. pp. 42–43.
33 Judy Sproxton, *The Women of Muriel Spark* (London: Constable, 1992), p. 155.
34 Ian Rankin, 'Surface and Structure: Reading Muriel Spark's *The Driver's Seat*', in *The Journal of Narrative Technique* 29 (1985), pp. 146–55.
35 This phrase is from Spark's poem, 'Verlaine Villanelle' (c. 1950).

I. SPARK, BIOGRAPHY, AND FEMALE EXPERIENCE

1. 'I knew what was what': Correspondence and the Meta-Archival in the Muriel Spark Archive[1]

COLIN McILROY

In Muriel Spark's short story 'The Executor', the character and narrator Susan Kyle, having been appointed literary executor by her uncle, says the following:

> Probably for the first time in his life all his papers were in order. I went into Edinburgh and bought box-files and cover-files and I filed away all that mountain of papers, each under its separate heading. And I knew what was what. You didn't catch me filing away a letter from Angus Wilson or Saul Bellow in the same place as an ordinary 'W' or 'B', a Miss Mary Whitelaw or a Mrs Jonathan Brown. I knew the value of these letters, they went into a famous-persons file, bulging and of value.[2]

Is this how Spark's real archive is arranged; are fiction and reality in concurrence? Perhaps not surprisingly, Spark exaggerates somewhat; there is no 'famous-persons file' as such (although as we will see, there is something very alike).[3] There are, though, marked similarities between Spark's fictional archives and the real one – not least the mountain of papers – and here one senses the writer poking fun at her own hoarding tendencies as well as her own archival arrangement. And this is not an isolated passage; Spark's fiction often features references to manuscripts, papers, executors, estates, and archives.

But lest one think that Spark is overly exaggerating, sections of her archive are constructed in a manner not dissimilar to that outlined in 'The Executor'. In the early parts of the archive (Acc. 10607), the 'correspondence' is subdivided into the categories of 'literary', 'general' and 'personal'. Later on, a distinction is made between 'letters' and 'correspondence' as two entirely separate categories. 'Letters' are from literary figures, politicians, royals, film stars, directors, artists, playwrights, performers – the fictional 'famous-person's file' – while the category 'correspondence' is, well, everyone else.

While some may question such a seemingly hierarchical delineation, any researcher seeking to find a letter from Graham Greene, Doris Lessing, Iris Murdoch, or Saul Bellow will be thankful they do not have to wade through fan mail, carburettor receipts, and boxes of correspondence from the likes of 'a Miss Mary Whitelaw or a Mrs Jonathan Brown' in order to find them (although these so-called ordinary files can often contain the most revealing material).[4] However, while there exists a distinction between categories ('letters' and 'correspondence'), researchers should be prepared to spend a significant amount of time in the archive, as Spark herself indicates in her 1992 autobiography *Curriculum Vitae*. Here she says that her archive contains:

> Almost every letter I have received, every note I have made, every cheque-book, every book of accounts, every appointments book, lists of names and addresses, my correspondence with publisher and agents throughout the world, with income tax departments, accountants, lawyers, turf accountants […] all and everything, I have conserved in a vast archive.[5]

And it is indeed vast. At around three hundred and sixty boxes totalling over one hundred and seventy feet or fifty-two metres of shelf space, the Spark archive is the largest modern literary archive of any single author held at the National Library of Scotland. And there is still more to arrive from Tuscany, where Spark spent the last few decades of her life with her closest friend and companion Penelope Jardine.

As noted, Spark's fiction often features archives, estates, executors, and manuscripts, but it is not just the fact that Spark talks about archives in her work that draws one to passages such as the above. It raises questions about the way in which she uses biographic and archival material in her fiction, and how this affects our understanding of her work. In *Curriculum*

Vitae, Spark writes, 'I transferred a number of my experiences in the Poetry Society, as I usually do, into a fictional background', and these experiences would form the foundation for her 1981 novel *Loitering with Intent*.[6] Notice that little aside 'as I usually do', suggesting that events from her life often make it into the pages of her fiction.[7] But in this process of transference from personal experience into fictional material, something intriguing happens. We know that in this instance, transfer really means transfigure. For example, when she suffered from textual hallucinations – whereby she began to see Greek codes and a 'word-game' embedded within the work of T. S. Eliot and others – she used elements of this experience in her debut novel *The Comforters* (1957).[8] Rather than simply recount the episode, Spark altered it to suit her new mode of expression at that point: the novel. She states that

> From the aspect of method, I could see that to create a character who suffered from verbal illusions on the printed page would be clumsy. So I made my main character 'hear' a typewriter with voices composing the novel itself.[9]

In this example, Spark adjusts her biographic source material to extract from it the desired fictional effect, but does so without losing aspects – the disorientation and paranoia – of the original experience.

Similarly, we should be cautious about over-simplifying the correlation between what is found in Spark's archive – what it reveals about her life events – and what this tells us about her work. As she says, 'From the aspect of method [that] would be clumsy'.[10] It is a point that was brought home powerfully, and in a sense literally, with the return of the manuscript of *The Prime of Miss Jean Brodie* (1961) to Scotland for the first time since early 1961, in the National Library of Scotland's 2017–18 exhibition 'The International Style of Muriel Spark'. The manuscript – kindly loaned by the McFarlin Library at the University of Tulsa – includes an author's note. This has never before been published, and it offers a fascinating insight into Spark's approach and her own evaluation of her work and methodology. In the note, Spark clarifies that 'The prime of MJB [*sic*]' is 'a work of fiction, not disguised autobiography'.[11] Spark also notes that any literal reading of the novel as such 'would be a blow to my pride of invention'.[12] And that phrase – 'my pride of invention' – tells us that the elements of transformation, of transfiguration, are essential to Spark's notion of what it means to be an artist.[13] One remembers the famous line from Proverbs 29.18 spoken by Miss Brodie: 'Where there is no vision [...] the people perish'.[14] But the act of seeing is not the same as vision; to see is not enough. In order to claim creative vision, the viewing act has to be combined with the imagination, and without due care, the positive requirements of noticing – or seeing – can decay into their murky antitheses of voyeurism and spying; a fruitful seam that Spark taps into regularly. Think of those who cannot transfigure what they see: Rowland Mahler in *The Finishing School* (2004), who – despite being a creative writing tutor – is only capable of viewing, a reality Spark alludes to in the title of his book '*The School Observed*'.[15] The implication is clear; this is a barely disguised diary – an inventory even – of events with no element of the vision, the imagination, or the 'pride of invention'[16] that Spark so values. We also have the comically inverse and reductive form of transfiguration whereby Teddy Lloyd paints endless Jean Brodies no matter the model who sits. Throughout Spark's fiction, artists and writers who fall foul of this lack of imagination come in for the sharp end of her belief in the 'arts of satire and of ridicule'.[17] What will become apparent, however, is the contrast between Spark's treatment of writers in her fiction, and those real-life cases in her archive where she is almost entirely kind to her fellow authors.

As Susan Kyle says of her uncle's archive, the Spark archive at the National Library of Scotland is literally a 'mountain of papers'.[18] And it is still growing. The Library recently received thirty-three boxes of material that relate to *The Golden Fleece: Essays* (2014) – or *The Informed Air* as it was titled in the United States. These boxes include Spark's essay on the twentieth-century Italian sculptor Giacomo Manzù, in which she writes: '[o]ne feels, with Manzù, that the art has chosen the artist. He troubles definition.'[19] These phrases have a familiar ring: 'the art has chosen the artist'[20] reminds us of Spark's words in *Curriculum Vitae*, where Spark's school teacher Miss Kay 'predicted my future as a writer in the most emphatic terms. I felt

I hardly had much choice in the matter.'²¹ And 'he troubles definition' is itself a definition that applies to Spark, the artist who evades classification, who defies categorisation.²² Spark is without doubt one of those distinctive voices, a writer who exists in that area between genres, in the liminal spaces that original artists populate.

Given the vast size of the Spark archive, any researcher consulting its papers is likely to make a new discovery, especially when viewing the more recently acquired material. So, what does the archive tell us and what has been discovered that might alter our understanding of Muriel Spark? Very briefly, the archive includes manuscripts and typescripts of Spark's poetry, with folders full of early drafts including those that Spark did not think worthy of publication. There are numerous short stories which she wrote in the 1950s, but revised and rewrote in the 1990s and which raise the intriguing critical possibility that Spark re-edited her work to a greater extent than previously thought. Also to be discovered is Spark's love of the wonderfully kitsch television soap opera *The Bold and the Beautiful*, and the remarkable correspondence which reveals that Spark wanted a film of the early part of her life to be made, going so far as to write a press release to be sent to the trade magazines. This movie was to be based on *Curriculum Vitae* and *Loitering with Intent*, and she wrote: 'I am sure this is the right thing. A film of this nature is very much what I want.'²³ But perhaps the most revealing material is to be found by consulting the entire stratification of 'letters' and 'correspondence' and analysing what can be revealed across these seemingly distinct areas. Following the publication of Spark's 1974 Watergate satire *The Abbess of Crewe*, she received a letter from Dr C. J. Wright, a member of staff of the British Museum. This was filed under the 'fan letters' section.

Dear Madam,

Much as I enjoyed reading *The Abbess of Crewe* I must object in the strongest possible terms to the detention of Sister Winifrede in the Gentlemen's Lavatory of the British Museum, wearing a Sidney

> Sussex tie, about which you add, somewhat gratuitously I thought, that it was 'emblematic of some university unidentified even by the Sunday press'. I only wish this were true. You will imagine the embarrassment to which, as a member of both institutions, I have been and will be subjected as a consequence of this passage. I would, therefore, greatly appreciate its amendment in any future edition. If you must choose a college, would not Jesus be more suitable? It is, after all, a former nunnery and I know of none of its men who work here.[24]

Entering into the spirit of things, Spark replies as though the entire Sister Winifrede episode is real, and not a character born of her imagination:

> I am truly sorry to learn that poor Sister Winifrede, who was snared by the harsh attendant of the British Museum while going about her normal business in the Gents, was careless enough to borrow your tie. I really think you should wear your tie during business hours and not leave it lying about for a defenceless nun to pick up. However, I apologize for having reported the incident in such detail as to embarrass you.[25]

When working through the archive, what soon becomes apparent is just how much time Spark gave to others, how generous she was in answering fan mail – such as this – and requests for her time. Her reply above is not the exception. This giving is reflected also in her support for other writers, particularly writers at the beginning of their careers, which is similarly heart-warming.

Readers and scholars of Spark will be aware of the support she received as she worked to establish herself early in her career, particularly from Graham Greene and Evelyn Waugh. Greene would commission Spark to read and review books, and pay her over the odds to do so. He also sent cheques accompanied with bottles of wine, which Spark famously said 'took the edge off cold charity'.[26] Waugh's support was – as far as the evidence in the archive shows – only verbal. However, what support. Her debut novel,

The Comforters, he described as 'Mrs Spark's remarkable book [...] brilliantly original and fascinating',[27] and it is worth revisiting his 1960 letter to her:

> Dear Mrs Spark
>
> How do you do it? I am dazzled by *The Bachelors*. Most novelists find there is one kind of book they can write (particularly humorous novelists) and go on doing with variations until death. You seem to have an inexhaustible source. *Bachelors* is the cleverest and most elegant of all your clever and elegant books [...] I suspect that you are still the sort of writer whom people rejoice to introduce to their friends; *Bachelors* shall take you clear through that phase into full fame. May you enjoy it.
>
> If your publisher wants a puff for you before the reviews appear he can quote 'I am dazzled by *The Bachelors*' and anything else in the foregoing note of homage.
>
> Yours sincerely,
>
> Evelyn Waugh
>
> I have gushed so about my delight in reading the book that I have neglected to thank you for the gift of it. Thank you.[28]

It is rare to come across higher praise from one writer to another – especially from an established author to one at the outset of their career. And Waugh was not known for his benevolence towards other writers. It is worth noting this to provide some context for Spark's similar generosity. There is no evidence that Spark provided financial assistance to any writers, and if she did one would assume that the publicity-averse Spark would have kept such generosity to herself. But her time – not only to reply, but to read what numerous writers sent her – as well as her subsequent encouragement, would have been invaluable to any writer, especially to those early in their career.

Spark's archive reveals her kindness repeatedly in evidence. In early 2000 the author Pearl Abraham writes: 'What a wonderful surprise to receive your letter, and to learn that you read and liked [my novel]'.[29] In the same file, the author Michael Arditti writes:

> Dear Dame Muriel, I wish to express my gratitude for your kindness in reading my novel [...] and for writing such a full and generous endorsement. On a personal level, it means an enormous amount to me that you enjoyed the book; on a professional one, it will make all the difference, when presenting the novel to the public, that it comes with the backing of a writer of your stature.[30]

Like Waugh, Spark knows that her endorsement will carry weight. And these are only two examples that form a recurring theme throughout the archive; where Spark's generosity, kind words, and encouragement towards other writers are in abundant evidence. When considered alongside the other examples of such benevolence found in the archive, a predominant pattern emerges that these are writers who, like Spark in the late 1950s and early 1960s, are trying to establish themselves. While examples are rarer, it is not just late in her career that she shows this. The early correspondence has her recommending Christine Brooke-Rose to her publisher during the 1960s, and she has kind words for established writers too. When Beryl Bainbridge writes, worrying that inspiration is drying up as she turns seventy, Spark replies that age is just a number, and that many authors have written great work late in their careers.[31]

    All of which makes for a stark contrast with the treatment of writers in her fiction, where she is anything but kind. But before considering such examples, it is worth looking at one writer who straddles both the fictional and the real categories. In Martin Stannard's *Muriel Spark: The Biography* he notes that in *The Ballad of Peckham Rye* (1960), the excerpts we hear from Dougal Douglas's ghost-biography of the wonderfully named Maria Cheeseman, are apparently written in the prose style of – in fact taken directly from – the novels of Spark's friend Pamela Hansford Johnson.[32] This was 1960, and in 1966 Muriel was still exchanging letters of close friendship with Johnson. So, there are exceptions, but here we see that Spark compartmentalises her obviously deleterious view of Johnson's prose style (or lack thereof) into her fiction, and omits it from the correspondence and friendship they maintained. And on the subject of characters who are writers, we might think of the cast of reprobates, diabolists, pontificators, and all-around narcissists of the poets'-pub scenes in *The Comforters*, or Hector Bartlett, the '*pisseur de copie*'[33] in *A Far Cry from Kensington* (1988), all the way through to the 'flamboyant literary success' Chris Wiley and the voyeuristic jealousy of Rowland Mahler in *The Finishing School*.[34] While there are exceptions – think of Freddy Hamilton in *The Mandelbaum Gate* (1965), for example, although Freddy is more of a committed amateur versifier – they are predominantly those fictional writers that most resemble Spark herself, such as Caroline Rose in *The Comforters* and Fleur Talbot in *Loitering with Intent*. One can recognise why Derek Stanford was rendered as the *pisseur*, given Spark's personal relationship with him (which became toxic), the inaccuracies he subsequently peddled, and the fact he sold their love-letters to a third party. With the exception of Stanford, Spark is reticent about denigrating other writers in her personal archive.

Spark was also kind to students of her work. There are numerous personal replies, and an entire file that includes articles to send to students, along with a bibliography of the Muriel-approved literary criticism of her work. It is the kind of generosity that we do not often hear about in relation to Spark, and the archive reveals that a number of these students would go on to become friends and correspondents long after their initial enquiries. It is perhaps too easy to say that such generosity is simply Spark paying back the generosity she received from Waugh and Greene. It would be disingenuous to suggest that Spark never crossed swords with friends or other writers, but the extent to which she did has been somewhat exaggerated. This is perhaps less the case in relation to the publishing world, where she had a number of disagreements with agents, publishers, editors, and where she could be especially short with those who altered or interpreted her work. On receiving a first draft of the BBC screenplay for *Memento Mori* (1959) in 1990, Spark writes back to say that the scriptwriters should scrap their first attempt, and start again from scratch. But this simply illustrates that she was protective of her work, as any writer or artist might be. As this next example attests, attempts to define her may fall foul of a stiff retort, this time from Penelope on Muriel's behalf. On being asked – again – to submit to a collection of women's writing, Penelope replies that (Muriel) 'considers herself a Writer. She writes for Women and Men. And she is still waiting for scientific proof that the intellect has a gender.'[35]

Looking after the Spark archive at the National Library of Scotland means dealing with Spark enquiries from readers and researchers. From a practical perspective, such requests often mean having to consult parts of the archive that remain as yet un-catalogued – or which were catalogued in the 1990s. The writer and journalist Alan Taylor requested the location of the correspondence regarding the incident of Muriel and the tax man, from 1952. Alan writes about this in his 2017 book *Appointment in Arezzo* in which he recounts how Muriel entered into a dialogue with said taxman, a Mr R. C. Mitchell. In her letter dated 18 May 1952, she says of her £250 prize for the *Observer* short story competition:

> [s]hould the inclusion of this sum in my income make me liable to tax, I should wish to appeal against its inclusion, for the following reasons: The prize was not, in any sense, professional earnings [...] I am not a short story writer. I am a critic and biographer. I doubt if I shall ever have another short story published. The only creative writing I do is poetry.[36]

On 28 May the taxman replies: 'looking at the matter financially it is hardly possible, I suggest, to draw a hard and fast line between one form of literary earnings and another'.[37] Having failed to convince the tax man to waive any deductions, Muriel takes a different tack. All is not lost (and this part of the episode follows on from that included in Taylor's book). She writes back on 1 June, saying that she had forgotten to include 'an important item in her list of expenses' – her rent.[38] She states: 'I live in London for the sole purpose of my literary work, and in order to be near publishers and editors. My own home is in Scotland, with my parents, and my son aged 14 lives in Scotland also.'[39] She goes on to appeal for sixty-eight pounds, half of her rent for the entire year, to be deducted. The tax man agrees and Spark wins, and in so doing ensures that whatever she stood to lose through taxation is negated by a reduction in her taxable income, because her London flat is used for the professional purpose of writing. This whole episode is illuminating in a number of ways. Spark does not simply reject authority for the sake of it (although she certainly does not accept authority unthinkingly), but here she refuses to take the initial ruling as the final word. It must have been difficult for Spark to make such a case to the tax man in the first instance, and her attempt to delineate between forms of literary earnings has a boldness that verges on impudence. Most of all, perhaps, it demonstrates her determination to assert herself as a writer. Spark was at this point struggling financially, yet she gave fifty of her two hundred and fifty pounds in winnings to Derek Stanford, equivalent to nearly eleven hundred pounds in today's money. The tax episode demonstrates Spark defending her career; she is clearly determined that the opportunity afforded by her win be grasped wholeheartedly. And yet her gift to Stanford again illustrates her generosity. One senses that Spark could see this opportunity evaporating before her eyes, money that would support her and her son Robin as well as her dreams of being a writer. Hence the need to cling to every penny that would extend the time available to her for writing.

We perhaps should not be surprised at Spark's tax – and then rent – appeals, because she already had demonstrated her capacity for standing up to authority figures, or certainly, figures with greater public standing. Her spat with Dr Marie Stopes – pioneer of birth-control clinics and aspirant poet – proved that Spark would stand her ground. Following Spark's securing of the editorial role at the Poetry Society's magazine the *Poetry Review*, Stopes writes to Spark to ask if it is true that Spark's husband had divorced her. Stopes accuses Spark of impertinence over her refusal to answer any such questions, before claiming that her position as Vice President of the Poetry Society affords her the right to seek such information. Spark replies:

> I have received your outrageously impudent letter of 27th May.
> My private affairs are no concern of yours and your malicious

> interest in them seems to me to be most unwholesome. [...] I must say your attitude fills me with contempt, as it would all right-thinking people.[40]

She then tells Stopes that the libel lawyers will be informed if there is a continuation of such requests. In reality the row had more to do with Spark's plans to publish modernist poetry in the *Poetry Review*, an editorial decision which outraged many of the members and led to a rupture that threatened the continuation of the Society.[41] The incident, however, is clear evidence that Spark would not accept being dictated to by a prominent figure, especially within a context in which Spark was by far the greater qualified. The Stopes episode is one of many during her tenure at the Poetry Society that awakens in Spark the necessity to accumulate and maintain an archive of textual proof, as she explains:

> After leaving the Poetry Society I became aware of the value of documentary evidence, both as a means of personal defence against inaccuracies and as an aid to one's own memory. Consequently, since 1949 onwards I have thrown away practically nothing on paper.[42]

From what she reveals here, it strongly suggests that Spark researchers arguably owe a debt to the likes of Stopes, Stanford, and those who inspired in her the need to record her life in an archival framework.

Throughout the period of the late forties and into the early fifties, incorporating her victory in the *Observer* short story competition, and the subsequent episode with the tax man, Spark was studying John Henry Newman. The Library holds a selection of books from Spark's personal library in the archive, including her annotated copy of Newman's *Apologia Pro Vita Sua*. It is a crucial text for Spark, one which – along with Newman's sermons – had a significant influence on her in terms of theology, psychology and literary style. In the *Apologia*, Newman argues that the Church is the site of an on-going, but necessary internal battle, and in this battle between

[a]uthority and Private Judgement [...] it is the vast Catholic body itself, and it only, which affords an arena for both combatants in that awful, never-dying duel. It is necessary for the very life of religion, viewed in its large operations and its history, that the warfare should be incessantly carried on.[43]

Here, Newman lays out his vision of the individual's crucial role within the body of the Church, outlining the need for 'The energy of the human intellect' to be brought to bear upon the Church's teachings.[44] This debate, he says, renders the 'Catholic Christendom [as] no simple exhibition of religious absolutism, but [...] a continuous picture of Authority and Private Judgement alternatively advancing and retreating as the ebb and flow of the tide'.[45] In addition to her admiration for Newman the man, Spark's recognition of the struggles he endured, and her love of his writing style, this passage suggests the possibility that Spark could become Catholic whilst continuing to express 'the energy of [her] human intellect', and not simply adhering to all aspects of Ecclesiastical authority.[46] This entanglement of the back-and-forth between the authority of the church and the private judgement of the individual reminds us of the narrator's words about Jean Brodie, who 'was by temperament suited only to the Roman Catholic Church; possibly it could have embraced, even while it disciplined, her soaring and diving spirit, it might even have normalised her'.[47] This concept of the Church embracing Miss Brodie's 'soaring and diving spirit'[48] is conceptually close, reminiscent even, of Newman's words where 'authority and private judgement [are] alternatively advancing and retreating as the ebb and flow of the tide'.[49] One senses, then, that Spark was fully aware of Newman's position, and embraced aspects of the authority of the Church at the same time as she welcomed the intellectual freedom he outlines.

The Spark archive contains an abundance of material which offers interpretive possibilities that may help to illuminate author and work. However, Spark does not often make the kind of pronouncement where such connections become easily straightforward. While examples such as Spark's annotated books are illustrative of the depth of her reading, one of the pleasures of working with the archive is that one encounters an abundance of fragmentary insights into Spark's daily life that are dispersed throughout. These insights serve to de-mystify Spark and her work and accentuate the routine aspects of her life which in turn serves to emphasise the time and work she invested. So, while researchers may be looking for the correspondence that reveals the motivation behind Spark's literary work, or intertextual allusions which add interpretive possibilities, sometimes the sheer range of material serves to reveal something that perhaps no one was looking for. There is plenty to sift through, as Spark outlines in *Curriculum Vitae* where she states: 'I am a hoarder of two things: documents and trusted friends.'[50] One example illustrates that the day-to-day life Muriel enjoyed in Tuscany with Penelope had a generous element of fun. Written on a post-it note, Muriel says 'I bet PJ (Penelope Jardine) 10,000 Italian lira Bush wins. PJ says Clinton wins' and then in Penelope's handwriting: 'Mr Clinton will win – the last word PJ'.[51] Of course Mr Clinton did win the 1992 US Presidential election, and Penelope netted the colossal sum of ten thousand lira – approximately £4.67.

Asked by a friend for advice on where to stay in Edinburgh, Muriel offers practical advice – one can imagine here the earliest seeds of Nina's *comme il faut* lessons in *The Finishing School*. She says: 'The Braid Hills Hotel still apparently flourishes, although it is inclined to be chilly. The Roxburghe is all right, but they are very stingy with the soap.'[52] Perhaps not as useful as Nina's advice to her students to wave a handkerchief at a charging elephant – apparently it confuses their legs – but nevertheless useful to know, as is the fact that she kept the brass plaque from outside her childhood home in Bruntsfield Place in Edinburgh, advertising her mother as a 'teacher of pianoforte'.[53]

Spark nurtured strong friendships from an early age. One of the most touching items in the archive is the handmade laurel wreath made from wax and paper, presented by Frances Niven, Spark's closest childhood friend, when Spark was crowned Young Poetess in 1932. Holding this fragile item, what is immediately evident is the tender care and attention that has gone into its construction, likewise the accompanying verse written by Frances to Muriel on a tiny fragment of paper. It reads:

> Though on fame's dizzy heights you stand,
> Though you climb ladders without end,
> Please don't forget me for I am
> Your dear and most devoted friend.[54]

Writing almost sixty years later, Spark says of the wreath and verse – 'which I still treasure' – that '"fame's dizzy heights" are more often than not a great pain in the neck'.[55] Spark did find such fame, and the 2018 centenary of Spark's birth afforded the National Library of Scotland the opportunity to stage an exhibition to celebrate her life and work by displaying selected contents of her archive. But how to tell the life of a writer such as Muriel Spark? As someone who lived in locations across the globe, and for whom style was not restricted to semantic systems and lexical choice, but appeared crucial to all aspects of her life, Spark was to be celebrated under the rubric of 'The International Style of Muriel Spark'. The exhibition was structured around the locations in which she lived, with six discrete sections: Edinburgh, Southern Rhodesia, London, New York, Rome, and Tuscany. Taking on the challenge that Spark's writing presents, these sections were presented out of linear chronology to reflect the narrative structure of novels such as *The Driver's Seat* (1970) and *The Prime of Miss Jean Brodie*. As a result, the visitor might read the exhibition in a way reminiscent of Spark's use of flash-forward and flashback in her work. Rather than present her life narrative in the familiar birth-to-death line starting in Edinburgh in 1918, the exhibition began at the height of her success, in her years in Rome starting from 1966, then narrated back to her struggling years in bedsit London, to her time in Southern Rhodesia, followed by Edinburgh, New York, and finally re-integrated chronologically with her last decades in Tuscany. There are of course numerous examples of analepsis and prolepsis in Spark's work, but it was the voice of Lister from *Not to Disturb* (1971) that provided textual justification for the structure of the exhibition: 'let us not strain after vulgar chronology', 'let us not split hairs [...] Between the past, present and future tenses'.[56]

Spark is of course a writer for whom style is crucial and whose prose is utterly unique, whether her rendering of dialogue, her style in the broad sense of her wonderfully pithy, concise, crystalline text, or the unsettling, partially omniscient, narrative position and tone she often adopts. But her work is often concerned with the broader context of style, particularly design, fashion, and art. Miss Brodie proclaims that 'pictorial art is my passion', with Dante Gabriel Rossetti, Botticelli, Giotto, and Leonardo all featuring in that novel alone.[57] Fashion is another recurring feature. One thinks of the central motif of the Schiaparelli dress in *The Girls of Slender of Slender Means* (1963), and Miss Brodie's myriad outfits. Similarly, Miss Kay's advice in *Curriculum Vitae*, to wear 'a grey coat and skirt [...] with a citron beret' – and note her specificity in adding: 'it is yellow with a sixteenth or so of blue' – and Lise's intentionally alarming visual cacophony of an outfit in *The Driver's Seat*.[58]

Having come up with a title and a concept for dividing the exhibition space and the narrative into non-chronological 'location and era' sections, the next question was how would we present the display material in terms of design? Following a conversation with Professor Robert Hosmer of Smith College, his suggestion that we include a recreation of Muriel's Tuscany writing desk was expanded upon, and the designers came up with the concept of imaginative recreations of Spark's writing spaces for five of the six locations. In so doing they managed to evoke a tangible sense of these locations – of specific places at a point in time – through design style. Presenting the archival material in these recreations of Spark's writing spaces aligned with her own words, that 'a famous writer's house is irresistible; I find sheer magic in the rooms'.[59] This was proven to be the case with strong evidence in the archive of Muriel's visits to the houses of writers, musicians, and philosophers. Such material includes a National Trust booklet for visitors to Thomas Hardy's cottage, and similar leaflets from the houses of Edvard Grieg, Anne Frank, and Jean-Jacques Rousseau. Also, there are notes by Spark about her visit to Lamb House, Henry James's home in Rye, East Sussex. Somewhat ironically, when asked to contribute to a BBC programme where writers would talk about their house, Penelope replies on Muriel's behalf, saying Muriel is unable to participate because 'she does not have a house. She lives in the house of a friend.'[60] This succeeds in both being true, whilst also being a charmingly evasive way of saying no.

CORRESPONDENCE AND THE META-ARCHIVAL

A number of Spark's original manuscripts were on display in the exhibition, including pages from her most famous work *The Prime of Miss Jean Brodie*, as well as *The Driver's Seat*, and *Curriculum Vitae*. But the majority of the manuscript exhibit was drawn from Spark's voluminous correspondence and included all of the names that one would expect, such as Jackie Onassis's offer for the rights to *Curriculum Vitae*, and Liz Taylor's expressing her admiration – and that of Richard Burton – for Spark's work. Other correspondents included were Harold Macmillan, T. S. Eliot, Gore Vidal, Iris Murdoch, John Updike, Doris Lessing, Evelyn Waugh, Graham Greene, George Mackay Brown, Beryl Bainbridge, Sir Alec Guinness, Dame Maggie Smith, and Vanessa Redgrave. Despite his brilliance, Saul Bellow – mentioned in 'The Executor' – did not make it.

To return to the earlier point, the correspondence on show – with the notable exception of Dr Marie Stopes – shows Spark's capacity for warmth and wit. And in addition to the friendships she sustained over decades, she also reveals how she saw herself. While researching former Poet Laureate John Masefield for her critical study, Spark writes to him, requesting to meet at Oxford train station, stating: 'I could be recognised by my green coat, small stature, and (as I am told) bewildered air.'[61] Perhaps the most insightful gaze into her time in Southern Rhodesia is contained in the correspondence between Spark and Nobel Prize winner Doris Lessing. They lived close to each other but did not meet and correspond until many years later. In 2003 Lessing writes to ask 'how and why were you there. [*sic*] You must see it is a fairly improbable combination, Muriel Spark and Southern Rhodesia.'[62] Spark, with typical economy, reveals, 'I had secretarial jobs. I preferred Bulawayo to Salisbury […] I won a poetry competition […] I was really very young and rather dumb. I would have loved to meet you.'[63] Spark lists her African stories, four of which would appear in her 1958 collection *The Go-away Bird*. Reflecting on their experiences, Lessing notes that '[o]ne woman in her time may play many parts. Well we both have.'[64] In another identity-questioning philosophical sentence, Lessing writes: 'we under-estimate how poses and styles and affectations can eat into the mask and become the face'.[65] John Updike is another correspondent across decades. His letters are full of expressions of his respect for Spark's work. This warm admiration was mutual. Writing to Updike in 1991, Spark says:

> Dear John, [...] It was truly good to hear from you. Your feeling for my work has always meant a great deal to me [...] You are so prolific and so talented and expressive, I don't know how you do it, I admire your work more than I can say. *Rabbit at Rest* has just arrived and sits beside me on the desk. I smile before I even open it.[66]

In subsequent correspondence – almost forty years after his first letter to Spark in 1963 – Updike reveals his pleasure at reading all of Spark's works as they are published. In addition to these decades-long relationships, Spark corresponded with a number of other well-known figures. Iris Murdoch writes repeatedly during the 1970s, encouraging Spark to move back to London, which – for a time – Spark was considering. Former Prime Minister Harold Macmillan claims to be too old to party, but manages to attend a number of soirees at Spark's apartment in Rome. On the subject of one such party Miriam Margolyes – who starred in the BBC's adaptation of Spark's novel *The Girls of Slender Means* – writes, 'for me it was a particularly special occasion, infinitely glamorous, socially devastating, for I have never met all in one go such a number of distinguished people. I felt honoured and privileged.'[67] The day after she wins the Best Actress Oscar for her performance as Jean Brodie, Dame Maggie Smith writes to Spark to thank her 'for creating such a wonderful character for me to play'.[68] Vanessa Redgrave, writing in 1966 during the run of *The Prime of Miss Jean Brodie* in London's West End, writes that 'Jean Brodie and the play seem to enthral the audience'.[69] In addition to such stars, Spark was always closely involved with the creative and artistic community wherever she lived, and this meant a range of friends who were neither affluent nor famous.

What all these letters illustrate is that Spark sustained friendships. When working with the Spark archive, one almost expects to encounter a frosty, aloof, difficult personality in the correspondence. Muriel and Penelope can often display a forceful directness when dealing with the business side of her writing career, but while there are disagreements, what emerges in the correspondence is something else. Spark was determined; she knew she wanted to write, and she pursued that. What might have appeared as an anti-authoritarian streak was rather the expression of her fierce intelligence; she was stylish in both work and life, and utterly original in her art. But the archive also reveals a character who could be kind, warm, generous, and giving.

While Spark outlines the need to accumulate an archive for proof and accuracy, what is notable is the way in which the process of retaining an archive becomes part of her writing, rather than simply anterior to it. In *Loitering with Intent*, her brilliant 1981 novel, the character Fleur Talbot asks herself:

> Why did I keep all these letters? Why? They are all neatly bundled up in thin folders, tied with pink tape, 1949, 1950, 1951 and on and on. I was trained to be a secretary; maybe I felt that letters ought to be filed, and I'm sure I thought they would be interesting one day.[70]

Here Spark writes her own archive into the story – some of her letters were indeed tied with pink tape – and through Fleur's questioning of why she retains her letters, Spark opens up the novel's interrogation of what it means to create an archive, and it leads to one of Spark's favourite subjects: blackmail. This passage encapsulates Spark's use of archives in her fiction: archives are not just the product and the evidence of a writing life; they contain it, and they in turn sustain it. While many writers keep an archive, not all write their archives into their fiction.

For Spark, then, her archive is not only 'a means of personal defence against inaccuracies and [...] an aid to one's own memory', crucially it is also material from which new fictions can be created.[71] This is true not just in the sense that she returns to unfinished ideas and previous fragments of work, although she does do this. Rather, the evidence suggests that Spark sees the whole endeavour of archives and archiving as also containing the moral and ethical dilemmas that she explores in her work. Or to put it another way, she takes the materiality of her archive, and uses it to question fundamental archival choices. One can imagine her asking herself: how do

I categorise my correspondence? – do I discard or embargo anything? – what should remain private? – should I sell or donate my papers? – and to whom? She realises that these archival questions are themselves full of the dilemmas, possibilities, and tensions from which fiction can be made. Spark makes archives a territory within which to interrogate greed, loss, duplicity, loyalty, blackmail, empathy, even identity itself. In other words, the moral, ethical, philosophical, and spiritual questions that she examines throughout her oeuvre. For example – returning to the story 'The Executor' – Susan Kyle, in finding the manuscript of her deceased uncle's unfinished novel, decides to finish it herself. When she later returns to the manuscript, a note has eerily appeared in her dead uncle's hand, which says: 'Well, Susan, how do you feel about finishing my novel? Aren't you a greedy little snoot, holding back my unfinished work, when you know the Foundation paid for the lot? What about your puritanical principles?'.[72] Here the ethical dilemma, the greed, the opportunism, and the supernatural – all recurring elements throughout Spark's fiction – are created from the potential fictional energy that an unfinished manuscript offers. There are other examples: as mentioned, the use of archival autobiography becomes the foundation for blackmail in *Loitering with Intent*. 'Open to the Public' culminates in the destruction of Henry Castlemaine's papers, his daughter and ex-husband burning his archive rather than succumbing to 'the same old industry [of] Letters from students, letters from scholars'.[73] Without this act of destruction, the afterlife of the archive would ensure that they 'would never be free […] those ghosts, would never let us go'.[74] The poem 'Created and Abandoned' and the re-written version of the short story 'Harper and Wilton' have archives woven into their narratives. We might think of these lines in Spark's poem 'Going Up to Sotheby's':

> And now the grandchildren are selling the manuscript.
> Bound and proud, documented and glossed
> by scholars of the land, smoothed out
> and precious, these leaves of paper
> are going up to Sotheby's.[75]

Unlike in 'Open to the Public', here we glimpse the wider legacy of the writer's papers being realised, with their archive now entering the cultural landscape, analysed by readers and academics. But this broadening of scope is in contrast to the narrower matters of family and finance, with the descendants in line to benefit; a situation reminiscent of her story 'The Executor', and full of ethical and moral possibilities that the tale explores. These are just a few examples from Spark's work where she utilised her knowledge of generating and sustaining – and even destroying – an archive to create fiction and poetry referring to this process and its materiality. They leave no doubt as to the importance she placed on the real thing, whether her own papers, or the archives of others. In a fax from November 1996, Spark writes a touching message to the writer and critic Frank Kermode, following a fire at his home:

> Dear Frank, Hearing about a frightful loss of some of your papers I was about to write you a consolatory letter. I don't know if such an event is consolable and can only hope that some part, maybe a good part of your archives were saved.[76]

Spark's sympathy for Kermode's loss of his papers is palpable, and in the phrase 'I don't know if such an event is consolable', we hear her real voice, not mediated through fiction or character or plot, but the voice of one writer to another, lamenting the loss of his archive.[77]

If meta-fiction is the practice of writing fiction that foregrounds its very fictionality – or in other words, writing fiction about writing fiction – then Muriel Spark is a meta-archival writer. Not only is her work replete with references to archives, manuscripts, executors, and estates, but in a feedback loop of archival self-referentiality, Spark has created an archive from writing, then created writing from an archive that she clearly treasured.

Endnotes

1. My thanks to all those who granted permission to be quoted, particularly to Penelope Jardine for permission to quote from the Spark archives at the National Library of Scotland, and the University of Tulsa, Oklahoma. Also, thank you to the Estate of Doris Lessing for permission to quote from the Lessing correspondence, and to the Estate of Evelyn Waugh and the Wylie Agency (UK) for permission to quote from the letters of Evelyn Waugh. My gratitude also to the following for their kindness in allowing their correspondence with Muriel Spark to be quoted: Pearl Abraham; Michael Arditti; Miriam Margolyes; Vanessa Redgrave; Dame Maggie Smith; and Dr C. J. Wright.

    Sections of this essay have appeared in the following: Colin McIlroy, '"A Social History in Itself": The Muriel Spark Archive at the National Library of Scotland', *Broadsheet* 46 (Summer 2018) www.scottisharchives.org.uk/wp-content/uploads/2018/10/Issue-46-Summer-2018-1.pdf; Colin McIlroy, 'The Denial of the Self: The Romantic Imagination and the Problem of Belief in Muriel Spark's *The Prime of Miss Jean Brodie* (1961)' (unpublished master's thesis, University of Glasgow, 2011). www.theses.gla.ac.uk/2918/.

    Please note: all references to the Spark accessions 11621, 11344, 11870, 12082, and 13508 held at the National Library of Scotland may be subject to change as these are currently in an interim arrangement while being listed.

2. Muriel Spark, 'The Executor', in *Muriel Spark: The Complete Short Stories* (Edinburgh: Canongate, 2011), pp. 252–63, (p. 254).
3. Ibid.
4. Ibid.
5. Muriel Spark, *Curriculum Vitae* [1992] (Manchester: Carcanet, 2009), p. 185.
6. Ibid., p. 184.
7. Ibid.
8. Ibid., p. 204.
9. Ibid., pp. 206–07.
10. Ibid.
11. Muriel Spark, Manuscript Notebook 1, *The Prime of Miss Jean Brodie*, the Muriel Spark papers 1957–88, Department of Special Collections & University Archives Repository, McFarlin Library, University of Tulsa (UT), 1983.003.1.59.2-5.
12. Ibid.
13. Ibid.
14. Muriel Spark, *The Prime of Miss Jean Brodie* [1961] (Harmondsworth: Penguin, 1971), p. 7.
15. Muriel Spark, *The Finishing School* [2004] (London: Penguin, 2005), p. 154.
16. UT, 1983.003.1.59.2-5.
17. Muriel Spark, 'The Desegregation of Art', in *Critical Essays on Muriel Spark*, ed. Joseph Hynes (New York, NY: G. K. Hall & Co., 1992), pp. 33–37 (p. 35).
18. Spark, 'The Executor', p. 254.
19. Muriel Spark, 'Giacomo Manzù', in *The Golden Fleece: Essays*, ed. Penelope Jardine (Manchester: Carcanet Press Limited, 2014), pp. 23–26 (p. 24).
20. Ibid.
21. Spark, *Curriculum Vitae*, p. 66.
22. Spark, 'Giacomo Manzù', p. 24.

23 Muriel Spark (*pp* Penelope Jardine), Fax to Ruth Arnaud of Casarotto Ramsay Ltd., 24 September 1992. The Muriel Spark archive, National Library of Scotland (NLS), Acc. 11344/Box 4, File: 'Enders, Bob, c. 1987–'95'.
24 Dr C. J. Wright, Letter to Muriel Spark, 11 December 1974. NLS, Acc. 10607/86.63.
25 Muriel Spark, Letter to Dr C. J. Wright, 19 December 1974. NLS, Acc. 10607/86.64.
26 Spark, *Curriculum Vitae*, p. 205.
27 Evelyn Waugh, Letter to Mr Fielding, 29 October 1956. NLS, Acc. 10607/92.156. The Estate of Evelyn Waugh, used by permission of The Wylie Agency (UK) Limited.
28 Evelyn Waugh, Letter to Muriel Spark, 11 October 1960. NLS, Acc. 10607/91.145. The Estate of Evelyn Waugh, used by permission of The Wylie Agency (UK) Limited.
29 Pearl Abraham, Letter to Muriel Spark, 11 October 2000. NLS, Acc. 12082/Box 9 (Letters vol V), File: 'Abraham – Jones'.
30 Michael Arditti, Letter to Muriel Spark, 10 January 2000. NLS, Acc. 12082/Box 9 (Letters vol V), File: 'Abraham – Jones'.
31 Beryl Bainbridge, Letter to Muriel Spark, 25 August 2004. NLS, Acc. 13508/Box 78.
32 See: Martin Stannard, *Muriel Spark: The Biography* (London: Weidenfeld and Nicolson, 2009), pp. 266–67.
33 Muriel Spark, *A Far Cry from Kensington* [1988] (London: Penguin, 1989), p. 45.
34 Spark, *The Finishing School*, p. 137.
35 Penelope Jardine, Fax to Gina Dobbs of David Higham Associates, 28 May 1990. NLS, Acc. 11344/Box 17, File: 'David Higham Associates, Permissions, Jan–June 1990'.
36 Muriel Spark, Letter to Mr R. C. Mitchell, Her Majesty's Inspector of Taxes, 18 May 1952. NLS, Acc. 10607/6.
37 R. C. Mitchell, Letter to Muriel Spark, 28 May 1952. NLS, Acc. 10607/6.
38 Muriel Spark, Letter to R. C. Mitchell, 1 June 1952. NLS, Acc. 10607/6.
39 Ibid.
40 Muriel Spark, Letter to Dr Marie Stopes, 29 May 1948. NLS, Acc. 10607/101.334.
41 See Spark, *Curriculum Vitae*, pp. 174–75, and p. 178, for more on the fall-out with Stopes.
42 Spark, *Curriculum Vitae*, p. 185.
43 John Henry Newman, *Apologia Pro Vita Sua* (Glasgow: William Collins Sons & Co Ltd, 1977), p. 286. For an illuminating consideration of Newman's influence on Spark, see Benilde Montgomery, 'Spark and Newman: Jean Brodie Reconsidered', in *Twentieth Century Literature* 43.1 (Spring 1997), pp. 94–106.
44 Ibid.
45 Ibid., p. 286; p. 286.
46 Ibid.
47 Spark, *The Prime of Miss Jean Brodie*, p. 85.
48 Ibid.
49 Newman, *Apologia Pro Vita Sua*, p. 286; p. 286.
50 Spark, *Curriculum Vitae*, p. 11.
51 Muriel Spark and Penelope Jardine, Note, undated (although it can reasonably be assumed to be 3 November 1992, the date of the presidential election in the United States). NLS, Acc. 11344/Box 17, File: 'Houghton Mifflin, C.V. Production and Promotion, 1992 – 1994'.
52 Muriel Spark, Letter to Barbara Morey, 23 April 1991. NLS, Acc. 11344/Box 14, File: 'Letters from Public in response to CV, 1989 – 1995'.

53 Brass plate of Mrs Bernard Camberg (Muriel Spark's mother), teacher of pianoforte, Edinburgh. NLS, Acc. 12730.
54 Frances Niven (later Cowell), in Spark, *Curriculum Vitae*, p. 69. Original item: NLS, Acc. 11870/4.
55 Spark, *Curriculum Vitae*, p. 69.
56 Muriel Spark, *Not to Disturb* [1971] (London: Granada, 1981), p. 40; p. 6.
57 Spark, *The Prime of Miss Jean Brodie*, p. 66.
58 Spark, *Curriculum Vitae*, p. 60.
59 Spark, 'Footnote to "The Poet's House"', in *The Golden Fleece: Essays*, ed. Penelope Jardine, pp. 70–72 (p. 71).
60 Penelope Jardine, Fax to Rachel Linton, 25 September 1996. NLS, Acc. 11621/194.
61 Muriel Spark, Letter to John Masefield, 1 December 1950. NLS, Acc. 10607/89.68.
62 Doris Lessing, Letter to Muriel Spark, 1 February 2002. NLS, Acc. 13508/Box 78.
63 Muriel Spark, Fax to Doris Lessing, 25 January 2002. NLS, Acc. 13508/Box 78.
64 Doris Lessing, Letter to Muriel Spark, 1 February 2002. NLS, Acc. 13508/Box 78.
65 Ibid.
66 Muriel Spark, Letter to John Updike, 26 January 1991. NLS, Acc. 10607/103.511.
67 Miriam Margolyes, Letter to Muriel Spark, 20 April 1975. NLS, Acc. 10607/103.474.
68 Dame Maggie Smith, Telegram to Muriel Spark, 8 April 1970. NLS, Acc. 10607/89.89.
69 Vanessa Redgrave, Letter to Muriel Spark, 27 May 1966. NLS, Acc. 10607/88.46.
70 Muriel Spark, *Loitering with Intent* [1981] (London: Virago, 2003), p. 3.
71 Spark, *Curriculum Vitae*, p. 185.
72 Spark, 'The Executor', p. 257.
73 Muriel Spark, 'Open to the Public', in *Muriel Spark: The Complete Short Stories*, pp. 205–20 (p. 220).
74 Ibid.
75 Muriel Spark, 'Going Up to Sotheby's', in *Going Up to Sotheby's and Other Poems* (London: Granada, 1982), p. 11.
76 Muriel Spark, Fax to Frank Kermode, 23 November 1996. NLS, Acc. 11621/18.
77 Ibid.

2. Muriel Spark's Waywardness

CAROLE JONES

Spark as Wayward

'Critics are fond of describing Muriel Spark as ruthless', Zoë Strachan points out,[1] and Janice Galloway confirms, 'Malcolm Bradbury is on record as reading Mrs Spark's essence as "hardness"'. Others – mostly chaps – sum her up as 'steely', 'aloof', 'brusque', 'capricious' and 'queer'.[2] I interpret the surfeit of judgemental descriptions as commenting on or targeting Spark's womanliness or, rather, her lack in that area. She is seen as calculating and cold, which signify a lack of feminine softness, nurturance and propriety with Ian Gregson going so far as to state that Spark is the 'least feminine of women writers'.[3] My aim in this chapter is not to directly dissect or resist the pejorative nature of the assessments often intended in these comments but to engage constructively with an aspect of Spark's writing that they implicitly and hysterically foreground: her refusal to comply with the expectations, in various periods, of the 'woman writer'. In taking this stance I employ the term 'wayward' to describe Spark's work and situate her in a discourse which is not entirely oppositional but aptly describes her askew sensibility; one that has proved adept at irking her critics. The notion of the 'wayward' provides us with a small hand-hold on the inexplicable but brilliant conundrum of Spark's writing that leaves us more often than not, as she says in her lecture 'The Desegregation of Art', 'with a sense of the absurd and a general looking-lively to defend ourselves from the ridiculous oppressions of our times'.[4]

Waywardness resonates with other more penetrating descriptions of Spark's work: with James Bailey's disorientation and obliqueness, Jonathan Kemp's queerness, Gutkin's camp,[5] Marilyn Reizbaum's strangeness, Martin McQuillan's contrapuntality, and Patricia Waugh's 'not quite', in her description of Spark as 'familiar and yet displaced; almost realist, but not quite; seemingly postmodern, but not'.[6] Moreover, waywardness plays merrily in the same discursive playground as Spark's own 'nevertheless': as she writes in 'What Images Return',

> my whole education in and out of school, seemed even then to pivot around this word [...] I believe myself to be fairly indoctrinated by the habit of thought which calls for this word [...] I find that much of my literary composition is based on the nevertheless idea.[7]

I am associating the 'nevertheless' moment, that quixotic or even perverse point of *turning* in a discourse – the moment of 'however', of 'in spite of what has just been stated I will now state the contrary' – with the wilful disruption of waywardness.

Here I am engaging the notion of 'wayward' as a quality often, but not always, associated with the feminine. According to the *Oxford English Dictionary* the term signifies 'disposed to go counter to the wishes or advice of others, or to what is reasonable; wrong-headed, intractable, self-willed, perverse [...] Capriciously wilful; conforming to no fixed rule or principle of conduct; erratic'. Unreasonable, contrary, perversely turning from fixed rules and principles – many of Spark's texts, with their frequently foregrounded women, are recognisable here. Angela Carter deliberately associates waywardness with females in her edited collection of short stories by women writers, *Wayward Girls and Wicked Women*. In the introduction she points out that all the stories she has chosen 'are reflections in some kind of squinting, oblique, penetrating vision',[8] a wayward sensibility situated in the rebellious, constricted feminine position of the patriarchal reality. Carter says of the women in these stories, 'even in defeat, they are not defeated',[9] and though this may not feel entirely true of a character such as Lise in *The Driver's Seat* (1970), Spark's writing and her characters pulse with the clarity and control of the undefeated, even if her vision is one of macabre indifference and indeterminacy. Spark's more difficult feminine representations, such as Lise, Elsa of *The Hothouse by the East River* (1973) and Annabelle of *The Public Image* (1968), present us with intriguing portraits of wayward women, each in their own particular way fulfilling a wilfully perverse snubbing of male reality.

Defining Waywardness

As defined, waywardness involves a wilful and erratic wandering from what is reasonable and the fixed rules of propriety. The precarious position of the straying self is suggestively described by Judith Butler:

> The 'I' that I am finds itself at once constituted by norms and dependent on them but also endeavours to live in ways that maintain a critical and transformative relation to them. This is not easy, because the 'I' becomes, to a certain extent unknowable, threatened with unviability, with becoming undone altogether, when it no longer incorporates the norm in such a way that makes this 'I' fully recognizable. There is a certain departure from the human that takes place in order to start the process of remaking the human. I may feel that without some recognizability I cannot live. But I may also feel that the terms by which I am recognized make life unlivable. This is the juncture from which critique emerges, where critique is understood as an interrogation of the terms by which life is constrained in order to open up the possibility of different modes of living; in other words, not to celebrate difference as such but to establish more inclusive conditions for sheltering and maintaining life that resists models of assimilation.[10]

Waywardness, a knowing engagement with the disjunction between how things are and how they could otherwise be, creates such a 'juncture from which critique emerges' and Spark's writing inhabits that space.

Waywardness in its unreasonableness may offer an opportunity to consider thought, being and action away from the hegemonic constrictions of everyday existence. As Nicola Pitchford argues in relation to Kathy Acker's writing,

> I have called Acker's novels 'unreasonable' because this word offers a third term, a way out of the binary opposition between the rational and the irrational. To be unreasonable frequently carries connotations of protest, of someone's stubborn refusal to acknowledge the

superiority of the logic of the person using the term. [...] To be irrational, on the other hand, is simply to be incomprehensible or hysterical, to remove oneself from contestation entirely.[11]

Waywardness is just such a useful third term, or in-between concept, that suggests a refusal within the terms of the comprehensible, that works to disrupt from within the power relations of the here and now, and so to expand and mobilise our conceptions of the possible. In this I conceive of it as an analytic tool with which to trouble and perhaps explore escape routes from binary formulations of the contemporary moment.

A wider argument could hypothesise that waywardness is evoked in many aspects of contemporary Scottish women's writing. Such a sensibility may be found in the playful challenges and serious play of Ali Smith's and Jenni Fagan's writing, as well as the gender and genre implications of the work of earlier authors such as Nan Shepherd and Jessie Kesson. In this genealogy, though, Spark stands out as a practised purveyor of the wayward. Most obviously it is evoked in the presentation of unruly, disobedient and rebellious female characters, who challenge authority and the strictures of femininity – women's constrained place in society. However, waywardness is also present in the form of this writing, the jumps and swerves it may take from the present to the future, from the realist to the Gothic fantastic, in the reversals of relations, roles and authority, from being to non-being, from the dead to the living and back again, with an oblique engagement with narrative progress and resolution. This is an experimental writing which aims to defamiliarise reality, to challenge and question dominant world views, and to undo our ideas and ideals of identity, subjectivity, the human. Waywardness illuminates possibilities of springing the trap of fixed selves and fixed relations to understand and experience both differently.

This chapter aims to celebrate Spark's representations as executing a poetics of waywardness, a literary mode which I contend reveals, in Judith Halberstam's words, 'counterintuitive modes of knowing'[12] such as refusal and failure, to present a cogent critique of the injustices of the oppressive and constraining pressure of the here and now. This engagement with waywardness resonates with other recent approaches that seek to escape contemporary critical modes and language and the bounds of academic habit that limit analytical imagination and systematically confine. A re-thinking of concepts such as 'the wild', 'wilfulness', and the undoing of subjectivity in failure and refusal has produced a rich critical groundswell of contemporary cultural engagement.

Halberstam, for example, drafts in new terms – 'wildness',[13] 'gaga feminism'[14] – to 'attempt to stretch our critical vocabularies in different directions – away, for example, from the used-up languages of difference, alterity, subversion, and resistance, and toward languages of unpredictability, breakdown, disorder, and shifting forms of signification'.[15] Calling on the work of José Esteban Muñoz and Fred Moten, Halberstam aims to engage in cultural analysis which seeks out the spirit of the unknown and the disorderly to find alternatives to the discourses of neoliberalism 'as a normative order of reason'[16] which 'configures all aspects of existence in economic terms'.[17] Halberstam invokes an alternative focus for analysis: on a resistance of mastery that prioritises 'counterintuitive modes of knowing such as failure and stupidity',[18] re-assessing methods of refusal in scenes of negation, absence, passivity, unknowing in order to set forms of 'unbeing' and 'unbecoming' against a positivist complicity with hegemonic discourses of self-realisation and subjectivisation, such as neoliberalism. Halberstam's 'gaga feminism', for instance, 'expresses itself as excess, as noise, as breakdown, drama, spectacle, high femininity, low theory, masochistic refusal, and moments of musical riot'.[19] I contend that all these characteristics can be observed in Spark's writing, in one way or another. For instance, in the excess of Lise, Elsa and Annabel's high feminine style, in the noise of *The Driver's Seat*, the scenes of civil unrest and the unruly musical riot of the parties and nightlife of *The Public Image* and *The Hothouse by the East River*, all of which present us with drama and spectacle, as does the infamous masochistic refusal of Lise's quest for destruction. As texts that act out rather than psychologise the pathologies of femininity, they can be described as 'low theory', a concept Halberstam adapts from the work of Stuart Hall in order to 'look for a way out of the usual traps and impasses of binary formulations'.[20] In line with this, the characteristics of Halberstam's gaga feminism signal 'potentials'[21] for theorising alternatives to the hegemonic 'within an undisciplined zone of knowledge production',[22] an interesting label to apply to Spark's novels. Employed in cultural analysis, then, these terms can evoke and identify oblique ways of reading to refresh, recalibrate and re-vision our sensibilities.

This chapter associates the concept of waywardness with approaches such as Halberstam's and suggests that it is particularly useful in identifying disturbances in the fabric of consensus and drawing attention to the significance of moments of refusal for the conceptualisation of feminine subjectivity, a specific interest of Spark in these texts. Fred Moten, in his work in relation to blackness, asks an explosive question regarding the implications of *refusing the rights that have been refused to you*, and he extends his crucial interrogation of such refusal:

> What does it mean to be against or outside of the law of the home and the state, the home and the state that you constitute and which refuses you? What's it mean to refuse that which has been refused you? What new infusion is made possible by such a refusal?[23]

In evoking the condition of living outside of state forms of regulation and governance, Moten embraces a concept of fugitivity – the state of flight, banishment or exile, or as Moten would put it, a 'being separate from settling'[24] – and this route leads him to a counterintuitive call for a 'being together in homelessness', where homelessness 'is a state of dispossession'[25] to be sought and embraced as 'a way of being together in brokenness'.[26] Spark, the 'constitutional exile' who embraced 'the conditions of exiledom' as a 'calling',[27] would perhaps be intrigued by, if not cognisant of, this sensibility, one which infuses a text such as *The Driver's Seat*.

Waywardness is also usefully associated with Sara Ahmed's thoughtful theorising of 'willful subjects' where wilfulness 'is a diagnosis of the failure to comply with those whose authority is given'.[28] As she observes, to be identified as wilful is to become a problem; it is thought of as a fault of character, an attribution of error. In contemporary culture the will is transformed into 'willpower', making individuals the problem when they cannot 'will themselves out of situations in which they find themselves'.[29] However,

Ahmed asks what it would mean to understand the will as not *residing in* the subject, as this approach implies. Her problematising of will emanates from her theorising of emotions as socially and culturally produced, happiness in particular, as that which 'starts from somewhere other than the subject'.[30] Paying attention to how subjects become invested in particular structures, relations and objects causes us to think about the social construction and production of affect, in a challenge to the drive to privatise emotions under the neoliberal order of reason.[31] Ahmed argues that to refuse happiness or refuse to be made happy or hopeful in the 'right way' is to occupy a difficult position. In *The Promise of Happiness* she delineates what she calls figures who become cultural containers for this refusal and in doing so traces resistance to the various hegemonic regulatory effects of happiness. This is a genealogical method enabling a challenge to the 'assumption that happiness follows relative proximity to a social ideal', such as, for instance, the 'happy housewife'.[32] She writes, 'Feminist genealogies can be described as genealogies of women who not only do not place their hope in the right things but who speak out about their unhappiness with the very obligation to be made happy by such things'.[33] In making her 'unhappiness archives' Ahmed offers 'an alternative history of happiness [...] by considering those who are banished from it, or who enter this history only as troublemakers, dissenters, killers of joy'.[34] It is 'assembled around the struggle against happiness'[35] to challenge the commands and injunctions of the contemporary 'happiness turn' and dominance of 'positive psychology' from the point of view of those excluded or who exclude themselves.

This chapter presents 'wayward' as an equally suggestively mobile term; wayward connotes an erratic, deviationary movement, a turning, wandering or straying from the straight, right path while, perhaps, keeping that path in view. It can be rebellious, harmful, euphoric or celebratory, but there is rarely a satisfyingly logical resolution to the wayward narrative. If waywardness informs Spark's textual productions, it does so by repudiating the settled and the housed and embracing the wilful. From this perspective wayward femininity in these texts is often working towards an unravelling and an undoing of the unified model of the subject and the whole and wholesome female self.

In this, Spark's wayward writing takes its place among other provocative explorations of femininity in the work of Scottish women writers from the early twentieth century on: for example, Violet Jacob's 'Thievie', Nan Shepherd's *The Quarry Wood*, Willa Muir's *Imagined Corners*, and Jessie Kesson's *The White Bird Passes*. However, in the period in focus here Spark lights the touchpaper on explosive versions of femininity in part by embracing experimental writing strategies, specifically those which caught her imagination in her formative period of the 1950s such as the *nouveau roman* and the work of Alain Robbe-Grillet, and other metafictional techniques that would become pervasive in postmodern fiction. It is fair to say that she took advantage of these movements in fiction in developing them for her own purposes but without becoming overwhelmed by them. As David Herman argues, Spark 'chose a third path' in relation to the clashing antimodernist realists (such as Kingsley Amis) and postmodernists (such as John Barth) of her time: 'her fiction embraces (or rather extends and radicalises) the modernist emphasis on technique while *also* projecting complex social worlds'.[36] However, in the years surrounding 1970 Brian Cheyette proposes that Spark 'utilizes the anti-novel [the *nouveau roman*] as a means of substituting conventional concerns with the inner self for a more chilling and dehumanized account of the "times at hand"', in a 'pitiless and heartless tone' described by Angus Wilson as 'machine made'.[37] It is this 'heartless and chilling' Spark that I find wayward in her refusal to enact heart-warming feminine proprieties in her fiction and, consequentially, in creating some of the more incendiary representations of femaleness of her time.

Reading Spark as Wayward

In reading Spark as wayward, novels from that vigorously creative period around 1970, including *The Public Image*, *The Driver's Seat* and *The Hothouse by the East River*, are prime examples. Lise, the central character of *The Driver's Seat*, exemplifies this waywardness, spending the narrative seeking and organising her own murder. Not only wayward in character and content, the form of the narrative is also adeptly dissonant. Narrated in the present tense by an extra-diegetic narrator who never accesses the inner lives of the characters, the text often reads like a police report in its objective observational style. It is also an infamous example of Spark's use of prolepsis; we know the end from near the beginning – from page 14 in the Penguin edition – creating the effect that Lise's violent demise appears to be fated and fixed all along. Also, crucially, this writing strategy undermines the reader's drive to know, to get to the end of the story. There is 'rather', writes Judith Roof, 'a drive to narrate – to inhabit the point of tension, the middle, the *détour*, the deviance'.[38] This deviation providing intimate knowledge of Lise's predetermined fate, the predetermined script that is outside her control, illustrates Lise's choice to be complicit with this fate; as Gerardine Meaney argues, 'She is a figure for the feminine subject whose options are no options. She can either choose a subjectivity which kills her or lose subjectivity and all ability to act.'[39] Spark strongly hints at that lack of subjectivity near the beginning of the text when she refers to Lise's job in an accounts' office where 'her lips [...] are normally pressed together like the ruled line of a balance sheet' and her one-room flat which is 'clean-lined and clear to return to after her work as if it were uninhabited'.[40] In her life Lise is a silent absence until she chooses to take control, to take a holiday and have 'the time of my life'.[41]

Lise's choice of 'a subjectivity which kills her' is enacted as a position of excess in relation to accepted behaviours of the humdrum everyday, signalled through unnerving demonstrations of intemperance. At the start of the text, Lise's reaction to the offer of a non-staining dress is extreme in its affront – 'I won't be insulted!'[42] – and her subsequent choice of outfit is seen as outlandish: a dress with 'a lemon-yellow top' and 'a skirt patterned in bright V's of orange, mauve and blue'[43] topped with a 'summer coat with narrow stripes, red and white'.[44]

> The girl is saying, 'You won't be able to wear them together, but it's a lovely coat over a plain dress' [...]
> 'They go very well together,' Lise says [...] 'Those colours of the dress and the coat are absolutely right for me. Very natural colours.'
> [...] 'If only you knew! These colours are a natural blend for me. Absolutely natural.'[45]

Her refusal of sartorial propriety delineates her waywardness, and here her repeated assertion of the suitable 'naturalness' of her choice, in defiance of the judgement of expert others, demonstrates her determination to perversely overturn and undermine acceptable norms of behaviour within their own terms. Her refusal of normative constrictions is also expressed in her excessive laughter: she 'laughs hysterically',[46] 'heartily',[47] giggles 'merrily',[48] 'laughs harshly'[49] and 'very loudly',[50] 'longer than expected' so that 'Mrs Fiedke looks frightened as the voices of the bar stop to watch the laughing one'.[51] Such laughter is associated with unconstrained women, such as the 'hacking cough-like ancestral laughter of the streets'[52] of the female porter as she ridicule's Lise's outfit, or that of the passing woman whose laughter at Lise is 'without possibility of restraint, like a stream bound to descend whatever slope lies before it'.[53] This lack of inhibition in both the laughing and being laughed at gives Spark's narrative an edge of abandon, hinting at a wild, bubbling, underlying danger which is also exposed in scenes of riot that unexpectedly catch up with Lise in their chaotic flow.

As well as gestures of protest, Lise's actions also signal a refusal to live within the law; she stuffs her passport down the back seat of a taxi,[54] an action interpreted as one of the clues she leaves throughout the narrative regarding her presence, her journey, and her fate. However, such an action is symbolic of her position outside the state, in relation to her stunted citizenship as a woman, and outside the home as a single woman. In this moment we could say that she is embracing homelessness or a state of dispossession or, in Fred Moten's words, stepping into fugitivity. Her refusal of what she has been refused – full selfhood or subjectivity or agency as a woman – is staged in her pursuit of her own murder. Such an end, the text suggests, is the only possible outcome of taking control in the present circumstances. Ultimately, what Lise is refusing, as a woman, is vividly demonstrated in the novel – it is the objectification of women, specifically their sexual objectification, and the demand for their sexual availability to men. Twice in the narrative she escapes rape – with the macrobiotic man and the garage mechanic. She is less successful with her murderer who, contrary to her wishes that 'I don't want any sex', 'all the same, plunges into her, with the knife poised high'.[55] The phrase 'all the same', a 'nevertheless' turn in the narrative, signals the moment of the re-imposition of hegemonic authority. *The Driver's Seat*, then, is an unreasonable rather than an irrational narrative, in Pitchford's terms, demonstrating the full implications of a fundamental misogynist narrative: that 'she was asking for it'. The text provokes the reader with the implications of how it looks and feels when that particular social script is followed through to its conclusion. By 'asking for it' Lise paradoxically stages her protest at the objectification of women by exposing the ultimate consequences of such a view of femininity. She constitutes a spectacle of masochistic refusal of the conditions for female survival, characterising an 'antisocial feminism' in Halberstam's words, that 'refuses conventional modes of femininity by refusing to remake, rebuild, or reproduce and that dedicates itself completely and ferociously to the destruction of self and other'.[56] In relation to this Halberstam refers to a notion of radical passivity which has the power to unravel the subject and dramatise unbecoming in order to resist mandatory, liberal, patriarchal formulations of the self. However, though we can conceive of Lise's end as a sacrifice, it is less radically passive and more aggressively protesting and strident in illustrating the difficulty of controlling the journey to unbecoming within the scripts of femininity, exposing as it does the 'invisible contracts we make with violence'[57] in just being ourselves.

The Driver's Seat's extreme nihilism in the face of the feminine condition is present but more tempered in the next novel, *The Hothouse by the East River*, by an uncanny narrative which incorporates Spark's wartime experiences in a tale of life after death in contemporary Manhattan. To begin with, though, it is madness not death that is undoing subjectivity here, with strange interruptions in the fabric of reality creating dissonant hauntings of the present by the past. The central female character Elsa and her husband Paul met when they worked for 'a small outpost of British Intelligence'[58] during the Second World War. Nearly thirty years later characters from that time pop up in the environs of their New York lives causing tensions over uncertain events in the past; most significantly a German collaborator, Helmut Kiel, now apparently works in a shoe shop nearby. Kiel's appearance, as well as other uncanny unexplainable events, are associated with Elsa. Her 'excess' is marked in other ways: she is characterised by extravagance and extreme wealth and is a lavish consumer and wayward performer of femininity. Spark's attention is once again drawn to sartorial excess, revelling in the detail of Elsa's choice of outfit for attending a fringe theatre 'away downtown':

> Elsa comes into the drawing-room. Paul gasps. She is wearing a flame-coloured crepe evening dress with dark beads gleaming at the hem and wrists. She wears a necklace and earrings made of diamonds and rubies. Her fingers are a complex of the same sparkling stones. She is wearing a diamond bracelet [...] Elsa is wearing a long coat of white fox fur.[59]

Like laughter in the *The Driver's Seat*, Elsa's clothes signal an elemental connection to something wild and dangerous: the 'flame-coloured' dress; a sable coat, 'the furs, mysterious and rich, spilling over the brown satin lining'.[60] The frisson of threat around her is magnified in her most uncanny characteristic; her shadow falls the wrong way, 'falls the way it wants'.[61] It is 'unnatural',[62] 'like a webby grey cashmere shawl',[63] 'trailing at the wrong angle, like the train of an antique ball-dress',[64] 'like a flung coat',[65] the clothing associations reverberating with the sartorial excesses. Paul's panic is total: 'He will not sleep beside her in bed any more. Never again, never again. No man can sleep with a woman whose shadow falls wrong and who gets light or something from elsewhere.'[66]

Elsa's 'cloud of unknowing',[67] as her shadow is dubbed in the final line of the novel, is 'a radical disruption of all discourse' and a challenge to dominant ideology, argues Meaney: 'It defies the laws of physics and disrupts the specular economy in which power resides in the gazing subject rather than the object gazed upon.'[68] This wayward shadow, a simple but fundamental adjustment in the fabric of the world, signals for Meaney Elsa's 'truth-telling' and her challenge to the labels of madness and schizophrenia levelled at her and their implication that she is beyond reason. Instead, she is the agent of exposure of Paul's anxious delusions. The truth she is telling is of death as the fated end of everyone, the final undoing of the sovereignty of the subject in relation to which Paul is in denial. Elsa reminds him that they were both killed by a V-2 bomb near the end of the war and that he is the author of this present haunted place: 'It was you with your terrible and jealous dreams who set the whole edifice soaring.'[69]

> 'You died, too,' says Elsa. 'That's one of the things you don't realise, Paul.'
> 'Don't be silly,' he says. 'I remember standing by the side of the track when they pulled your body out of the wreck. I remember too many things to be dead.'
> 'No, Paul,' says Elsa. 'That was your imagination running away with itself.'[70]

Elsa, it would seem, is fully a part of Paul's imagined world, where he believes himself to be the rational, sovereign subject, diagnosing his wife's schizophrenia and committing her to an asylum sometime in the past. However, Elsa's waywardness exposes the limits of this world; she stages a refusal of his values and proprieties, his control: 'She's not my original conception any more. She took a life of her own. She's grotesque. When she died she was a sweet English girl.'[71] Elsa's 'grotesque' excess is a logic that runs counter to the masculine imagination. Behaving inappropriately and unreasonably, she undoes this male-defined world and they finally leave it and embrace the unknown.

Conversely, in Annabel, the successful actress of *The Public Image*, we have a conclusion other than death. The final lines see her escaping her perfect public image, waiting for a flight with her baby son:

> having moved the baby to rest on her hip, conscious also of the baby in a sense weightlessly and perpetually within her, as an empty shell contains, by its very structure, the echo and harking image of former and former seas.[72]

Though acknowledging Susan Sellers' reading of these closing lines as Annabel's 'escape into maternal plenitude',[73] we can also read her as a wayward character in touch with the ineffable, the inexpressible, the unpresentable, an exemplar of a waywardness which defies the hegemony, the regulatory matrix and normativity predicated on patriarchal certainty, predictability and control. Annabel is refusing her carefully honed 'public image' as the 'English Lady-Tiger' film star, a perfect blend of wife and lover, where surface domesticity gives way in private to an underlying sexual passion. This image is responsible for her major success in the Italian film industry, manipulated as it is in the popular media of the day to engage with the hegemonic feminine stereotypes scripted and promoted by this media. Annabel, of all these three heroines, is the most obviously trapped within the constricting discourses of femininity as Spark spells out the parameters, demands and effects of this public image and its construction. However, Spark also demonstrates the waywardness which characterises Annabel's refusals.

Annabel is another heroine who refuses to engage with masculine values and ideals. From the beginning she is described as 'stupid', principally by her husband Frederick:

> In those earlier times [...] she had no means of knowing that she was, in fact, stupid, for, after all, it is the deep core of stupidity that it thrives on the absence of a looking-glass. Her husband [...] tolerantly and quite affectionately insinuated the fact of her stupidity, and she accepted this without resentment for as long as it did not convey to her any sense of contempt.[74]

In the first thesis that Halberstam proposes for engagement with 'subjugated knowledges', the exhortation to 'resist mastery' prescribes stupidity as a 'counterintuitive mode of knowing'[75] along with failure; 'stupidity could refer not simply to a lack of knowledge but to the limits of certain forms of knowing and certain ways of inhabiting structures of knowing'.[76] What is remarkable about Spark's Annabel is her lack of upset at the accusation of stupidity, her calm indifference to its provenance:

> In those early days when she was working in small parts her stupidity started to melt; she had not in the least attempted to overcome her stupidity, but she now saw, with the confidence of practice in her film roles, that she had somehow circumvented it.[77]

Stupidity here is not the binary opposite of cleverness; its circumvention is a wayward movement which renders it insignificant and undermines its power to oppress: 'She did not need to be clever, she only had to exist'.[78] In fact, this oblique, nullifying relation with stupidity is signalled from the very beginning of the novel when on the first page we are informed of Annabel's 'calm achievement'[79] in her practical approach to organising accommodation in Rome. The novel goes on to similarly undermine masculine logic and priorities, much as Elsa cuts through Paul's certainties in *The Hothouse by the East River*. Frederick's preoccupation with 'depth' – 'he was exasperated, seeing shallowness everywhere'[80] believing acting should be 'from the soul outward'[81] – is countered by Annabel's comfort with the superficial: 'He continued to enunciate. "Please do not talk of 'significance', because you do not understand it. And that is because you are insignificant yourself." Annabel said immediately, "D'you think so? Oh, well, minority opinions are always interesting."'[82] In such ways she unravels the power of the discourse of Enlightenment reason by waywardly skirting its binary traps.

As well as her nulling of the effects of stupidity, Annabel also refuses to be made happy, in Sara Ahmed's words, by her 'proximity to the social ideal'[83] signalling a resistance to the various hegemonic regulatory effects of happiness. The constructed image of the happy marriage does not satisfy either herself or Frederick, another jealous husband who kills himself as part of a plot to bring about Annabel's downfall. In one of those quixotically surprising 'nevertheless' plot-turns that populate many of the conclusions of Spark's novels, Annabel gives up her public image rather than give in to blackmail. In contrast to the accusation of emptiness consistently voiced by Frederick, particularly in his suicide note addressed to her – 'You are a beautiful shell [...] but empty, devoid of the life it once held'[84] – those closing lines finally and elegantly counter such a characterisation in what has been the typical wayward style of the novel. At the end the 'empty shell' that Annabel is compared to 'contains, by its very structure, the echo and harking image of former and former seas', as she is conscious of her baby son 'perpetually within her'.[85] If death in the case of this novel is associated with Frederick and his violent and selfish self-murder, Annabel undoes the subject in a different manner, through breaking down the boundary of the one, the sovereign individual, the oppositional relation of self and other. This breakdown goes beyond herself into the breakdown of language itself as 'she felt both free and unfree'.[86] This is a 'new infusion', in Moten's words, that sees and hears and feels and understands the world differently.

Conclusion

Of the novels I have explored here, *The Public Image* was the first to be published and in it Annabel enacts a constructive waywardness that constitutes an opening optimistic engagement with the difficulty of femininity in a patriarchal world. This is a problem not to be circumvented in the later novels where it is addressed principally through death. It is interesting to note that, published between 1968 and 1973, these texts suggest that as the counter-cultural 'sexual revolution' of that period proceeded so did Spark's scepticism increase regarding the tenets of freedom made possible in extant feminine identities. Spark's representations, though, are not fully oppositional, conflictual, aggressive, angry or mad; wayward in all aspects – from sentence construction to character to invented world – this writing demonstrates and enacts her hopes for the deployment of ridicule as a more politically incisive way to engage the reader in critique, as she sets out in 'The Desegregation of Art'. What is ridiculed here are the male-centred narratives that dominate patriarchal culture. Such radical female refusals as she sets out in these texts are resistant but not actively, positively oppositional. Instead, such tactics posit the possibility of undoing binary conceptions of social being and action that 'opposition' putatively takes part in. Waywardness in these texts facilitates such an undoing, asking questions of contemporary conceptions of gendered selfhood. These female characters veer away from the straight and narrow yet, like Lise, they leave traces in their wanderings which expose existential conundrums within apparent certainties; these wayward female characters leave behind the regular routes of female selfhood and contest the inevitability of their prescribed destinations. The danger involved in moving out of sight, of losing the recognition of others through these detours creates a precarious position for the straying self, as suggestively meditated on by Butler in her observation that 'the "I" becomes, to a certain extent unknowable, threatened with unviability, with becoming undone altogether, when it no longer incorporates the norm in such a way that makes this "I" fully recognizable'. In running towards and inhabiting this dissonance, Spark's wayward women present us with what Butler terms a 'juncture from which critique emerges'. Her critique of the terms of feminine life resonates profoundly through our own postfeminist epoch.

Endnotes

1. Zoë Strachan, 'Muriel Spark', *The Dangerous Women Project*, 2013 www.dangerouswomenproject.org/2016/07/31/muriel-spark/ [consulted June 2019].
2. Janice Galloway, 'Introduction', in Muriel Spark, *The Complete Short Stories* (Edinburgh: Canongate, 2011), p. xi.
3. Ian Gregson, *Character and Satire in Postwar Fiction* (New York, NY: Continuum, 2006), p. 107.
4. Muriel Spark, 'The Desegregation of Art', in *The Golden Fleece: Essays*, ed. Penelope Jardine [1970] (Manchester: Carcanet, 2014), p. 30.
5. Len Gutkin, 'Muriel Spark's Camp Metafiction', in *Contemporary Literature* 58.1 (2017), pp. 53–81 (p. 55).
6. James Bailey, 'Salutary Scars: The "Disorientating" Fictions of Muriel Spark', in *Contemporary Women's Writing* 9.1 (2015), pp. 34–52 (p. 47); Jonathan Kemp, '"Her Lips are Slightly Parted": The Ineffability of Erotic Sociality in Muriel Spark's *The Driver's Seat*', in *Modern Fiction Studies* 54.3 (2008), pp. 544–57 (p. 545); Len Gutkin, 'Muriel Spark's Camp Metafiction', p. 55; Marilyn Reizbaum, 'The Stranger Spark', in *The Edinburgh Companion to Muriel Spark*, eds. Michael Gardiner and Willy Maley (Edinburgh: Edinburgh University Press, 2010), pp. 40–51 (p. 40); Martin McQuillan, 'Introduction: "I Don't Know Anything About Freud": Muriel Spark Meets Contemporary Criticism', in *Theorizing Muriel Spark: Gender, Race, Deconstruction*, ed. Martin McQuillan (Basingstoke: Palgrave, 2002), pp. 1–33 (p. 14); Patricia Waugh, 'Muriel Spark and the Metaphysics of Modernity: Art, Secularization, and Psychosis', in *Muriel Spark: Twenty-First-Century Perspectives*, ed. David Herman (Baltimore, MD: Johns Hopkins University Press, 2010), pp. 63–93 (p. 66).
7. Muriel Spark, 'What Images Return', in *Memoirs of a Modern Scotland*, ed. Karl Miller (London: Faber and Faber, 1970), pp. 151–52 (p. 152).
8. Angela Carter, *Wayward Girls and Wicked Women* (London: Virago, 1986), p. xii.
9. Ibid.
10. Judith Butler, *Undoing Gender* (New York, NY: Routledge, 2004), pp. 3–4.
11. Nicola Pitchford, *Tactical Readings: Feminist Postmodernism in the Novels of Kathy Acker and Angela Carter* (London: Associated University Presses, 2002), p. 103.
12. Judith Halberstam, *The Queer Art of Failure* (Durham and London: Duke University Press, 2011), p. 11.

13. Jack Halberstam, 'Wildness, Loss, Death', in *Social Text* 32.4 (2014), pp. 137–48.
14. Jack Halberstam, 'Go Gaga: Anarchy, Chaos and the Wild', in *Social Text* 31.3 (2013), pp. 123–34.
15. Ibid., p. 126.
16. Wendy Brown, *Undoing the Demos: Neoliberalism's Stealth Revolution* (New York, NY: Zone Books, 2015), p. 9.
17. Ibid., p. 17.
18. Halberstam, *The Queer Art of Failure*, p. 11.
19. J. Jack Halberstam, *Gaga Feminism: Sex, Gender, and the End of Normal* (Boston, MA: Beacon Press, 2012), p. 125.
20. Halberstam, *The Queer Art of Failure*, p. 2.
21. Halberstam, *Gaga Feminism*, p. 126.
22. Halberstam, *The Queer Art of Failure*, p. 18.
23. Fred Moten, 'Gestural Critique of Judgment', in *The Power and Politics of the Aesthetic in American Culture*, eds. Ulla Haselstein and Klaus Benesch (Munich: Bacarian American Academy, 2007), pp. 96–114 (p. 105).
24. Stephano Harney and Fred Moten, *The Undercommons: Fugitive Planning and Black Study* (New York, NY: Minor Compositions, 2013), p. 11.
25. Ibid.
26. Ibid., p. 12.
27. Spark, 'What Images Return', p. 151.
28. Sara Ahmed, *Willful Subjects* (Durham and London: Duke University Press, 2014), p. 1.
29. Ibid., p. 7.
30. Sara Ahmed, *The Promise of Happiness* (Durham and London: Duke University Press, 2010), p. 1.
31. Sara Ahmed, *The Cultural Politics of Emotion* (Edinburgh: Edinburgh University Press, 2014), p. 12.
32. Ahmed, *The Promise of Happiness*, p. 53.
33. Ibid., p. 59.
34. Ibid., p. 17.
35. Ibid., p. 18.
36. David Herman (ed.), 'Introduction', in *Muriel Spark: Twenty-First-Century Perspectives*, pp. 1–20 (p. 2).
37. Brian Cheyette, *Muriel Spark* (Tavistock: Northcote House, 2000), p. 72. He is quoting Angus Wilson, 'Journey to Jerusalem', *Observer*, 17 October 1968, p. 28.
38. Judith Roof, 'The Future Perfect's Perfect Future: Spark's and Duras's Narrative Drive', in *Theorizing Muriel Spark: Gender, Race, Deconstruction*, ed. Martin McQuillan, pp. 49–66 (p. 59).
39. Gerardine Meaney, *(Un)Like Subjects: Women, theory, fiction* (London: Routledge, 1993), p. 185.
40. Muriel Spark, *The Driver's Seat* [1970] (London: Penguin, 2006), p. 15.
41. Ibid., p. 10.
42. Ibid., p. 9.
43. Ibid., p. 10.
44. Ibid., p. 11.
45. Ibid., p. 11; p. 12.

46 Ibid., p. 10.
47 Ibid., p. 13.
48 Ibid., p. 22.
49 Ibid., p. 42.
50 Ibid., p. 51.
51 Ibid., p. 56.
52 Ibid., p. 17.
53 Ibid., p. 69.
54 Ibid., p. 52.
55 Ibid., p. 106.
56 Halberstam, *The Queer Art of Failure*, p. 138.
57 Ibid.
58 Muriel Spark, *The Hothouse by the East River* [1973] (Edinburgh: Birlinn, 2018), p. 18.
59 Ibid., p. 81; p. 84.
60 Ibid., p. 113.
61 Ibid., p. 59.
62 Ibid., p. 3.
63 Ibid., p. 30.
64 Ibid., p. 32.
65 Ibid., p. 75.
66 Ibid., p. 12.
67 Ibid., p. 136.
68 Meaney, *(Un)Like Subjects*, p. 181.
69 Ibid., p. 91.
70 Ibid., p. 122.
71 Ibid., p. 104.
72 Muriel Spark, *The Public Image* [1968] (Edinburgh: Birlinn, 2018), p. 116.
73 Susan Sellers, 'Tales of Love: Narcissism and Idealization in *The Public Image*', in *Theorizing Muriel Spark: Gender, Race, Deconstruction*, ed. Martin McQuillan, pp. 35–48 (p. 46).
74 Spark, *The Public Image*, p. 5.
75 Halberstam, *The Queer Art of Failure*, p. 11.
76 Ibid., p. 12.
77 Spark, *The Public Image*, p. 7.
78 Ibid.
79 Ibid., p. 1.
80 Ibid., p. 7.
81 Ibid., p. 12.
82 Ibid.
83 Ahmed, *The Promise of Happiness*, p. 53.
84 Spark, *The Driver's Seat*, p. 85.
85 Ibid., p. 116.
86 Ibid.

3. Spark's Spinsters: Bedsits and Boarding Houses in the Novels of Muriel Spark

SUSANNAH THOMPSON

Before Bridget Jones, the reactionary 1990s caricature of the single woman living alone, mid-twentieth-century British literature teemed with more enviable unmarried role models. From Miss Roach in Patrick Hamilton's 1947 *The Slaves of Solitude*, Josephine Tey's Marion Sharpe in the 1948 novel *The Franchise Affair* or Barbara Pym's protagonists of the 1950s (Belinda in *Some Tame Gazelle* from 1950 or Mildred Lathbury in her 1952 *Excellent Women*) the spinsters of these works were women of substance and depth of character: adventurous, intellectual and charismatic. In taking centre stage as protagonists, these subversive spinsters (and other unmarried women of all types) appear in spite of, or perhaps in response to, the dogged literary trope of the marginalised, desperate, lonely 'old maid'. Appearing in literature when they do, these characters also reflect the historian Katherine Holden's point that there was an 'invisible majority' of women after the war who were not living within family structures, who 'lived in lodgings, boarding houses or institutions or who had no permanent home'.[1]

If 'the bedsit's modest dimensions have been seen to be spinster spaces, fit and proper for the woman who is neither an Angel of the House nor a mistress of the streets',[2] this chapter contends that in their bedsits and boarding houses, Muriel Spark's spinsters – and Spark herself – both single-handedly and collectively undermine the loaded associations of the 's' word. As Judy Little has noted, 'the spinster character, transformed several times, seems to have a special attraction for Spark, herself single for most of her life'.[3] In many of Spark's novels written or set in the 1950s and 1960s, spinsterhood and bedsit living was not a problem to be solved but a lifestyle which afforded considerable freedom, even when those freedoms were not always economic.

By the time Muriel Spark began her career as an editor and writer in the late 1940s, Virginia Woolf's classic 1929 lecture-essay 'A Room of One's Own' had already explored the connection between material conditions and the ability to think and write.[4] Woolf famously proposed that the requirements for women's creative freedom were a room of one's own and independent means. Having both, according to Woolf, would provide the space and time requisite for writing. Woolf deemed an income of around five hundred pounds per year necessary – the precise amount left to her by an aunt in 1918, the year of Spark's birth. By 1929, following the publication of the 1928 lecture as 'A Room of One's Own', Woolf's own room was presumably comfortable, warm, and decorated Omega Workshop-style. The lock on the door of 'one's room' avoided interruption and distraction while 'five hundred a year' (equivalent to around thirty-two thousand pounds in 2020[5]) at a time when a miner earned one hundred and fifty-six pounds a year[6] removed the need to be economically dependent on a man or to have to take on paid employment outside of writing.

To Spark, Woolf was a 'spoilt brat'.[7] Melinda Harvey has argued that Woolf's 'class-blind rubric of the room of one's own' has posited the bedsit 'as a utopian site of female creativity and freedom' for a number of feminist scholars 'confused with the kind of rooms that money – and five hundred pounds a year is real money – could supply'. Rather, she claims, the bedsit has been overlooked 'for what it usually is: a locus of economic hardship and social deprivation as well as a site of intellectual and sexual freedom'.[8] In Muriel Spark's case, apart from the occasional lifelines thrown *in extremis* by friends and supporters, her material conditions were far more meagre than those of Woolf. Until the publication of *The Comforters* in 1957 her income was earned through editing and secretarial work that she undertook alongside writing criticism, short stories and poems. Far less than Woolf's five hundred, she had no legacy or invisible means of support and endured periods of extreme poverty and hunger. Spark was 'from a background quite at odds with the tenor of her prose' and claimed that she 'had always had to struggle'.[9] Her London years have been described as 'years of striving and obscurity' where 'she lived by her pen, in poverty, in a succession of tiny abodes'.¹⁰ As such, Spark's 'succession of tiny abodes' were 'one's own' only to the extent that she had a dedicated room to herself within larger communal residences. She lived in five different rooms in a decade, but it was these circumstances, as frugal as they could be, which allowed her to produce such a prolific body of writing in a relatively short period. The very conditions necessary for Spark to create her early novels (solitude, time, the absence of housekeeping responsibilities and dependents) became rich material for her work. The bedsit was both a site of production and representation and her domestic arrangements during her bedsit years were reflected in semi-autobiographical novels and stories throughout her life.¹¹ Spark once wrote that in order to describe someone's life you needed little more than just 'a glance through an open door as you're going up the stairs [...] a glimpse of the room before the door shuts'. If this is the case, it is hard to think of an arrangement more suitable for a writer than the observation and character study provided by space of the bedsit or boarding house.¹²

While Spark does not avoid describing the discomfort, claustrophobia, and practical hardships of bedsits and boarding houses, she was not concerned with the self-pity and melancholia of upper-class women who have found themselves in reduced circumstances (such as Sara in Virginia Woolf's 1937 *The Years* or Anna in Jean Rhys's 1934 *Voyage in the Dark*). As Parul Sehgal has noted, Spark 'simply seemed to find no romance in female abjection'. She may have been 'fascinated by suffering' but 'it was an active, robust kind of suffering that she liked, whereby hunger whetted one's wits. Her women are not enamoured of their anxiety, of their moods and wounds'.¹³ Spark's struggles with her mental and physical health – directly related to lack of money during her period in London – are well documented.¹⁴ Her characters similarly experience problems at work, have run-ins with fellow lodgers and boarders, deal with intrusive, interfering landladies, suffer delusions and paranoia and eke out a living in cramped quarters. But in spite of this, Spark – and her leading spinsters and widows – are, for the most part, cheerful, resourceful, capable and determined. Sometimes they thrive in the conditions of the bedsit and boarding house, enjoying the relative freedoms, opportunities and pleasures offered by affordable rooms in the capital. Spark's protagonists are not confined by their living spaces but rather seem to move between and across class barriers with impunity. They move outside and beyond their rooms using public transport, walking to parks and cafes, going to work, playing *flâneuse*. In Spark's novels, women are not excluded from the sites and spaces of modernity and participate fully in public life, but they also reveal a number of environments and experiences specific to women. There is little sense of spatial confinement in Spark's novels, either inside or outside the home. In *A Far Cry from Kensington* (1988), sacked for the second time for her forthright opinions, Mrs Hawkins whiles away her time riding around London suburbs on the tops of buses, eavesdropping on fellow passengers' conversations (disappointingly dull – never a 'general topic') as she sails through Dagenham, Southall, Ewell and Surbiton.[15] *Loitering with Intent* (1981) begins in a Kensington graveyard on a sunny day, where Fleur Talbot is writing a poem and avoiding her landlord, to whom her rent is overdue. Despite being alone and struggling financially, Fleur is happy, working on her first novel, living in a bedsit and making ends meet through secretarial work.[16]

In her 2017 book *British Boarding Houses in Interwar Women's Literature*, Terri Mullholland has argued that a distinct literary sub-genre emerged in Britain between the wars in which women writers used the space of the boarding house to articulate women's changing social roles.[17] Though this is never explicitly addressed in Spark's novels, many of her characters reflect such changing gender roles in the world of work. In particular, her early novels such as *The Comforters, The Girls of Slender Means* (1963) and *The Prime of Miss Jean Brodie* (1961), written in London in the late 1950s and early 1960s, feature the interconnected themes of single women, creative work and boarding houses. These interests reappear in two of Spark's later novels published in the 1980s which return to mid-century London (*A Far Cry from Kensington*; *Loitering with Intent*). Over a quarter of Spark's twenty-two novels are set in small rented flats, bedsits and boarding houses and many feature unmarried women in central roles. Her autobiography, *Curriculum Vitae*, published in 1992, similarly contains lengthy, detailed descriptions of her life in the bedsits and boarding houses which formed the mainstay of her accommodation between the mid-1940s to the mid-1960s.[18] In a further six novels, her characters live outside conventional or nuclear family homes in 'closed world' communal settings including a nursing home (*Memento Mori*, 1959), a hospital (*Reality and Dreams*, 1996), a hotel (*The Driver's Seat*, 1970), a convent (*The Abbess of Crewe*, 1974), an upstairs/downstairs style 'big house' (*Not to Disturb*, 1971) and a Swiss finishing school (*The Finishing School*, 2004).

After a childhood living with her family in a tenement flat in Bruntsfield, Edinburgh, Spark married and moved to Zimbabwe (then Southern Rhodesia) and it was there that her experience of boarding house living began. Spark's 1961 story 'The Curtain Blown by the Breeze', was based on a story told to her 'by a smug, self-satisfied South African Dutch woman of about forty-five, whom I met in one of the many boarding-houses I lived in during my married life'.[19] Her 1982 short story 'Bang-bang You're Dead' is another fictionalised account of boarding house life which recounts the death of Spark's friend and fellow lodger Nita McEwan, who was shot in 1939 in the house they shared. Spark returned to the UK in 1944 after separating from her husband and making arrangements for the care of her son. Initially, she lived at the Helena Club at 82 Lancaster Gate, a model for the May of Teck Club in the 1963 novel *The Girls of Slender Means*. Cheap but elegant, the Helena Club housed up to 120 working women, provided two meals per day and had maids to clean rooms and change beds. For £1 12s. 6d. per week including meals, Spark had one of the more expensive single rooms on the top floor. The social hierarchy of the boarding house (once a private residence) is described by Spark in *The Girls of Slender Means*: the ground floor houses the dining room, offices, recreation room and drawing room; the first floor is occupied by the youngest residents in curtained-off cubicles; the second floor offers shared rooms for two to four young women looking for bedsits; the third floor mixes prim young women and slightly older career women; while the top floor, paralleling the Helena Club in real life, accommodates the most sophisticated and cultured women. With periodic returns to the Helena Club, Spark moved into different bedsits and lodgings in the South Kensington area over the next few years including a ground floor room in a Georgian house at 1 Vicarage Gate on Kensington Church Street (1949), larger furnished fourth floor rooms at

8 Sussex Mansions on Old Brompton Road (1950), and a room at 1 Queens Gate Terrace (1953). She left Kensington to move to 13 Baldwin Terrace in Camberwell in the mid-1950s, her home for over a decade before leaving the UK for good in the mid-1960s. Even after moving to New York City and Rome, she repeatedly returned to her attic rooms at Baldwin Terrace where she wrote *Memento Mori*, *The Ballad of Peckham Rye* (1960), *The Bachelors* (1960) and much of *The Girls of Slender Means* – three of the four are set in boarding houses and bedsits.

In Spark's novels the liminal, transient space of the boarding house functions as far more than a mere backdrop, allowing plot devices to emerge with ease (eavesdropping, overhearing, spying, stealing) while also acting as an essential aspect of characterisation, particularly in her representations of middle-aged and elderly women (and also, less flatteringly, of middle-aged bachelors). The apparently trivial, quotidian details of the domestic lives of characters such as Collie, Greggie and Jarvie in *The Girls of Slender Means*, for example, reveal insights about women's lives that do not conform to 'the marriage plot'. Gerard Carruthers argues that 'while not a feminist in any conventional sense', Spark's 'charting of the experience of the female protagonist in her fiction represents a profound fictional essaying of the woman in society and the world'.[20] In Spark's own words, the 'old maids of settled character' in *The Girls of Slender Means* lived alongside flighty debutantes, sharing with them 'the graceful attributes of a common poverty'.[21] Of the younger women, it is only Jane Wright who remains a spinster at the book's end, and yet it is only Jane who is described as 'intellectually glamorous'. As Hope Howell Hodgkins has observed,

> [Jane] is no pathetic single woman, but a tough observing consciousness, like the author herself [...] it is not the Schiaparelli-stealing Selina but the unalluring Jane that [Nicholas] recalls 'years later in the country of his death – how she stood, sturdy and bare-legged on the dark grass'.[22]

Even where Spark's spinsters eventually marry or go on to form partnerships, as Nancy Hawkins does in *A Far Cry from Kensington*, there is little sense that these attachments have been sought out or that prior to them the women felt diminished by their absence. Rather than actively seeking relationships, in fact, it is often the spinsters and widows who are sought after, propositioned or pursued by would-be suitors, suitors who are usually rebuffed or strategically diverted. In creating sexually desirable, sometimes sexually active, middle-aged women within novels that often treat sex as 'small potatoes'[23] when compared with what else life can offer, Spark again rejects the 'loser in love', Havisham-esque spinster caricature. Even Miss Brodie's long-lost lover Hugh is relegated to the status of a literary MacGuffin in the narrative. With Hugh gone, rather than sleep with the married Teddy Lloyd, Brodie is simply 'working it off' with Gordon Lowther.[24] Fleur Talbot, in *Loitering with Intent*, seems to like men, but ultimately regards them as too time-consuming, a distraction from her writing. When the tiresome Beryl Tims asks if Fleur is going to get married, she responds 'No, I write poetry. I want to write. Marriage would interfere'. When Beryl suggests she could get married, have children and write after the children have gone to bed, Fleur simply smiles and makes Beryl Tims furious. In another episode, Dottie, the 'awful wife' of her lover, Leslie, confronts Fleur with the affair, only to be told:

> I love him on and off when he doesn't interfere with my poetry and so forth. In fact, I've started a novel which requires a lot of poetic concentration because, you see, I conceive everything poetically. So perhaps it will be more off than on with Leslie.[25]

Similarly, in *The Comforters*, Caroline finds her lover Lawrence, and men in general, secondary if not dispensable. Writing about this novel, Hope Howell Hodgkins cites John Updike's bemused question, 'Where else in the fiction of the fifties do we find a heroine whose heterosexuality is so calmly brought forward and assigned a secondary priority?'[26] If it puzzles Updike, the question puzzles Spark's male characters more.

Almost all of Spark's central characters, both men and women, live lives out of sync with conventional family structures. In 2007, the Scottish literary critic and novelist Jenny Turner, discussing the critic James Wood's claim that Spark's novels eluded the features usually associated with 'greatness', wrote:

> One of Spark's disqualifications from 'greatness' is her lack of interest in families – was there ever a 'great' novelist who could manage without this mighty social and fictional institution? Did Spark ever write with conviction about even one? [...] it is exactly the way the novels swerve round family, child-bearing, romantic love and so on that lends them their delightful perversity, their very sense of self.[27]

And not only does Spark swerve around family, her characters are often frankly dismissive of pregnancy, children and child-rearing. This stands in contrast to contemporaneous work by writers such as Lynne Reid Banks or Margaret Drabble, whose novels share a number of thematic elements with Spark but centre on bedsit-bound motherhood as a profound journey or rite of passage. Spark's work is rather more wry in her handling of the subject. *Loitering with Intent*'s Fleur Talbot tells us that Edwina, Sir Quentin's mother, 'bore very well the fact she had spawned a rotter'.[28] For Dorothy in *The Girls of Slender Means*, an unwanted pregnancy is announced in passing amidst 'a waterfall of debutante chatter'. 'Filthy luck. I'm preggars', says Dorothy, as she pops her head around Jane's bedroom door.[29] And in *A Far Cry from Kensington*, Mrs Hawkins is irritated by the assumption, on the part of fellow lodger Isobel and her overbearing father, that she is, almost by default, 'motherly' and therefore interested in Isobel's unplanned, extra-marital pregnancy. To Mrs Hawkins' anger, Isobel continues to visit the rooming house even when she secures a flat of her own. On arriving home to find Isobel sitting on the bed with William (Mrs Hawkins' new boyfriend and fellow lodger) we are told by the protagonist that Isobel 'didn't for a moment think I could be the part of his life I now was [...] She continued to think, speak and act as if I was motherly, and she was wrong [...]. To be motherly, I felt, was her role'.[30] Isobel herself treats the matter as an inconvenience at worst. In Spark's own life, it is almost tiringly and gender-specifically well documented that Spark's parenting skills were less than sparkling, and that while officially a mother, she was not mother*ly*. Paraphrasing Cyril Connolly,

Spark's biographer Martin Stannard has noted that 'her "pram", her domestic responsibilities, were to remain in someone else's hall'.[31] In many of Spark's novels, the reader is offered a portrait of male and female experience largely unbound by 'significant others', be they romantic partners or dependents. Spark's spinsters in particular are very rarely presented as characters to be pitied, unlike the persistent stereotype – in literature and in life – of the vulnerable, desperate, childless single woman. In *Loitering with Intent*, Spark reimagines herself as Fleur, describing her 'autobiographical artist figure as a spinster, even though Spark herself had been married', choosing to 'reimagine her early life as if she had been a cheerful, self-assured, never-married woman'.[32]

If spinsterhood was a terrifying prospect in much eighteenth- and nineteenth-century fiction (Miss Bates in Jane Austen's *Emma* is one such example), its literary legacy has been hard to shake even in the twenty-first. Whatever their literary merit, recent novels such as Zoe Heller's *Notes on a Scandal*, Harriet Lane's *Alys, Always*, Claire Messud's *The Woman Upstairs*, Ottessa Moshfegh's *Eileen*, Sayaka Murata's *Convenience Store Woman* or Gail Honeyman's *Eleanor Oliphant is Completely Fine* continue to cast spinsters variously as odd, lonely, obsessive, creepy or downright sinister. The spinster in popular culture is still frequently defined by Charles Dickens's mad, dusty and doomed Miss Havisham, the apotheosis of the jilted woman in *Great Expectations*, while the 'thrum' of 'spinster-dread' abounds in the novels of Jane Austen and their endless television adaptations.[33] But in spite of the dominance of 'the marriage plot', the role of the spinster in both fiction and society began to change in the late nineteenth and early twentieth century, as writers and scholars including Chiara Briganti, Kathy Mezei, Sheila Jeffreys, Laura L. Doan, Niamh Baker, Katherine Holden, Emma Liggins, and Judy Little have explored, often in relation to the specific living arrangements of single women as landladies, nannies, boarders or lodgers. In this period, a range of more interesting single women began to appear in literature: bluestockings, sleuths, detectives, activists and suffragettes. The tragic spinster trope continued, but it had competition. By the time Spark came to write her post-war novels, the image of the spinster in society had changed again and some of the more positive role models of the spinster in fiction had again begun to dissipate as Britain attempted to restore the social order and re-establish gender roles in the inter- and post-war periods. By the 1930s, images of women living in an impoverished state of 'spinster-dread' were combined with a broader suspicion of 'the surplus', and plucky, adventurous, intellectually curious spinsters had, by the 1950s and 1960s, given way to increasing representations of single women *in extremis*: themes of alcoholism, unwanted pregnancy, back street abortion, abandonment, betrayal, sex work or affairs proliferated. Among these are Olivia Manning's *The Doves of Venus*, Lynne Reid Bank's *The L-Shaped Room*, Nell Gunn's *Up the Junction*, Shena Mackay's *Music Upstairs*, Margaret Drabble's *The Millstone* and many others. Heterosexual relationships (or the want of them) formed the central plot, with spinsters often cast as beleaguered, melancholy, lonely and desperate. That is not to say that we do not find such characters or themes in Spark's novels. Wanda, the Polish dressmaker in *A Far Cry from Kensington*, is tormented and driven to suicide, while Lise in *The Driver's Seat* is perhaps the ultimate alienated spinster in fiction and is the only one of Spark's spinsters to live completely alone (in an immaculate, self-contained apartment). Of all Spark's women, only Lise is truly isolated – there is no sign in her life of friends, neighbours or housemates who might have offered companionship, support or alleviated boredom. Yet however morbid or macabre her intentions, Lise is nevertheless more active than the passive, bedsit-bound spinsters of many of Spark's literary peers, whose characters wait in vain to be rescued or simply fade into diminished lives. Spark's single women – debutantes, spinsters, widows and divorcees – are varied and distinctive. January Marlow, Joanna Childe, Jean Brodie, Barbara Vaughan, Caroline Rose, Louisa Jepp, Nancy Hawkins, Fleur Talbot, Jane Wright, Milly Sanders, Wanda Podolak, Lise and Collie, Greggie and Jarvie: all of these women differ enormously in terms of personality, appearance, age and occupation. Across her novels and short stories Spark's women get married, take lovers, go mad, pursue careers, die young, write novels, commit and solve crimes. They are complex, multi-faceted, and not always likeable.

Unlike the single lodgers and landladies in the work of male writers such as Rudyard Kipling (*Mary Postgate*), William Platt (*The Passionate Spinster*),

George Orwell (*A Clergyman's Daughter*) or Brian Moore (*The Lonely Passion of Judith Hearne*), Spark's women lodgers and landladies are independent, idiosyncratic, with rich, complex inner lives. Their circumstances are rarely cause for regret or self-pity, even when they are beset with challenges and obstacles: scheming blackmailers, plagiarists, sexual predators. If anything, they are regarded by other characters as rather too capable, too independent or too smart. As such, Spark comments on the way unmarried women, especially those of a certain age, are perceived. On one hand they are seen as having few responsibilities, and therefore available to attend to others' needs on demand (much to their ire), and on the other, their resolute and cheerful single-ness confounds those around them. Why do Jean Brodie and Nancy Hawkins turn down proposals? Why are they not as amenable as they appear? How can they resist? What else would they be doing? Why are they so obstinate? Spark's self-determined spinsters are fearless. Less lonely and frustrated than their married counterparts, they lead active social lives and make friends easily. Friendship, in fact, is treated as a crucial aspect of life: 'there they were', writes Fleur in *Loitering with Intent*, 'like your winter coat and your meagre luggage'.[34] These platonic friendships are what Armistead Maupin has deemed 'logical' rather than 'biological' family structures formed between colleagues, neighbours, lodgers and landladies.[35]

Hope Howell Hodgkins points out that much of the comedy of Spark comes through the fact that spinsters, usually the object of pity, neglect or scorn, take pride of place as never before, and become the subject.[36] Their character's or narrator's focus on apparently trivial domestic details works both to celebrate individual female perception and to satirise traditionally grand literary ideals. These women are aware when other characters are being condescending towards them; they have an all-too-conscious sense of their being potential objects of ridicule; and they strive to validate their own subjectivity in the face of prejudice and dismissal. Nancy Hawkins's refusal to adjourn to the next room with the 'ladies' at a formal dinner party is both a *faux pas* and a statement of intent: she will not be categorised and she will not follow convention. When Spark herself was referred to as a 'dear little thing' (by John Bayley), she wrote to Doris Lessing about the encounter, saying 'I hated that "dear little thing" – f**k him'.[37] In *The Comforters*, Louisa Jepp's crimes are hidden in plain sight – who would suspect an old lady, living alone and devoted to home baking, of diamond smuggling? And in *The Prime of Miss Jean Brodie*, 'it is not the sexpot but the girl with piggy eyes who becomes the mistress'.[38] Spark delights in confounding the expectations of her readers and characters.

Kate Macdonald writes of lodgings as 'having the capacity to test character', that the socially low setting of the lodging house allowed characters to respond to the circumstances that had brought them there.[39] The bedsit and boarding house was inhabited not only by single, heterosexual women, of course, but by many other people otherwise marginalised, excluded or otherwise on the fringes of 'conventional' family life. Spark's boarding houses include immigrants, homosexuals, bachelors, refugees, criminals, those with religious callings – housemates and bedfellows of diverse backgrounds and nationalities who are brought together to create a vibrant cast of characters. In these spaces, the spinster is less an 'odd woman', and becomes part of a community made up of co-habiting 'foreigners' and others. Bedsit and boarding house living held a similar appeal for some of Spark's fellow writers in early to mid-century London, including her friend and contemporary Doris Lessing. Reflecting on a slightly earlier period, Dodie Smith's autobiographies also include long, detailed descriptions of her time living in rented rooms in London. Her nostalgic account of this period evokes 'a lost world where young career women had a different sort of independence'.[40] Smith's contemporary, the Scottish playwright and novelist Elizabeth MacKintosh, who wrote plays under the pen name Gordon Daviot and novels as Josephine Tey, also wrote positively about lodgings before she was forced to return to Inverness to live with and care for her elderly father. Many of MacKintosh's spinster characters were similar to Spark's in their defiance of convention and their enthusiasm for life beyond romantic relationships (*The Franchise Affair*; *Miss Pym Disposes*) while her 1934 play *The Laughing Woman* is 'an attempt to understand why a woman would give up her creative dreams for a man'.[41]

For women, and for Spark in particular, the removal of domestic drudgery and the absence of family responsibilities allowed for a focus on other occupations. Miss Brodie is only allowed to be a teacher, Gerard Carruthers notes, *because* of her spinsterhood in a period where women teachers were expected or required (by the 'marriage bar') to relinquish their career when they married.[42] According to Barbara Pym's Mildred Lathbury, even the burden of keeping three people in toilet paper seemed rather a heavy one.[43] In catered accommodation – boarding rather than lodging houses – where occupants took meals together before retreating to their individual rooms, the experience sounds remarkably similar to a long-term writing residency. It is surely no accident that, like their author, many of Spark's women are either writers or work in publishing: Caroline Rose, Fleur Talbot, Mrs Hawkins, Jane in *The Girls of Slender Means*. *Loitering with Intent*, as Spark acknowledged, was a semi-autobiographical novel which drew on her experiences as a woman living alone in post-war London. Like *A Far Cry from Kensington*, it is written in the first person, framed as a memoir and features Fleur Talbot, a celebrated writer, reminiscing on a period during which she lived in a bedsit and worked on her first novel, supporting herself through paid employment for the Autobiographical Association. The parallels to Spark's period as a jobbing writer in the late 1940s – for a jewellery trade magazine, *Argentor*, the political magazine *European Affairs* and then as General Secretary for the Poetry Society and Editor of the *Poetry Review* – are abundantly clear.

The bedsit in Spark's novels, then, represents artistic freedom for women, allowing for a lifestyle which provides both solitude to focus on work and diverse companionship and opportunity through living communally. Jenny Turner has highlighted that the opening pages of *Loitering with Intent* present details of what she calls 'a mid-century room of one's own',[44] complete with a gas ring operated by pennies. The detailed description of Fleur Talbot's bedsit room in the novel is remarkably similar to the account of Spark's own room, described in Martin Stannard's biography. In *Loitering*, we are told that the room contained

> [A] gas ring for cooking, a bed for sitting and sleeping on, an orange box for food stores and plates, a table for eating and writing on, a wash basin for washing at, two chairs for sitting on or (as on the

present occasion) hanging washing on, a corner cupboard for clothes, walls to hold shelves of books and a floor on which one stepped over more books, set in piles.⁴⁵

When Fleur's friend, Maisie Young, comes to visit she is described as 'ignorant about penniless realities'. Clearly horrified, she repeatedly remarks on the room's 'compactness': 'Compact, compact, it's really … it's really … I didn't know they had this sort of thing in Kensington […] how do you keep everything so clean, yourself?'⁴⁶ Describing Spark's own rooms, Stannard writes: 'the table was a folding card table; the bed, single: everything temporary, functional, convential in its austerity – and dominated by books, books, books'.⁴⁷ Even the makeshift orange box cupboard in *Loitering*'s Vicarage Gate appears again in Spark's own account of how her rooms were furnished. And yet, in spite of the relatively low status of these lodgings, and the clear sense of austerity and making do, we are reminded by their inhabitants that this is in no way cause for self-pity – quite the opposite. Rather, we are told repeatedly in *Loitering with Intent* 'how wonderful it feels to be an artist and a woman in the twentieth century'.⁴⁸

The contingent relationship between the material conditions of a writer's life and her ability to think and write regularly for uninterrupted periods of time is still regarded as one of the most significant requirements for women who want to write.⁴⁹ In *The Girls of Slender Means*, Jane is on a constant quest to find peace and quiet to concentrate on her 'brain-work'.⁵⁰ According to Alan Taylor, being a writer 'was of paramount importance' to Spark and 'demanded a degree of sacrifice not required in other professions. To achieve her aims she had to distance herself from demands on her time and emotions.' Taylor claims that 'Spark was not in the least domesticated':

> From an early age, she told me, her mother had instilled in her the idea that if you don't know how to do something – ironing, washing dishes, vacuuming – you'll probably not be asked to do it. Spark took this advice to heart and never wavered in her avoidance of such chores.⁵¹

As Paul Delany has noted, both Spark and Doris Lessing accepted the bedsit as a suitable place for those unwilling or unable to become housekeepers: 'It was a question not just of avoiding "female" domestic obligations, but also of being free to do something else, to sit and smoke and contemplate the blank page.'[52]

Spark 'made a career of escaping when she thinks something is going to stop her writing'[53] to the extent that a room – or the solitude a room provided – was as crucial to her writing as it was for her literary characters. In a trailer for her online writing masterclass, Joyce Carol Oates, an admirer of Spark, has similarly identified quiet and solitude as crucial to a writer's success, claiming that 'the great enemy of writing isn't your own lack of talent, it's being interrupted by other people'. For Oates, 'constant interruptions are the destruction of the imagination'.[54] Spark's friend and contemporary Doris Lessing also noted that 'writers, and particularly female writers, have to fight for the conditions they need to work'.[55] Spark's spinsters, and Spark herself, assumed that paid employment was part of life, a necessity that would allow for a lifestyle and occupation they chose – work allowed them to live outside of family networks. Like their author, most of Spark's women characters regard relationships (with partners or children) as secondary concerns in their life's narrative: 'to Spark, everything comes second to the story: sons, lovers, health and welfare'.[56] Mary Taylor, an early feminist activist and close friend of Charlotte Brontë, published numerous essays between 1865 and 1870 to persuade her readers that to be truly free, women should earn their own living. She believed that to marry for money was degrading and had criticised Charlotte Brontë for subscribing to the idea that women were bound in duty to sacrifice themselves for others. Spark's life and work appear to follow all of Taylor's edicts.[57]

Muriel Spark is not, of course, the only writer to have foregrounded the lives of unmarried women, or to have presented them as admirable, interesting and vibrant. We laugh with, rather than at, Spark's spinsters, who have their literary ancestry in George Gissing's Rhoda Nunn in *The Odd Women* or Sylvia Townsend Warner's *Lolly Willowes*. Similarly robust, confident and complex spinsters can be found in the works of Winifred

Holtby, Vita Sackville-West, Stevie Smith, Elaine Dundy, Barbara Comyns, Doris Lessing, Sarah Dunant, Margaret Atwood and many others. In contrast to the dominant portrayal of the spinster in culture, Spark's spinsters are characterised by their modernity – they are Londoners: urban, autonomous, sophisticated, intellectual, decisive. They go wherever they please and see whomever they choose. They do not live with extended family as 'maiden aunts', neither are they 'spinsters of the parish', arranging flowers in the village church and assisting the curate. Laura Doan argues that as a historical subject and literary representation the character of the spinster 'is defined by absence; she lacks a primary relationship with a man to fulfil her role as wife and mother. Other available kinship roles achieve only marginal importance and cannot compensate for the inadequacy of her single status'.[58] We might see that in this perceived lack, the spinster's lack of 'other' results in her being other*ed*. But equally, spinsterhood allows women to define themselves. For Spark, bedsits and boarding houses became spaces of production, where she engaged in participant observation with her fellow boarders and lodgers – living cheek-by-jowl with people thrown together by circumstance yielded rich rewards in terms of subject matter. The odd juxtapositions, idiosyncratic dialogue, strange couplings and – for a writer so spare and economical – the rich attention to domestic detail in Spark's novels surely find their source in lived experience.

In 1903, Arnold Bennett found that reviewers 'were staggered by my hardihood in offering a woman of forty as a subject of serious interest to the public'.[59] Over fifty years later, in *Quartet in Autumn*, Barbara Pym's Letty writes, 'might the experience of "not having" be regarded as something with its own validity?'.[60] It is perhaps disappointing, then, to read an entry in Pym's diary which initially appears to comply with literary convention in overlooking the spinster as an active subject: 'the position of the unmarried woman – unless, of course, she is somebody's mistress, is of no interest whatsoever to the reader of modern fiction'. In the next line, she adds a note: 'the beginning of a novel?'.[61] For Muriel Spark, writing furiously in her lodging rooms in the late 1950s, the position of the unmarried woman was the beginning of some of her most celebrated and memorable works, works which brought spinsters off the shelf.

Endnotes

1. Katherine Holden, *The Shadow of Marriage: Singleness in England, 1914–60* (Manchester: Manchester University Press, 2007), p. 26, quoted in Terri Mullholland (ed.), 'Introduction: Reading the Single Room in the British Boarding House', in *British Boarding Houses in Interwar Women's Literature* (London: Routledge, 2017), pp. 1–21 (p. 5).
2. Melinda Harvey, 'Dwelling, Poaching, Dreaming: Housebreaking and Homemaking in Dorothy Richardson's Pilgrimage', in *Inside Out: Women Negotiating, Subverting, Appropriating Public and Private Space*, eds. Teresa Gómez Reus and Aránzazu Usandizaga (Amsterdam: Rodopi, 2008), pp. 167–88 (p. 169).
3. Judy Little, '"Endless Different Ways": Muriel Spark's Re-visions of the Spinster', in *Old Maids to Radical Spinsters: Unmarried Women in the Twentieth-Century Novel*, ed. Laura L. Doan (Urbana, IL: University of Illinois Press, 1991), pp. 19–35 (p. 20).
4. Virginia Woolf and Michèle Barrett, *A Room of One's Own / Three Guineas* (London: Penguin, 2000).
5. This figure accords with the modern-day real wage or real wealth value to be found at www.measuringworth.com/calculators/ukcompare [accessed 15 June 2021]. The site offers even higher sums as equivalent depending on which economic measure of inflation is applied.
6. House of Commons, *Hansard's House of Commons Debates* (7 June 1928, vol 218, cols 343–44) [online] www.api.parliament.uk/historic-hansard/commons/1928/jun/07/coal-miners-wages [accessed 15 June 2021]. The annualised figure is based on a working week of six shifts.
7. Muriel Spark, quoted in Martin Stannard, *Muriel Spark: The Biography*, paperback ed. (London: Phoenix, 2010), p. 480.
8. Harvey, 'Housebreaking and Homemaking', p. 169.
9. Emma Brockes, 'The Genteel Assassin', *Guardian*, 27 May 2000. www.theguardian.com/books/2000/may/27/fiction.books [accessed 2 January 2020].
10. Joseph O'Neil, 'Killing Her Softly', *Atlantic*, September 2010. www.theatlantic.com/magazine/archive/2010/09/killing-her-softly/308180/ [accessed 2 January 2020].
11. In 1998 Spark published an essay titled 'Bedsits I Have Known' in US interiors magazine *Nest*, in which she presented a taxonomy of bedsits and boarding houses, describing the characteristics of each type. Spark also recounts her own exponentially improving financial fortunes, culminating, before she left the US for a permanent home in Italy, in the luxurious rooms rented in the Beaux-Arts Hotel between 1964 and 1968 on the East River in New York. Spark kept on her rooms in London after her move to New York, as though the bedsit represented a form of escape and productive solitude. When finances allowed, she would later check into retreats or hospitals because of illness but also because she wanted to be alone 'and gather her thoughts'.
12. Robert Hosmer, 'Muriel Spark: A Glance through An Open Door', in *Scottish Review of Books*, 3 October 2013. www.scottishreviewofbooks.org/free-content/muriel-spark-a-glance-through-an-open-door/ [accessed 2 January 2020].
13. Parul Sehgal, 'What Muriel Spark Saw', *New Yorker*, 8 April 2014. www.newyorker.com/books/page-turner/what-muriel-spark-saw [accessed 2 January 2020].
14. For example, in Martin Stannard's biography.
15. Muriel Spark, *A Far Cry from Kensington* [1988] (London: Penguin Books, 1989), p. 113.

16 Muriel Spark, *Loitering with Intent* [1981] (London: Virago, 2009).
17 See Mullholland, 'Introduction', pp. 1–21.
18 Muriel Spark, *Curriculum Vitae: A Volume of Autobiography* [1992] (Manchester: Carcanet, 2009).
19 Alan Taylor, 'Memento Mori', in *Scottish Review of Books*, 14 October 2009. www.scottishreviewofbooks.org/2009/10/memento-mori/ [accessed 2 January 2020].
20 Gerard Carruthers, 'Ghost Writing: The Work of Muriel Spark', in *The Bottle Imp* 22, November 2017. www.thebottleimp.org.uk/2017/10/ghost-writing-work-muriel-spark/ [accessed 2 January 2020].
21 Muriel Spark, *The Girls of Slender Means* [1963] (Harmondsworth: Middx Penguin Books, 1982), pp. 84–85.
22 Hope Howell Hodgkins, 'Stylish Spinsters: Spark, Pym, and the Postwar Comedy of the Object', in *MFS Modern Fiction Studies* 54.3 (2008), pp. 523–43. www.doi.org/10.1353/mfs.0.1544.
23 Carruthers, 'Ghost Writing', op. cit.
24 Little, 'Spark's Re-visions of the Spinster', p. 25.
25 Spark, *Loitering with Intent*, p. 17.
26 John Updike, quoted in Howell Hodgkins, 'Stylish Spinsters', p. 537.
27 Jenny Turner, 'Rereading: On my way rejoicing', *Guardian*, 21 April 2007. www.theguardian.com/books/2007/apr/21/fiction.murielspark [accessed 2 January 2020].
28 Spark, *Loitering with Intent*, p. 108.
29 Spark, *A Far Cry from Kensington*, p. 44.
30 Ibid., p. 176.
31 Stannard, *Muriel Spark*, p. 77.
32 Little, 'Spark's Re-visions of the Spinster', p. 31.
33 Rachel Cooke, 'The 10 Best … Spinsters', *Guardian*, 3 July 2015. www.theguardian.com/culture/2015/jul/03/the-10-best-spinsters [accessed 2 January 2020].
34 Spark, *Loitering with Intent*, p. 82.
35 Armistead Maupin, *Logical Family: A Memoir* (New York City, NY: Harper Collins, 2017).
36 Howell Hodgkins, 'Stylish Spinsters', op. cit.
37 Hosmer, 'A Glance through an Open Door', op. cit.
38 Susannah Clapp, 'Pisseurs', in *London Review of Books* 10.11 (2 June 1988). www.lrb.co.uk/the-paper/v10/n11/susannah-clapp/pisseurs [accessed 2 January 2020].
39 Kate Macdonald, 'The Use of London Lodgings in Middlebrow Fiction, 1900–1930s', in *Literary London Journal* 9.1 (March 2011). www.literarylondon.org/london-journal/march2011/macdonald.html [accessed 2 January 2020].
40 Jennifer Thomson, *Josephine Tey: A Life* (Dingwall: Sandstone Press, 2015), p. 85.
41 Ibid., p. 160.
42 Carruthers, 'Ghost Writing', op. cit.
43 Barbara Pym, *Excellent Women* (London: Penguin, 2006), p. 16.
44 Turner, 'On my way rejoicing', op. cit.
45 Spark, *Loitering with Intent*, p. 66.
46 Ibid., pp. 66–67.
47 Stannard, *Muriel Spark*, p. 104.

48 Spark, *Loitering with Intent*, p. 15.
49 In the acknowledgements for her novel *Milkman*, Anna Burns thanked a housing charity, Lewes District Churches Homelink, for their support in 'helping her find quiet accommodation in order to write'. After winning the 2018 Man Booker Prize, Burns continued to acknowledge the housing charity and Newhaven food bank reinforcing the need for writers – particularly women from lower socio-economic backgrounds – to secure accommodation and domestic arrangements that allow for writing time.
50 Spark, *The Girls of Slender Means*, p. 44.
51 Alan Taylor, 'Where did Muriel Spark's difficult reputation come from?', *Telegraph*, 7 November 2017. www.telegraph.co.uk/authors/alan-taylor/ [accessed 2 January 2020].
52 Paul Delany, 'Writing in a Bedsitter: Muriel Spark and Doris Lessing', in *Living with Strangers: Bedsits and Boarding Houses in Modern English Life, Literature and Film*, eds. Chiara Briganti and Kathy Mezei (London; New York, NY: Bloomsbury Academic, 2018), pp. 63–74 (p. 64).
53 Alan Taylor, quoted in Brockes, 'The Genteel Assassin', op. cit.
54 Joyce Carol Oates, 'Masterclass Trailer', online video recording. www.youtube.com/watch?v=MhtfIwcSN5Y [accessed 2 January 2020].
55 O'Neil, 'Killing her Softly', op. cit.
56 Taylor in Brockes, 'The Genteel Assassin', op. cit.
57 See, for example, Janet Horowitz Murray, 'The First Duty of Women: Mary Taylor's Writings in "Victoria" Magazine', in *Victorian Periodicals Review* 22.4 (Winter 1989), pp. 141–47.
58 Laura L. Doan (ed.), 'Introduction', in *Old Maids to Radical Spinsters: Unmarried Women in the Twentieth-Century Novel*, pp. 1–16 (p. 5).
59 Chiara Briganti and Kathy Mezei, *Domestic Modernism, the Interwar Novel, and E. H. Young* (Aldershot; Burlington, VT: Ashgate, 2006), p. 131.
60 Barbara Pym, *Quartet in Autumn* (London: Picador, 2015), p. 20.
61 Barbara Pym, quoted in *A Very Private Eye: The Diaries, Letters and Notebooks of Barbara Pym*, eds. Hazel Holt and Hilary Pym (London: Macmillan, 1984), p. 1.

4. Between Desire and Control: The Fashioned Image in Muriel Spark's Life and Fiction

MONICA GERMANÀ

> Bluebell was what I called my grandmother's lovely blue silk brocade going-away dress the colour of cornflowers. I have never seen anything quite so beautiful, nor touched anything so sensuous before or since.[1]

Muriel Spark's glamorous image and elegant writing style are intertwined with the author's lifelong interest in *couture*. In the above excerpt from Muriel Spark's memoir, *Curriculum Vitae* (1992), her grandmother's silk brocade dress is personified not merely by virtue of being named 'Bluebell', but because it embodies a stable image of her grandmother's former character against the background of her deteriorating mental and physical health. Sartorial recollections such as this punctuate Spark's memoir, signalling the author's deep fascination with the meaning of garments, and offering a new way to decode the key thematic and formal preoccupations in her life and fiction.

Viewed from a combined sartorial and textual perspective, the complex dynamics of image control become a productive framework within which to explore the tension between human agency and destiny in her fiction. With particular reference to *The Prime of Miss Jean Brodie* (1961), *The Girls of Slender Means* (1963), *The Public Image* (1968), *The Driver's Seat* (1970) and *A Far Cry from Kensington* (1988), this chapter explores the 'fashioned image', as it emerges from the competing narratives of self-representation at work in each novel. Fashion's elusive visual language, its fraught relationship with female desire, and its non-linear temporality, all feed into Spark's treatment of the fashioned image.

Fashion is a complex cultural practice and its language and structure resist closure and stability on many levels. Giving 'form' to the body, as Alexandra Warwick and Dani Cavallaro note, 'dress simultaneously promotes the myth of a unified identity and atomizes the subject into a plethora of alternative masks'.[2] Indeed, rather than a fixed system of signs, as a language, Fred Davis argues, fashion 'can best be viewed as an incipient or quasi-code, which, although it must necessarily draw on the conventional visual and tactile symbols of a culture, does so allusively, ambiguously, and inchoately'.[3] Therefore, while garments may express identity, they never do so in absolute or essentialist terms, but rather to convey the continuously shifting paradigms of self. The fashioned image is, by definition, subject to change, and it is the loose fluidity of sartorial language that enables Spark to articulate the complexities of image and self-representation.

In addition to the instability of its codes, and the images it produces, the element of consumption, central to the industry of fashion, adds a further layer of complexity to the notion of female agency. Often charged with reducing women to mindless consumers of whimsical fads, a long-standing anti-fashion discourse, indiscriminately supported both by misogyny and feminism, has persistently portrayed women as the vain victims of profit-led trends set by fashion designers: 'More intimately than her knick-knacks, rugs, cushions and bouquets, she prizes feathers, pearls, brocade and silks that she mingles with her flesh', pronounced Simone de Beauvoir's mid-century critique, adding that 'their shimmer and their gentle contact compensate for the harshness of the erotic universe that is her lot'.[4] While to Beauvoir, fashion consumption is the symptom of unfulfilled female desire and a consequence of patriarchal oppression, more recent criticism has focused on the fact that fashion, which has placed increasing emphasis on female consumption since the nineteenth century,[5] relies, for its sustenance, on female desire: 'A garment is not an independent, fully formed entity that is superimposed on the blank canvas of a woman's body', argues Alison Bancroft, '[o]n the contrary, it exists only when it is in the process of being worn'.[6] Such interdependence is behind the shifting dynamics of the fashioned image in Spark's fiction; propelled by the desire to assert agency and yet competing for power against forces beyond one's own control, the act of self-representation is a process of constant negotiation.[7]

Spark's narratives also arguably mirror fashion's non-linear temporal structure. 'Fashion [...] overtly flouts the demand for any clear points of origin', claim Warwick and Cavallaro, 'owing not only to its penchant for ceaseless recycling but also to its patently anti-chronological admixture of past and present, the old and new'.[8] Cyclical by nature, fashion's non-linear time, is never quite completely located in the present, but liminally placed between past and future; designers always work ahead of seasons, because, as put by Elsa Schiaparelli, whose work is directly referenced in Spark's *The Girls of Slender Means*, 'as soon as a dress is born it becomes a thing of the past'.[9] Commenting on *The Girls of Slender Means* and *The Prime of Miss Jean Brodie*, Gerard Carruthers reminds us that the narrative flashbacks used in these novels 'take the reader outside chronological time and give a sense of a larger controlling hand'.[10] In other words, the omniscient narrators of Spark's proleptic narratives, like fashion designers, operate with a prescient knowledge of the future. As well as admitting that the flashback 'device is quite deliberate', Spark confirms its dual-purpose in interview with Robert E. Hosmer: '[t]o give the show away in a strange way, strange manner, creates suspense more than the withholding of information does. Secondly, [...] it has an eschatological function'.[11] Just as fashion's non-linear chronology is preoccupied with manipulating the appetites of the future, Spark's proleptic narratives expose the tension between her characters' desire to stabilise their own image and a narrative technique, which, by virtue of its foreshadowing devices, exposes the fallacy of character progress and agency.

Biographical information offers evidence of Spark's long-standing interest in clothes since, by her own admission, she 'was fascinated from the earliest age [...] by how people arranged themselves'.[12] Childhood memories are frequently framed by sartorial references, especially when these become signifiers of social difference, exemplified by her mother's make-up and coiffed hair, 'decidedly out of place amongst the northern worthies who came to collect my friends',[13] and Spark's own 'pre-school dresses [...] knitted in silk and wool [...] in a variety of colours'.[14] Her interest in clothes increased while she worked for William Small and Son's Women's Department Store in Edinburgh, 'where employees were allowed a discount on any purchases they made': 'I made as many as I could afford', she recalls, 'for I always cared for charming clothes [...] [and] I thought often that I would like to write an amusing book called *The Department Store*.[15] Unsurprisingly, in 1951, Spark marked the first significant acknowledgement in her writing career (the award of the *Observer* short story prize) with the purchase of 'a blue velvet dress for six pounds and a complete set of Proust's *A la Recherche du Temps Perdu*'.[16]

Each subsequent phase in Spark's life has reflected her persistent fascination with fashion, and, more specifically, the image she self-consciously pursued. Her move to New York, and the professional changes it brought about, are described by her biographer Martin Stannard in sartorial terms: 'In just four months she had renovated her entire professional life [...] as though she had walked into a store wearing a serviceable British outfit and emerged undetectably Fifth Avenue'.[17] Indeed, at a 1963 New York party, she is described as 'a strikingly dressed woman', distinctly styled with 'white fox furs and diamonds and a very sophisticated hair-do'.[18] As Spark's writing career blossomed, so did her sartorial appetite which led to experimentation in different looks and styles; in Rome, 'her bedroom wardrobes bulge with long glamour evening outfits so her day clothes have to take their chance in the kitchen cupboards', writes Beryl Hartland of the *Daily Telegraph* from Spark's Roman house in 1971.[19]

Although, throughout her life, Spark acquired a large and varied wardrobe, fashion was not just a frivolous pastime; rather the different images she cultivated were the result of careful negotiation within the different social contexts she inhabited. 'She was transforming herself into a work of art', claims Stannard of her time in New York, who also suggests that, while '[c]lothing interested her', it also 'provided a screen'.[20] Her Italian diaries, and, in particular, the years she spent in Rome, are filled with references to fitting and alteration appointments at some of the high fashion houses such as Fendi, Sorelle Fontana and Andre Lang, and purchases made at exclusive jewellery stores.[21] 'She loved dressing up and eating out. She was a dedicated follower of haute couture, a religious reader of *Vogue*, and a keen appraiser of *la bella figura*', confirms her biographer and friend Alan Taylor, who, upon first meeting with Spark in July 1990, remembers '[s]he was dressed elegantly and expensively'.[22] Even in her later life, spent in the calmer setting of the Tuscan countryside, the appeal of glamour was never too far from Spark's life.[23]

Fashion has complex ramifications for and within Spark's understanding of desire and pleasure in life and literature. By her own admission, her interest in fashion's attention to form is distinctively Catholic; the Protestant tradition, which arguably influences her in other ways, is devoid of the fascinating mundanity that informs Spark's literary taste: 'there's no primping yourself, making yourself beautiful. It's frightfully suppressed', she said of the Brontës and George Eliot's fiction.[24] Significantly, although her decision not to go to university was dictated by her family's limited financial resources, Spark also felt stylistically at odds with the bland aesthetics of student dress:

> At that time the girls who went to university looked as if they'd just put on a dark blue dress and they left it at that for the winter. They were so dreary. And I liked to look nice, go dancing, too, and things like that.[25]

The sensual associations between clothes and other objects of desire point not only to the material pleasure afforded by clothes, but to the pivotal function of apparel in self-fulfilment, as well as self-representation.

Since cutting is an essential part of garment-making, there is also a manifest parallel between Spark's fascination with couture and her distinctly economic narrative style. It is no coincidence that, instead of going to university, Spark enrolled on a précis writing course: 'I've always liked to keep it short', she noted of her interest in concise expression.[26] Like couture, Spark's idiosyncratic terseness speaks of the result of formal control, a preoccupation which, in turn, she also applied to her lifestyle. In addition to garments, Spark's expense-books and personal diaries list appointments for treatments at Elizabeth Arden, and purchases for items such as curling tongs for hair, freckle cream, eyebrow wax, and body stockings – tools revealing a desire to contain and control, rather than simply beautify, the body.[27] 'Spark's shopping wasn't just about having clothes', Andrew O'Hagan observes, 'it was about inhabiting a world of style and basking in the ordinary rituals of maintenance and self-improvement'.[28] Indeed, looking back on her sartorial evolution, Spark has intimated that behind her appreciation for couture is a significant investment in image control:

> From 1944 to 1954 I had absolutely nothing. But then I bought some couture clothes. You could keep a family on what they cost now, but then, for £100 or £200, you could get a really smart dress – and, do you know, I still have them. *More important, I can still wear them.*[29]

Spark's interest in fashion, therefore, cannot be defined solely in pleasure-seeking terms, but also in terms of economy and control, strategies also reflected in the eating problems she experienced in the post-war years.[30] What links précis writing, appetite suppressants, 'well-cut' clothes, and the discipline required to fit into them over time, are Spark's personal and fictional preoccupations with self-representation.

This transpires most prominently in *The Girls of Slender Means*, a novel which revolves around the concepts of self-discipline and control through its historical post-war setting and simultaneous references to both rationing and couture. Set in the May of Teck Club, an institution 'for the Pecuniary Convenience and Social Protection of Ladies of Slender Means below the age of Thirty Years', the narrative focuses on the group of mostly young female residents between February and August 1945, at a time when '[e]veryone carried a shopping bag in case they should be lucky enough to pass a shop that had a sudden stock of something off the rations'.[31] Within this context, *Girls* unfolds as a narrative centred on the appetites of the main characters involved:

> Love and money were the vital themes in all the bedrooms and dormitories. Love came first, and subsidiary to it was money for the upkeep of looks and the purchase of clothing coupons at the official black-market price of eight coupons for a pound.[32]

The novel captures a very specific fashion moment, situated between wartime rationing (still to be in place in the United Kingdom for several years) and the longing for the return of haute couture luxuries, epitomised by the relaunch of French *Vogue* in February 1945 and the inauguration of Christian Dior's 1947 'New Look' collection.[33] As historical fashion magazines reveal, particular emphasis was then placed, on the one hand, on the practicality, versatility, and 'coupon-value' of new clothes and, on the other, on the mending and recycling of existing garments:

> 'Old clothes' is a loose term and does not necessarily mean that the cloth they are made from is worn out. They may be old-fashioned, attacked by moths, or no longer useful. There may be in them a quality you can now no longer obtain. These clothes are worth the trouble of remodelling.[34]

The Schiaparelli dress, owned by Anne, one of the 'girls of slender means', is one such commodity, being

> a taffeta evening dress which had been given to her by a fabulously rich aunt, after one wearing. This marvellous dress, which caused a stir wherever it went, was shared by all the top floor on special occasions, excluding Jane whom it did not fit.[35]

The 'top-floor' collectively refers to 'the most attractive, sophisticated and lively girls' whose rooms are located on the fourth floor of the house.[36] They all share the dress, which Anne lends in exchange for other commodities including soap, used to 'facilitate the exit' 'through the lavatory room' for the girls' unofficial *rendezvous* on the rooftop.[37] Indeed, as Frank Kermode remarks, '[t]he girls at the May of Teck Club are mostly, though not without exception, of slender bodies', as well as of 'slender means', and the question of shape is central to this 'exquisitely formed' novel.[38]

Body shape and appetite control emerge as joint preoccupations in the parallel stories of the girls, concerned simultaneously with fulfilling their own desires and keeping in shape. Rationing means that, while only the stodgier and fattier food is served at the May of Teck Club canteen, the much-coveted clothing coupons are hard to get hold of. An article from a 1945 issue of *Vogue* proclaims that 'the clothes of 1945 need a figure everywhere',[39] and it is partly in response to such sartorial pressures, that '[t]he question of weight and measurement was very important on the top floor'; as Selina admits, 'I only eat a little bit of everything [...] I feel starved all the time'.[40] At the other end of the sartorial spectrum is Jane Wright, 'who was miserable about her fatness and spent much of her time in eager dread of the next meal'.[41] Seemingly unconcerned by the debates about 'food, whether it contained too many fattening properties',[42] is Joanna Childe, whose past history of self-harm (she has plucked her right eye and cut off her right hand) reflects her spiritual antipathy to the body as an obstacle to pure love.[43]

Juxtaposed to Joanna's ascetic self-mutilation is Selina's devotion for 'the Poise Course', an auto-suggestion course which insists on the repetition of 'the Two Sentences' twice a day: 'Poise is perfect balance, an equanimity of body and mind, complete composure whatever the social scene. *Elegant dress, immaculate grooming,* and *perfect deportment* all contribute to the attainment of self-confidence.'[44] The course is an explicit prelude to the return to the 'feminine' in late 1940s and 1950s fashion. *Vogue*'s 'Victory issue' from June 1945, sporting a charcoal etching of a unicorn with a horn in the colours of the Union on its cover, features 'Myself Again', a catalogue of head-to-toe grooming resolutions. Echoing Selina's Poise Course, the article concludes that 'I shall bear in mind that good beauty depends upon well-organised, constant routine, and discipline myself accordingly'.[45] Much like the Poise Course, the new beauty regime ushered in by peacetime prompts a renewed emphasis on femininity as spectacle, and a return to a more conservative conception of womanhood, based on youthfulness, prettiness and softness rather than the wisdom, practicality and toughness predicated by wartime and austerity fashion.

Central to this apparently conservative regression, however, is the paramount question of discipline. This is reflected in Spark's novel, where a central concern is the 'slenderness' of the title, referring not only to the girls' financial resources, but also their physical condition, because slenderness enables the young women who are thin enough to get through the lavatory window to have more freedom and enjoyment – enhanced by the Schiaparelli dress, which only fits the slimmest girls. As Joori Joyce Lee observes of Spark's characters, however, while '[t]he women's slenderness seems to benefit them in many ways, [...] the slender body operates against the empowerment of the women'; this, Lee argues, is particularly manifest in Selina's predicament, 'surrendered [...] to the gaze of male spectators who treat her body as an aesthetic object, devoid of corporeal qualities'.[46] According to this logic, therefore, it is the 'fat' girl, Jane, who, in resisting the pressure to succumb to the desirable thin body, should ultimately emerge, 'sturdy and bare-legged', truly victorious on VJ Day. Meanwhile, Selina is apparently shocked by her fortuitous escape from the explosion outside the May of Teck which leaves Joanna dead.

To attribute absolute agency to any of Spark's characters is as dubious as suggesting absolute freedom of choice exists in a fashion system; in fact, as argued earlier, agency and freedom are never unproblematic in the complex dynamics that underpin both. Jane's apparent disregard for the paradigms of beauty projected upon the girls by the fashion industry also induces constant frustration, and her autonomous desire is compromised, at the end, by the image of non-consensual sexual euphoria on VJ Day: 'A seaman, *pressing* on Jane, kissed her passionately on the mouth; *nothing whatsoever could be done* about it. She was at the *mercy* of his beery mouth.'[47] On the other hand, Selina's last-minute rescue of the Schiaparelli dress from the building on fire speaks of her image-awareness and determination not to lose the power the dress stands for: '[e]mpty hunger for commodity is allowed to survive the war', notes Adam Piette, 'whilst the fervour for religious mysticism which occurred during the war is killed off'.[48] Though fashionable Selina is far from untouched by the course of events, like Jane she survives in a narrative that points to her desire to control as central to self-survival. The same is not true of ascetic Joanna, who, as well as her image, has sabotaged her own desire, and whose death may also signal the end of wartime spiritualism.

Spark's awareness of the doors that clothes may open to women who know how to use them nevertheless raises questions about the agency attributed to those apparently in charge of their own sartorial choices. 'What is shopping, what is a purchase if not a more or less intense moment of desire settled by a sudden act of volition?',[49] asks Andrew O'Hagan in his introduction to *The Driver's Seat*, a novel that pushes the boundaries of agency through a character whose actions contribute to her meticulously planned death by murder. While the novel, which was Spark's own favourite and originally titled *Predestination*,[50] leaves an unsettling mystery about the character's motive open, it also ambiguously subverts accepted notions of (female) passivity and victimhood: 'Spark deconstructs the murder mystery novel [...] turning everything on its head', argues O'Hagan, 'not least the easy separation of killer and killed'.[51]

Within the apparently ordinary context of a shopping expedition at the start of the novel, Lise's rejection of a garment on the ground that 'the material doesn't stain' casts a sinister light on her obscure quest for the 'the necessary dress'. A sense of uncanny uneasiness persists when her final selection, '[a] lemon-yellow top with a skirt patterned in bright V's of orange, mauve and blue', matched with 'a summer coat with narrow stripes, red and white, with a white collar',[52] is at odds with her otherwise functional and minimalist lifestyle. While she 'keeps her flat as clean-lined and clear to return to after her work as if it were uninhabited',[53] Lise's garish sartorial choices provide, as Frank Kermode notes, the novel's sole source of (dark) humour,[54] pointing to her grotesque appearance as echoing the circus, the fairy tale and the carnival.[55]

In a novel that, in Jonathan Kemp's words, is 'almost cinematic in its attention to surface detail and action', the reasons behind Lise's deliberate choice of an outfit designed to look strange remain undisclosed, but are in no doubt connected with the image Lise attempts to fashion for herself; thin, pale-brown haired, with dull blue-grey eyes, and 'neither good-looking nor bad-looking', her looks are inconspicuous. But Lise's plan requires enhanced visibility: 'Her conspicuousness is [...] doubly significant', explains Kemp, 'not only does it mark her out from [...] all the other women in their "dingy" clothes [...], but it is also a signal to her murderer',[56] a passenger sitting next to her on the plane. In contrast with both her and the other women's invisibility, Lise's lurid-coloured clothes perform a specific function, which is to manipulate the gaze of those around them and purposefully re-direct it towards her, when she would otherwise be unnoticed.

Lise's exhibitionist turn signals a reversal of the male gaze; in the context of film, Laura Mulvey argues that the patriarchal politics of cinematic narrative places female characters in a position of passive exhibitionism, an object controlled by the active voyeurism of the male gaze.[57] Lise's self-aware sartorial choices, however, reveal 'the active dimension of exhibitionism [...] and the passive dimension of voyeurism'.[58] No longer relegated to the function of passive consumption, fashion serves the female consumer's desire to achieve visibility where they would normally lack it: 'women may be successful exhibitionists', Michael Walker claims, and 'the voyeur's sense of power' can be undermined 'by the exhibitionist's uninhibited élan'.[59]

Although Lise's purchase cannot be categorised as an 'impulse' buy, it is nevertheless her *élan*, or dynamic impulse, that drives the narrative forward, and, unlike other male-gaze-controlled narratives, her sartorial exhibitionism does not 'minimise the extent to which display (and, by implication, femininity) is a troublesome phenomenon'.[60] That this is the case in *The Driver's Seat* is made clear by Lise's preoccupation that her clothes be 'ostentatious enough' to provoke a desired reaction from fellow travellers, who 'look at her as she walks past, noting without comment the lurid colours of her coat, red and white stripes, hanging loose over her dress, yellow-topped, with its skirt of orange, purple and blue'.[61] The effect of the deliberately gaudy ensemble is one of 'magnification' of Lise's ordinarily dull appearance, whereby the carefully arranged attire manipulates the gaze, and thus takes active control over her own narrative of self-destruction. Moreover, Lise's stylistic manipulation undermines the narrative's linear progression and logic, as the skewed aesthetics of Lise's active exhibitionism subvert the notion of passive victimhood foreshadowed in the post-murder 'identikit picture' at the beginning of Chapter 2.

As the plot unfolds, the reader becomes gradually more acquainted not only with the details of Lise's end – 'dead from multiple stab-wounds, her wrists bound with a silk scarf and her ankles bound with a man's necktie'[62] – but also with the disquieting realisation that Lise's desire has orchestrated it. Having taken care of each meticulous detail down to the choice of place, weapon and perpetrator (both of which are indirectly supplied by Mrs

Fiedke, an older woman Lise casually meets in the city of her murder), Lise bullies Mrs Fiedke's disturbed nephew into committing her murder.

While Lise's assertiveness showcases her position of control, as always in Spark's fiction, the narrative insinuates doubts about Lise's agency. Although she does not buy the knife herself, 'a paper-knife will end up in her handbag', Ian Rankin notes, '[c]hance, or Lise's creator, is coming to her aid and breaking into the autonomy she is trying to create'.[63] Most worryingly, the final scene signals her apparent inability to control her murderer's desire, as, 'he plunges into her, with the knife poised high' when she is still alive, despite her firm condition from the outset – 'I don't want any sex [...] You can have it afterwards'.[64] As Carruthers observes '[t]he one piece of contingency which she fails to control [...] represents a particularly bleak puncturing of the omnipotence of the individual human'.[65] Yet there is also the possibility, proposed by Vassiliki Kolocotroni, that if Lise's self-destructive plan has involved rape all along, then the only way she can fulfil her perverse desire is to deny consent up front: 'Scarily, magnificently, Spark here turns the horrific logic of misogyny inside out: the standard line of defence implies that a woman "asks for it" by saying "no" [...], and that's what Lise does'.[66] Unlike other characters whose sartorial pursuits are wrecked by the unstable dynamics of the fashioned image, it is precisely because of the terminal nature of her desire that, with her dress stained, Lise succeeds in holding on to the image she has conceived for herself from the start.

Active exhibitionism also emerges in *The Prime of Miss Jean Brodie*, which revolves around the complex mechanics of self-fashioning through the interaction between a charismatic teacher and her susceptible pupils. Throughout the novel, Miss Brodie's attention-seeking strategies are conveyed through a self-conscious performance of her self-proclaimed image. Sartorial details – such as the 'long black gown with a lace mantilla' worn when meeting the Pope, or the 'silk dress with the large red poppies' chosen for a visit to A. A. Milne – turn the mundane references to the teacher's summer holidays snapshots into opportunities to cement her fashioned image by making her the centre of the representation; her self-praising remarks that she 'looked magnificent' and that red 'is just right for my colouring', deliberately move the focus away from the iconic figures in the pictures and place it, instead, on the glamorous Miss Brodie, whose body image becomes as captivating as her 'glowing amber necklace', the 'magnetic properties' of which she demonstrates in one of her unorthodox lessons.[67]

Miss Brodie's self-centred sartorial narrative, nevertheless, retains the ambivalence of the language of clothes seen in *The Girls of Slender Means* and *The Driver's Seat*. Rather than accepting her 'war spinster' predicament, as Hope Howell Hodgkins suggests, Miss Brodie thus 'endeavours to impose her subjective self-vision on her students and so to control her body as perceived effect'.[68] Indeed, adornment, fashion's primary function, as Georg Simmel explains, 'intensifies or enlarges the impression of the personality by operating as a sort of radiation emanating from it'.[69] But the ambiguous politics of Miss Brodie's sartorial strategy, and carefully choreographed poise, also reveal her dubious glorification of Italy's fascist politics, captured in her charismatic performance of the Roman salute, 'in her brown dress like a gladiator with raised arm and eyes flashing like a sword'.[70]

Indeed, as much as a character like Miss Brodie seeks to promote a coherent image for herself, as a cultural narrative, the body is not a stable, unchangeable entity, but a blank canvas which multiple gazes may inscribe with different narratives; the body is 'a fluid object of both representation and analysis', Warwick and Cavallaro claim, 'the melting-pot where discourses of power and sexuality, authority and desire, mix and collude'.[71] The body's inherent formlessness and fashion's change-led *modus operandi* mean that no fashioned image can ever be final, especially when this is also determined by the gaze of the other, as seen in the ways in which Sandy sees multiple, inconsistent versions of Miss Brodie:

> Some days it seemed to Sandy that Miss Brodie's chest was flat, no bulges at all, but straight as her back. On other days her chest was breast-shaped and large, very noticeable, something for Sandy to sit and peer at through her tiny eyes while Miss Brodie on a day of lessons indoors stood erect, with her brown head held high, staring out of the window like Joan of Arc as she spoke.[72]

The effect of Miss Brodie's 'shape-shifting' is also amplified by the various cultural references, from Britannia to the Mona Lisa, that frame her charismatic presence. Such changes to Miss Brodie's fashioned image are as much the result of her self-conscious sartorial performance, as of the pupils' fantasies projected onto her body. Either way, this proliferation of images undermines the foundations of the Brodie 'brand' which, as the narrative foreshadows, collapses when Sandy betrays her seemingly in pursuit of her own autonomous desire.

Discussing the dual drives behind modern sartorial behaviours, Georg Simmel argues that fashion simultaneously accommodates the human desire to conform to an existing model and the opposite tendency to mark one's own individualism.[73] Both tendencies are visible in the ways in which the Brodie set fashion themselves. Their 'fame' at the Marcia Blaine School for Girls is primarily attached to Miss Brodie herself and, as such, they constitute a cohesive, uniform group. Simultaneously, 'while they remained unmistakeably Brodie [...] they had no team spirit and very little in common with each other outside their continuing friendship with Jean Brodie'.[74] Their individualisms significantly emerge in the different ways they choose to arrange their hats:

> The girls could not take off their panama hats because this was not far from the school gates and hatlessness was an offence. Certain departures from the proper set of the hat on the head were overlooked in the case of fourth-form girls and upwards so long as nobody wore their hat at an angle. But there were subtle variants from the ordinary rule of wearing the brim turned up at the back and down at the front. The five girls, standing very close to each other because of the boys, wore their hats each with a definite difference.[75]

Placed at the beginning of the narrative, this passage draws attention to the distinctiveness of the Brodie set simultaneously as it foreshadows the rise of the girls' individual taste, expressed through the ways in which they choose to fashion their own images. Where Miss Brodie would have wanted to stir the girls' lives in the specific directions dictated by her own will, they all in fact end up pursuing their own individual journeys. In a process comparable to the trickle-down effect whereby the styles chosen by the elite have a direct impact on lower-class consumption trends,[76] Miss Brodie's individualism and cult of her own image, has a visible effect on the girls' collective 'look'. At the same time, just as fashion ultimately relinquishes power to the consumer, this incipient act of self-fashioning preludes to the loss of Miss Brodie's own agency.

Fashion's tension between original and replica captures the conflict between self-image and narrative authority that lies at the heart of the novel; each character strives for their own autonomy, and yet there is a sense in which there is always a higher force controlling every choice each of them makes. Exemplary of fashion's reiteration of replicas is the series of portraits painted by Mr Lloyd which, despite the use of different models, all bear an unmistakeable Brodie 'look'.[77] Yet it is this uncontrolled proliferation of the Brodie image that signals, simultaneously, its apex and decline. Because fashion is change-led by definition, sartorial narratives keep being rewritten; when a particular item reaches its peak, this also signals its falling out of fashion. The same could be argued about Miss Brodie's 'prime' which, in a way, also signals the beginning of her decline. Significantly, towards the end of their relationship, while Miss Brodie 'looked admirable in her heather-blue tweeds', it is 'a folkweave shirt' that Sandy acquires when looking for new clothes with the art master's trendy wife.[78] In turn, despite her betrayal, Sandy's own 'choice' to 'take the habit', and become a Catholic nun, would appear to have been influenced by 'a Miss Brodie in her prime', as she explains while she 'clutched the bars of her grille more desperately than ever'.[79] Like a garment from a previous fashion, Miss Brodie returns, revenant-like, to possess a new chapter of Sandy's life.

The fragility of 'image control' distinctly permeates *The Public Image*, where the life of an apparently insignificant actress, Annabel, is turned around by her sudden fame. Annabel's public image as the 'English Tiger-Lady', chiefly puppeteered by the Italian filmmaker Luigi Leopardi, the business brain behind her big cinematic break, exists in contrast to her apparent weak appearance described, throughout, as 'a puny little thing', 'a little chit of a thing' and 'a little slip of a thing'.[80] The necessary public-facing image is also carefully cultivated with the help of her husband Frederick through an accurate choice of venues, events, and, of course, clothes, as shown when the couple, after a meeting with the Pope, are '[m]uch photographed, Frederick in correct morning suit and Annabel shrouded in black lace set'.[81]

Annabel's apparent weightlessness is seemingly both a threat to her public image, and the very reason for it: 'You are a beautiful shell, like something washed up on the sea-shore, a collector's item, perfectly formed, a pearly shell – but empty, devoid of the life once held', accuses her husband Frederick in his suicide letter.[82] Yet, it is precisely Annabel's malleable lack of substance – both in the physical and intellectual sense – that allows for her manipulation, first by her husband, then her director: 'Annabel is a cipher, more acted upon than acting', notes Kolocotroni.[83] Her 'lightness', therefore, becomes a blank canvas and stands as a void, as Susan Sellers suggests, to be filled with her public image, perfectly symbolised by the novel's opening 'in a series of empty rooms'.[84] As the public image becomes gradually more pervasive in Annabel's existence, her character is replaced by a fuller, though paradoxically hollower, public persona:

> Annabel was still a little slip of a thing, but her face had changed, as if by action of many famous cameras, into a mould of public figuration. She looked aloof and well bred. Her smile had formerly been quick and small, but now it was slow and somewhat formal; nowadays she was vivacious only when the time came, in front of the cameras, to play the tiger.[85]

That Annabel's face shifts 'into a mould of public figuration', means that her image becomes, temporarily, 'public' property, an asset controlled by the PR machine of the film industry behind her, and capable of turning her 'well-cut clothes' and even her 'ordinary string of pearls' into fame.[86]

As the hollow foundations of her public image begin to crack, paradoxically, the strength of the artificial image triggers Annabel's desire to control her own image. As with the complicated relationship that exists between Miss Brodie and the girls she wishes to 'form' with her own image, Annabel's act of re-appropriation coincides with her temporary downfall caused by Frederick's suicide staged to occur at the same time as a wild party he has arranged at Annabel's apartment. It is then that her ability to manipulate the appearance of things, which she has internalised from Frederick and Luigi, replaces her submissiveness. Her rejection of Leopardi's suggestions – 'We'll have to get a new image for you. You'll have to play wild, mad girls when you come back from your vacation' – points to Annabel's determination to pursue a new life (and image) – autonomously, and away from the limelight. As noted by Rankin, by the end of the story, Annabel is 'director of, author of, and leading actress in her own destiny'.[87] Ready to board a plane for Greece, where she intends to move, the ambiguous ending returns to Frederick's shell metaphor to subvert its meaning:

> Waiting for the order to board, she felt both free and unfree. The heavy weight of the bags was gone; she felt as if she was still, curiously pregnant with the baby, but not pregnant in fact. She was pale as a shell. She did not wear her dark glasses. Nobody recognized her as she stood, having moved the baby in a sense weightlessly and perpetually within her, as an empty shell contains, by its very structure, the echo and harking image of former and former seas.[88]

Echoing Frederick's words, the novel's circular structure points to Annabel's re-appropriation of her own image, which she can now control.

The ambivalence of clothing, which gives the illusion of stable form to the formless without itself being a secure mould, is reflected in this paradoxical body image. Having been stripped of the cumbersome armour of her public persona, now pale and unscreened by her dark glasses, Annabel is simultaneously free and unfree, her body pregnant with a weightless child, embodying, in Kolocotroni's words, 'the spiritual potential of female materiality'.[89] As Pamela Church-Gibson reminds us, 'fashion *is* material, in two senses: on the one hand, the world of fashion is a world of material things; on the other it is a world of constant change, transformations, shifting surfaces'.[90] Perpetually thrust in the dynamic process of self-fashioning, '[t]he echo and harking image of former and former seas' of Annabel's 'empty shell', points to the fashioned image as the paradoxical holder of surface and depth, substance and weightlessness, meaning and form.

A Far Cry from Kensington also investigates similar strategies of image control, although, in contrast to Annabel's diminutive presence, the main character and narrator, Nancy Hawkins (known for most of the story as the widowed Mrs Hawkins) is, by her own admission, 'massive in size, strong-muscled, huge-bosomed, with wide hips, hefty long legs, a bulging belly and fat backside'.[91] While not affected by Annabel's inconspicuousness, Mrs Hawkins's weight is just as problematic with regard to her image: 'abundance was the impression I gave. [...] It was, of course, partly this physical factor that disposed people to confide in me. I looked comfortable.'[92] Though child-free and young, Mrs Hawkins's size traps her within the essentialist image of the motherly and the maternal body. It is precisely this image that her second employer, a dubious publisher, exploits to manage authors' complaints to his own advantage. Having noticed the physical oddities in all public-facing staff, Mrs Hawkins's realisation that her weight is the very reason she has been employed is a pivotal moment:

> What was *wrong* with me? Why had I been chosen by Mackintosh and Tooley? It was then the reason dawned on me: I was *immensely too fat*. [...] It was plain to me that no-one who had a complaint to utter or anything against the firm, especially an aggrieved author, could express themselves strongly to me. It would have been unkind. It would have been like attacking their *mother*. Above all, it would have *looked* bad.[93]

Mrs Hawkins's body awareness does not simply indicate that the extra weight has suddenly become apparent to her. It rather unveils the implications that body shape holds in relation to the image others have fashioned for her, and, consequently, the role she can play in her self-representation thereafter.

In her influential work, *Fat is a Feminist Issue*, Susie Orbach argues that patriarchy controls women's bodies through the perpetuation of essentialist arguments about gender roles: 'since women are taught to see themselves from the outside as candidates for men,' she claims, 'they become *prey* to the huge fashion and diet industries that first set up the ideal images and then exhort women to meet them'.⁹⁴ While the visual objectification of women is undeniably central to the paradigms and tradition of Western art,⁹⁵ this position does not give women any sense of their own agency in the process of fashion consumption. Consequently, some feminist fashion critics lament feminism's fraught relationship with fashion, and propose, as Church-Gibson does, that fashion is 'crucial to the destabilization or deconstruction of identity politics'. Rejecting the notion that fashion is primarily linked to the function of female display in heterosexuality, Church-Gibson also reminds us that '[w]omen [...] dress for "each other"', signalling the centrality of dress in the process of female self-representation.⁹⁶

In this sense, Mrs Hawkins's decision to lose weight can be framed more as a result of her enhanced self-awareness than to please the male gaze, a notion supported by her decision to revert to her first name, Nancy, rather than the less correct (she is not married) and more formal 'Mrs Hawkins'. To paraphrase Orbach then, it is weight loss that becomes a feminist issue, fuelled by Nancy's own desire to control her image through a conscious and methodical transformation of her own body. To those in the same predicament, she advises:

> [I]f there's nothing wrong with you except fat it is easy to get thin. You eat and drink the same as always, only half. [...] On the question of will-power, if that is a factor, you should think of will-power as something that never exists in the present tense, only in the future and the past. At one moment you have decided to do or refrain from an action and the next moment you have already done or refrained.⁹⁷

As in *The Girls of Slender Means*, weight loss is not framed in aesthetic terms only, but as a means for Nancy to fashion her image which, in turn, helps her regain control of her own narrative.

Significantly, willpower, the discipline required to lose weight, is characterised here by the similarly disrupted temporality that randomly punctuates fashion. This lack of linearity signals Nancy's resistance to narrative determinism. While previously presented as the passive recipient of her body shape as *telos*, or predetermined typecast characterisation, Nancy's dietary performance enacts a form of sartorial subversion rebelling against the visual narrative imposed on her body: 'I was hungry, but I took pride in that',[98] she claims throughout the process, the success of which is measured against the alterations that Wanda, the Polish dressmaker, applies to her 'black lace evening dress [which] needed to be taken in a good inch both sides'.[99]

Like Spark's dual interest in couture and précis writing, Nancy's systematic approach to weight loss has echoes in her professional career as an editor, and her temporary downfall due to her uncompromising attitude to Hector Bartlett. Bartlett is a Radionics charlatan and mediocre writer to whom she continually refers as a '*pisseur de copie*'; literally, 'a urinator of journalistic copy', the metaphor conjures up the image of an incontinent, out of control, body. Hector's bodily and textual incontinence stands in contrast to Nancy's new image, carefully edited to suit the narrative she wants for herself. Her new shape is the form she chooses for the text of her body; in her words: 'I wanted to be Nancy with my new good shape.'[100]

As with *The Public Image*, *Far Cry* also warns against the sinister consequences to the manipulation of another person's image. As a dressmaker, and much like an editor, Wanda helps the body's visual narrative take its shape. Sartorially, this gives her considerable control over the self-fashioning narratives of others, such as Mrs Hawkins, who put their trust in her ability to fashion their sartorial image:

> Wanda made all my clothes for me. The only other place I could get clothes to fit me at a reasonable price was an Outsize Shop in Oxford Street: these were clothes suitable for everyone, only larger. Wanda, on the other hand, had a flair for divining her clients' personalities.[101]

When, however, under the malicious influence of Hector, who has become her lover, Wanda attempts to alter more than the cut of Mrs Hawkins's clothes, in turn, Wanda's own body image is engineered into pornographic poses by Vladimir, an unscrupulous photographer hired by Hector. Such 'monstrous' fashioning of another person's image bears a significant comparison with Victor Frankenstein's egotistical act of creation in Mary Shelley's 1818 novel: 'it struck me they were trying to reconstruct Wanda, and I thought of a passage in *Frankenstein* where the scientist-narrator dabbles in the grave for materials to construct his monster', Nancy notes upon seeing the images which send Wanda to an early grave.[102]

There is plenty of evidence to suggest that Spark's personal interest in couture, amply referenced in her biographical materials, bears relevance to her writing's investment in formal control. In addition to the elegant economy of her style, the simultaneously liberating and controlling mechanics of fashion consumption and sartorial performance underpin the author's complex treatment of free will and predestination. Central to Spark's exploration of human agency is the fashioned image, which results from the triangulation of character desire, external manipulations, and overarching narrative control. In its complex dynamics, fashion articulates the unresolved conundrum of self-representation, which, in Spark's fiction, is always a dynamic process of negotiation between the desire to control one's own image, and the other, external, and often inscrutable, forces that attempt to manipulate it.

Endnotes

1. Muriel Spark, *Curriculum Vitae: A Volume of Autobiography* [1992] (London: Penguin, 1993), p. 89.
2. Alexandra Warwick and Dani Cavallaro, *Fashioning the Frame: Boundaries, Dress and the Body* (Oxford: Berg, 1998), p. 53.
3. Fred Davis, *Fashion, Culture, and Identity* (Chicago, IL: University of Chicago Press, 1992), p. 5.
4. Simone de Beauvoir, *The Second Sex* [1949], transl. Constance Borde and Sheila Malovany-Chevallier (London: Jonathan Cape, 2009), p. 586.
5. See John Flügel's analysis on the 'end' of gentlemen's fashion which he defines as 'The Great Masculine Renunciation': John Flügel, *The Psychology of Clothes* [1930] (London: Hogarth Press, 1950), p. 111.
6. Alison Bancroft, *Fashion and Psychoanalysis: Styling the Self* (London: I. B. Tauris, 2012), p. 2. Specific case-studies on the most controversial items in fashion history such as the stiletto heel and the corset demonstrate that the popularity – and longevity – of these 'unlikely' objects derives precisely from consumer demand. See, for example, Lee Wright, 'Objectifying Gender: The Stiletto Heel', in *Fashion Theory: A Reader*, ed. Malcolm Barnard (London and New York, NY: Routledge, 2007), pp. 197–207, and Valerie Steele, *The Corset: A Cultural History* (New Haven, CT: Yale University Press, 2001).
7. It could also be argued that Spark's treatment of self is 'queer' because it points to 'a loss or lack of authority'; see Jonathan Kemp, '"Her Lips Are Slightly Parted": The Ineffability of Erotic Sociality in Muriel Spark's *The Driver's Seat*', in *Modern Fiction Studies* 54.3 (2008), pp. 544–57 (p. 545).
8. Warwick and Cavallaro, *Fashioning the Frame*, p. 97.
9. Elsa Schiaparelli, quoted in Ilya Parkins, *Poiret, Dior and Schiaparelli: Fashion, Femininity and Modernity* (Oxford: Berg, 2012), p. 82.
10. Gerard Carruthers, 'Muriel Spark and the Politics of the Contemporary', in *The Edinburgh Companion to Muriel Spark*, eds. Michael Gardiner and Willy Maley (Edinburgh: Edinburgh University Press, 2010), pp. 74–84 (p. 82).
11. Robert E. Hosmer Jr., '"Fascinated by Suspense": An Interview with Dame Muriel Spark', in *Hidden Possibilities: Essays in Honor of Muriel Spark*, ed. Robert E. Hosmer Jr. (Notre Dame: University of Notre Dame Press, 2014), pp. 227–55 (p. 246).
12. Spark, *Curriculum Vitae*, p. 25.
13. Ibid., p. 37.
14. Ibid., p. 36.
15. Ibid., p. 110; p. 113.
16. Ibid., p. 199. Spark also shared part of her prize money with Derek Stanford, 'who had not been keen on my wasting my time on story-writing', and her parents, 'to pay for a party for his [her son Robin's] bar mitzva' (*Curriculum Vitae*, p. 199).
17. Martin Stannard, *Muriel Spark: The Biography* (London: Phoenix, 2009), p. 282.
18. Ibid., p. 283.
19. Beryl Hartland, 'Step into Muriel Spark's Palazzo, and You're in Velvet', *Daily Telegraph*, 24 March 1971, p. 15.
20. Stannard, *Muriel Spark: The Biography*, p. 302.
21. See Diaries, record no. 323 (1968), 325 (1972), 327 (1973), 328 (1975), 329 (1976), 330 (1977), Account No. 10607. The Muriel Spark archive, National Library of Scotland (NLS).

22 Alan Taylor, *Appointment in Arezzo: A Friendship with Muriel Spark* (Edinburgh: Polygon, 2017), pp. 87–88. Taylor also remembers his first meeting with Spark in Arezzo in July 1990, when, after his request for help with buying trousers in Florence, 'she couldn't have shown more concern'. Not only did she display interest in Taylor's sartorial needs, but her appearance, too, displayed her long-lasting interest in style: 'She was dressed elegantly and expensively. Her dress was a riot of yellow and black. Round her neck she wore a string of white pearls and a canary-yellow scarf.' (pp. 9–10).
23 In 2004 on a casual visit to a branch of Cartier to have a watch repaired, the then eighty-six year-old Spark and Penelope Jardine (the artist who became her life-long companion after a fortuitous encounter at a hair salon in Rome) left the shop having bought a couple of diamond rings and a diamond watch. See Emily Bearn, 'The Mistress of Mischief', *Telegraph*, 8 March 2004. www.telegraph.co.uk/culture/books/3613439/The-mistress-of-mischief.html.
24 Muriel Spark, quoted in Rhoda Koenig, 'Bella Donna Muriel Spark', *Vogue* (UK edition), September 1990, p. 420.
25 'Muriel Spark', *The John Tusa Interviews*, BBC Radio 3, 6 January 2002. www.bbc.co.uk/sounds/play/p00nc8vq [accessed 11 March 2020].
26 Ibid.
27 See Expenses Book, record no. 383 (1968–70), and Diaries record no. 323 (1968), 328 (1975). Account No. 10607. NLS.
28 Andrew O'Hagan, 'Introduction', in *The Driver's Seat* [1970] (Edinburgh: Canongate, 2018), p. x.
29 Muriel Spark, quoted in Koenig, pp. 368–69, 420; p. 430 (my emphases). Similarly, talking to the BBC Scotland programme *Scope* in 1971, Spark spoke about her appreciation for 'well-cut clothes', noting also that, she'd 'been making up for' her frugal childhood 'ever since'. Muriel Spark, *Scope*, BBC Scotland (1971), quoted in O'Hagan, p. x.
30 As documented in *Curriculum Vitae*, as well as in all of her biographies, as a consequence of ration-sharing with her then partner Derek Stanford, Spark suffered from malnutrition, a condition aggravated by Dexedrine appetite-suppressant pills she took 'so that I would feel less hungry' (Spark, *Curriculum Vitae*, p. 204). Stannard gives additional information on the addictive nature of dextro-amphetamine, and its associations, discovered later, with symptoms similar to schizophrenia, which Spark also suffered from when she experienced a breakdown in 1954 (p. 154).
31 Muriel Spark, *The Girls of Slender Means* [1963] (Edinburgh: Polygon, 2017), p. 3; p. 2.
32 Ibid., p. 17.
33 See *Vogue*, 1 February 1945.
34 'Do your own remodelling', *Vogue*, 1 January 1945, pp. 70–71 (p. 70).
35 Spark, *The Girls of Slender Means*, p. 24.
36 Ibid., p. 20.
37 Ibid., p. 23.
38 Frank Kermode, 'Unrivalled Deftness', in *Hidden Possibilities*, ed. Robert E. Hosmer Jr, pp. 107–18 (p. 113).
39 'New clothes need a figure!', *Vogue*, 1 February 1945, pp. 29–33 (p. 29).
40 Spark, *The Girls of Slender Means*, p. 22; p. 24.
41 Ibid., p. 22.
42 Ibid., p. 16.

43 See Adam Piette, 'Muriel Spark and the Politics of the Contemporary', in *The Edinburgh Companion to Muriel Spark*, eds. Michael Gardiner and Willy Maley, pp. 52–62 (p. 59).
44 Spark, *The Girls of Slender Means*, p. 37 (my emphases).
45 'Myself again', *Vogue*, 1 June 1945, p. 62.
46 Joori Joyce Lee, 'Discipline and Slenderness: Docile Bodies in Muriel Spark's *The Girls of Slender Means*', in *A Quarterly Journal of Short Articles, Notes and Reviews* 29.4 (November 2016), pp. 250–54 (p. 252).
47 Spark, *The Girls of Slender Means*, p. 115 (my emphases).
48 Piette, 'Muriel Spark and the Politics of the Contemporary', p. 59.
49 O'Hagan, 'Introduction', p. xi.
50 See Hosmer, 'Fascinated by Suspense', p. 233; see also *The Driver's Seat*, p. xiii.
51 O'Hagan, 'Introduction', p. xii.
52 Muriel Spark, *The Driver's Seat* [1970] (Edinburgh: Canongate, 2018), p. 3; p. 1; p. 4.
53 Ibid., p. 8–9. As Ian Rankin notes, this could be read as a self-reflective, metafictional comment on Spark's own stylistic minimalism, concealing accomplished complexity beneath the surface of utilitarian simplicity: 'The flat, as well as being symbolic of owner, also represents Spark's fictional technique. She presents us with a bare room of prose, beneath the surface of which may lie many ornaments and gadgets. This is Spark's house of fiction'. See Ian Rankin, 'Surface and Structure: Reading Muriel Spark's *The Driver's Seat*', in *Journal of Narrative Technique* 15.2 (1985), pp. 146–55 (p. 148). Further references to this text are given in brackets after quotations.
54 See Kermode, p. 115.
55 Spark, *The Driver's Seat*, p. 9; p. 19; p. 56.
56 Jonathan Kemp, '"Her Lips Are Slightly Parted": The Ineffability of Erotic Sociality in Muriel Spark's *The Driver's Seat*', in *Modern Fiction Studies* 54.3 (2008), pp. 544–57 (p. 545; p. 551).
57 See Laura Mulvey, 'Visual Pleasure and Narrative Cinema', in *Screen* 16.3 (1975), pp. 6–18.
58 Pam Cook, *Fashioning the Nation: Costume and Identity in British Cinema* (London: BFI Publishing, 1996), p. 48.
59 Michael Walker, *Exhibitionism / Voyeurism / The Look* (Amsterdam: Amsterdam University Press, 2005), p. 168; p. 166.
60 Cook, *Fashioning the Nation*, p. 48.
61 Spark, *The Driver's Seat*, p. 42; p. 13.
62 Ibid., p. 18.
63 Rankin, 'Reading Muriel Spark's *The Driver's Seat*', p. 149.
64 Spark, *The Driver's Seat*, p. 89.
65 Gerrard Carruthers, 'Muriel Spark as Catholic Novelist', in *The Edinburgh Companion to Muriel Spark*, eds. Michael Gardiner and Willy Maley, pp. 74–84 (p. 83).
66 Vassiliki Kolocotroni, '*The Driver's Seat*: undoing character becoming legend', *Textual Practice* 32.9 (2018) pp. 1545–62 (p. 1548).
67 Muriel Spark, *The Prime of Miss Jean Brodie* [1961] (London: Penguin, 1965), pp. 44; p. 53. The red poppy dress is a style directly borrowed from Spark's biography where her own teacher, Miss Kay, describes a dress with 'large red poppies on a black background' (*Curriculum*, p. 62).

68 Hope Howell Hodgkins, 'Stylish spinsters: Spark, Pym, and the Postwar Comedy of the Object', in *Muriel Spark: Twenty-First-Century Perspectives*, ed. David Herman (Baltimore, MD: Johns Hopkins University Press, 2010), pp. 129–49 (p. 134).
69 Georg Simmel, 'Adornment' (1950), in *Simmel on Culture: Selected Writings*, eds. David Frisby and Mike Featherstone (London: Sage, 1997), pp. 206–11 (p. 207).
70 Spark, *The Prime of Miss Jean Brodie*, p. 46.
71 Warwick and Cavallaro, *Fashioning the Frame*, p. 6.
72 Spark, *The Prime of Miss Jean Brodie*, p. 11.
73 Georg Simmel, (1957) 'Fashion', in *American Journal of Sociology* 62.6 (1957), pp. 541–58, p. 543.
74 Spark, *The Prime of Miss Jean Brodie*, p. 6.
75 Ibid., p. 1.
76 Simmel, 'Fashion', pp. 544–55.
77 Spark, *The Prime of Miss Jean Brodie*, p. 111; p. 112.
78 Ibid., pp. 99–100.
79 Ibid., p. 128.
80 Muriel Spark, *The Public Image* [1968] (Harmondsworth: Penguin, 1970), p. 5; p. 6; p. 7.
81 Ibid., p. 33.
82 Ibid., p. 92.
83 Vassiliki Kolocotroni, 'Poetic Perception in the Fiction of Muriel Spark', in *The Edinburgh Companion to Muriel Spark*, eds. Michael Gardiner and Willy Maley, pp. 16–26 (p. 21).
84 Susan Sellers, 'Tales of Love: Narcissism and Idealization', in *The Public Image, Theorising Muriel Spark: Gender, Race, Deconstruction*, ed. Martin McQuillan (Basingstoke: Palgrave, 2002), pp. 35–48 (pp. 35–36).
85 Spark, *The Public Image*, p. 35.
86 Ibid., p. 29.
87 Rankin, 'Reading Muriel Spark's *The Driver's Seat*', p. 146.
88 Spark, *The Public Image*, pp. 124–5.
89 Kolocotroni, 'Poetic Perception in the Fiction of Muriel Spark', p. 23.
90 Pamela Church-Gibson, 'Redressing the Balance: Patriarchy, postmodernism and feminism', in *Fashion Cultures*, eds. Stella Bruzzi and Pamela Church-Gibson (London; New York, NY: Routledge, 2000), pp. 349–362 (p. 355).
91 Muriel Spark, *A Far Cry from Kensington* [1988] (London: Penguin, 1989), p. 10.
92 Ibid., p. 10.
93 Ibid., p. 86 (my emphases).
94 Susie Orbach, *Fat is a Feminist Issue* [1982] (London: Arrow Books, 2006), p. 17 (my emphases).
95 See John Berger, *Ways of Seeing* [1972] (London: Penguin Classic, 1990), p. 41.
96 Church-Gibson, 'Redressing the Balance', p. 356; p. 350.
97 Spark, *Far Cry*, p. 11.
98 Ibid., p. 106.
99 Ibid., p. 88.
100 Ibid., p. 162.
101 Ibid., p. 26.
102 Ibid., p. 158.

5. 'Unfortunately you have left out all the love poems': Spark in Love[1]

WILLY MALEY AND DINI POWER

This chapter takes as its starting point a little-known, uncollected poem of Spark's entitled 'Anniversary' which can instructively be placed among her other poems of the period as one of a sequence she published in the wake of her love affair with poet and editor Howard Sergeant. When we look at the poems of 1948, at least two are intense, almost obsessive, love poems: 'A Letter to Howard', published in *Poetry Quarterly* in autumn 1948, the same season as 'Anniversary', invokes a kind of religious fervour with its biblical phrasing, repetition and imagery, while 'He is Like Africa' is a celebration of masculine strength and sensuality. Sergeant was the inspiration for other poems of that year, including 'Lost Lover' and 'She Wore His Luck on Her Breast', both of which appeared in *Outposts*, edited by Sergeant. Like 'Anniversary', 'He is Like Africa' draws on imagery from Spark's African experiences. Spark and Sergeant's courtship was conducted in the colonial imagery of that continent. Although the two lovers briefly collaborated, her next lover, kindred spirit Derek Stanford, proved a more long-term and ultimately more problematic figure. This essay explores the links between love, poetry and collaboration in Spark's early work, before she emerged as a novelist.

What does Muriel Spark have to say to us about love and romance? Most of her published pronouncements on love and relationships are cool, distant, ironic. In her memoir, *Curriculum Vitae* (1992), Spark observed: 'From my experience of life I believe my personal motto should be "Beware of men bearing flowers".'[2] Her marriage to Sidney Oswald Spark (SOS), who had ingratiated himself by bringing flowers when she had flu, did not end well. She was unlucky in love, she declared; a 'bad picker', and love had nothing to do with her decision to marry SOS.[3] Pity, flowers, and foreign travel had played a part, but there was another incentive: 'I also liked the proposition that I wouldn't have any housework to do "out there" in Africa, that I would be free to pursue my writing.'[4]

Yet despite her protestations against romantic love, in May 1947, ten years after her African wedding, Spark came first in a Love Lyric competition run by the *Poetry Review*. Her entry was 'a metaphysical sonnet' entitled 'The Robe and the Song', but rather than being based on experience or personal reflection it was, she insisted, 'merely an old-fashioned exercise in what I thought would win that poetry prize'.[5] If this is true, the exercise achieved its aim. The poem comes across like the devotional verse of Donne or Herbert, and the theme is reminiscent of Marvell in 'To His Coy Mistress':

> Hesitant lover, claim my favour soon
> Lest Pride enfold me like a winding-shroud
> And harsh Resentment sing my threnody.[6]

The competition judges – who were generally unimpressed by the standard of entry – said of Spark's poem: 'It has an air about it. It is complete in design, form and texture. "Hesitant", perhaps, in the last line but two, might have been strengthened, but it is a lovely poem as it stands.'[7]

In her writing Spark tends to depict love and lovers with deep cynicism; where romance occurs in her novels it is often revealed with a sly, knowing humour. Think of Leslie and Wally in *Loitering with Intent* (1981), for example, neither of whom seem fit partners for budding novelist Fleur Talbot, Spark's alter ego. There are a few apparently sincere romances in her work, like that between Barbara Vaughan and Harry Clegg in *The Mandelbaum Gate* (1965), and Nancy Hawkins and William Todd in *A Far Cry from Kensington* (1988); but we could easily conclude from both her fiction and her biographical writing that falling in love was not something Spark had ever done, or allowed herself to do. We know she had a number of relationships with men after her marriage ended, but she did not reveal a great deal about her feelings during those affairs and tended to cast aspersions on the men in question. It is usually suggested by biographers that these were relationships doomed to fail for a variety of reasons, not least being her lack of commitment to the men involved, or her unwavering commitment to her art, or both.

Spark only uses the word 'lovers' in her memoir in a literary sense on one occasion, and disparagingly: 'There is something about a passion for poetry that brings out a primitive reaction, especially in non-poets, that is, the "poetry lovers".'[8] In sharp contrast to the 'poetry lovers' were the submissions she received as editor of the *Poetry Review*: 'The young poets brought me poetic tributes – poems dedicated to myself – which I lapped up contentedly, without letting them influence me in the slightest.'[9] Yet we know of at least two serious 'poetry lovers' who did indeed influence her while she was an emerging writer, men with whom she collaborated and shared a love of literature, as well as romantic love. The best documented of these is Derek Stanford.[10] Although latterly she fell out with him over what she saw as a betrayal of trust, Spark initially declared that she loved Stanford, and found in him a close ally. They became close before her feelings about him became ambivalent. Martin Stannard speaks of 'the intensity of their early feelings for each other', evident from their letters: 'Addressing him as her beloved prince, she assured him that she would never betray him; that the affection she felt was uniquely wonderful in her life.'[11] Stannard sees the fruitful collaborative years of the 1950s – when Spark and Stanford published several critical and biographical studies together, as part of a rich and productive literary apprenticeship of which her occasional poetry was also a key component – in entirely negative terms: 'Joint publication was a form of literary wedlock – one of the worst mistakes she ever made.'[12]

When she began her relationship with Stanford she was on the rebound from a more romantically interesting, yet often overlooked, lover: the married poet and editor Howard Sergeant (1914–1987). Their eighteen-month relationship is lightly dismissed in her autobiography, but Sergeant clearly played a key role at a crucial period in Spark's formation as a writer. In fact some of her lesser-known poetry strongly suggests that she fell head-over-heels in love with him, despite later protestations to the contrary.

In a little-known uncollected poem of hers entitled 'Anniversary', published in autumn 1948, she handles the subject of love in a quite visceral way, using imagery suggesting the movement of the wildlife she would have seen on the African plains:

> Our love approaches the last episode
> of pitiless flight;
> the young albino animal reaching
> his soft neck
> to the friendly year
> fears no more the hot herd-breath
> > behind him.¹³

We are not told which particular anniversary she is writing about in this poem, but it is clearly a lover's anniversary – it's about 'our love', described in animal metaphor: the 'young albino [...] reaching / his soft neck / to the friendly year'. But what lies ahead for the young animal, the yearling, is not 'friendly'. It is doomed:

> So wise beyond his age, this
> white yearling shall not grow
> rotten and rheumy, dull
> as to wit, dyspeptic
> as to heart,
> who has lain fugitive
> from the black and bellowing others,
> and suffered the enchantment of stars
> > too bright.

At first sight it could be assumed that the anniversary in question was her wedding anniversary with her ex-husband, since they married in Africa, in Salisbury on 3 September 1937. But the wistful tone suggests otherwise, based on what we know of their marriage, and the poem laments not the end of a ten-year marriage but the end of a short-lived relationship, the 'white yearling' which shall not grow old. Might she be referring to a real-life relationship? Let's look at where it was placed: a 'free verse' pioneering poetry quarterly called *Variegation*, launched in Los Angeles in 1946, the first to publish Kerouac and Ginsberg.¹⁴ This was a serious setting for what was clearly not a light verse.

Then look at *how* it was placed among Spark's other poems of the period. It is one of a sequence Spark published in 1947 and 1948, a period about which Spark is decidedly vague in her memoir. We do know that during that time she was involved in an affair with Howard Sergeant to whom she gave a signed photograph that year, but the general view has been that the affair was not a particularly serious one on her part, since Sergeant does not come off well in *Curriculum Vitae*, published five years after his death. Spark refers to him dismissively as her 'boyfriend of eighteen months' and alludes to his 'hundreds of letters' to her and his poems which 'independent readers' assured her were 'quite good'.[15] Spark's response to this rather weak endorsement of her former (and late) boyfriend's verse is telling: 'They are written to an egocentric idea, or an impossible ideal.'[16] You can imagine her saying this with a dismissive sweep of the hand. But if we look at a poem of Spark's in *Variegation* earlier in 1948 entitled 'Standing in Dusk' it tells a different story.[17] Spark dedicated a copy of this poem to Sergeant on 10 November 1947, and in it we find an explicit expression of intense longing. The speaker reaches

> in the long night of extremity
> for you, my love,
> needing your steadfast sun
> wherewith my whirling earth
> would make a dawn.

It seems to have been part of a complex call and response in 'personalist poetry' as the lovers conducted a poetic dialogue.[18] In its yearning, 'Standing in Dusk' is quite poignant, a word which Spark herself uses in the poem, presumably invoking the same absent lover:

> high trees and parapets
> assert their structure,
> being silhouetted made poignant
> by your absence.

'A Letter to Howard', published in *Poetry Quarterly*, autumn 1948, sees Spark throwing caution to the wind, explicitly addressing her beloved in the title and in the form of address at the start of the poem. Biblical phrasing and rhythms, and the imagery of vast eternally unchanging landscapes invoke a pantheistic religious fervour:[19]

> My love, full of wonder today I call you by everlasting,
> I call you by tide and by rock, by the name of those
> Fowl and fishes that people them. Trees have affinity
> With shells, anemones with leopards since I gather
> Their differences together in your name.[20]

This invocation of her lover as a force of nature is repeated in other poems. The leopard-like Howard also seems to be the inspiration for 'He is Like Africa', later revised, retitled and reprinted as 'Like Africa'. As in 'Anniversary', the continent represents her lover's magnificence in terms of vast landscapes. He is a phenomenon of the natural world, like the sun:

> His light, his stars, his hemisphere
> Blaze like a tropic, and immense
> The moon and leopard stride in his blood
> And mark in him their opulence.[21]

He is a continent, a proud wild animal, the Zambesi River. He is Africanised, lionised, idolised in passionate exotic terms. He is clearly Howard, who shared Muriel's fascination with Africa and later compiled an anthology of African poetry. He was intrigued by Muriel's romanticised images of the place, and references to that continent recur time and again in their literary courtship. As she recalled of her decision to leave Scotland as a young woman, 'the call of adventure in a strange continent was very strong'.[22] According to Martin Stannard:

> When the imaginative impulse of her work was charged by love or
> hate, it moved restlessly back to Africa. In love, Africa was light,

> space, freedom, exotic and mysterious, its savage power offering glimpses of the transcendental. Images of strange energies erupt: the moon, the leopard, muffled drums; above all, the rush of the Zambesi, that 'seraphic river', towards the thundering falls, the epitome of ecstasy, the very thrust of creation.[23]

By the time she was writing 'Anniversary' the African imagery had been somewhat tamed. Their love was by then like a vulnerable young albino animal, a 'white yearling' that would not survive to grow 'rotten and rheumy [...]'. It was an animal that could not come out into the open. It had to hide itself; it lay 'fugitive from the black and bellowing others'. The poem may have marked the first anniversary of their love, while lamenting the fact that it would be the last.

Howard also seems the likely inspiration for other poems of Spark's from later that same year: 'Song of the Divided Lover', published in *Poetry Commonwealth*, and 'Lost Lover' and 'She Wore His Luck on Her Breast', both of which appeared in *Outposts*.[24] These three poems are undoubtedly about a love affair from a personal viewpoint, and while they are quite cryptic, in them we can detect signs of an ending. 'Song of the Divided Lover' is a first-person address, her wordplay invoking robbery, plunder, Adam and Eve and the splitting of ribs:

> Even who lacks a rib shall lie believing
> the robber innocent and you shall lie
> witless what loot establishes your lover.[25]

The speaker is 'the one who could never properly handle / so large a plunder', the 'I' 'sitting and sober in your house [...] / the unexpected rowdy arrived at your threshold'. It is tempting to see Spark as 'the unexpected rowdy', the robber of the rib, the one who has inserted herself into someone else's domestic arrangement, stolen the husband, but still 'believing / the robber innocent'. The poem is full of revelry, 'merry half-bones are clattering [...] like castanets', and suggestions of dancing, sex, 'the merry midnight'. It is a celebration of the excitement of a clandestine relationship, the intensity of their stolen moments, yet it is tinged with regret:

> I was the one who could never properly handle
> so large a plunder, but the hands that dropped it
> lamented the whole of the year that the rib split.

'The whole of the year' is an echo of the 'yearling' in 'Anniversary'. Here the speaker admits to always having struggled to hold the forbidden plunder of their love. The pivotal word 'but' might suggest that the other is to blame for dropping it, for severing the bond, and for a year laments its loss; but the syntax is ambiguous and leaves us wondering where the blame lies. If we look for parallels in their real lives, Spark's biographer Stannard wrote that Sergeant was the one to draw an end to the relationship: 'She had looked to him for strength and permanence, to discover only a timorous beastie cautious of his reputation. She frightened him and, just four months later, he wrote finally to crush what remained of their love.'[26] But in *Curriculum Vitae*, Spark describes the end of the relationship in terms that suggest it was she who ended it. Referring to 'the nastiest, meanest letter (21 April 1949) from Howard that it is conceivable to imagine, especially in contrast to his previous voluminous effusions of love and admiration', she says: 'I believe I had already told him that I could not tie myself permanently to him, but that I could be a friend'.[27] The feuding that followed, according to her, was bitter on his part, while she maintained a sense of detachment. Yet, in 'She Wore His Luck on Her Breast' there is a clear acknowledgement of romantic disappointment, based around the conceit of a lucky charm gifted to the poet by the lover, which 'turned in upon her', became 'a live coal' that burned between her breasts. The poem picks up on earlier metaphors of this lover as the sun – this time the morning sun, which shall

> never more kindle
> beacons on her two hills, who once had stood in the
> thrice-woven circles of fire.[28]

The poem 'Lost Lover', as the title suggests, is based around a similar theme, but there is a less personal tone. Spark seems to stand at a distance as she draws on the imagery of Greek mythology and the Odyssey, referring to Achilles, Pallas, Hellespont, Phryxus and Penelope. She shifts into a more controlled and formal poetic register as if to revert to the style of 'an old-fashioned exercise in what [...] would win that poetry prize'.[29] Yet there is something odd about the title when set beside this poem: it seems discordant, incongruous, as if promising frankness then failing to deliver, offering a hint at personal relevance. But she unfolds her account of lost love in mythical terms, to deflect any sense that it is autobiographical.

It was hard to hide your love away in the small world of literary London that centred on the Poetry Society, where passions ran high, sides were taken, criticism was heartfelt, and collaboration could lead to something more.[30] The practice of dedicating poems to fellow lyricists was of course common, but could prompt jealousy within a small coterie, as Martin Stannard notes: 'At that time, February 1948, she had written a poem for Stanford, "On Music for Statues", which Sergeant not unreasonably construed as an expression of love, although it was more about her relationship to the Poetry Society generally'.[31] *Music for Statues* was a collection of verse published by Stanford that same year.[32] This post-war period was a time of intense debate on the nature of poetry and love. Stanford had published a critical work a year earlier entitled *The Freedom of Poetry* in which he spoke of the wish 'to create a poetry of love' when discussing the young war poet Sidney Keyes, who was killed in action at the age of twenty.[33]

Love poems, circulating in manuscript and in print, were a strange mix of public and private, a sharing of secrets. But could these romantic thoughts be collected for publication? In a letter he wrote to Spark from Glasgow on 5 February 1948, Sergeant referred to a collection of poems she had sent him, perhaps for prospective publication:

> I have been trying to build up a picture of you as the intellectual in exile [...] Didn't you try hard to be worldly-wise and mature? Unfortunately you have left out all the love poems – which are the

most interesting from my point of view – and I see you as you were then [...] Oh, the years in Africa take away the innocence of us all.³⁴

As with Stanford, once the relationship had turned sour, Spark seemed keen to write him out of her history or at least to erase any hint of his emotional significance. Sergeant refers to 'all the love poems' being 'most interesting from my point of view' and it seems reasonable to conclude that many, if not all, were indeed addressed to him. Her withholding of these particular poems when contemplating a collection – she would publish her first slim volume of verse four years later³⁵ – may well have been because she felt they revealed too much; she regretted allowing herself, briefly, to expose deeper emotional needs, desires and longings. It was important to reassert their relationship as a professional one and set aside their affair, no matter how difficult the break-up had been. And it is worth stressing here that Spark's affair with Sergeant was bound up with poetic theory as well as poetry. In addition to publishing poems in *Outposts*, the journal Sergeant edited, Spark co-authored that same year a pamphlet with Sergeant entitled *Reassessment*, setting out their joint approach to poetry and criticism. However, that proved to be the last time they worked together. Though her wistful poetry shows she mourned the end of the affair, its ending had a silver lining because it coincided with the beginning of her career. Spark has insisted that her 1954 conversion to Catholicism opened the door to her life as a writer, but since she had won the *Observer* short story award and published poetry, criticism and biographies ten years before *The Comforters* appeared in 1957, that claim has always seemed odd. The end of the affair with Howard Sergeant carries greater weight as an earlier crossroads and crisis of faith. As Fleur Talbot says of this period in *Loitering with Intent*: 'This was the last day of a whole chunk of my life but I didn't know that at the time'.³⁶

In *Curriculum Vitae* Spark refers to meeting Sergeant many years after the affair, by which time she had 'enjoyed a lot of success' with her novels. 'He said he felt he had behaved badly towards me. I looked at him politely. I really could not like that man.'³⁷ And with these words she dismisses him, a little too hastily. It seems, in the light of the love poems, that Spark's downplaying of Sergeant's importance came about not because he was insignificant to her, as critics often claim, but quite the opposite.

In a short essay written in 1984 simply entitled 'Love', Spark acknowledges the fact that love is difficult to pin down, to define or understand: 'The most unlikely people may fall in love with each other; their friends, amazed, look for the reason. This is useless; there is no reason.'[38] According to Spark, 'Falling in love is by nature an unforeseen and chance affair, but it is limited by the factor of opportunity.'[39] As a character in one of her most remarkable short stories observes, 'Love is an expedition of discovery into unexplored territory'.[40] This haphazard happenstance of the heart is the key to Spark's view of love. She tells us that 'love is inexplicable [...] like poetry', and that 'it includes a certain amount of passion and desire, a certain amount of madness while it lasts'.[41]

In this essay she appears to be speaking, characteristically, from experience yet at the same time maintaining a distance from the subject. She discusses love mainly in the third person and concludes, rather peculiarly, that the mating behaviour of animals – young hares, or horses – is more pleasing to her than that among humans. She ends this essay with clichés: 'But certainly, as the old songs say, love is the sweetest thing, and it makes the world go round.'[42] She seems keen to close down the subject. She tended to be reluctant to talk about love openly, other than comically or in dismissive terms, perhaps because of the pain it had caused her. This pain is spoken of literally in a poem Spark published in 1949 in the wake of her affair with Sergeant. 'The Voice of One Lost Sings Its Gain' includes the lines,

> It is the pain I move in and the best
> of a woman is lost somewhere in me.
> O pain, pain, pain.[43]

Part of this poem later resurfaces as Fleur Talbot's verse entitled 'Metamorphosis' in *Loitering with Intent*, her novel set in the years of transition from Sergeant to Stanford, and it appears again, depersonalised, as 'Flower into Animal' in Spark's collected poems in 2002, where the lines quoted above are altered to read:

> It is a pain to choke with, when the best
> of a species gets lost somewhere.
> Different, indifferent pain.⁴⁴

In this later form, of course, it is much less clear that the poem refers to the pain of a broken heart.

In his biography of Spark, Martin Stannard tends to view her lovers through her eyes, and so he sees the character of Leslie in *Loitering with Intent* as an unflattering composite of Sergeant and Stanford that represents a reckoning with the two rejected partners:

> In *Loitering* Muriel writes Sergeant / Stanford out of her life in the form of the repulsive Leslie (no surname), a married boyfriend who annoys her 'in the extreme by small wants of courtesy. [...]. He was ambivalent about my writings, in that he often liked what I wrote but disliked my thoughts of being a published writer.' This was Sergeant. Lesley's [sic] inaccuracy, inefficiency, selfishness; his 'proprietary way' with her food, writing paper, reputation, reflect how she came to regard Stanford. In retrospect, the first was a bully, the second a sponge.⁴⁵

But time changes perspective. Ten years later, reflecting on his experience as Spark's biographer and on her determination to control the narrative of her life, Stannard remarks: 'All those who had been hurt by her – her husband, her son, her first editor (Alan Maclean), her lovers (Derek Stanford and Howard Sergeant) – she wanted written out, or down, as liars.'⁴⁶ And to some extent Stannard is complicit with Spark's wishes. Further study might find more merit in Sergeant and Stanford than has hitherto been the case in Spark criticism. Deeper understanding of the richness and complexity of the material arising from this period of Spark's life will certainly yield fresh insights into her formation as a writer. She declared in her memoir: 'I was destined to poetry by all my mentors'.[47] The poetry is the thing, and there are hidden gems among Spark's uncollected verse that will repay attention for poetry lovers and critics alike. Incidentally, 'Love' is the last word of Spark's quoted in Stannard's account of her life: 'The recording of her last major interview was delayed by the baying of her dog outside. "Poor thing," she said. "It's howling for love."'[48] Spark knew the feeling.

Endnotes

1. An earlier version of this essay was given as the opening lecture at the Muriel Spark Centenary Symposium, University of Glasgow on 1 February 2018. Willy Maley remains grateful to the organisers and editors for the invitation and this commission. The original title was 'Spark's Anniversaries: Memoirs of a White Yearling', in keeping with the centenary theme. This revised and co-authored version focuses more directly on Spark's early love lyrics.
2. Muriel Spark, *Curriculum Vitae: A Volume of Autobiography* (Harmondsworth: Penguin, 1992), p. 116.
3. Ibid., p. 209.
4. Ibid., p. 116.
5. Ibid., p. 167. 'The Robe and the Song' was published in *Poetry Review* 38.3 (May–June 1947), pp. 192–93.
6. Spark, 'The Robe and the Song', p. 193.
7. Ibid., p. 192.
8. Spark, *Curriculum Vitae*, p. 173.
9. Ibid., p. 174.
10. See Simon Jenner, 'Derek Stanford: Poet, critic and former lover of Muriel Spark', *Guardian*, 26 March 2009. www.theguardian.com/books/2009/mar/26/derek-stanford-obituary [accessed 28 January 2020].
11. Martin Stannard, *Muriel Spark: The Biography* (London: Weidenfeld and Nicolson, 2009), p. 105.
12. Ibid., p. 107.
13. Muriel Spark, 'Anniversary', in *Variegation. Free Verse Quarterly* 3.4 (Autumn, 1948), p. 17.
14. 'in 1955 [...] the West Coast had only one well-established magazine willing to print members of the Beat generation such as Ginsberg, Kerouac, and Whalen; it was located in Los Angeles. Grover Jacoby, Jr., the editor of *Variegation* magazine, accepted the poems by Kerouac and Ginsberg before the Six Gallery reading took place, indicating that at least one editor in the nation was open to their work before any publicity about the Beat generation occurred'. Bill Mohr, *Hold-Outs: The Los Angeles Poetry Renaissance, 1948–1992* (Iowa City, IA: University of Iowa Press, 2011), p. 8.
15. Spark, *Curriculum Vitae*, pp. 180–81.

16 Ibid., p. 181.
17 Muriel Spark, 'Standing in Dusk', in *Variegation* 3.3 (Summer 1948), p. 3.
18 Bruce Miller Meyer, 'Sergeant of *Outposts*: One Editor's Role in Post-War British Poetry 1944–1981' (unpublished doctoral thesis, McMaster University, 1988), p. 134.
19 The relationship between love and religion in Spark's poetry, bound up with crisis of spirit and with conversion, is worthy of further exploration. For an excellent essay on this topic see Martin Stannard, 'Nativities: Muriel Spark, Baudelaire, and the Quest for Religious Faith', in *The Review of English Studies*, New Series 55.218 (2004), pp. 91–105.
20 Muriel Spark, 'A Letter to Howard', in *Poetry Quarterly* 10.3 (Autumn 1948), p. 152.
21 Muriel Spark, 'He is Like Africa', in *New English Weekly* (1948); reprinted in Roy MacNab (ed.), *Towards the Sun: A Miscellany of Southern Africa* (London: Collins, 1950), p. 80; revised and reprinted as 'Like Africa', in Muriel Spark, *All the Poems* (Manchester: Carcanet, 2004), p. 71. The thing about *All the Poems* is that it is emphatically not 'all the poems'.
22 Spark, *Curriculum Vitae*, p. 116.
23 Stannard, *Muriel Spark: The Biography*, p. 100.
24 Muriel Spark, 'Song of the Divided Lover', in *Poetry Commonwealth* 1 (Summer 1948), p. 5; 'Lost Lover', in *Outposts* 11 (Autumn 1948), p. 3; and 'She Wore His Luck on Her Breast', in *Outposts* 12 (Winter 1948), p. 10.
25 Spark, 'Song of the Divided Lover', p. 5.
26 Stannard, *Muriel Spark: The Biography*, pp. 100–01.
27 Spark, *Curriculum Vitae*, p. 182.
28 Spark, 'She Wore His Luck on Her Breast', p. 10.
29 See note 5.
30 On this period see Susan Sheridan, 'In the Driver's Seat: Muriel Spark's Editorship of the *Poetry Review*', in *Journal of Modern Literature* 32.2 (2009), pp. 133–42.
31 Stannard, *Muriel Spark: The Biography*, p. 94.
32 See Derek Stanford, *Music for Statues* (London: Routledge & Kegan Paul, 1948).
33 Derek Stanford, *The Freedom of Poetry: Studies in Contemporary Verse* (London: Falcon Press, 1947), p. 30.
34 Stannard, *Muriel Spark: The Biography*, p. 93.
35 Muriel Spark, *The Fanfarlo, and Other Verse* (Aldington: Hand and Flower Press, 1952). Spark had sent Sergeant the title verse, 'The Ballad of the Fanfarlo', in 1951, only for him to reject it for *Outposts*. Stannard, 'Nativities: Muriel Spark, Baudelaire, and the Quest for Religious Faith', pp. 92–93.
36 Muriel Spark, *Loitering with Intent* [1981] (London: Virago Modern Classics, 2007), p. 1.
37 Spark, *Curriculum Vitae*, p. 183.
38 Muriel Spark, *The Golden Fleece: Essays*, ed. Penelope Jardine (Manchester: Carcanet, 2014), p. 8.
39 Spark, *The Golden Fleece*, p. 9.
40 These words are uttered by Ralph Mercer to his lover Daphne du Toit in 'The Go-away Bird', which appeared as the title tale in a collection dedicated to Derek Stanford. See Muriel Spark, *The Go-away Bird & Other Stories* [1958] (Harmondsworth: Penguin, 1969), p. 115. This story draws on Spark's experiences in Africa and after, when anecdotes of her sojourn there became the stuff of romance. Daphne's response to Ralph pumping her for information is to realise that it is a useful prompt: 'To Daphne

this approach had such force of originality that it sharpened her memory. She remembered incidents which had been latent for fifteen years or more. She sensed the sort of thing that delighted him' (p. 115).
41 Spark, *The Golden Fleece*, p. 8.
42 Ibid., p. 11.
43 Muriel Spark, 'The Voice of One Lost Sings Its Gain', in *Poetry Quarterly* 11.4 (Winter 1949–50), p. 221.
44 Spark, *All the Poems*, p. 17.
45 Stannard, *Muriel Spark: The Biography*, p. 104.
46 Martin Stannard, 'Estate Management: Evelyn Waugh and Muriel Spark', in *A Companion to Literary Biography*, ed. Richard Bradford (West Sussex: Wiley Blackwell, 2019), pp. 357–72 (p. 371).
47 Spark, *Curriculum Vitae*, p. 64.
48 Stannard, *Muriel Spark: The Biography*, p. 536. This can be set alongside another comment cited by Stannard: 'Someone once put it to Spark that she did not much like the people she wrote about. "Oh no", she replied, "I love them all; when I'm writing about them I love them most intensely, like a cat loves a bird. You know cats do love birds; they love to fondle them."' Stannard, 'Nativities: Muriel Spark, Baudelaire, and the Quest for Religious Faith', p. 104.

II: WRITING MATERIALS

6. Muriel Spark and J. M. Barrie

CAIRNS CRAIG

In her autobiography, *Curriculum Vitae* (1992), Muriel Spark recalls that she and her schoolfriend, Frances Niven, buried 'under an ancient tree in the botanical gardens' a manuscript with 'a lot of the Celtic Twilight culture woven into it'.[1] The 'Celtic Twilight culture' seems to have been inspired by J. M. Barrie's *Mary Rose*, a play of 1920: 'There was a room at the top of the school where the wind was especially rumorous. Frances and I called it the *Mary Rose* room. *Mary Rose* was a play by J. M. Barrie.'[2] Barrie's play about a girl who twice disappears on a Hebridean island and, on the second occasion, does not return till twenty-five years later, unaffected by the passage of time, is, as Andrew Nash has pointed out,[3] one of the explicit references to Barrie's work in Spark's novels. It appears in her fifth novel, *The Bachelors* (1960), in which *Mary Rose* has been the favourite childhood reading of Patrick Seton, a spiritualist who earns his living in séances as a believable but fraudulent medium. We are told that, as a child, he was 'a dreamer of dreams' and that '*Mary Rose* by J. M. Barrie is Patrick's favourite'.[4] Seton's enthusiasm for Barrie's tale of Highland romance about a timeless other world is repeated by the ways in which Seton encourages his clients to believe in his own spiritualist invocation of an apparently timeless afterlife with which he can help them communicate. The other explicit Barrie reference in Spark's work is her invocation of *Peter Pan* in *The Hothouse by the East River* (1973), in which a satirical version of Barrie's play has all the children performed by old people. This novel is, however, also an invocation of the Mary Rose theme, since its characters have returned to live in a time which they ought not to inhabit, having been for many years dead.

In both cases, the implication of the Barrie intertexts might be read as revealing the emotional and moral inadequacies of Spark's characters – an interpretation which would conform to the ways in which, as R. D. S. Jack argued,[5] Barrie himself came to be read. Barrie, it was suggested, was a writer whose lack of seriousness, despite his many successes, made him a minor literary figure as compared with such contemporaries as Bernard Shaw: Barrie's work, just like Patrick Seton or the characters in *Hothouse by the East River*, evaded the real world for sentimental aesthetic alternatives. Barrie's Scottish critics added a further charge, that Barrie held up his Scottish characters to the ridicule of metropolitan audiences, who found them comically parochial in their intense but irrelevant religious concerns.

Such interpretations, however, fail to acknowledge the underlying concerns of Barrie's art. *Mary Rose* is more than a slight fabrication of belated Celtic Twilightism: it was first produced in 1920 and its focus is on an Australian soldier who has returned to the house in England where he spent his childhood only to discover that it cannot now be sold because it is said to be haunted. In the context of imperial soldiers fighting in the First World War, Mary Rose's twenty-five year disappearance becomes symbolic of the gulf between the Victorian world into which she had been born and the modernising world to which she returns – a world of telegrams and the threat of war.[6] At the same time, her disappearance and return is also symbolic of the gulf between the world before the First World War and the world subsequent to it that she continues to haunt, the Australian soldier being, in fact, her missing son, who had run away from the grandparents to whose care he had been consigned after her disappearance. However romantic Barrie's play might have seemed to the young Muriel Spark, the Muriel Spark who returned from Africa during the Second World War and left her son behind with her parents in Edinburgh when she went off to London would have had very different reasons for identifying with Barrie's heroine. Mary Rose's story is not just a piece of supernatural mythmaking. It is an event that can be seen as representative of the many disappearances brought about by mass emigration in the late nineteenth and early twentieth centuries – Spark herself, of course, left for Rhodesia where her husband planned to settle – as well as the destructive losses incurred during the First World War. Mary Rose's husband is a ship's captain who would have spent almost as little time with her as she did with him after her disappearance, and he was eventually drowned at sea during the war. Spark herself had experienced a similar loss when, during her divorce in Rhodesia, she became involved with a young flight lieutenant 'who had been through the blitz' but whose ship was torpedoed just as it set off for home: 'Arthur and his companions went down with it that night'.[7] Barrie's world is full of ghosts not because of Highland 'glamourie' – though what Mary Rose calls 'misty, eerie Highland stories'[8] may be the inspiration of the plot – but because the post-war world is full of the ghosts of those who have, one way or another, been forced to depart. When she returns, unchanged, the play juxtaposes present and past in a state of mutual incomprehension: her father breaks down – 'I cannot cope'[9] – while Mary Rose's demand to know where she can find her baby cannot be answered: 'the stage darkens and they are blotted out'.[10] Neither she nor they can live in this world of crossed times, a theme all too pertinent to the original audience in 1920. The gulf between a lost past and an unrecognisable present results in her failing to see in the Australian soldier the child – Harry – from whom she was cut off by her disappearance. There can be no recognition between those who have escaped from, and returned unchanged to, the world of time and those who have continued to live in its unilinear inevitability.

In *The Hothouse by the East River*, the main characters are all, like Mary Rose, ghosts from an earlier era who are trapped in a time they should not inhabit, living as they do in New York after the Second World War, despite having died in England in 1944. The characters are tormented both by the memory of their actual lives during the war years and the lives they hoped to live in its aftermath before they, like Mary Rose's family, were 'blotted out'. It is in this context that *Peter Pan* provides a series of ironic intertexts to the events of the novel, in which Paul's wife Elsa has a shadow that falls the wrong way, as though, like Peter Pan's, it has been chopped off but then wrongly re-attached. As a ghost, she can have no shadow cast by a body that does not exist, so her shadow is an unreal and false extension of her self. Similarly, her children – Pierre and Katerina – are people who could never have been born since their parents were already dead before their conception. The children cannot exist and yet they do, and the ontological discrepancy of their existence is mirrored in Pierre's version of Barrie's play, which transforms the Neverland of eternal childhood into the everland of geriatric forgetfulness. The intertext underlines that Pierre's parents may have escaped from death into an apparent afterlife but, as his and his sister's very existence demonstrates, they have not escaped from time: even as ghosts they continue to age. This reversal of the Mary Rose effect is played out when Elsa goes to see the play's first performance and announces to the police who are trying to arrest her for throwing tomatoes at the actors, 'I'm the mother of the author'.[11] Elsa can be neither the real mother of Pierre since, like Peter, he does not actually exist, nor, obviously, can she be the real mother of J. M. Barrie. Fiction and reality collide unresolvably in this performance of *Peter Pan*, because art, which seems, like Peter himself, to defy time is suddenly transformed into the very medium of time. The play reveals the truth about the aged ghosts who make up its *dramatis personae*: they are people who had hoped that their ghostly afterlives could, like the characters in a play, be released from time into some kind of eternity but instead they have only departed from one temporal sequence to find themselves in another. Just as the ghost of Mary Rose haunts the world of time from which she has apparently been released, so Paul and Elsa haunt the world of time which they did not live to see. Peter Pan, of course, haunts the world of time by his continual return to find children to take with him to his Neverland:

> As you look at Wendy, you may see her hair becoming white, and her figure little again, for all this happened long ago. Jane is now a common grown-up, with a daughter called Margaret; and every spring-cleaning time, except when he forgets, Peter comes for Margaret and takes her to the Neverland, where she tells him stories about himself [...].[12]

Like Mary Rose, such characters escape from time only to discover that the world of time always lies in wait for them.

The complexities of Spark's invocation of *Peter Pan* in *The Hothouse by the East River* do not, however, only travel in one direction: they force us to reconsider the nature of Barrie's original play as well as its role in Spark's novel. There have been many 'postcolonial' readings of *Peter Pan* in recent years, which emphasise the extent to which the Neverland corresponds to Edward Said's account of how 'orientalism' substitutes a fiction of the 'other' in colonised territories for any real encounter with the people who actually inhabit those territories.[13] There have also been readings which suggest that childhood is itself a 'colonised' territory taken over by adults who speak for the 'subaltern' child.[14] But these readings do not go far enough, for *Peter Pan* is written to be understood in different ways by different kinds and ages of spectators. To children, the narrative of *Peter Pan* corresponds with recognisable fantasies of children's literature – the ability to fly, to interact with fairies – while taking place in the recognisable locations of certain popular kinds of children's adventure stories – islands inhabited by native peoples and by pirates. In apparently real form the island repeats the games that children play beneath the table at home. But the island is also a simulacrum of the realities of imperial conquest and domination: the peaceful world of the Darlings in London is maintained only by the expropriation of the land of native peoples, is sustained by commercial brigandage and piracy, and by the endless infliction of cruelty, war and killing:

> Let us kill a pirate, to show Hook's method. Skylights will do. As they pass, Skylights lurches clumsily against him, ruffling his lace collar; the hook shoots forth, there is a tearing sound and one screech, then the body is kicked aside and the pirates pass on.[15]

The Neverland can appear 'real' to the children who fly there because, implicitly, it reveals the 'reality' on which the 'civilised' world of imperial domination is actually founded:

> 'Who is Captain Hook?' he asked with interest when she spoke of the arch enemy.
> 'Don't you remember,' she asked, amazed, 'how you killed him and saved all our lives?'
> 'I forget them after I kill them,' he replied carelessly.[16]

Pan is the spirit of British colonialism in the Edwardian period which provides the assets on which the Darlings live: Mr Darling 'was one of those deep ones who know about stocks and shares'.[17] Mr Darling remains innocent, for he does not see or acknowledge what is done to accumulate the wealth in which he trades – and Pan forgets it. But the tradition that the actor who plays Mr Darling also plays Hook makes it visually evident that the wealth in which Darling trades is the outcome of piratical extortion. The Neverland is not an escape from the historical world of colonisation and wealth extraction but a compressed model of the world system which makes the civilisation of London possible. Equally, the characters in *The Hothouse by the East River* cannot acknowledge the violence upon which their wealthy lives in New York are actually based, since they were themselves among the victims of that violence. But they inhabit the New York which the Second World War made possible, a place of wealth that has no idea where the wealth comes from or how it is obtained; as Elsa declares in the final pages, 'I never had any money in my life. It's all a myth'.[18] The 'money empire' of New York, based on the Bretton Woods agreement that tied the dollar to the value of gold and all other currencies of the signatory states to the value of the dollar, had, by the 1970s, when Spark was writing, become a fiction.[19] Currencies had ceased to have any connection with the material reality of the gold supply, and simply floated against each other according to the sentiments of investors. Spark's characters inhabit an apparently materialist and materialistic world that has no substance: as with Barrie's Neverland in *Peter Pan*, her unrealistic presentation captures the essence of the 'reality' of the modern world.

In his novel *Tommy and Grizel*, Barrie's narrator defines genius as 'the power to be a boy again at will',[20] presciently anticipating the birth of Peter Pan two years later in *The Little White Bird*. Peter's defiance of time is possible because he is the spirit of Pan, part human, part animal (he started life by discovering he could fly like a bird), part god.[21] He is Nietzsche's Dionysos – the ancient force which allows the Apollonian transformation of the world into art, and, through art, defies time. In *The Birth of Tragedy*, Nietzsche challenged his reader about how he responded to what took place in a theatre: for many the test will reveal that,

> he belongs [...] to the community of Socratic men, he may ask himself honestly with what emotion he responds to the *miracle* on the stage; whether he feels that his historical sense, trained to look everywhere for strict psychological causation, has been outraged, whether he admits the miracle as a phenomenon that seems natural to child minds but rather remote from himself [...].[22]

The ability to recover a child's response to the world allows the spectator entry into 'myth, which, being a concentrated image of the world, an emblem of appearance, cannot dispense with the miracle.'[23] What Spark learned from *Mary Rose* and from *Peter Pan* was the aesthetics of the miraculous, of the ability to recover a world where 'strict psychological causation' is no longer the only way in which the world can be understood and in which the logic of myth is as significant as the logic of causation. In its combination of fantasy and realism, of artful self-consciousness and a determination to reveal the true – and ultimately fictional – nature of the modern world, Spark's novels rework many of Barrie's concerns.

That Barrie's *Mary Rose* shares a name with the central character of Spark's first novel, Caroline Rose, points to the fact that both, in their different ways, have risen into forms of spirituality which their contemporaries cannot understand. In *The Comforters* (1957), Caroline Rose is not a Celtic Twilight ghost but a Catholic convert, as well as a theorist of the nature of the novel who aims herself to become a novelist. Caroline is, however, as haunted and haunting as Mary Rose, and finds apparently immaterial voices intercepting her thoughts:

> '[...] I am being haunted. I am not haunting myself.' Meantime, she was trembling, frightened out of her wits, although her fear was not altogether blind.
> *Tap-click-tap.* The voices again: *Meantime, she was trembling, frightened out of her wits, although her fear was not altogether blind.*
> 'Christ!' she said, 'Who *is* there?'[24]

As a Catholic she is the inheritor of an ancient spiritual tradition but as a character in a novel she is the product of a modernity (the typewriter as opposed to the chanting voices) from which she cannot escape. The collision between these two ontologies produces the car crash which leaves her trapped in a hospital bed for the second part of the novel, locked, like Mary Rose, in a plot which she cannot control but cannot help but influence: 'Caroline among the sleepers turned her mind to the art of the novel, wondering and cogitating, those long hours, and exerting an undue, unreckoned influence on the narrative from which she is supposed to be absent'.[25] Art itself is the means of exerting an apparently supernatural influence on the world and the novel we are reading gradually evolves into the novel that Caroline is writing, just as *Peter Pan* is the story of the narrative that Peter is constructing about events in the Neverland. Thus, Hook is pursued by the crocodile that has swallowed a clock (the world of time that he, like Peter, has tried to escape), but the crocodile becomes Peter in disguise:

> Only when Hook was hidden from them did curiosity loosen the limbs of the boys so that they could rush to the ship's side to see the crocodile climbing it. Then they got the strangest surprise of the Night of Nights; for it was no crocodile that was coming to their aid. It was Peter.[26]

Peter takes control of the narrative just as Caroline, despite being immobilised in hospital, takes control of her narrative. Peter and Caroline play the roles of both author and character, being apparently inside the narrative while, at the same time, remaining outside and controlling it. Art is a supernatural confluence of the real and the mythic in which author and character can exchange places. But the climax of *The Comforters* also involves a transposition between another of Barrie's dramas and Spark's plot. The climactic moment takes place on a riverside where Caroline Rose agrees to take a boat across to collect Georgina Hogg, the grotesque Catholic believer who has been trying to blackmail various characters in the plot and who declares that Caroline has 'a lot of the Protestant about you still'.[27] Georgina, however, cannot manage to step into the boat:

> Mrs Hogg had rubber-soled shoes which had picked up a good deal of mud. In spite of all her care she slipped on her heels, she tottered backwards with her hand still gripped in Caroline's so that the boat rocked wildly. In an instant she was loudly in the water and Caroline, still grasping the hand by the first compulsive need to overcome her horror of it, went with her.[28]

Caroline is saved by the man from the houseboat whose rowing boat she had borrowed. The setting and the scene recapitulate elements of Barrie's first successful play, *Walker, London*, produced in 1892, in which the major object on stage throughout the play is a large houseboat on a river along which various characters row or punt their vessels. As was often the case with Barrie's plays, the stage construction is as important as the plot, in this case allowing various characters to appear and disappear on the various parts of the houseboat – its deck, its roof, inside the saloon, or alongside it in a rowing boat. One of the female characters who has gone in chase of the man whose offer of marriage she has just refused, falls out of her punt and is apparently saved by a passing stranger who claims to be a famous African explorer, Colonel Neil. He is, in fact, Jasper Phipps, a barber, who is in flight from his own marriage to one Sarah Rigg, who has already arrived at the houseboat in search of him. The events of Bell's near drowning are recounted by the boat boy Ben:

> It was this way, ma'am. The young lady, she falls into the water as she has told you. It was a ticklish place just this side o' the weir, and before you could say Jack Robinson, I sees her being carried towards it. Ma'am, my first thought was, she's as good as a corpse, for I didn't think there was a man in England could ha' torn her out o' that rush of water. But there was – this gentleman – [...] I just sees him flash by me and jump into the water. It's UP with both of them I thinks, for by the time he gripped her she were just on the being shot over the weir [...] Three times, ma'am, it tore him back and I cries, 'Your only chance is to let her go'. He just shook his head and fought on

and on, and inch by inch he brought her nearer the bank, till they both fell on it senseless.²⁹

Neil/Phipps has achieved what was beyond Caroline in dealing with Mrs Hogg – 'The woman clung to Caroline's throat until the last'³⁰ – but nonetheless Caroline had to be saved by a stranger: 'Caroline had the sense of being hauled along a bumpy surface, of being landed with a thud like a gasping fish, before she passed out.'³¹ It turns out, however, in the case of *Walker, London*, that the events described by Ben are mere fiction, for it was he who got Bell out of only two feet of water with a boathook but has been paid by Phipps to make the role of Neil more heroic. Indeed, as the play goes on, Ben becomes the blackmailer of Phipps, declaring in words that could easily be repeated by Georgina Hogg, that he is 'not the kind to split on them as pays up'.³² Phipps has to extricate himself from the relationships he has entered into and the fabrications with which he has surrounded himself in the persona of Colonel Neil: as he departs they call to him for his address and he replies with the title of the play, 'Walker, London'. 'Walker' was a nineteenth-century colloquialism which the *OED* explains as 'an exclamation expressive of incredulity', and which Eric Partridge defines as 'a phrase signifying that something either is not true or will not occur'.³³ Barrie's play thus becomes a self-reflexive artifice: the play may be set near London, and present a set of typical contemporary characters, but it is all 'Walker'. Barrie seems to have been influenced in this by David Masson, whose lectures he attended at Edinburgh University and who argued that Shakespeare's late romances were his greatest achievements, precisely because they emphasised the anti-realistic nature of the theatrical medium.³⁴ It is an experience that the young Patrick Seton had found disturbing when, in *The Bachelors*, he is confronted with the actual play of *Mary Rose*:

> [...] He is taken to the theatre to see it acted, and is sharply shocked by the sight of the real actresses and actors with painted faces performing outwardly on the open platform this tender romance about the girl who was stolen by the fairies on a Hebridean island.³⁵

What, to Patrick, is shock at the 'reality' of theatrical illusion is precisely what audiences at the 511 performances of *Walker, London* delighted in – its self-conscious theatricality. And this was precisely the trick that Spark played at the end of *The Comforters* when the novel unveils itself as the novel that Caroline has been writing, and the 'character called Laurence Manders'[36] discovers that he is indeed a character in a novel, when a letter that he has torn up and thrown away actually reappears complete in the book. *Walker, London* was an early experiment in Barrie's exploration of non-realistic modes of fiction and theatre, a formal challenge which, from her first successful novel, would also become central to Spark's writings.

The implications of 'Walker' as an evasion of truth were to be revisited by Spark in her late novel *Aiding and Abetting* (2000), in which psychiatrist Hildegarde Wolf is confronted by two patients who both claim to be the missing Lord Lucan, who has been on the run since murdering his children's nanny in 1974. One calls himself Walker while claiming to be Lucan, the other goes by Lucan's nickname, 'Lucky'. Being near doubles they confuse the police and the press by appearing in different places, thus disguising each other's travels in search of funds that can 'aid and abet' Lucan's escape: 'Walker and Lucan, Lucan and Walker, they were bound together.'[37] In the case of Hildegarde, each is prepared to admit to his identity as Lucan because they have discovered that she, too, is on the run and have decided to blackmail her. Like Phipps trying to extricate himself from his double, Colonel Neil, the Lucans also need to extricate themselves from their expensive doubles: 'Lucan needed to rid himself of Walker, and soon; before Walker decided that Lucan must die, it was Walker's destiny to die.'[38] These characters are, of course, Muriel Spark's fictions, belonging to an alternative reality than the one in which the 'real' Lucan or his corpse might still be found: 'The story of his presumed years of clandestine wanderings, his nightmare existence since his disappearance, remains a mystery, and I have no doubt would differ factually and in actual feeling from the story I have told.'[39] But it is precisely Spark's point that fiction does not *represent* reality but transforms it; it has been 'metamorphosed into what I have written',[40] just as Lucan himself (in her story) is killed and absorbed into the African world that had been fictionally claimed by Neil as the location of his heroic exploits: 'Lucan is dead, not buried. He was roasted and consumed by all the male children of Delihu. Some of them were rather unwell after the feast, but they are all partly little Lord Lucans now.'[41] The illusory Lucan that is Walker 'walks' (he is assisted in escaping back to Mexico) while Lucan's remains remain as part of the ambition of the local chief to teach his children how to act like English lords: 'The three sons did very well under their tuition. They learnt to jump their horses over fences, they learnt to cheat at poker and so on, in the best tradition of a gentleman.'[42] The Africa invoked by Neil in Barrie's play becomes the last resting place of Lucan in Spark's novel: what escapes in both is Walker.

For both Barrie and Spark, 'Walker' is of the very nature of art, a self-conscious illusion whose purpose is not the revelation of reality but the revelation of how limited is that which we take to be reality. Thus, in Spark's second novel, *Robinson* (1958), three survivors of a plane crash find themselves on an island in the Atlantic which, by the end of the novel, will have been wiped off the map by a volcanic explosion – become quite literally a Neverland. Like the Darling children they have crash-landed in an alternative world, and they might indeed have died and be living, like the characters in *The Hothouse by the East River*, in some kind of afterlife. The person who owns the island is called Robinson, and the island too is called Robinson, the map of its territory looking strangely like a human form, as though in imitation of the humanism which has led Robinson to break with the Catholic church. When Robinson disappears, there is evidence that he has been murdered by one of the three survivors, and the terms in which the issue is posed recapitulates questions from the first appearance of Peter Pan in *The Little White Bird*, which revolves around whether or not he had a goat:

> If you ask your mother whether she knew about Peter Pan when she was a little girl, she will say, 'Why, of course I did, child'; and if you ask whether he rode on a goat in those days, she will say, 'What a foolish question to ask; certainly he did.' Then if you ask your grandmother whether she knew about Peter Pan when she was a girl, she also says, 'Why of course I did, child,' but if you ask her whether he rode on a goat in those days, she says she never heard

of his having a goat [...] Therefore there was no goat when your grandmother was a little girl.⁴³

The issue of the goat is also the issue in *Robinson*: did he have a goat on the night he disappeared, or had he already shot and disposed of it in the days before? The goat is the fulcrum of two different narratives about the trail of blood through the mustard field, and about whether the scatter of blood-stained clothes was accidental – like the accident of the plane crash – or intentional:

> I said, 'Those blood-stained articles of clothing must have been planted by someone.'
> 'Oh, must they?'
> 'They wouldn't have been scattered about in quite such an obvious manner if they had been dropped accidentally.'
> 'Oh, wouldn't they?'⁴⁴

The possible narratives by which the central character, January Marlow, is surrounded turn on the issue of cause and effect: who is the cause of Robinson's death? – 'he has been killed by Jimmie or Tom Wells, or by both together';⁴⁵ what is the cause of Robinson's death? – Tom Wells suggests, 'A supernatural force [...] had done away with Robinson, in revenge for some sacrilege done to the lucky charms which Robinson had confiscated',⁴⁶ whereas Jimmie declares, 'Ah me! Man is born, he suffers, he dies',⁴⁷ as if individual processes of causation are irrelevant to the final outcomes of existence. Robinson's death puts in doubt the relation of cause and effect, just as Peter's activities in the Neverland defy the normal causal relations: Tinkerbell is saved from death not by medical intervention but by the applause of the audience of the book we are reading: 'The clapping stopped suddenly; as if countless mothers had rushed to their nurseries to see what on earth was happening; but already Tink was saved.'⁴⁸ An ontological bridge between text and audience provides the medium for Tink's salvation: causes, it appears, can operate at a distance, such that the actions in one dimension of existence can have consequences in another. If this is the issue with which January has to deal in *Robinson*, it is also the basis of the plot structure of *Symposium* (1990), in which Margaret Murchie is continually linked to, though not actually responsible for, a series of deaths, as though she can somehow bring them about without actually being their cause. She wants to do away with her partner's mother, Hilda Damien, but 'in the destiny of the event Margaret could have saved herself the trouble, the plotting. It was the random gang [...] of which Margaret knew nothing, who were to kill Hilda Damien for her Monet'.[49]

Barrie's explorations of cause-at-a-distance provide the template for Spark's refusal to accept causal sequence as the basis of the plots of her novels. Thus, *Robinson* also invokes another of Barrie's plays, *The Admirable Crichton*, in which an aristocratic family are marooned on a desert island when their yacht runs aground in a storm. Their ship is named the *Bluebell* and 'Bluebell' is the name of the cat which January adopts in *Robinson*. In Barrie's play, the desert island leads to various kinds of transformations, in ways which defy the causality of the world in which they had previously lived. Thus, in Act Three of Barrie's play, we are introduced to an apparently new character:

> *A stalwart youth appears at the window, so handsome and tingling with vitality that, glad to depose* CRICHTON, *we cry thankfully, 'The hero at last.' But it is not the hero; it is the heroine. This splendid boy, clad in skins, is what Nature has done for* LADY MARY.[50]

Lady Mary's apparent gender change and her transformation from an upper-class woman, constrained by the expectations of her society, into an androgynous creature capable of dominating the environment into which she has been cast, is matched in Spark's novel by January's transformation into an adventure story heroine, capable of challenging masculine assumptions about her gender identity.

Such disruptions of causality and transformations of personality are typical of Barrie's narratives; in *The Little Minister*, for instance, Babbie is both the ward of an English landowner in Scotland and the impersonator of a wild, Scots-speaking gypsy girl:

> She was still fifty yards away, sometimes singing gleefully, and again letting her body sway lightly as she came dancing up Windyghoul. Soon she was within a few feet of the little minister, to whom singing, except when out of tune, was a suspicious thing, and dancing a device of the devil. His arm went out wrathfully, and his intention was to pronounce sentence on this woman.
>
> But she passed, unconscious of his presence, and he had not moved or spoken [...] The grace of her swaying figure was a new thing in the world to him. Only while she passed did he see her as a gleam of colour, a gypsy poorly clad, her bare feet flashing beneath a short green skirt, a twig of rowan berries stuck carelessly into her black hair. She had an angel's loveliness.[51]

At the end of the chapter the doubleness of this gypsy figure is revealed to the reader but not to Gavin Dishart, the 'little minister':

> 'Mr Dishart,' the mole-catcher cried, 'hae you seen that Egyptian? May I be struck dead if it's no' her little leddyship.'
> But Gavin did not hear him.[52]

As the complications of the narrative are worked through, Gavin and Babbie find themselves on opposite sides of a weavers' revolt – she secretly bringing them word of an attack by the constabulary, Gavin insisting that they obey the law. They are, however, later married in a 'gypsy wedding' that allows them to defy Lord Rintoul, Babbie's guardian, who has been planning to marry her himself, thereby forcing Gavin to acknowledge the reality of Babbie's adopted culture. It is a story which, like Spark's *The Prime of Miss Jean Brodie* (1961), was enormously successful not only as a novel, but as drama and as film (starring Katharine Hepburn in the 1934 version), and that resurfaces in Spark's novel *The Takeover* (1976), which tells of the travails of rich people living in Italy who are constantly threatened by thieves, conmen and extortionists. The central character is Hubert Mallindaine, who insists, on the basis of a tale told by his aunts but inspired by J. G. Frazer's account of classical gods in *The Golden Bough*, that he is actually descended from the goddess Diana. He is, therefore, another incarnation of Peter Pan, part human, part god. On this basis he asserts his right to live in a house overlooking the lake at Nemi, which is the starting point of Frazer's vast narrative of magic and religion, even though the house actually belongs to his rich friend Maggie Radcliffe. Mallindaine acts as though his divine ancestry makes him immune to the effects of time as well as the constraints of law. Thus, at the start of the novel he is trying to recreate the pleasures of a previous summer with his four young male 'secretaries' and later he will go on to found a cult of Diana which defies the history by which the Catholic Church sought to suppress such cults. Thereafter Mallindaine claims through his inheritance from Diana to have recovered the spiritual truths of a repressed and ecologically oriented religion. Mallindaine and Maggie have a kind of Peter and Wendy relationship: she initially indulging – and funding – his fantasies but later trying to make him wake up to the nature of a world (around 1974) in which wealth has not only ceased to be real, but in which those who are believed to possess it are under continual threat from extortion and blackmail. Just as, in *The Little Minister*, the heroine has to disguise herself as a gypsy in order to escape from the home of her guardian and the ethics of a landed elite, so Mallindaine encounters Maggie towards the end of *The Takeover*:

> Suddenly Hubert saw a shape approaching, an old woman, it seemed, probably a gypsy, picking her way towards him [...] The crone, dressed drably with a scarf round her head, came close and was about to pass him with the usual 'Buona sera' of the countryside. 'Maggie!' said Hubert.[53]

Maggie's gypsy disguise is to protect her from kidnap but also to conceal her identity, since she has actually herself become the kidnapper of the lawyer who had embezzled her money. Maggie and Babbie live in very different social worlds, but both need a gypsy disguise to negotiate the conflicts between those social worlds and the 'natural' energies of their pre-social emotions which cannot help but disrupt the apparent order of the worlds that they are forced to inhabit.

Such recapitulations of the plots of Barrie's works in Spark's writings are, however, indicative of a much more profound parallel in their attitudes to their art. Both are deeply aware that the artist is a conscious deceiver, and their moral disapprobation is, therefore, directed at those characters who attempt to treat life as though they had the equivalent of an authorial power over the rest of the characters around them. In effect, art has to announce within its own plot structures the fact that it rejects the lie upon which it is founded. Barrie's Sentimental Tommy is not just an author, he is an author who tries to treat everyone as characters in a drama of his own creation, just as Peter Pan constructs the Neverland adventures of which he will be the hero. The usurpation by a character within a narrative of the power of the author over that narrative is the crime which shapes Spark's novels from *The Ballad of Peckham Rye* (1960) through to *Symposium*. It is the moral failing of Jean Brodie in *The Prime of Miss Jean Brodie*, who attempts to become the controlling author of the destinies of the girls in the 'Brodie set', deciding their futures as though they were characters in a fiction of her own devising:

> And Miss Brodie said to Sandy: 'From what you tell me I should think that Rose and Teddy Lloyd will soon be lovers.' All at once Sandy realized that this was not all theory and a kind of Brodie game [...] Miss Brodie meant it [...] there was nothing new in the idea, it was the reality that was new.[54]

Sandy's realisation that Miss Brodie was projecting her own emotions on to Rose, in order that Rose should fulfil the narrative that Miss Brodie had imagined for herself, transforms Rose (in this, again, a version of Barrie's Mary Rose) into a character no longer allowed to make choices about her own future.

Such displacements of the role of author cannot help, however, but turn our attention back on the role of the 'actual' author of a text. In *Tommy and Grizel*, for instance, there is a point at which the narrator invites the reader to sympathise with Tommy: 'What do you say to pitying, instead of cursing him?' Having done so, however, the narrator then declares not only his self-interest but his knowledge of the narrative future: 'It is a sudden idea of mine, and we must be quick, for joyous Grizel is drawing near and this, you know, is the chapter in which her heart breaks.'[55] The narrator's 'sudden idea' that may bring events to a happy conclusion takes place in an immediate present in which the future is apparently, as yet, undecided, but those possibilities are then countermanded by a knowledge of the future from which there is no escape: this 'is the chapter in which her heart breaks'. We are both inside the unfolding time of the narrative in which there are many possible futures and, at the same time, outside of it, in a temporality which is already completed, finished and final. Barrie's play with this double perspective is one of the key elements in the emotional dynamics of *Tommy and Grizel*. As early as Chapter 5, the narrator tells us that Tommy had come into the room to kiss his sister goodnight: 'he had never once omitted doing it since they went to London, and he was always to do it, for neither of them was ever to marry'.[56] This is a sentence poised between its intra-temporal significance – neither of them, at this point in time, had any *intention* of ever marrying – and its extra-temporal suggestion, that neither of them *would* ever marry. The latter implication is, however, overthrown when Tommy's sister marries the doctor in Thrums, an event which is supposed to release Tommy from his commitment to his sister and so make it possible for him to marry Grizel. His sister's unexpected marriage, however, simply makes Tommy conscious of his need to be free from social constraints in order to fulfil his ambitions as an artist. Grizel is to be denied the marriage for which her whole life had seemed to be a preparation, an outcome that seems to break the contract between narrator and reader about how the narrative was to develop:

> She is not so heart-broken, after all, you may be saying, and I had promised to break her heart. But, honestly, I don't know how to do it more thoroughly, and you must remember that we have not seen her alone yet.[57]

'We' hovers ambiguously between the intra-temporal readers who cannot yet know the future and the narrator who has access to the extra-temporal perspective in which the future is already determined. It is an ambiguity which Barrie can also use in the other direction, implying that readers already know the outcome of the narrative which they are reading: 'We have now', he suddenly declares at the end of Chapter 33, 'come to the last fortnight of Tommy's life'.[58] The reader is assumed already to be aware of Tommy's death, because it is a public event, even though, in terms of the intra-temporal narrative, we have been given no indication of it. Indeed, Tommy's possible death has been discounted when Grizel's fears about his health lead her to journey to Switzerland to care for him, to discover him not only healthy but amorously in pursuit of an upper-class English woman. From the intra-temporal perspective there is nothing to suggest that Tommy is anything but a boyish young man headed towards a long middle age. He dies, however, when he falls off a wall while in pursuit of the woman he had met in Switzerland and is strangled by his coat that has been caught on an iron stanchion. Our foreknowledge of his death thus turns accident into a retrospective predestination: Tommy was bound to die of the emotional excesses that had been the foundation of his success as a writer but were also his fundamental weakness as a human being.

If Barrie's narratives insist that his characters are simply characters in a story whose ultimate outcomes are beyond their control, his tragi-comic play with the structure of fiction allows him, at the same time, to reduce the author from a god-like omniscience to the mere plaything of casual impulses:

> I had made up my mind that when the time came to describe Grizel's mere outward appearance I should refuse her that word beautiful because of her tilted nose. But now that the time has come I wonder at myself. Probably when I am chapters ahead I shall return to this one and strike out the word beautiful, and then as likely as not I shall come back afterwards and put it in again. Whether it will be there at the end God knows.[59]

The fixed order of narrative time, in which all events have their necessary place, dissolves into the flux of a world in which choices can be made, unmade and remade and we cannot know, therefore, what the appearance of the word 'beautiful' finally denotes. The tragi-comic ethos of Barrie's writings underlines not only the partiality of the author but how warped is a literary text's version of reality:

> Ever since the beginning of the book we have been neglecting Elspeth so pointedly that were she not the most forgiving creature we should be afraid to face her now. You are not angry with us, are you, Elspeth? We have been sitting with you, talking with you, thinking of you between the chapters, and the only reason why you so seldom got into them is that our pen insisted on running after your fascinating brother.
>
> (That is the way to get round her.)[60]

The fictional character who can only come into existence through the text is assumed to have an extra-textual reality of which both author and reader are aware – 'we have been sitting with you' – with the result that they can interact with the character in the spaces between the actual chapters of the book. Barrie's deployment of these double perspectives is adopted and adapted by Spark in many of her novels – most potently, perhaps, in *The Prime of Miss Jean Brodie*:

> She had reckoned on her prime lasting till she was sixty. But this year, the year after the war, was in fact Miss Brodie's last and fifty-sixth year. She looked older than that, she was suffering from an internal growth. This was her last year in the world and in another sense it was Sandy's.[61]

The extra-temporal perspective – 'This was her last year in the world' – is juxtaposed with the intra-temporal perspective – 'this year, the year after the war' – to produce a fundamental ambiguity about the character's relationship to time. From the intra-temporal perspective, the character lives forwards, toward the apparent openness of a future – her ever mobile 'prime' – that is still to be made by her choices; from the extra-temporal perspective, however, the future is already complete and finalised. By switching back and forward between these two perspectives, Spark, like Barrie, produces a sense of the tragic incompatibility between human beings' belief in their freedom of choice and the necessities of a world from which there is no escape. Reality, it turns out, is only too like a novel, with all our choices determined by a conclusion that, unknown to us in the midst of the action, cannot be evaded. Such ontological disjunctions Spark was to exploit in the opposite direction in *The Comforters* when she has Mrs Hogg disappear not just from the text but from existence itself: '[…] as soon as Mrs Hogg stepped into her room, she disappeared, she simply disappeared. She had no private life whatsoever. God knows where she went to in her privacy.'[62] When she is not being written about, Mrs Hogg is not part of reality: she is not a reality represented by the text but a reality of the text. When the text no longer engages with her, despite her very material presence in the narrative, she simply ceases to exist.

Barrie's parodic play with the relations between the text and world it is supposed to represent opened up, for Spark, not only the aesthetics of the 'miraculous' but a way of challenging the whole realist tradition of the novel, including the psychological realism of the 'stream of consciousness' techniques which had been so important to her modernist precursors. Barrie's self-conscious awareness of how the writer is *playing* with the expectations of the reader at the same time as inviting the reader to empathise with his characters, provided Spark with a model of how the novel might be reshaped to escape not only the traditions of realist fiction but its modernist challengers. By going back to her Scottish precursor, Spark found ways to give an entirely new direction to fiction in the second half of the twentieth century and thus challenged those critics who would deny to her – as they did to Barrie – a place in a specifically Scottish literary tradition.

Endnotes

1. Muriel Spark, *Curriculum Vitae: A Volume of Autobiography* (London: Penguin, 1992), p. 70.
2. Ibid.
3. Valentina Bold and Andrew Nash (eds), *Gateway to the Modern: Resituating J. M. Barrie* (Glasgow: Scottish Literature International, 2014), p. 114.
4. Muriel Spark, *The Bachelors* (London: Macmillan, 1960), p. 171.
5. R. D. S. Jack, *The Road to the Neverland: A Reassessment of J. M. Barrie's Dramatic Art* (Aberdeen: Aberdeen University Press, 1991).
6. A. E. Wilson (ed.), *The Plays of J. M. Barrie in One Volume* [1928] (London: Hodder and Stoughton, 1943), p. 1136.
7. Spark, *Curriculum Vitae*, p. 136.
8. Barrie, *Plays*, p. 1119.
9. Ibid., p. 1140.
10. Ibid.
11. Muriel Spark, *The Hothouse by the East River* [1973] (Harmondsworth: Penguin, 1975), p. 93.
12. J. M. Barrie, *Peter Pan* [1911] (London: William Collins, 2015), p. 159.
13. See, for instance, Pradeep Sharma, 'Peter Pan: A Colonial Myth', in *Barrie, Hook and Peter Pan: Studies in Contemporary Myth*, eds. Alfonso Muñoz Corcuera and Elisa T. Di Bias (Newcastle-on-Tyne: Cambridge Scholars, 2012), pp. 138–50.
14. See Jacqueline Rose, *The Case of Peter Pan or The Impossibility of Children's Fiction* (London: Macmillan, 1984).
15. Barrie, *Peter Pan*, pp. 47–48.
16. Ibid., p. 152.
17. Ibid., p. 2.
18. Spark, *Hothouse by the East River*, p. 137.
19. See for instance, www.investopedia.com/terms/b/brettonwoodsagreement.asp.
20. J. M. Barrie, *The Uniform Edition of the Works of J. M. Barrie: Tommy and Grizel* [1900] (London: Cassell, n.d.), p. 214.
21. See Allison B. Kavey, 'The History and Epistemology of Peter Pan', in *Second Star to the Right: Peter Pan in the Popular Imagination*, eds. Allison B. Kavey and Lester D. Friedman (New Brunswick, NJ: Rutgers University Press, 2009), pp. 79–80.
22. Friedrich Nietzsche, *The Birth of Tragedy* and *The Genealogy of Morals*, transl. Francis Golffing (New York: Doubleday, 1956), p. 136.
23. Ibid.
24. Muriel Spark, *The Comforters* [1957] (London: Penguin, 1963), pp. 44–45.
25. Ibid., p. 137.
26. Barrie, *Peter Pan*, p. 127.
27. Spark, *The Comforters*, p. 32.
28. Ibid., p. 196.
29. Barrie, *Plays*, pp. 15–16.
30. Spark, *The Comforters*, p. 197.
31. Ibid.
32. Barrie, *Plays*, p. 38.

33 Eric Partridge, *A Dictionary of Slang and Unconventional English* (London: Routledge and Kegan Paul, 1949), p. 403.
34 See David Masson, *Shakespeare Personally*, ed. Rosaline Masson (London: Smith, Elder, 1914), pp. 162–63.
35 Spark, *The Bachelors*, p. 171.
36 Spark, *The Comforters*, p. 202.
37 Muriel Spark, *Aiding and Abetting* [2000] (London: Penguin, 2001), p. 152.
38 Ibid., p. 153.
39 Ibid., pp. vii–viii.
40 Ibid., p. viii.
41 Ibid., p. 210.
42 Ibid., p. 209.
43 Andrew Nash (ed.), *Farewell Miss Julie Logan: A Barrie Omnibus* (Edinburgh: Canongate, 2009), p. 99.
44 Muriel Spark, *Robinson* (London: Macmillan, 1958), p. 109.
45 Ibid., p. 111.
46 Ibid., p. 111–12.
47 Ibid., p. 112.
48 Barrie, *Peter Pan*, p. 118.
49 Muriel Spark, *Symposium* [1990] (London: Penguin, 1991), p. 176.
50 Barrie, *Plays*, p. 390.
51 J. M. Barrie, *The Works of J. M. Barrie: The Little Minister* (London: Cassell and Company, nd.; 1890), pp. 35–36.
52 Ibid., p. 37.
53 Muriel Spark, *The Takeover* [1976] (London: Penguin, 1978), p. 188.
54 Spark, *The Prime of Miss Jean Brodie*, p. 119.
55 Barrie, *Tommy and Grizel*, p. 276.
56 Ibid., p. 68.
57 Ibid., p. 287.
58 Ibid., p. 403.
59 Ibid., p. 43.
60 Ibid., p. 169.
61 Spark, *The Prime of Miss Jean Brodie*, p. 56.
62 Spark, *The Comforters*, p. 156.

7. All the Abbess's Nuns: Muriel Spark and the Idioms of Watergate

COLIN KIDD

Is *Animal Farm* a story about livestock management? Is *Gulliver's Travels* an exploration of body size in different populations across the globe? Only by the same token is Muriel Spark's *The Abbess of Crewe* (1974) a Catholic novelist's enquiry into the hierarchy and operations of a nunnery. The affinities with *Gulliver's Travels* and *Animal Farm* are, however, very close. *The Abbess of Crewe*, like *Animal Farm* and *Gulliver's Travels*, involves the satirical displacement of well-known political referents from their native heath to an unfamiliar location. Where Swift satirised post-Reformation politics and the disputes of Whigs and Tories in the settings of Lilliput and Brobdingnag, and Orwell the rise of Communism and the Russian Revolution in the porcine takeover of Manor Farm, so Spark transplanted the unfolding Watergate scandal, from Washington D. C. to a Benedictine nunnery in the English Midlands. The immediate effect of the contrast is both deflationary and rich in comic absurdity. What comes clearly into focus is the farcical fumbling of Nixon and his aides. Spark pricks the pompous punditry and hyperbolic media exaggeration surrounding the Watergate affair, and brings a dose of bathos to the tragic fall of a president. Here Spark follows the similar satiric strategies of Swift and Orwell, employing mock-heroic allegories of reduction. Nevertheless, unlike the efforts of Swift and Orwell, whose interests, respectively, in body size and livestock farming, were somewhat limited, Spark, a Roman Catholic convert and self-declared Catholic novelist, leaves open the tantalising possibility that *The Abbess of Crewe* contains a richer seam of commentary on the ostensible matter in hand than the comedy of juxtaposition and comparison. Is the story of the Abbess and her nunnery about more than preposterous parallels and ridiculous comparisons? Is it, in some measure, a Catholic novel after all?

Spark's idea for a Watergate parable came to her when reading a story about Watergate in a Ceylonese newspaper when visiting the newly renamed Sri Lanka in November 1973. Watergate was not the lead item in the Sri Lankan press, but a tiny below-the-fold paragraph. That, she said later to a *Guardian* interviewer, put Watergate in perspective. It clarified matters for her, which she now saw for the first time in due proportion.[1] Certain remarks in *The Abbess of Crewe* suggest that Spark saw the mundane farce behind the high-flown constitutional issues:

> Such a scandal could never arise in the United States of America. They have a sense of proportion and they understand human nature over there; it's the secret of their success. A realistic race, even if they do eat asparagus the wrong way.[2]

In her following novel, *The Takeover*, published in 1976, but set in the disordered Italy of 1973 to 1975, a character relaxes with 'a couple of tranquillizers' and a pile of newspapers and magazines, as he manages to 'hypnotize himself with the current American government scandals of which everyone's latent anarchism drank deep that summer'.[3] There was nothing edifying about the popular clamour surrounding the Watergate affair, just as there was nothing inherently tragic about the fate of the far-from-Hamlet-like, clumsy Malvolio in the White House. Spark took everybody involved in Watergate down a peg or two.

However, an episode that is all bathos and bungling would not be worthy of sustained allegorical treatment, even at the length of a novella. More is going on here, more is at stake, than Spark's sense that the excessive fanfare surrounding Watergate ought to be downplayed. It is very hard to believe that the entire inspiration behind Spark's intricate plot was negative, simply one of noise abatement. In a contemporary interview with BBC Radio 4's *Kaleidoscope* on the book's publication, Spark revealed that she 'thought the whole Watergate thing was greatly exaggerated. I didn't want to do a direct satire on Nixon and I haven't done that'.[4] But what exactly? For all that Spark's declared aim was to diminish Watergate as it was presented by a febrile, hyperbolising media, the lineaments of Watergate obtrusively dominate the plot of *The Abbess of Crewe*.

Although a satirist of sublime gifts, Spark is not immediately thought of as a political writer or as an observer of America and its institutions. Why Watergate? At one level, of course, the answer is obvious. If no educated middle-class person, anywhere on the globe, at the time of Spark's centenary in 2018 could get through a day without seeing some article about President Trump on their computers or smartphones, so no educated person in the years 1973 and 1974 could get through a day without seeing Watergate unfold in their newspapers or on their television screens. For Watergate was the great scandal of the analogue era, and the daily televised deliberations of the Senate Watergate Committee became a fix for many viewers.

The Watergate scandal and its investigation made household names of several figures from the Rosencrantz and Guildenstern class of American politics – backroom advisers, political aides of various kinds, judges and prosecutors, reporters and editors, including, far-from-exhaustively, Haldeman and Ehrlichman, Colson, Butterfield, Liddy and Hunt, Judge Sirica, Cox, Jaworski, Woodward and Bernstein, Ben Bradlee. A useful index of celebrity: the *Washington Post* reporter Carl Bernstein who did so much to uncover the scandal was portrayed on screen by both Dustin Hoffman (in *All the President's Men*) and Jack Nicholson (in *Heartburn*). Indeed, Watergate's impact on the wider culture was significant and enduring. Just as the idioms of Shakespeare and the Authorised Version of the Bible are ubiquitous in the English we speak, so the idioms of Watergate became fixtures in journalese from the mid-1970s onwards. Most obviously, the addition of the mischievous suffix '-gate' became the standard way of designating any political scandal or even minor shenanigans, and not only in the United States. Moreover, several memorable expressions entered the language – 'third-rate burglary', 'cancer on the presidency', 'Deep Throat', 'expletive deleted', 'smoking gun', 'Saturday Night Massacre', the 'inoperative' statement, and the 'long national nightmare'. The idioms of Watergate have become clichés, though for Spark, writing *The Abbess of Crewe* as the scandal entered its final days, they remained fresh, and, along with a casuistical Nixonspeak, constitute a central strand of her novella. For her subject is as much about language and modes of communication as it is about the abuses of authority (something about which Spark is pointedly ambivalent).

The Election Campaign and 'Watergate'

Watergate is the name of a hotel, office and apartment complex at Foggy Bottom in Washington D. C. Here the Democratic National Committee had its headquarters. On the night of 17 June 1972 five burglars were arrested trying to plant a bugging device on the Democrats.[5] Those arrested were four anti-Castro Cubans and James McCord, an ex-CIA man who was an electronics expert working with Nixon's campaign, unhappily known by its acronym CRP (pronounced CREEP), the Committee to Re-elect the President. The burglars were being run by two underlings, Gordon Liddy at CRP, and Howard Hunt, another former CIA man who acted as a White House consultant. Evidence soon linked both Liddy and Hunt, and thus both the campaign and the White House, to the burglary. However, at first it seemed that Liddy and Hunt had been moonlighting, and that higher-ups were not implicated in the scandal.

Nixon was fighting a re-election campaign in 1972, and the immediate response of the White House to the break-in was political, the need for containment of the episode lest it contaminate Nixon's campaign. There was, however, a further concern. A wider investigation might uncover other dirty tricks and illegal actions performed by Nixon's irregulars, known as the Plumbers, as they had originally been used to plug leaks from the administration. This was because Nixon and his National Security Adviser, the German-born Henry Kissinger, had been engaged in a dramatic set of openings to both Mao's China and the Soviet Union, intricate and sensitive manoeuvres which were highly secret, even within the administration, with both the Pentagon and the State Department deliberately kept out of the loop. Kissinger would eventually hold the National Security Adviser's role in tandem with the role of Secretary of State, and won global fame in 1973 for his jetsetting efforts to reconcile the superpowers as well as for his shuttle diplomacy in the Middle East. The Abbess's long-distance telephone conversations with the disembodied, guttural and German-accented voice of the globetrotting missionary Sister Gertrude provide a comic chorus on events at the Abbey, and a familiar and amusing echo of Kissinger's immense vanity and grandiosity.

Watergate is in fact a collective name for a whole trail of monkey business, misdemeanours and outright crimes, as well as attempts to cover them all up. As the Watergate scandal later revealed, Nixon's dirty tricks during the primary season had been designed to undermine the candidacies of credible Democrat opponents. The break-ins and bugging of the Democratic headquarters at Watergate gave the scandal its name, but beneath the distracting pranks and skulduggery of the President's men, the ultimate offence of the catalogue of chicanery known collectively under the synecdoche 'Watergate', was this interference with the electoral process. A Republican should not be able to select the Democrat opponent he would prefer to run against.

To begin with, Watergate unfolded – at least in its public aspect beyond the hidden work of the prosecutors and other investigators – very slowly and tentatively. Campaign contributions were diverted to pay off the burglars and their minders, as a means of sweetening their silence. Watergate did nothing whatsoever during 1972 to dent Nixon's electoral popularity. Containment worked, up to a point. Nixon achieved a landslide victory in the presidential election in November, nearly six months after the botched burglary. Notwithstanding what were then easily dismissed as the off-piste capers of insubordinate and freelancing subordinates, Nixon won forty-nine states in the electoral college, losing only Massachusetts and the District of Columbia to his Democratic challenger, the ultra-liberal Senator George McGovern.

Nevertheless, soon after Nixon's re-election, the strategy of containment burst at the seams. Although the burglars were found guilty at the conclusion of their trial in January 1973, the presiding judge at the trial of the burglars, John Sirica, was not convinced that the whole story had come out. James McCord, the convicted electronics expert, wrote to Judge Sirica, admitting that his testimony was perjured under compulsion, and that senior figures in the Nixon regime had known what was afoot. Nixon's White House legal counsel John Dean, to whom the cover-up had been entrusted, anticipated where the investigation was heading, and seized the opportunity to barter with the prosecutors, hoping to win a lighter sentence for himself by implicating the President in the cover-up. As the scandal engulfed his Presidency, Nixon was forced to part with some of his senior advisers, including his chief of staff H. R. Haldeman and his principal counsellor on domestic affairs, John Ehrlichman, as well as the turncoat Dean. It was now Dean's story against the President's denials, but with seemingly no way of deciding the issue. Then in the summer of 1973 a minor functionary in the White House, Alexander Butterfield, revealed to prosecutors that Nixon had installed recording equipment in his office, and that all of his meetings there had been taped.

A special prosecutor, Archibald Cox, who had been appointed at arm's length from the Justice Department, lest the executive branch be seen to be investigating itself, now challenged the President for the relevant tapes. Nixon attempted various ploys to avoid giving Cox the tapes, and eventually had him sacked in the famous Saturday Night Massacre of October 1973, a month before Spark was inspired to begin her novella. In the ensuing furore, Nixon was forced to appoint a successor to Cox, Leon Jaworski, who continued the investigation and the quest for the tapes. Nixon eventually released edited transcripts of the tapes, notoriously with 'expletives deleted'. However, this was insufficient. Eventually, in the summer of 1974, Jaworski won a decisive Supreme Court case forcing Nixon to disgorge relevant tapes. These included a 'smoking gun' tape which showed Nixon at an early stage in the cover-up conspiring to use national security to frustrate the investigation of the burglary. At this point Spark's novel was in press, and it was published in the months following Nixon's resignation and subsequent pardon by his successor President Gerald Ford. Spark did not know the eventual outcome of the Watergate affair, but she could see that it had jeopardised Nixon's presidency; something that was evident by late 1973 when she embarked upon *The Abbess of Crewe*.

Transposing the Watergate Affair

Spark cleverly transposes the Watergate affair – or at least the events of 1972 and 1973 – to the setting of the Abbey. Spark's initial inspiration for the novella came to her in November 1973, in the month after the Saturday Night Massacre in the Justice Department, and she was still adding significant material as late as May 1974 when the House Judiciary Committee began hearings preliminary to an impeachment motion. The memorable detail, near the beginning of the story, that even the row of poplars in the Abbey grounds was bugged, came to Spark as a result of a dinner party in Rome Spark hosted in honour of her publisher, the former Prime Minister, Harold Macmillan, on 12 May 1974. Spark asked Macmillan if he had ever bugged anyone. He replied with circumspection to the effect that at least he had never been 'such a damn fool as to bug myself'. Macmillan then proffered an arresting anecdote: when he had met the Soviet leader Khrushchev in Moscow in 1959, they walked in the garden to evade KGB eavesdroppers, though Macmillan suspected that there were microphones in the trees.[6] The memorable conceit of the 'secret police of poplars'[7] at the opening of the novella and the information that the trees were indeed bugged emerged from the dinner party in mid-May. However, publication in the autumn of 1974 suggests that Nixon's resignation in August of that year came too late for the novelist to include in her allegorical whimsy, though by the early summer Nixon already seemed doomed, politically, one way or the other, though whether he would be impeached, or would be forced to resign, or indeed be prosecuted in the criminal courts, was unknown to Spark.

The humour lies primarily in the ingenious parallels Spark concocts between the Abbess's entourage and President Nixon's, between the activities of the Abbess's nuns and those of the President's men. The two contenders to succeed the dying Abbess Hildegarde at the nunnery, the conservative Alexandra and the ultra-liberal Sister Felicity, represent Nixon and his Democrat opponent, Senator George McGovern of South Dakota. Felicity's message of free love, which appeals to some of the younger nuns, is pitched as a version of McGovern's appeal to America's student protesters and anti-Vietnam War counterculture. As in real life the eventual election was never in doubt, resulting in the expected landslide for the conservative candidate.

The *dramatis personae* of the Watergate scandal have their appropriate counterparts in *The Abbess of Crewe*. Nixon's two principal advisers, his chief of staff H. R. 'Bob' Haldeman and his chief counsellor for domestic affairs John Ehrlichman, appear in Spark's novella as, respectively, the Prioress Walburga and Mildred, the Novice Mother. John Dean, the White House counsel, who was set up as the fall guy for Watergate but who eventually ratted (truthfully) on his superiors, is captured in the role of Sister Winifrede: 'the scandal stops at Winifrede'.[8] Gordon Liddy and Howard Hunt, who were the immediate begetters of the Watergate burglary and stationed across the road from the Watergate in a room at a Howard Johnson's motor lodge, are depicted as the Jesuits, Father Baudouin and Father Maximilian. The Cubans they hired to carry out the burglary appear in Spark's allegory as the novice Jesuits, Gregory and Ambrose.

The events of Watergate too have their faithful correspondences in the novella. The work of the Plumbers unit is all too obviously depicted in the training which the nuns at Crewe receive in electronics. The break-in and bugging of the Watergate are allegorised in the theft of Sister Felicity's silver thimble and then the return job to get her love letters out of the secret drawer in her sewing basket. The Watergate cover-up and the payments out of CRP campaign funds to Hunt and the burglars are satirised in Alexandra's doctoring of the tape recordings of conversations in the nunnery and in the attempts of the dismissed Jesuit novices, who had been commissioned to break into the sewing room and who burgled Sister Felicity's silver thimble, to blackmail the Abbess's co-conspirators.

There are also miscellaneous allusions to Watergate matters which would have been obvious to the readers of 1974, but are perhaps now more recondite. We learn, for instance, that Sister Felicity is seeing a psychiatrist,[9] and here her character (which is, to some extent, the archetypal liberal) represents not McGovern but Daniel Ellsberg, the consultant who had leaked the Pentagon Papers to the press, and whose psychiatrist's office, as it emerged during Watergate, Nixon's aides had raided in an attempt to find material with which they could smear the whistleblower. Similarly, Nixon's constitutional argument for not disgorging the tapes, the Executive Privilege enjoyed by the Presidency which protects confidential conversations between a President and his advisers, surfaces in Alexandra's defence of her own position: 'I won't part with the tapes. I claim the ancient Benefit of Clerks. The confidentiality between the nuns and the Abbess cannot be disrupted.'[10]

The funniest passages are those which capture telephone conversations between Alexandra and the Kissinger character, the globetrotting ecumenical missionary with the deep Germanic voice,[11] Sister Gertrude. She is clever, a philosopher manquée who is compared, in a pejorative backhanded compliment, with her totalising philosophical 'compatriot',[12] Hegel. Gertrude is an accommodationist with vaingloriously global horizons, a jest perhaps at the expense of Kissinger's celebrated jetsetting, so routinised in fact that it became known as 'shuttle diplomacy'. However, Gertrude's preposterous syncretism is also the *reductio ad absurdum* of Jesuit attempts to accommodate cultural variations to the core truths of Christianity, at least on matters of supposed indifference. Indeed, Gertrude seems to subscribe to the universal reconciliation and concordance of all religions, under the auspices of a very notional, indeed loosely heretical, Roman Catholicism.

Gertrude supplies an intermittent comic chorus. She reports in, variously, to the order's headquarters at Crewe, from the Congo, the Andes, the Himalayas, and Iceland. From the Congo we learn that Gertrude is 'reconciling witch doctors' rituals with a specially adapted rite of the Mass'.[13] Gertrude preaches in favour of birth control in the Himalayas,[14] where she also intervenes in a dispute between two sects 'on a point of doctrine which apparently has arisen from a mere spelling mistake in English'.[15]

In the case of the jokes about Gertrude's planet-wide missionary efforts a decidedly Gulliverian seam is evident in the complex layering of the novel. There are evocations of *Gulliver's Travels*, and perhaps even a very particular allusion to Voltaire's intercontinental anti-Catholic satire *Candide*, in which he describes a tribe of fastidious Amerindian cannibals who eat only Jesuits.[16] Gertrude at the end of a phone line in the Andes describes how she is 'at a very delicate point' in her 'negotiations between the cannibal tribe and that vegetarian sect on the other side of the mountain'.[17] Kissinger-like, Gertrude has fashioned a solution which will accommodate these culturally disparate Andean converts: 'The cannibals are to be converted to the faith with dietary concessions and the excessive zeal of the vegetarian heretics suppressed'.[18] Alexandra wonders how the cannibals 'will fare on the Day of Judgment'.[19] Who shall then arise, the eaters or the eaten? Later, we learn that 'the vegetarian tribes have guaranteed to annihilate the cannibals, should they display any desire to roast' Gertrude.[20]

Kissinger's foreign policy achievements on behalf of Nixon, his opening to China, détente with the Soviet Union, protracted negotiations over Vietnam and the Arab-Israeli conflict, were, politically – though not legally or constitutionally – Nixon's best claim to retain office in the face of possible impeachment proceedings. In *The Abbess of Crewe*, Sister Gertrude's 'magnificent work abroad' which 'had earned universal gratitude' becomes the Abbess's best defence against her critics.[21]

However, there is more – much more – to *The Abbess of Crewe* than a spoof on the characters and episodes of the Watergate scandal. There are, it seems, layers of meaning here beyond that of the allegory itself. However, Spark goes further than mirroring the characters and deeds of Watergate in the nunnery's cast and their preposterously cynical, undignified and un-nun-like actions. Indeed, one of Spark's primary concerns is with the idioms of Watergate. Spark is entranced by the political argot – simultaneously cynical and pompous – of the President and his aides. This is a book with language at its core. Most obviously, Spark makes play with Nixonese. When on 30 April 1973 Nixon was forced to sacrifice Haldeman and Ehrlichman, he described them in a televised address as 'two of the finest public servants it has been my privilege to know'. This finds its echo in *The Abbess of Crewe*, when Alexandra describes Walburga and Mildred as 'two of the finest nuns I have ever had the privilege to know'.[22]

At a deeper level Spark explores the languages of dissimulation and evasion, which are part of the professional deformation of character associated with politicians, but not only politicians. For Roman Catholic priests had also been traditionally associated with a certain economising with the truth. In *The Abbess of Crewe* Spark deploys Alexandra and her co-conspirators as mouthpieces for discourses of indulgence, self-exculpation, apologia, and casuistry: 'The more truths and confusions the better.'[23] This is something for which the Jesuits were particularly notorious in anti-Catholic polemic. Why, the reader wonders, is the convent a hybrid institution, quasi-Benedictine, quasi-Jesuit? The most plausible answer is that it gives

Spark licence to make sport of Jesuit casuistry, or more precisely to use the Jesuits as cover for an exploration of the stratagems of exculpation.

Rhetoric, scenarios and poetry are essential elements in Spark's story. Indeed, without these features, the allegory itself is, however congruent with the affairs of Watergate, somewhat thin gruel for the reader. Weightier matter comes in the form of the arguments used by Alexandra to justify herself. She notes that 'there is one particular tape in which I prove my innocence of the bugging itself'.[24] Nixon indeed resorted to such devious ploys on the tapes; knowing that he was being taped, as his interlocutors, on the whole, did not, he could choreograph conversations to project his blamelessness (though at other times he forgot that he was on tape and unwittingly incriminated himself). The Abbess says at one point, in pure Nixonese, 'The more money they demand the less I like it', then segues cleverly into innocence, for the tapes: 'Actually, I heard about these demands for the first time this morning.'[25] There is a marvellous casuistry in the Abbess's argument that 'electronic surveillance', far from being prohibited by the traditional monastic rule, is in effect positively encouraged by it, for it 'does not differ from any other type of watchfulness'.[26] The Abbess Alexandra encourages her senior nuns to pay off blackmailers and confuse those authorities, temporal and ecclesiastical, investigating the nunnery, all the while slyly distancing herself, as Nixon did, from the particulars of the cover-up: 'plainly I can take no personal party in what you have in mind'.[27] 'I must remain,' she insists, 'in the region of unknowing'.[28] The bishops who come to investigate the Abbey leave 'with soothed feelings', though also 'a curious sense of being unable to recall precisely what explanation Alexandra had given'.[29]

Alexandra says of Gertrude that 'she fits the rhetoric of the occasion'.[30] The 'rhetoric of the occasion' is cleverly aped; but to ulterior ends. Sister Gertrude, based on the power-worshipping Kissinger, proclaims at one point that 'a rebellion against a tyrant is only immoral when it hasn't got a chance'.[31] Gertrude advises Alexandra to consult Machiavelli – 'a great master, but don't quote me as saying so; the name is inexpedient'.[32] At one point Sister Winifrede asks Alexandra 'What are scenarios?' 'They are an art-form', replies Alexandra, 'based on facts'. She then proceeds to classify casuistical scenarios: 'A good scenario is a garble. A bad one is a bungle. They need not be plausible, only hypnotic, like all good art.'[33] Alexandra is obsessed with 'scenarios'; what they are, their significance, above all their aesthetic qualities. This brings us to the very nub of the book. Arguably, Spark's real subject is style.

This is a novella about aesthetics, a dimension of life which seems to have mattered little to Nixon, Kissinger and their hardboiled associates. Indeed, deliberately, it seems, the Watergate parallels are far from complete in Spark's story. There is a major divergence between the two stories. Nixon and Alexandra share a certain cack-handed ruthlessness, but here the parallels stop. Abbess Alexandra is not a copy of Nixon; if anything, she is Nixon turned-inside-out. Nixon was a self-made man from a poor background whose career was propelled in good part by his resentment of the good fortune, easy manner and seductive style of the various elites he had encountered, whether at Whittier College in California or, later, in fierce political competition with the Kennedy dynasty. Abbess Alexandra is an anti-Nixon, embodying precisely the aristocratic pedigree, discrimination, aesthetic sense, swank and swagger which he lacked and so detested. According to John Updike's contemporary review of the novella, Alexandra is 'the very opposite of Nixon, a print from the negative'. Alexandra's confident hauteur is a world away from Nixon's 'painfully self-conscious' attempts at human contact, for the Watergate tapes revealed to Updike the President's inability to hit the right note in human relationships, his alighting on mere 'toadying' when trying to establish 'fellowship' with even his 'inner circle'.[34] The novella is certainly replete with anti-bourgeois sentiment. Who are we meant to side with, the free-loving bourgeois liberal Felicity, with her renegade Jesuit lover, or the aristocratic, Machiavellian Abbess? Certainly, Spark tends to view the action, albeit by way of an impersonal narrator, through the eyes of Alexandra and her lieutenants. And should we even begin to contemplate fictional worlds in terms of moral categories? Who among us is fit to judge between the good and the reprobate? 'We are corrupt by our nature in the Fall of Man', Alexandra proclaims.[35]

Alexandra is a charismatic leader of a sort Nixon could never aspire to be; her effect is 'mesmeric rather than satiric', as Ruth Whittaker notes.[36] It is unclear whether Spark appreciated Nixon's dark grudges and decided to give him a comic makeover, transforming the President into an obtrusively anti-Nixonian character. However, Alexandra is much more than a Swiftian disfiguration of Nixon. The parallels here are not simply with the world of Watergate, but with enduring themes in Spark's own fictional world. It seems just as likely that Spark was, with typical autobiographical swish, recreating yet another wilful, qualm-free, stylish, formidable and capricious woman in the Brodie mould. After all, there are other close resemblances. This story too concerns a female ensemble in an institutional setting presided over by an arbitrary and despotic queen bee. Indeed, Spark's oeuvre contains several arbitrary, goddess-like creators and manipulators, who make others dance to their sly, willed choreographies. There is, for example, the phony psychologist in *Aiding and Abetting* (2000) who makes sport with the two self-confessed Lord Lucans who come to her practice needing counselling;[37] or the cunning and ingenious Fleur Talbot of *Loitering with Intent* (1981).[38] The Abbess Alexandra is similarly blessed with smeddum and devilment. Indeed, as Whittaker suggests, she is a most unusual fictional character who seems almost to chafe against the confines of the plot.[39] Alternatively, Allan Massie sees the darker side – theologically inflected – of a stream of such characters who parade through Spark's oeuvre, exhibiting a wilful solipsism, which insists on remaking the world to suit their own egoism and vanity. No modern novelist, Massie notes, is so alert to evil and the many 'deceptively attractive guises' it is capable of assuming.[40]

Alexandra is a seeming bundle of contradictions. She is a traditionalist, but she encourages the nuns to educate themselves in electronic eavesdropping techniques. She despises Sister Felicity's liberal notions, describing Felicity's religion as 'morbid', a species of 'sentimental Jesusism'.[41] (Is Alexandra here, one wonders, acting as Spark's alter ego, articulating the novelist's own firmly held conception of what Catholicism was, and what it was – very decidedly – not?) Moreover, Alexandra herself, heretically, blasphemously indeed, prefers the diction and rhythms of English poetry to the sacred words of the nunnery's religious services. Poetry is Alexandra's private vice; Nixon's venial sin was swearing of a fairly mild sort. Indeed, 'Expletives deleted' on his selected transcripts of the tapes suggested that the cussing was saltier than it was in fact. At the conclusion of the novella Alexandra asks her aides to mark 'Poetry deleted' on the transcripts of her recordings.[42] But how are we to read Alexandra's love of secular poetry, a profane idiom which she prefers to the sacred liturgy?

Politics and Religion: Satire and Parable

The Abbess of Crewe is a flawed jewel. There are undoubted blemishes, and some of the jokes are heavy-handed: the pet food fed to the rank-and-file nuns, for example, and the payoffs in drag to the blackmailers in public lavatories. On the other hand, there are almost certainly cryptic jokes, largely inaccessible to American readers and connoisseurs of Watergate, concealed in plain view at the heart of the story.[43] Moreover, where does Spark take her allegory? Unlike *Animal Farm*, *The Abbess of Crewe* does not yield a deeper insight into the political process. The events just happen, with characteristic Sparkian arbitrariness. Of course, this in itself presents a puzzle. Is Spark here, as ever, portraying the unknowable – the undecodable, unpredictable operations of divine providence? Or is it, less charitably, evidence that Spark, unlike Orwell, lacked a profound understanding of politics?[44]

There is no apparent insight into what is being satirised. But is this the wilful obtuseness of the Catholic novelist who views all political machinations, all terrestrial affairs in the light of the eternal? Spark herself attributed her reckless satirical outlook to her grounding in her new-found Catholic faith.[45] Why, she seems to ask, should the Catholic novelist read the hearts of men? Rather, all too often in Spark's novels, providence simply and arbitrarily disposes. By contrast, realism, context and explanation verge on extenuation, and are appropriate to the secularising late Protestant or post-Protestant novel, but have no place, as Spark sees it, in her fictions. Is *The Abbess of Crewe* then a Catholic novel *faute de mieux*? Neither of her supporters, Graham Greene and Evelyn Waugh, was a conventional Catholic novelist. Heresies abound in the twentieth-century Catholic novel, and Spark's own Catholic plotting was of a similar cast.

Collectively, contemporary reviewers caught the novella's unmistakable Watergate tints. That much they agreed upon; more difficult to parse was the ulterior significance of Spark's enigmatic tale. Was it even a satire? David

Lodge, in the *Tablet*, thought not. While the novella 're-enacts the Watergate affair', it was 'not a satire on the Nixon regime'. While the cunning twinning of 'two utterly different worlds' created a 'comedy of incongruity', the novella's 'tone' was not one of 'satiric indignation'. Rather, the mood was one of 'gaiety and glee'. Lodge preferred to describe *The Abbess of Crewe* as a 'parable', one in which the 'familiar theme that absolute power corrupts absolutely' was defamiliarised. For, as Lodge notes, the story is narrated 'from the point of view of the conspirators, never allowing the liberal moral consciousness to have its say'. Indeed, Lodge reckoned that the Catholic novelist had 'no moral response at all' to the sublunary affairs of Watergate.[46] Lorna Sage, in the *Observer*, followed a parallel path. While 'worldly' novelists seemed 'to have their noses put a bit out of joint by the rival productions of the White House fiction machine', Spark had paid 'a magnanimous tribute' to the Watergate conspirators. The Catholic novelist saw more clearly than secular writers that all profane history partakes of sin; therefore, 'the only heroism is to sin in style'. Alexandra achieves, Sage argues, 'a state of euphoric wrongdoing', which draws the reader 'irresistibly to conspire with the heroine's sheer style'.[47] On a related note, Gabriele Annan in the *Times Literary Supplement* also found the novella a parable, 'a parable about art and its incompatibility with religion', except 'in paradoxical coexistence'. The effect, Annan contended, was like a 'trance', but short-lived, for the story itself was so 'silly'.[48]

Indeed, according to Updike, in the *New Yorker*, Spark's 'paradoxes' made for 'indifferent satire', indeed he found the Watergate allegory inappropriately thin, 'a rather lame echo of a plot that in real life never wearied of thickening'. Rather the novella worked best as 'a transfiguration' of Watergate, and was at its least compelling when it was mechanically 'aping' political events.[49] A similar note is struck by Patricia Mayer Spacks in the *Yale Review*. Spacks perceived the direct comparison with *Gulliver's Travels*. Spark's tale of a nunnery thrown into convulsions by the theft of a thimble succeeded in 'miniaturizing political concerns' after the fashion of Swift's Lilliput. While Spacks enjoys the 'ingenuity of the equivalences' in Spark's Watergate novella, she also senses the limitations of the genre: 'Once you've thought of big men and little men, as Dr Johnson pointed out, the rest is easy.' Thus, Spark is most entertaining when she engages in 'deliberate violations of parallelism', as in the Abbess's taste for the English poetic canon.[50]

But were the novella's primary concerns religious at all? Emma Tennant, in the *Listener*, detected class – the ubiquitous leitmotif of the English novel – at the heart of Spark's tale. Everything about Sister Felicity screamed bourgeois bad taste, and what Alexandra could not abide was Felicity's 'irremediable middle-class-ness'.[51] Inevitably, this calls to mind the fiction of Waugh in which it is hard at times to distinguish the social from the theological components of recusant aristocratic Catholicism. Spark, however, had little truck with the psychological realism so characteristic of the English novel of class; she, like Alexandra, was an imposer, not an observer.

Nevertheless, there was, and is still, clearly disagreement about what is at stake in *The Abbess of Crewe* beyond an allegory of Watergate, and the puzzlement remains. The novella certainly transcends satire and is possibly in some remote sense a Catholic parable. Moreover, the Abbess Alexandra is an utterly memorable character; once encountered, never forgotten. The novella perches precariously in a zone of studied ambiguity between judging Alexandra for her various deceits, her petty tyranny over the Abbey, her use of others as instruments rather than as fully human co-equals, and an indulgent complicity verging on admiration for Alexandra's stylish, uncompromising, highly aestheticised approach to life. Allegory is also overlaid, arguably, with deliberate self-satirising, a portrait of the artist's own whimsical authorial despotism. Alternatively, of course, this revelation of the capricious side of Spark's character is unconscious and inadvertent: an accidental glimpse, perhaps, of the Devil's cloven hoof.[52]

Endnotes

1. Alex Hamilton, 'Alex Hamilton Interviews Muriel Spark', *Guardian*, 8 November 1974, p. 10.
2. Muriel Spark, *The Abbess of Crewe* [1974] (New York, NY: New Directions, 1995), p. 19.
3. Muriel Spark, *The Takeover* [1976] (Harmondsworth: Penguin, 1978), p. 54.
4. Muriel Spark, Interview on *Kaleidoscope*, BBC Radio 4; abridged as 'Bugs and Mybug', *Listener*, 28 November 1974, p. 706.
5. Amidst a huge literature on Watergate – much of it partial and much written by the protagonists themselves – there are some comprehensive surveys, including Stanley I. Kutler, *The Wars of Watergate* [1990] (New York, NY: Norton, 1992); Fred Emery, *Watergate: The Corruption and Fall of Richard Nixon* [1994] (London: Touchstone, 1995).
6. D. R. Thorpe, *Supermac: The Life of Harold Macmillan* (London: Chatto & Windus, 2010), p. 426; Martin Stannard, *Muriel Spark: The Biography* (London: Weidenfeld and Nicolson, 2009), p. 402.
7. Spark, *Abbess*, p. 7.
8. Ibid., p. 18.
9. Ibid., p. 82.
10. Ibid., p. 101.
11. Ibid., p. 24.
12. Ibid., p. 23.
13. Ibid., p. 23.
14. Ibid., p. 68.
15. Ibid., p. 70.
16. Voltaire, *Candide* (Oxford: Oxford University Press, 2006), Ch. 16.
17. Spark, *Abbess*, p. 42.
18. Ibid., p. 42.
19. Ibid., p. 42.
20. Ibid, p. 44.
21. Ibid., p. 103.
22. Ibid., p. 92.
23. Ibid., p. 21.
24. Ibid., p. 96
25. Ibid., p. 84.
26. Ibid., p. 26.
27. Ibid., p. 46.
28. Ibid., p. 62.
29. Ibid., p. 104.
30. Ibid., pp. 27–28.
31. Ibid., p. 43.
32. Ibid., p. 44.
33. Ibid., p. 88.
34. John Updike, 'Topnotch witcheries', *New Yorker*, 6 January 1975, reprinted in Updike, *Hugging the Shore: Essays and Criticism* [1983] (Penguin: Harmondsworth, 1985), pp. 341–50 (pp. 344–45).
35. Spark, *Abbess*, p. 48.

36 Ruth Whittaker, *The Faith and Fiction of Muriel Spark* (Basingstoke: Palgrave Macmillan, 1982), p. 103.
37 Muriel Spark, *Aiding and Abetting* [2000] (London: Penguin, 2001).
38 Muriel Spark, *Loitering with Intent* [1981] (London: Penguin, 2007).
39 Whittaker, *Faith and Fiction*, p. 102.
40 Allan Massie, 'Calvinism and Catholicism in Muriel Spark', in *Muriel Spark: An Odd Capacity for Vision*, ed. Alan Bold (London; Totowa, NJ: Vision; Barnes & Noble, 1984), pp. 94–107 (esp. pp. 99–101; p. 107).
41 Spark, *Abbess*, p. 49.
42 Ibid., p. 106.
43 Why Crewe? Why Alexandra? Crewe Alexandra, the English association football team?
44 Not that Spark was entirely apolitical, or altogether ignorant of American politics. See her brief anthologies of extracts: Muriel Spark, 'Poetry and Politics', in *Parliamentary Affairs* 1 (1948), pp. 12–23; Muriel Spark, 'Poetry and the American Government', in *Parliamentary Affairs* 3 (1949), pp. 260–72. I am indebted to Prof. Willy Maley for these references.
45 Muriel Spark, 'My Conversion', in *Twentieth Century* 170 (Autumn 1961), pp. 58–63 (p. 60; pp. 62–63).
46 David Lodge, 'Prime Spark', *Tablet*, 7 December 1974, p. 1185.
47 Lorna Sage, 'Bugging the Nunnery', *Observer*, 10 November 1974, p. 33.
48 Gabriele Annan, 'Holy Watergate', *Times Literary Supplement*, 15 November 1974, p. 1277.
49 Updike, 'Topnotch witcheries', p. 343; p. 345.
50 Patricia Meyer Spacks, 'New Novels: In the Dumps', in *Yale Review* (Summer 1975), pp. 583–94 (pp. 589–90).
51 Emma Tennant, 'Holy joke', *Listener*, 14 November 1974, p. 649.
52 Cf. Bryan Cheyette, *Muriel Spark* (Tavistock: Northcote House, 2000), p. 88, where he identifies Alexandra as one of 'Spark's novelists manqués', her 'wilful determiners of society', and describes her as 'Spark's most complete and sympathetic fictional double'.

8. 'Making patterns with facts': Unmaking History in *The Prime of Miss Jean Brodie*

CATRIONA M. M. MACDONALD

The setting (Edinburgh) and the context (the inter-war years) of *The Prime of Miss Jean Brodie* (1961) have been foregrounded in much literary criticism to the extent that, to speak of the work as an historical novel, would appear to be trite, self-evident, a given. Yet Muriel Spark throughout the work hints strongly at how easily history and story are conflated. Early on in the novel, Miss Brodie appears to suggest that history is simply composed of stories: '"They are moved by a story I have been telling them. We are having a history lesson," said Miss Brodie, catching a falling leaf neatly in her hand as she spoke.'[1] More profoundly, when the 'Brodie set' are later challenged by the headmistress about their teacher's practice, the girls identify history as a source of safe stories – for them, claiming history is a defence against allegations of impropriety that is certain to silence Miss Mackay.

> 'And what are *your* cultural interests?' [...]
> 'Stories, ma'am,' Mary said.
> 'Does Miss Brodie tell you stories?'
> 'Yes,' said Mary.
> 'What about?'
> 'History,' said Jenny and Sandy together, because it was a question they had foreseen might arise one day and they had prepared the answer with a brainracking care for literal truth.[2]

It would appear disingenuous, therefore, to treat *The Prime of Miss Jean Brodie* as a straightforwardly historical novel: rather, it is a work that problematises the nature of history, history's relationship with fiction, and history's claims on truth. In so doing it de-historicises Miss Brodie whose 'prime' strains against the boundedness of time and resists the historian's craft. That said, it is only by considering the history of the novel itself; the use of history in the novel; the history of the times in which the novel is set; and the narratological struggle through which Miss Brodie is dispossessed of a past and a present, while her future is foreclosed, that we can appreciate just how unhistorical (or alternatively, superhistorical) this novel is.

History

Like any novel, however, *The Prime of Miss Jean Brodie* has a history all of its own. It was written by Muriel Spark over the course of four weeks in December 1960 at her family home, after a period of intermittent absence from Edinburgh. Spark thus wrote in an environment where she was acutely aware of her status as a daughter and of her own schooldays: days when she, like Sandy, interlaced the novels of Robert Louis Stevenson with her own life and was the 'Poet and Dreamer' of James Gillespie's School.[3] But we do not need to claim that Sandy is Muriel to make the point that there is strong contextual evidence at least to suggest that Spark in *The Prime of Miss Jean Brodie* was writing (in part) from the perspective of youth, and that the voices of the 'Brodie set', as much as those of Miss Brodie herself or the anonymous narrator of the novel, might be the authoritative sources to which we ought to listen most acutely and perhaps more carefully than we have done to date. We will return to this in due course.

The novel itself was published in the *New Yorker* in October 1961, and following publication in book format in both the UK and the US, was the inspiration for a stage play by Jay Presson Allen that eventually hit Broadway in 1968 and which went on to provide the basis of the 1969 Twentieth Century Fox 'classic' film starring Maggie Smith, who won an Academy award for her performance as Miss Brodie. The speed at which the book inspired high-profile theatrical and film versions meant that the novel itself had little time to establish its own worth before its reception was mediated by versions which, in both obvious and subtle ways, at times do not resemble the book in the slightest. Where Spark is experimental with narrative, character and plot, both play and film pretend to a comforting realism that Spark's novel simply does not offer.[4] As David Lodge notes of the film: 'it rendered *only* the literal and linear dimension of the story' – a tendency that is evident elsewhere in critical readings of the work.[5]

Alan Bold's evocation of Brodie's Edinburgh as a city 'haunted by its historic past' is suggestive of a critical tradition that claims *The Prime of Miss Jean Brodie* as Spark's 'Edinburgh novel', and its author as 'Scottish', descended from a long literary lineage.[6] There are, however, relatively few Scottish historical analogies (as distinct from literary analogies) in the novel, and Spark often subtly undercuts their significance. So, while the battle of Flodden is evoked in references made to the 'Flowers of the Forest' who fell, like Miss Brodie's beau, in the Great War, Brodie's girls do not know the date of the original battle (1513) or – a fact of apparently equal significance – the capital of Finland.[7] Similarly, when the class 'ought to be doing history [...] according to the timetable', Miss Brodie shares tales of her holiday in Italy and her appreciation of Rossetti, instructing the girls to 'Keep your history books propped up in case we have any further intruders': history thus cloaks story and disguises art.[8] Even Eunice, who shows promise in History in the senior school, retreats into historical romances:

> Eunice Gardiner discovered the Industrial Revolution, its rights and wrongs, to such an extent that the history teacher, a vegetarian communist, had high hopes of her which were dashed within a few months when Eunice reverted to reading novels based on the life of Mary Queen of Scots.[9]

It is a Scottish *literary* inheritance rather than a *historical* inheritance that delivers the time depth of the novel: Burns, Scott, Hogg, Stevenson story this past, conflating history and fiction, and intruding 'out of time' voices which compromise as much as enrich what constitutes the 'where' and 'when' of the novel itself.

Others disagree. *The Prime of Miss Jean Brodie* is, according to Philip E. Ray, 'a novel of Edinburgh', and has been described by Trevor Royle as one of the best portraits of Edinburgh as it was in the 1930s.[10] When writing the book, Spark relied much on memory, but also undertook research to ground her observations: amongst other titles, she read C. L. Mowat's *Britain Between the Wars*, taking note of Scotland's disproportionate suffering in these years, and consulted Theo Lang's *Edinburgh and the Lothians*.[11] Comparing the novel with the Third Statistical Account of Edinburgh, published in 1966, it is clear that there is much on the surface to support Royle's claim. There is certainly evidence to ground the 'small village' feel that Spark evokes: the population of the capital was just around 440,000 in 1931, and ninety per cent of the population of Edinburgh at that time was Scottish.[12] Ever since 1801 at least, Edinburgh had also been a female city, with proportionately more women than men: in 1931 the number of women exceeded men in the capital by nearly 40,000.[13] And at the turn of the twentieth century, half of Edinburgh's adult women were single (compared to a Scottish average of forty-four per cent).[14] Miss Brodie was thus typical in many respects of other women in the city in the inter-war years, although clearly Edinburgh had known this type long before the ravages of the Great War had created a generation of 'spinsters'. There were, indeed, 'legions of her kind' and a history to ground Spark's claims of a particular kind of 'Edinburgh spinster'.[15]

The famous 'walk' scene, where the girls encounter the 'Idle', is also well judged (historically at least), when further evidence is explored: Edinburgh did not suffer as much as other Scottish cities from the ravages of the Great Depression and so it is not surprising that many of the privileged 'Brodie set' had never seen the squalor of the Old Town. It was also inevitable, however, that there they would find poverty: the worst slums and the biggest common lodging houses were located in the Old Town, in the Grassmarket, and the Cowgate.[16] By contrast, the golfing scenes are also apt: Edinburgh has a long golfing heritage, and boasted hundreds of acres of municipal courses when Sandy and Brodie teed off in the thirties.[17] In Cramond, Mr Lowther's sailing boat would have been one of many, and his housekeeper would have been one of thousands attending Presbyterian church services in Edinburgh in the 1930s. Even in the 1960s, the communicant roll of the Presbytery of Edinburgh was 126,899 (i.e. twenty-seven per cent of the population).[18]

The wider political context is also well observed by Spark.[19] Stanley Baldwin regularly played the 'Scottish card' to shore up the Unionist vote in Scotland in the 1930s and was remarkably successful at the time: it is thus hardly surprising that Miss Mackay, the 'Safety First' headmistress, is shown as responding positively to his message and perhaps equally predictable that Jean Brodie would have found him dull in contrast to fascist alternatives ('Mussolini has performed feats of magnitude').[20] Indeed, Brodie's interest in fascism was far from rare in Scotland in the 1930s: with unemployment over thirty per cent in some Scottish towns, it would have been strange had no-one sympathised with governments that appeared to prioritise full employment and the renewal of national pride. Scots-Italians responded positively to the message: over forty per cent of Italian-Scots were full members of the Italian Fascist Party.[21] Spark herself remembered Blackshirts on the streets of Edinburgh, and among pro-Franco sympathisers in Scotland was Lady Maxwell-Scott, wife of General Sir Walter Maxwell-Scott (great grandson of the Scottish novelist): she was honorary president of the Scottish branch of the Friends of National Spain.[22] At the University of Glasgow, the Regius Professor of Law, and a co-founder of the Scottish National Party (est. 1934), Andrew Dewar Gibb, maintained his Germanophile sympathies well after the declaration of war with Nazi Germany, although – unlike Brodie – he was not forced to retire.[23]

One could take this approach further. A detailed treatment of education is certainly possible – many have compared Spark's time at Gillespie's with the depiction of the Marcia Blaine school within the wider context of the Scottish educational tradition, and linked Spark's teacher, Christina Kay, with Miss Brodie.[24] But to what end? Both Brodie and Kay visited Egypt; both were experimental teachers; and Brodie's famous phrase ('the crème de la crème') may first have been Kay's. So what?

Spark has offered sufficient clues both within the novel and beyond that ought to make us suspicious about reading too much into historical coincidence and apparent biographical precedent. In correspondence with Alasdair Roberts, Spark was sceptical of over-reading the novel for historical 'fact'. 'In general', she noted, 'one can make fiction out of fact but not fact out of fiction'.[25] Stannard, for example, confirms that Muriel Spark did not see Miss Brodie as a fascist,[26] and – while Trevor Royle made much of Spark's choice of Brodie as Jean's surname, with its explicit connections to the famous Edinburgh deacon[27] – in *Curriculum Vitae* (1992), Spark admits that she '[did] not know exactly why [she] chose the name', musing that it might have been an association with the maiden name of a woman known to her in her infant years.[28]

The point is a simple but important one: the story of Miss Brodie does not depend on her being real or potentially realisable in human form. That there was a Miss Kay does not make Miss Brodie any more or less probable for those who read only the novel. Indeed, probability in this sense really ought not to come into it, as Brodie exists only within the world of the book and even in that environment she matters less for herself than for the impact she has on the girls and what they infer from her actions and protestations. Spark is explicit about this: this is an Edinburgh uncoupled from its past and its present. Sandy observes that 'there were other people's Edinburghs quite different from hers [...]. Similarly, there were other people's nineteen thirties'.[29] There is no stable essence about either setting or context, meaning that Edinburgh variously dissolves and is dissolved by the apparent specificity of time and place. As Gerard Carruthers has noted of Scotland more generally: it is 'a place conjugated by Spark'.[30]

In sum, this is not a historical novel at all. Spark herself limits time by interspersing the girls' schooldays with intimations of their fate (flashforward) without the chain of causal connections that take them there. This matters. Context and setting are *not* the same as history. History requires causal connections and recognisable sequential narrative approaches even if they are contested and far from linear. Critics previously have touched on this obliquely. In her compelling essay in the *Edinburgh Companion to Muriel Spark,* Marilyn Reizbaum comments on how Brodie's 'prime' by necessity 'delimits pastness', and how the teacher uses the word as a noun almost to make time stand still.[31] Indeed, throughout the novel things temporal and matters contextual appear at times interchangeable with character, and Brodie's 'prime' – as the explanation for everything – negates the need for causality. Things just are as they are, because it is her prime. Similarly, the younger Sandy's ability to tune out of or further into her environment to realms of fantasy, literature and make-believe, suggest that we ought not to read too much in to 'when' and 'where'. Indeed, even in later life, when they meet at the Braid Hills Hotel, Miss Brodie accuses Sandy of not listening: not being fully there.³² The fact that the novel is set in the 1930s, the fact that the novel is set in Edinburgh, may just be incidental. It is an interesting if, perhaps, unpopular suggestion to pose (at least in Scotland).

Narratology

Having set aside the biography of the author and the book, and released the narrative from an overly determined reading of its place and times, the most likely discernible route for the pursuit of any demonstrable historical imperative in the novel is to seek to historicise Miss Brodie herself. This, in turn, demands a thorough-going analysis of Spark's narratological approach.

First, however, it is essential to start with some basic facts: who Brodie is and what she does, for example. Born – 1890 (do we know this for sure?); suffered the death of her fiancé – 1918 (did Hugh Carruthers exist?); retired (or forced out?) – 1939; died – 1946 (at least for that we have a gravestone).³³ Even at this most mundane level, there are recognisably historical challenges when it comes to the provenance and authenticity of the evidence and the authority and bias of sources. In short, it is a question of 'who says?': in sum, it is a question of narration. Even Brodie's physical appearance is not straightforward:

> Some days it seemed to Sandy that Brodie's chest was flat, no bulges at all, but straight as her back. On other days her chest was breast-shaped and large, very noticeable [...].

> They kept an eye on Miss Brodie's stomach to see if it showed signs of swelling. Some days, if they were bored, they decided it had begun to swell. But on Miss Brodie's entertaining days they found her stomach as flat as ever [...]

> Miss Brodie's masterful features became clear and sweet to Sandy when viewed in the curious light of the woman's folly.³⁴

Spark, as her own biographer, was alert to the dangers of 'false data [...] false premises and [...] false conclusions', stressing the need for documentary evidence and setting the 'record straight', even if she at times fell short of that herself.³⁵ She cautioned: 'In my case, the truth is often less flattering, less romantic, but often more interesting than the false story. Truth by itself is neutral and has its own dear beauty [...].'³⁶ The narrative voice in *The Prime of Miss Jean Brodie* is anonymous, and stands at times as close as one might hope to get to, in Spark's terms, 'truth by itself'.³⁷ If that is the case, and if that voice is to be trusted – Spark does not offer unqualified assurances – Miss Brodie, unmediated by the gossip of the girls, is less romantic and – unlike her creator – less interesting: 'there was nothing outwardly odd about Miss Brodie'.³⁸

For example, the 'truth by itself' of the walk in the Old Town amounts to little. One Friday in March 1931 the school's central heating system broke down, and instead of sending all her pupils home, Miss Jean Brodie took a small group of girls from her class on a walk, despite the poor weather. Stated in such bland terms, it is not quite how it is recalled by readers, and that is the point. Spark reflected in her autobiography that Miss Kay at James Gillespie's School was to her 'a character in search of an author'. Miss Kay 'fell into my hands'; she 'entered my imagination' at an age when Spark enjoyed 'watching teachers' and even wrote about them.³⁹ In contrast to some critics who see Miss Brodie as the transformative presence in the lives of the girls, it is the girls – Spark as schoolgirl and in later life, writing in her family home – who create Miss Brodie. It is largely through Sandy's imaginative re-writing of *Kidnapped* as the girls walk the cobbled streets, and her association of Brodie's attitude to Girl Guides with Mussolini's Blackshirts, that important characteristics typically associated with Brodie – her literary allusions, her politics – become compelling, and the walk becomes more than simply a way to avoid a cold classroom.⁴⁰ There is arguably little evidence beyond that offered by the pupils to suggest that Brodie is more than a lonely middle-aged woman – a prime, after all, is only divisible by itself and '1'. For example, as an adult, Eunice seems not to be able to decide whether Miss Brodie was 'an Edinburgh Festival all on her own' or 'just a spinster', although, reading closely, it is clear that the carnival element was provided by the girls ('I did the splits and made her laugh, you know').⁴¹

One ought not to exaggerate this line of reasoning, of course. In the second half of the novel the narrative emphasis shifts quite dramatically, once the girls enter the senior school. Nevertheless, in the novel as a whole there is a narratological struggle – not just between Brodie and Sandy, as Randall Stevenson has noted – but between Brodie, Sandy and the narrator (or 'truth by itself').[42]

Miss Brodie is a narratological presence in the book mainly as a focal point for others who story these years and as a source of imperatives largely untested in the real world. She herself is permitted no 'interior' beyond that deduced by the girls and states truths rather than seeking them. Her claims regarding her educational philosophy are not borne out in practice.

> '[…] I follow my principles of education and give the best in my prime. The word "education" comes from the root *e* from *ex*, out, and *duco*, I lead. It means a leading out. To me education is a leading out of what is already there in the pupil's soul. To Miss Mackay it is a putting in of something that is not there, and that is not what I call education, I call it intrusion, from the Latin root prefix *in* meaning in and the stem *trudo*, I thrust. Miss Mackay's method is to thrust a lot of information into the pupil's head; mine is a leading out of knowledge, and that is true education as is proved by the root meaning.'[43]

In reality, Brodie practices an uncompromising didacticism and dogmatism regarding (a) life and (b) art which suggests an assured counter reality, tending almost to a belief in self election.[44]

> (a)
> 'It is important to recognize the years of one's prime, always remember that.'
>
> 'You little girls, when you grow up, must be on the alert to recognize your prime at whatever time of your life it may occur. You must then live it to the full.'

'You girls,' said Miss Brodie, 'must learn to cultivate an expression of composure. It is one of the best assets of a woman, an expression of composure, come foul, come fair.'

(b)
'[...] Who is the greatest Italian painter?'
  'Leonardo da Vinci, Miss Brodie.'
  'That is incorrect. The answer is Giotto, he is my favourite.'

'Art is greater than science. Art comes first, and then science.'

'Art and religion first; then philosophy; lastly science. That is the order of the great subjects of life, that's their order of importance.'[45]

In the end we agree with Miss Mackay – as does Sandy, whose daydreams are never 'led out' by her teacher – that Miss Brodie 'put ideas into your young heads'.[46]

Sandy's role is crucial here, although in contrast to Brodie's assertiveness, Sandy's contribution to the narratological struggle is to be found in her non-sequiturs, inferences and imaginative associations which drive the plot in subtle and dramatic ways. Indeed, it is often these that stand in for the absence of uncontested causal connections. Just as Spark 'sensed' romance and sex in her teacher's accounts of waltzing in long skirts, so Sandy reads sex into Brodie's accounts of her tragic romance with Hugh, and writes stories and fictional epistolary exchanges between them.[47] (Though we only have it on Brodie's authority that Hugh ever existed and doubts grow when she embroiders her old love story about him with details of her romance with Mr Lowther.)[48] Throughout the novel, it is telling how often Spark deploys suggestive rather than definitive verbs in relation to Sandy's observations and reflections. She 'feels', she 'senses', she 'thinks':

Sandy had the definite feeling that the Brodie set, not to mention Miss Brodie herself, was getting out of hand.

> In this oblique way she began to sense what went to the makings of Miss Brodie [...]
>
> She thinks she is Providence, thought Sandy, she thinks she is the God of Calvin [...] And Sandy thought, too, the woman is an unconscious Lesbian.[49]

And at times, we suspect the narrator ventriloquises Sandy. Soon after being told that 'Sandy was almost as sure as could be that the singing master was in love with Miss Brodie and that Miss Brodie was in love with the art master', the narrator takes up the theme in similarly equivocal terms: 'It was impossible to imagine Miss Brodie sleeping with Mr Lowther, it was impossible to imagine her in a sexual context at all, and yet it was impossible not to suspect that such things were so.'[50] Frequently, these thoughts and inferences have consequences: it is Sandy who deduces that Brodie's cultivation of Teddy Lloyd's relationship with Rose has sexual intent, and it is Sandy who condemns Brodie's politics on the basis of a confession of intent. Yet Spark casts doubt repeatedly on Sandy's 'logic', as the narrator juxtaposes Sandy's thoughts alongside Miss Brodie's reported speech.

It is 'plain' only to Sandy that Miss Brodie wanted Rose 'to start preparing to be Teddy Lloyd's lover'.[51] Indeed, the origins of the 'plan' are arguably in Sandy's mind: 'even if these plans were as clear to her own mind [Miss Brodie's] as they were to Sandy's, the girls were too young'.[52] When Miss Brodie later suggests to Sandy that Rose 'will be a great lover', however, Mr Lloyd is not mentioned. And yet, grounded only on this inference, 'for over a year Sandy entered into the spirit of this plan'.[53] The 'truth by itself' is more prosaic: Rose was famed for sex, but was more accurately famous for being famous about sex. There is no evidence that the petals ever fell from this Rose. And Miss Brodie's absence from Cramond was not, as Sandy infers, because 'her sexual feelings were satisfied by proxy', but because Mr Lowther had taken up with Miss Lockhart, the science teacher.[54] Rather, as Miss Brodie shares with Sandy, she deduced that Rose and Lloyd were lovers based on Sandy's own testimony ('what you tell me'), and only after this dialogue appears to conclude, 'Yes, of course, it's inevitable'. From this remark, however, Sandy concludes, 'this was not theory, Miss Brodie meant it. Sandy looked at her, and perceived that the woman was obsessed by the need for Rose to sleep with the man she herself was in love with.'[55] It is only after Sandy tells Miss Brodie 'again and again' that Lloyd's portraits were of her, that Brodie concedes that 'I am his Muse but Rose shall take my place'.[56] It is only after having heard that Sandy rather than Rose was Lloyd's lover, that Miss Brodie concedes: 'I wanted Rose for him, I admit.' In the end, even Sandy has to admit to Miss Mackay that 'you won't be able to pin [Miss Brodie] down on sex. Have you thought of politics?'.[57]

Joyce Emily's death *en route* to Spain is the cause of Miss Brodie's ultimate undoing:

> 'Did she go to fight for Franco?' said Sandy.
> 'That was the intention. I made her see sense.'

We are denied a resolution – whose intention is referred to? Politics was, both Sandy and Miss Brodie tell us, only an 'excuse' for the teacher being forced to retire early.[58] Miss Brodie long before predicted that 'As for impropriety, it could never be imputed to me except by some gross distortion on the part of a traitor'.[59]

Unlike David Lodge, it is unclear to me that Miss Brodie 'for her own devious psychological reasons, tries to create, in the manner of a romantic novelist, a love affair between Rose and Mr Lloyd'.[60] Rather, Sandy's role in this regard demands greater consideration, as does the context of her adolescence.[61] Exchanges early on between Sandy and Jenny confirm the girls' sexual inexperience and ignorance, despite their commitment to 'research' – 'piecing together clues from remembered conversations illicitly overheard, and passages from the big dictionaries':[62]

> 'Do you think Miss Brodie ever had sexual intercourse with Hugh?' said Jenny.
> 'She would have had a baby, wouldn't she?'
> 'I don't know.'[63]

These are the girls, after all, who embark on a scheme to view a statue of a naked Greek god in the Royal Museum, and with their classmates express 'a collective quiver of mirth' when taught about the physical forms of Botticelli's *Primavera*.[64]

All this begs the question of whether we ought to treat as authoritative the testimony of a girl at this age and stage when it comes to the non-affair between Rose and Mr Lloyd, particularly as Spark has already shown Sandy to be a dreamer as well as an avid and oft-times misguided seeker after truth who has a tendency to resolve unknowns in the realm of the imagination. So, a suggestive smile between Miss Brodie and Mr Lloyd transforms Miss Brodie into a 'goddess with superior understanding', and when exhaustive questioning of Jenny fails to yield sufficient details about the policewoman who investigated the Water of Leith incident, Sandy is compelled to invent for her a name (Sergeant Anne), a look, and even an accent and appropriate vocabulary.[65]

Sandy is aware of leading a 'double life' from early on; and later we are told that she listens with 'double ears'.[66] Spark herself admitted a delight in writing characters that have a 'double-edged tongue'.[67] But it is Sandy's eyes that tell us most about the distorted reality that emerges from her flights of fancy. Sandy is introduced as being 'notorious for her small, almost non-existent eyes'; tears drop from 'Sandy's pig-like eyes' when she hears of the death of Hugh Carruthers; but tellingly (given her later role as Brodie's 'spy'), when imagining Mr Lloyd having sex with his wife, Sandy must '[screw] her eyes even smaller in the effort of seeing with her mind'.[68] Sandy's perception of the sex act is a cerebral exercise, an interior imagining, not necessarily supported by fact. In a similar fashion, a premonition of Sandy's later betrayal emerges just before Monica reveals she had seen Mr Lloyd kiss Miss Brodie. Sandy's 'little eyes' look at Miss Brodie 'in a slightly smaller way' when she is forced to respond to her teacher's prompt that 'discretion is the better part of valour'.[69] Still, Sandy takes on the role of Monica's cross-examiner after the kiss, challenging what she saw while 'desperately trying to visualise the scene in the art room to goad factual Monica into describing it with due feeling.'[70] A turning point in the narrative is marked when

Monica's inquisition ends and Miss Brodie interrupts the girls, Sandy 'photographing this new Miss Brodie with her little eyes'.[71] Again, Spark is hiding in plain sight that Sandy is an unreliable witness: it is not simply that she is literally 'short sighted', but that her narrow eyes, taking in less of life as it is lived, make her more reliant on her imagination and her will when making sense of the world.[72]

Conclusion

Sandy is fascinated with 'making patterns with facts', and Spark leaves sufficient spaces between what is and what might be to give these 'patterns' the patina of history, the appearance of both truth and its opposite.[73] Spark was conscious that children were most alive to these potentialities, but in Sandy's case, these patterns are deployed with sinister effect, to address her 'pressing need to prove Miss Brodie guilty of misconduct'.[74] And yet, there is more to this. Spark, by leaving unmediated the interface between truth and fiction, fantasy and reality, makes Miss Brodie at the same point at which she is un-made (her prime), from stories, rather than histories. Further, by compromising chronology, Spark makes it impossible to distinguish Miss Brodie's past, present and future, although – knowing what happens next – we are thrown back on how and why, but without the conventional comfort of a realisable chain of cause and effect. It is in this space that Sandy – not Miss Brodie – transfigures the commonplace by the act of writing both in her youth and in later life. Reizbaum, Carruthers, and Lodge all assume that Sandy's book, *The Transfiguration of the Commonplace*, like her school-day scribblings, is about or is inspired by Brodie.[75] I argue that only insofar as youthful ideas of Miss Brodie inspired Sandy's later reflections on 'the nature of moral perception' might this be true, although, of course, we will never know.[76] In a way, that is the point: we are denied 'truth by itself'. Sandy becomes a psychologist, not a historian; a nun, not a chronicler. And in her youth, by substituting imaginative inference for causality, intent for culpability, fantasy for fact, Sandy (aided by a complicit narrator) de-historicised Jean Brodie and in the act of doing so transfigured the commonplace. *The Prime of Miss Jean Brodie* does not accord with historical analysis, hence, it is unhistorical. It also, however, places emphasis on the significance of matters beyond historical processes: in this way it is superhistorical. For these reasons, perhaps, we might conclude that Miss Brodie's prime denied her a history.

Endnotes

1 Muriel Spark, *The Prime of Miss Jean Brodie* [1961] (London: Penguin, 2000), p. 13.
2 Ibid., p. 65.
3 Spark, *Prime of Miss Jean Brodie*, pp. 28–29, p. 37; Muriel Spark, 'How I Became a Novelist', in *Books and Bookmen* 7.2 (November 1961), p. 9; Muriel Spark, 'Edinburgh-born', in *New Statesman* 64, 10 August 1962, reprinted in *Critical Essays on Muriel Spark*, ed. Joseph Hynes (New York, NY: G. K. Hall, 1992), pp. 21–23 (p. 22).
4 Martin Stannard, *Muriel Spark: The Biography* (London: Weidenfeld and Nicolson, 2009), p. 325.
5 David Lodge, 'The Uses and Abuses of Omniscience: Method and Meaning in Muriel Spark's *The Prime of Miss Jean Brodie*' in *Critical Essays on Muriel Spark*, ed. Joseph Hynes, pp. 151–73 (p. 157).
6 Alan Bold, *Muriel Spark* (London: Methuen, 1986), p. 64; Trevor Royle, 'Spark and Scotland', in *Muriel Spark: An Odd Capacity for Vision*, ed. Alan Bold (London: Vision Press, 1984), pp. 147–66.
7 Spark, *Prime of Miss Jean Brodie*, p. 6.
8 Ibid., pp. 45–46.
9 Ibid., p. 83.
10 Philip E. Ray, 'Jean Brodie and Edinburgh: Personality and place in Muriel Spark's *The Prime of Miss Jean Brodie*', in *Studies in Scottish Literature* 13.1 (1978), pp. 24–31 (p. 24); Royle, 'Spark and Scotland', p. 154.
11 Muriel Spark, MS, the Muriel Spark papers 1957–88, Department of Special Collections & University Archives Repository, McFarlin Library, University of Tulsa (UT), 1983.003.59.1.
12 Third Statistical Account of Scotland, *City of Edinburgh* (Glasgow: Collins, 1966), p. 99.
13 GB Historical GIS / University of Portsmouth, Edinburgh City through time | Population Statistics | Males and Females, *A Vision of Britain through Time*. www.visionofbritain.org.uk [accessed 21 June 2019].
14 Third Statistical Account of Scotland, *City of Edinburgh*, p. 97.
15 Spark, *Prime of Miss Jean Brodie*, p. 26; p. 42.
16 Third Statistical Account of Scotland, *City of Edinburgh*, pp. 468–69.
17 Ibid., p. 531.
18 Ibid., p. 173.
19 Muriel Spark, MS, UT, 1983.003.1.59. Muriel Spark mapped the chapters of *The Prime of Miss Jean Brodie* against a contemporary historical timeline, detailing key historical events, e.g. the abdication crisis.
20 G. Ward-Smith, 'Baldwin and Scotland: more than Englishness', in *Contemporary British History* 15.1 (2001), pp. 61–82; *Prime of Miss Jean Brodie*, p. 10; p. 45.
21 Gavin Bowd, *Fascist Scotland: Caledonia and the Far Right* (Edinburgh: Birlinn, 2013), p. 81.
22 Ibid., p. 97.

23 Catriona M. M. Macdonald, 'Andrew Dewar Gibb', in *Scottish National Party Leaders*, eds. James Mitchell and Gerry Hassan (London: Biteback, 2016), pp. 105–26.
24 Alan Taylor, 'The Prime of Miss Jean Brodie', in *Scottish Review of Books* 13.1 (2018), pp. 10–11. See also Alasdair Roberts, *Crème de la Crème: Girls' Schools of Edinburgh* (London: Steve Savage, 2007); Stannard, *Muriel Spark*, pp. 23–35.
25 Roberts, *Crème de la Crème*, p. 13.
26 This seems to be ignored in Judy Suh's essay, 'The familiar attractions of Fascism in Muriel Spark's *The Prime of Miss Jean Brodie*', in *Journal of Modern Literature* 30.2 (2007), pp. 86–102.
27 Royle, 'Spark and Scotland', p. 155.
28 Muriel Spark, *Curriculum Vitae: A Volume of Autobiography* (London: Constable & Co., 1992), p. 56.
29 Spark, *Prime of Miss Jean Brodie*, p. 33.
30 Gerard Carruthers, '"Fully to Savour Her Position": Muriel Spark and Scottish Identity' in *Hidden Possibilities: Essays in Honor of Muriel Spark*, ed. Robert E. Hosmer Jr. (Notre Dame: University of Notre Dame, 2014), pp. 86–106 (p. 104).
31 Marilyn Reizbaum, 'The Stranger Spark', in *The Edinburgh Companion to Muriel Spark*, eds. Michael Gardiner and Willy Maley (Edinburgh: Edinburgh University Press, 2010), pp. 40–51 (pp. 41–42).
32 Spark, *Prime of Miss Jean Brodie*, p. 56; p. 60.
33 See Andrew Caink, 'Experiencing meanings in Spark's *The Prime of Miss Jean Brodie*', in *Journal of Literary Semantics* 41.2 (2012), pp. 121–38.
34 Spark, *Prime of Miss Jean Brodie*, p. 11; p. 53; p. 111. See also Stannard, *Muriel Spark*, p. 32.
35 Spark, *Curriculum Vitae*, pp. 11–12. See also A. Kirkwood, 'Muriel Spark as auto-biographer in *Curriculum Vitae*', in *Groundings* 1 (2007), pp. 1–12 (p. 5). Here, Spark's reliance on memory is emphasised.
36 Spark, *Curriculum Vitae*, pp. 11–12. In an interview with Philip Toynbee in 1971, Spark admitted that in her early writing career she considered fiction 'an inferior form'. 'Muriel Spark Limited Edition', *Observer* Colour Supplement, 7 November 1971 (Box 60, Spark Archive, McFarlin Library, Tulsa).
37 Colin McIlroy encourages a clear distinction between Spark and the narrator in *The Prime of Miss Jean Brodie*: see Colin McIlroy, 'The denial of the self: the romantic imagination and the problem of belief in Muriel Spark's *The Prime of Miss Jean Brodie* (1961)' (unpublished master's thesis, University of Glasgow, 2011), pp. 69–70. In similar fashion, Reizbaum notes more generally that 'Spark's narrative voices […] always seem anonymous' in Reizbaum, 'The Stranger Spark', p. 41.
38 Ibid., p. 43.
39 Spark, *Curriculum Vitae*, pp. 56–57.
40 Spark, *Prime of Miss Jean Brodie*, pp. 28–30; pp. 21–32.
41 Ibid., p. 27.
42 Randall Stevenson, 'The Postwar Contexts of Spark's Writing', in *The Edinburgh Companion to Muriel Spark*, eds. Michael Gardiner and Willy Maley, pp. 98–109.
43 Spark, *Prime of Miss Jean Brodie*, p. 36.
44 McIlroy, 'The denial of the self', p. 14.
45 Spark, *Prime of Miss Jean Brodie*, p. 10; p. 22; p. 63; p. 11; p. 25.

46 Ibid., p. 124.
47 Spark, *Curriculum Vitae*, p. 62.
48 Spark, *Prime of Miss Jean Brodie*, pp. 71–72.
49 Ibid., p. 102; p. 109; p. 120.
50 Ibid., p. 61.
51 Bower is mistaken in suggesting that 'The fantasies [...] occur only during the time the girls are in the junior division – 1930-32': See Anne Bower, 'The Narrative Structure of Muriel Spark's *The Prime of Miss Jean Brodie*', in *Midwest Quarterly* 31.4 (1990), pp. 488–98 (p. 494).
52 Spark, *Prime of Miss Jean Brodie*, p. 109.
53 Ibid., p. 110.
54 Ibid., p. 113.
55 Ibid., p. 119.
56 Ibid., p. 120.
57 Ibid., p. 124.
58 Ibid., p. 121; p. 126. Lodge refers to the ultimate allegation of fascism as merely an 'expedient' in Lodge, 'The Uses and Abuses of Omniscience', p. 164.
59 Ibid., p. 39.
60 Lodge, 'The Uses and Abuses of Omniscience', p. 163.
61 Stannard notes that '*Brodie* is, as much as anything, a book about female adolescence'. See Stannard, *Muriel Spark*, p. 34.
62 Spark, *Prime of Miss Jean Brodie*, p. 17.
63 Ibid., p. 19.
64 Ibid., p. 20; p. 49.
65 Ibid., p. 50; p. 68.
66 Ibid., p. 21; p. 72.
67 Spark, 'How I Became a Novelist', p. 9.
68 Spark, *Prime of Miss Jean Brodie*, p. 7; p. 13; p. 17.
69 Ibid., p. 46.
70 Ibid., p. 52.
71 Ibid., p. 53.
72 Ibid., p. 107.
73 Ibid., p. 72.
74 In her autobiography, Spark notes that 'children are quick to perceive possibilities, potentialities: in a remark, perhaps in some remote context; in a glance, a smile' in Spark, *Curriculum Vitae*, p. 57; Spark, *Prime of Miss Jean Brodie*, p. 72.
75 Reizbaum, 'The Stranger Spark', pp. 44–45; Gerard Carruthers, 'Muriel Spark as Catholic Novelist', in *The Edinburgh Companion to Muriel Spark*, eds. Michael Gardiner and Willy Maley, pp. 74–84 (p. 81); Lodge, 'The Uses and Abuses of Omniscience', p. 161. The concluding lines of the novel only claim that Miss Brodie 'in her prime' inspired Sandy's 'school days', not her book, in *Prime of Miss Jean Brodie*, p. 127.
76 Spark, *Prime of Miss Jean Brodie*, p. 35. See also Gerard Carruthers, 'The Remarkable Fictions of Muriel Spark', in *A History of Scottish Women's Writing*, eds. Douglas Gifford and Dorothy McMillan (Edinburgh: Edinburgh University Press, 1997), pp. 514–25 (p. 519).

9. Muriel Spark and the 'Hired Grammarians'

HELEN STODDART

On 10 November 1961 John Updike wrote to Muriel Spark, both to thank her for the signed copy of *The Prime of Miss Jean Brodie* (1961) which she had gifted him ('It is a grand book, of course') and to attempt to establish a writerly *esprit de corps* via some humorous sniping about the *New Yorker*'s priggish editing practices.[1] The October edition of the magazine had showcased Spark's most recent novel in full (albeit in a shorter version of 40,000 words) and this had been preceded in the September edition by an enthusiastic review[2] by Updike who, now furnished with both this and Lippincott's first edition of the novel, was well-placed to observe the extensive range of omissions, alterations and translations into American English which characterise the relationship between the two versions of the text.[3] Since then, these differences have either been overlooked or dismissed as minor and negligible[4] – a matter of trimming to fit the exigencies of the magazine's limited space as well as accommodations for the American reader – but Updike's letter is intriguing for the way it perceives other more substantial issues at stake in the editing of Spark's original manuscript. While he concedes that the novel was not ruined by the process ('nothing really crippling or disastrous'), he is amused by the 'prudery that led them to cut the thingummyjig, Mr Lowther's stoppage, and the entire indecent exposure episode with Jenny and the consequent fantasy of Sergeant Anne Grey' and wonders why they removed Brodie's letter to Gordon Lowther, supposing that the excision of these episodes was the product of a pre-war prudery that stymied a more enlightened editorial outlook ('they were not quite willing to face up to the extent to which the story is about sex'). He is equally struck, however, by the 'most annoying' formal and stylistic 'fiddling' with Spark's paragraphing and style ('their relentless sprinkling of commas and "clarifying" dashes') which he satirically (but erroneously) characterises as the 'timid and stupid pedantry' of a bunch of 'hired grammarians' of 'extreme venerability' who are 'all called Miss Gaunt and have been with the magazine since 1925'.[5] The evidence of both these editorial tendencies – towards sexual censorship and a re-shaping of Spark's literary voice through commas and dashes – is less interesting for what it may reveal about the *New Yorker*'s editorial culture than for the way it throws into relief Spark's determined forging of a distinctive and unfamiliar literary aesthetic. An analysis of the previously unexamined yellow manuscript, received from Spark and worked on at the *New Yorker*, however, reveals a much more complex story about the history of the novel's progress at the magazine and challenges many of the suppositions made by Updike about Spark's role in generating the relative 'prudery' of the magazine version of the text.[6]

In fact, Spark's editor at the *New Yorker* was Rachel MacKenzie who took up her post there in 1956, aged 47, after a career as an academic. She first made contact with Spark on 28 March 1957 following a recommendation from Hamish Hamilton. Editorial copy of *Brodie*, typed on distinctive yellow pages and now part of the Spark Archive at Tulsa University, reveals that MacKenzie herself carried out most of the smaller editorial changes, though the manuscript had clearly been cut significantly before she began her work on it. The changes were accepted by Spark for the purposes of this prestigious publication event, but none made their way into the first (and final) edition of the novel which was already primed for immediate publication by Macmillan (and Lippincott in the USA) once the magazine version hit the racks – the *New Yorker* enforced a contractual obligation stipulating that its fiction must not have appeared elsewhere already. Despite the fact that, following MacKenzie's initial contact in 1957, Spark submitted several stories for publication (starting with 'The Ormolu Clock' in 1960), all were rejected, albeit with strongly encouraging words.[7] On receipt of the Brodie manuscript, however, the telegrammed response was unequivocal: 'THE PRIME OF MISS JEAN BRODIE IS MARVELOUS AND WE WANT IT IF MRS SPARK WILL CONSIDER SOME MODEST CUTTING'.[8] Spark had received excellent reviews for her first five novels – especially *The Comforters* (1957), *Memento Mori* (1959) and *The Ballad of Peckham Rye* (1960) – and had forged a strong critical reputation in the United Kingdom, but sales of her books remained disappointing and she was still awaiting an American breakthrough on both of these fronts. MacKenzie's offer, accompanied as it was by a payment of six thousand dollars and followed by a long-term 'first-reading' agreement with the magazine giving Spark a regular income for many years afterwards, must have announced itself as exhilarating and irresistible. It meant that finally Spark would be able to focus on making a living as a novelist, no longer reliant on book editing and other distractions.

Yet the evidence of Spark's career reveals the extent to which this request for cutting must have felt like a Faustian pact: the relinquishing of one power (complete autonomy over her literary discourse) in return for commercial success and the financial independence she had longed for as the magazine's 500,000 distribution promised an opening in the American market (and beyond) for her novels. Spark remains notorious for her claims that she didn't 'correct or re-write' her work[9] and for the most part she made a career of guarding against editorial meddling, though the archives at Tulsa which contain her hand- and type-written manuscripts contain much evidence of revision and correction as she worked, albeit on a relatively small scale. Still, editing and correction was not a role she liked to hand over to others. Martin Stannard claims that one of the reasons her archive is 'littered with disputes' is that she 'refused to concede to anyone the power to intimidate and correct her'.[10] He quotes Spark as lamenting: 'I'm paralysed as a writer unless I write according to this queer dictatorial sense that I have' and she said of *Brodie* in particular that 'I had it all in my mind [...] I put it down as if I had dreamed the book'.[11] It appears to have been a diktat to which she subjected not only herself but also others. Stannard reports an injunction issued to Alan Maclean, her editor at Macmillan, not to 'alter the punctuation' in the novel (*The Comforters*) which she insists is 'intentionally unorthodox' and requesting the re-instatement of passages removed on the grounds of 'mild indecency'.[12] A galley print of *Doctors of Philosophy* (1962) which had been returned from the printers for checking shows Spark taking great care over the composition of a curt note requesting an end to their stylistic interference[13] and confirms the sense that her submission to the editorial requests for the Brodie manuscript must have been a painful concessionary trade-off rather than a relaxing of authority. Publication in the magazine required a temporary relinquishment of authority on the one hand but it simultaneously laid the ground for the flourishing of Spark's writerly reputation and confidence such that she would soon be able to rebuff further attempts to subject her to moral and grammatical rules of convention.[14]

Despite Updike's sexist inference about narrow-minded and obsessive spinsters it was, according to Stannard, MacKenzie's editor-in-chief, William Shawn, who was the source of the magazine's fusty reputation as 'a grand institution' which, despite its commitment to publish and reflect upon the best of contemporary writing, was 'something like a church or an Ivy League college, with its own lore, clergy and faculty'.[15] His editorial style was known to be punctilious and insistent: 'Myth has it that, meticulous to the point of obsession, he once traced a writer to the jungle in order to request permission to alter a comma.'[16] Certainly MacKenzie appears to have been loyal to this meticulous culture, though there is no evidence that she was in communication with Spark over the revisions in order to obtain permission to the extent that the anecdote above suggests. Neither does her commitment to scrutinise and revise the presence and/or absence of every separator and terminator in Spark's manuscript necessarily amount to a consistent or entirely systematic editing programme. The changes, however, can be divided into five categories, three of which will form the focus of this argument. The first two are the correction of typos and the fairly straightforward translation from British to American English spelling and preferences ('recognize' for 'recognise', 'gray' for 'grey', 'favorite' for 'favourite', 'learned' for 'learnt', 'Mr.' for 'Mr' and so on) which do not demand scrutiny. Third is the revision of punctuation which mainly consists of adding and subtracting commas but which at times also extends to substituting more emphatic separators such as dashes or semi-colons for commas and occasionally to shortening sentences with full-stops (the first category bleeds into the second through the North American preference for the Oxford comma which is implemented throughout). Fourth is the alteration of Spark's distinctive spacing throughout the text to mark important narrative shifts or breaks and fifth is the excision of text, often resulting in a shortening of paragraphs or sentences by removing details that are included elsewhere thought to be either insignificant or of obscure significance to American readers, but which at times extends to the removal of sizeable episodes within the text. As the new evidence of the yellow manuscript indicates, however, Spark was, at the very least, involved in the selection of these lost episodes. Thus, the *New Yorker* manuscript is much more extensively edited than previously acknowledged, but what is it that was being amended and what was the 'grammar' that Spark sought so continuously to establish and defend throughout her career?

Separation Anxiety

As Updike notes with amusement, there is barely a paragraph in Spark's yellow *New Yorker* manuscript that has not been edited for punctuation. Occasionally commas are removed, but overwhelmingly they are added throughout the text in a manner that continually, if not consistently, alters the narrative's rhythms, emphases and even signification. This is the most insistent, if not dramatic, difference in the *New Yorker* edition. According to *Cassell's Guide to Punctuation* 'punctuation in the past was much heavier than it is today and […] personal computers have encouraged changes in punctuation preferences over the last quarter of a century', a change which is coupled with a greater use of shorter, more direct sentences.[17] Clearly in 1961 Spark's was not a style being shaped by computer technology, yet the comment is relevant here both for the way that it suggests Spark is writing in a style that is more in tune with the direction of the prose fiction which dominates the second half of the twentieth century (more direct, less parenthetical), but also for the inadvertent suggestion made about the connection between heavy use of punctuation and a certain weightiness about the prose thus punctuated. For the function of additional punctuation may not only be to clarify, re-balance or re-orientate the meaning of a sentence; in doing so it may also stabilise and lend fixity to a sequence of words which are thus denied a more pliable quickness, energy or ambiguity. Spark often referred to the value of her first vocation as a poet in shaping the economy of her prose style.[18] It has almost become a critical commonplace to refer to the 'brevity'[19] and 'wit' of her prose style using adjectives such as 'economic',[20] 'minimalist',[21] 'sparkling',[22] 'tight',[23] 'light', 'sparse',[24] 'slim', 'firm',[25] 'precise' to identify a recognisably 'Sparkian' discourse on the basis of these ongoing characteristics in her work which all derive from or relate to an aesthetic of combined lightness and precision; it is writing that is powerful precisely for what it appears to have shed or done without. It startles, amuses and unsettles because of its apparent exactitude and is, therefore, a prose style that resonates more for the poise, balance and angles of its composition than the accumulation of detail or force of feeling captured within it. There is also a clear connection between this spare aesthetic and Spark's characteristic economy of humour. As Freud is careful to stress, humour depends on the sense of 'elevation' from raw worldly trauma to be truly itself (as opposed to comedy and jokes), indeed it repudiates reality by diminishing its force, therefore humorous fiction often hinges on a non-naturalistic twist.[26] More than any other fictional mode, humour depends on maintaining a careful balance – between what is said and only inferred, in the construction of a non-sequitur – and in resisting fixity. Both elements of this fragile economy may be thrown off course by the introduction or addition of punctuation which inevitably adds weight, shifts the balance and emphasis of a sentence and alters the tone, syntax or idiom of a purposefully stylised speaker when it occurs within direct speech. Spark's anxiety about interference with her sometimes unconventional punctuation (in this case through the addition of so many commas throughout the text) surely relate to their potential to act as an additional drag on the agility and tone of the development of her distinctive prose style.

There are indeed many examples of additional and more emphatic punctuation from the yellow manuscript which alter the style of the *New Yorker* text without appearing to clarify or sharpen the force or clarity of the prose. MacKenzie appears to embark on a battle of ownership for the manuscript, staking her claim with each newly planted or weeded comma. Occasionally she removes a comma to increase the flow of the prose, for example in Chapter 1 'but Sandy and Jenny got ink on their blouses at discreet intervals of four weeks, so that they could go and have their arms held by Miss Lockhart' (p. 24)[27] becomes 'but Sandy and Jenny got ink on their blouses at discreet intervals of four weeks so that they could go and have their arms held by Miss Lockhart' (pp. 017–18, YMS). Overwhelmingly, however, commas are added to the text, very often through MacKenzie's strict application of the rule that conjunctions such as 'and' must always be preceded by a comma even where the meaning as a whole is sometimes thrown off balance by the addition. In the next sentence two commas create an unnecessary, indeed slightly confusing, parenthesis describing Miss Lockhart. So, 'This long room was her natural setting and she had lost something of her quality when Sandy saw her walking from the school in her box-pleat tweeds over to her sports car like an ordinary teacher' (p. 24), becomes 'This long room was her natural setting, and she had lost something of her quality when Sandy saw her walking from the school in her box-pleat tweeds over to her sports car, like an ordinary teacher' (p. 018, YMS). The swift flow between strangely incongruous associations (fashionable tweeds, racy car and ordinariness), made sense of by the fact that the narrative has already indicated that Sandy's romantic vision of Lockhart dressed in a 'white overall' and surrounded by 'six inches of pure air' in the science room has now become disenchanted. The *New Yorker* interrupts the flow of Sandy's associations as the commas separate off Lockhart's actions from Sandy's humorously odd characterisation of her. The effect is an attempt to impose order and sense on a sentence conceived through the lens of a peculiar adolescent logic which has been warped through lost desire by somehow connecting 'her natural setting' around the parenthesis to 'like an ordinary teacher' in a way that does not now make sense. In another example, 'Sandy said, then "Mr Lloyd had a baby last week. He must have committed sex with his wife." This idea was easier to cope with and they laughed screamingly into their pink paper napkins' (p. 17) becomes 'Sandy said, then, "Mr. Lloyd had a baby last week. He must have committed sex with his wife." This idea was easier to cope with, and they laughed screamingly into their pink paper napkins' (p. 04, YMS). Here the sense of girlish hysteria is weakened by the orderly comma which introduces a more sober pace to the third-person narrative voice and marks a separation between spoken dialogue and narrative voice which Spark works hard to de-stabilise in the novel so that Brodie is not simply present as an isolated comic object or character in the narrative, but is the touchstone for a pervasive, highly flawed and complex shaping (or rather perversion) of youthful female desire, evidence of which is found throughout the third-person narration.

But even where Spark follows the conjunction rule, the impact of additional commas on Spark's brisk prose can be deadening. For example: 'Mary Macgregor, lumpy, with merely two eyes, a nose and a mouth like a snowman, who was later famous for being stupid and always to blame and who, at the age of twenty-three, lost her life in a hotel fire, ventured, "Golden"' has three additional commas in the *New Yorker*: 'Mary Macgregor, lumpy, with merely two eyes, a nose, and a mouth, like a snowman, who was later famous for being stupid and always to blame, and who, at the age of twenty-three, lost her life in a hotel fire, ventured, "Golden"' (p. 18, YMS). Further on, towards the end of Chapter 4, a discussion between Brodie and Jenny about the fact that Mr Lloyd has singled out the 'Brodie set' to invite to his studio is seized upon by Brodie: '"It is because you are mine," said Miss Brodie. "I mean of my stamp and cut, and I am in my prime."' (p. 97). In the *New Yorker* edition the second sentence becomes: '"I mean, of my stamp and cut, and I am in my prime."' Although the comma before a conjunction rule is followed here, the additional clutter of a comma after 'mean' significantly detracts from the brittle and direct force of Brodie's tone and logic: its certainty and ruthlessness.

Elsewhere in examples of shorter sentences the effect is sometimes more dramatic. In Chapter 3 the proleptic leap to Sandy's visit to a sixty-five-year-old Brodie in the last year of her life changes from 'This was her last year in the world and in another sense it was Sandy's' (p. 56), to 'This was her last year in the world, and, in another sense, it was Sandy's' (p. 0006, YMS). Here the additional separators slow down the pace and make the sentence seem more ponderous than it need be, almost over-egging the poignancy of the contrasting yet strangely parallel momentum of their relationships to worldliness. It also lends a sense of ending to a sentence that, although it belongs to the end of the story, has been purposefully shifted to the middle of the plot to provide an enigmatic narrative spike, an effect which is weakened by the way the commas slow the sentence down. To illustrate the impact of the application of this rule consistently in Spark's discourse, imagine what would happen to one of Spark's famously brutal short sentences from 'The Portobello Road': 'He looked as if he would murder me and he did' (p. 520).[28] Under Mackenzie's hand this would have become: 'He looked as if he would murder me, and he did'. The pace slower, the tone more thoughtful, it moves from indicating an irrevocable, pre-emptive and fatal logic (between looking, murder and the inevitable fact of her death) to an almost reflective separation of his murderous look from his (not necessarily inevitable) act of murder. Yet the concept of a world determined by inescapable predeterminations (above all death) is one that underwrites not only 'The Portobello Road' and *Brodie* but Spark's body of work as a whole; thus, Spark's widespread avoidance of separating punctuation may fall foul of strict 'grammarian' practice, but it does so in the service not only of a more agile and 'sparkling' aesthetic, but also an understanding of human lives underwritten by unfathomable predeterminations.

As the example of Sandy's view of Miss Lockhart above demonstrates, the absence of commas also functions at times to speed connections past the reader, the logic of which does not bear rational scrutiny. For example, in Chapter 1 Spark's text has: 'Sandy looked at it with her tiny eyes which it was astonishing that anyone could trust' (p. 100), whereas the *New Yorker* has: 'Sandy looked at it with her tiny eyes, which it was astonishing that anyone could trust' (p. 0056). Clearly the prejudicial association between facial characteristics and ethical confidence is a vehicle here for the text's sharp irony, of which there are many other examples throughout; the ironic humour is delivered with a swift, cold edge in Spark's which the *New Yorker* is missing as it works to separate out material observation from interpretation, as though it were the work of considered reflection rather than unquestionable and cruel fate. As well as the difference of punctuation, the *New Yorker* edition also reduces the impact of this line by changing the spacing around it. The following line, which starts a new paragraph ('The portrait was like Miss Brodie') is brought up into the preceding paragraph in a way that inevitably drains some of the discomfort and impact from the statement about Sandy by extending the paragraph back round to an observation about Miss Brodie's relationship to the painting. In another example, 'If the authorities wanted to get rid of her she would have to be assassinated' becomes, 'If the authorities wanted to get rid of her, she would have to be assassinated' (p. 10, YMS): again the comma in the *New Yorker* edition lends the content of the sentence a respectability – a sense of having been contemplated and narrated by a thoughtful if questionable overview – whereas Spark's narrative voice in *Brodie* is characteristically given to such bursts of quick, bright absurdity which reflect Brodie's warped thinking as well as the young minds she has bent towards it.

It is at points such as this that Brodie's characteristic idiom – of colourful, compelling and breathless instructions which mask a sinister and manipulative logic – leaks into, or rather mirrors, the text's third-person narrative voice. But even this voice, which is so famous for its pronouncements, is less present through direct rather than reported speech (within the third-person narration or in the girls' imagination and reportage), and is weighed down by the addition of commas. So 'If only you small girls would listen to me I would make of you the crème de la crème' (p. 14) becomes 'If only you small girls would listen to me, I would make of you the crème de la crème' (YMS, p. 18); 'But in this your last year with me you will receive the fruits of my prime' (p. 47) becomes 'But in this, your last year with me, you will receive the fruits of my prime' (YMS, p. 00011); 'That is the truth and there is no more to say' (p. 60) becomes 'That is the truth, and there is no more to say' (p. 000014, YMS); 'Cleopatra knew nothing of the team spirit if you read your Shakespeare' (p. 78) becomes 'Cleopatra knew nothing of the team spirit, if you read your Shakespeare' (p. 000017, YMS); 'I shall remain at this education factory where my duty lies' (p. 112) becomes 'I shall remain at this education factory, where my duty lies' (p. 0000073, YMS); 'I am his Muse but Rose shall take my place' (p. 120) becomes 'I am his Muse, but Rose shall take my place' (p. 181, YMS). Each of these examples shows how MacKenzie's impulse to follow proper conventions of punctuation by observing pauses and shifts in syntax which might normally be marked within a narrative voice are applied to Brodie's speaking voice in a way that modifies it, albeit gently, by reducing the sense of brittle certainty and sharp dictatorial style. In Brodie's own terms, the commas introduce a 'lump' to the 'leaven', though the 'leaven' (which refers to Sandy in this case), is shown to be a mysterious and treacherous thing indeed.

The tone and syntax are not only altered by the addition of commas. Elsewhere pauses become more emphatic as they are upgraded to dashes or full stops. For example: 'Take Helen of Troy. And the Queen of England, it is true she attends international sport, but she has to, it is all empty show, she is concerned only with the King's health and antiques' (p. 78) becomes 'Take Helen of Troy. And the Queen of England. It is true she attends international sport, but she has to – it is all empty show. She is concerned only with the King's health and antiques' (p. 0000017, YMS). Here the addition of full stops for two of the commas again introduces a grammatical formality to sentences that in the original are dominated by Brodie's characteristic voice with all its attendant drama and questionable reasoning.

Cutting the 'thingummyjig'

As Updike observes, the *New Yorker* edition of the novel is not only punctuated very differently, but is also without several significant passages from the original which concern sex, most notably the lengthy episode in Chapter 3, 'Towards the end of the Easter holidays […] and the fact that she had told her class first thing' (pp. 66–70) and 'What about […] was very thrilling' (p. 72) in which a man exposes himself to Jenny at the Water of Leith. Jenny's discussion of this with Sandy, and her subsequent interview with the policewoman, Anne Grey, is thus also removed. Having cut out this episode, all further references to it have been excised, and with this goes the important idea of Sandy and Jenny now sharing for the first time a sexual secret, an episode which then sets up the possibility of Sandy's further sexual secret from Brodie: her sleeping with Mr Lloyd. But beyond this, Sandy and Jenny's fictional letter from Brodie to Mr Lowther ('The last letter in the series […] With fondest joy, Jean Brodie', pp. 73–74) is also missing from the *New Yorker*, as are several much shorter, paragraph-length (or less) sections: for example, 'For the war-time romance of her life […] would get Monica Douglas into trouble' (p. 53) which relates Monica's witnessing of Brodie and Mr Lloyd's art room kiss to the girls' incredulity about a younger pre-war Brodie, 'hardly flesh and blood'; Jenny and Sandy's discussion about Mr Lowther's short legs around Miss Brodie ('When she was well out of the way […] with a housekeeper', p. 59) and a reference to the Silver Jubilee which is mixed in with a discussion between Brodie and Rose about her sitting for Mr Lloyd and Sandy's visit to this studio ('In the summer of nineteen-thirty-five [...] said Miss Brodie', p. 105). In fact, the reference to 'Mr Lowther's stoppage' is a very brief one (three lines of dialogue), as is the reference to the 'thingummyjig' (p. 20) on the naked statue in the art gallery (two lines). Yet not all the cuts indicate a bodily or sexually censorious inclination. The final section of Chapter 2 (from 'A very long queue of men lined this part of the street', pp. 39–41) which describes a dole queue of men and depicts the unsettling effects of the depression on the girls is absent, as is the account of Brodie's social group and their activities ('They went to lectures [...] holidays at North Berwick', pp. 42–43), Sandy's Pavlova fantasy ('Pavlova nodded sagely [...] will carry on the torch', p. 63), a passage about the diminishing impact of the novelty of the girls' experience of the 'Modern' and 'Classical' 'sides' ('A few weeks later [...] in passing on the wireless', p. 76), Brodie wondering with Sandy whether it was Mary who betrayed her ('And Miss Brodie [...] should have been kinder to Mary', p. 77), a passage about several of the girls' academic progress ('Even Monica Douglas [...] for her chemistry notes', pp. 82–83), a reference to Sandy's lack of understanding of social class ('She did not at the time [...] social class at all' p. 108), a comment on the school houses ('Nominally [...] For their own part and [...]', pp. 111–12), and the Brodie set's rejection of Joyce Emily ('but they [...] discredit Miss Brodie', p. 117). What is so startling about MacKenzie's editorial work in the yellow manuscript, however, is that the most significant of her cuts, certainly the ones which are most overtly sexual, had already been made before MacKenzie started her work. Whereas she has clearly crossed out some of the passages identified above for removal (Mr Lowther's 'stoppage', which would have required glossing for a North American readership, the Silver Jubilee, about the classical and the modern, the possibility of Mary Macgregor's having betrayed Miss Brodie, the girls' relative academic progress, the school houses, Miss Brodie's social circle), others (most notably the exposure episode, the girls' inability to imagine a 'flesh and blood' Brodie, Mr Lowther's legs around Miss Brodie, Jenny and Sandy's imagined letter from Brodie to Mr Lowther and the reference to the 'thingummyjig') are simply missing from the yellow manuscript she edited. This evidence throws a very different light on Updike's comments and begs a number of new questions, not only about Spark's relationship with the *New Yorker*, but also about her sense of her own writing – its perception by the wider reading public (especially a North American one) and its own internal priorities.

The process through which these cuts was decided upon, however, is not clear. What is the provenance of the yellow manuscript? Following on from this, do the omissions in this manuscript represent Spark's decisions about what should be removed from the narrative, or was she directed towards certain cuts on advice from MacKenzie? The yellow manuscript itself provides some evidence to help address these questions. The name and address of her literary agent's firm (Christy & Moore Ltd. of 52 Floral Street, Covent Garden) is typed on the title page and a comparison of the typeface used in the yellow manuscript and Spark's typescript for the first edition reveals differences and confirms that it was typed on a different machine; it also uses a completely different page numbering style.[29] The yellow manuscript, therefore, must have been produced for Spark through John Smith, her agent at Christie & Moore, and the dominance of British spelling and presentation conventions in the yellow manuscript confirms this, as well as the presence of many more typos than are characteristically present in Spark's own typewritten scripts. Unfortunately, despite Spark's conscientiousness about keeping correspondence, there is nothing in the Tulsa or Edinburgh archives which would explain the processes and conversations that shaped this manuscript. Did MacKenzie recommend or specify the longer cuts that are evident here? Or did she simply ask Spark to produce a shorter version of the novel to fit into the space available in the *New Yorker* and leave it up to her to decide which episodes should go? Did Smith, as her literary agent, play any role in this process? As evidence from the Edinburgh archive shows, he was certainly involved in relaying information from MacKenzie to Spark, but there is no suggestion that he was informed or consulted about the cuts.[30] For her part MacKenzie was clearly keen to establish a more personal relationship with Spark and wrote to her directly; this correspondence shows that she was very keen to obtain Spark's approval for the style and content of the new version of the text.[31] MacKenzie went on to carry out many further cuts (several of which are listed above), but the final version of the text was sent to Spark for rapid approval ahead of publication and was not met with objections or suggestions for alternative changes. Two things are clear: MacKenzie's cuts do not appear to be driven by any overt or covert puritanical agenda; they encompass a variety of subject matter and are mainly driven by a desire to trim away certain kinds of contextual information rather than censor entire episodes; the excision of the sexual episodes identified by Updike and confirmed above had already taken place since they are clearly absent from the yellow manuscript which means that Spark must have played a central role, if not the sole role, in their identification and removal. Any explanation of the rationale for the removal of these passages must remain speculative since there is no correspondence that would illuminate Spark's thinking about her textual priorities. They do not simply represent clearly freestanding episodes which could be cut without harming the central Sandy/Brodie plot because although the exposure episode, and Jenny and Sandy's letter arguably fall into this category, the short lines about Mr Lowther's legs around Brodie and the 'thingummyjig' do not and these constitute the most physical and sexual, if somewhat comical, references in the novel. Perhaps in removing them Spark was simply second-guessing MacKenzie's preferences on the basis of her knowledge of the *New Yorker*'s old school reputation under William Shawn, a reputation which Updike's letter certainly confirms must have been widespread amongst its contributors. Or perhaps the cuts represent an assumption of more widespread cultural prudery which Spark was projecting onto her North American readership. Yet, there is no evidence that any specific directions came from the *New Yorker* to downplay or remove the sexual content of the novel and MacKenzie's further excisions from the yellow manuscript, as the list above demonstrates, show no inclination to further edit this aspect of the novel, focusing instead on removing personal, cultural and historical material of a contextual nature, some of the detail of which MacKenzie may have judged either less crucial to the plot or less interesting to a North American readership. The evidence of this yellow manuscript, however, strongly indicates that Spark, despite her emerging reputation for rebuffing editor's attempts to direct or dictate to her about the shape and style of her work, appears to have either colluded in or initiated a set of excisions, several of which speak of a sensitivity about the novel's direct and humorous approach to the early sexual imaginings of the girls of Marcia Blaine School for Girls. There is no further correspondence in either the Tulsa or Edinburgh archive to indicate how or whether Spark explained any of this to Updike, but it does suggest that Spark's response to reading his mischievous letter of congratulations, with its haughty joke about the spinsters who missed the point of the novel, may not have been received with the sense of mutual self-congratulation he must have anticipated.

Conclusion

Close analysis of the relationship between the first edition of *The Prime of Miss Jean Brodie* and the shorter version of the novel published in the *New Yorker* demonstrates that the differences between the texts are not minor, nor does it seem likely that Spark would have regarded them as 'modest', as Rachel MacKenzie had hoped, since they involve meaningful and widespread changes to both the novel's plot and style. While the evidence of the previously unexamined yellow manuscript reveals that not all the textual excisions can clearly be attributed to MacKenzie, her zealous application of grammatical rules, especially the introduction of commas and additional forms of separation, not only changes the syntactical balance of Spark's prose, but demonstrably alters its meaning and impact in several places, weighing down and thus undermining the humorous impact of the text. The value of these editorial interventions for an understanding of Spark's aesthetic more broadly, however, is that they throw into sharp relief some of the distinctive qualities of what has come to be identified as the 'Sparkian discourse': a light, spare prose style marked by precision, wit and 'sparkle' in equal measure. Her more sparing use of commas reflects Theodor Adorno's caution in relation to commas, those 'most inconspicuous' of punctuation marks, which he regards as always in danger of 'making claims one would hardly expect of them' and of building in a separation between writing and voice and should therefore be 'thoughtfully avoided', where possible.[32] The additional commas in the *New Yorker* edition of the novel slow down the quick-witted prose, at times lending it a ponderous, hesitant quality that not only lets some of the air out of it, but also threatens the powerful sense throughout the novel that Brodie's brisk and absolutist approach to life and ethics has infiltrated the narrative voice of the novel as a whole. It is this style which, in speeding between observation ('tiny eyes') and assumption (untrustworthiness) ushers in a fiction of inescapable or fatalistic logic which emerges in *Brodie*, punctuated as it is by the certainty of its regular prolepses (Brodie's and Mary's deaths), and thus underlines the way that Spark's distinctive aesthetic at times echoes the logic of her plots. At the same time the yellow manuscript reveals a previously unacknowledged side to Spark who jealously guarded her reputation as an author whose work came to her through a form of authorial dictation and who fiercely protected her work from editorial interventions. Zadie Smith identifies Spark as one of three female writers who inspire particularly intense devotion amongst followers because of the apparently 'total control (over their form) they display'.[33] The yellow manuscript shows that even a writer like Spark, who was uncommonly protective of her work, felt the need to relinquish some of her authority to secure the *New Yorker* publication in a publishing world in which she felt undervalued in comparison with contemporary male writers whose work was being promoted and sold above hers. It also demonstrates that, even as publishing culture in Britain was taken up with working-class realism (Alan Sillitoe, John Braine, David Storey) firmly founded on the authenticity of voice based on the concepts of class and regional idioms, at stake in Spark's writing is an equally important concern: not to preserve and honour a neglected class or regional voice but rather to invent and defend a distinctive new narrative discourse unimpaired by grammarian orthodoxies.

Endnotes

1. Letter by John Updike to Muriel Spark, 10 November 1961. Copyright © 2021, John Updike, used by permission of The Wylie Agency (UK). National Library of Scotland, Spark Archive (Acc.10607/91, no. 127).
2. John Updike, 'Creatures of the Air', *New Yorker*, 30 September 1961, pp. 161–67.
3. At this point Lippincott & Co. published Spark in the United States while Macmillan were her British publishers.
4. See for example, Lisa Harrison, '"The Magazine That is Considered the Best in the World": Muriel Spark and *The New Yorker*', in *Modern Fiction Studies* 24.3 (Fall 2008), pp. 595–616.
5. Letter from Updike, 1961, op. cit. Miss Gaunt is the strict teacher from the Western Isles who shocks the Brodie set with her insistence on 'industrious learning' (*Jean Brodie*, p. 57).
6. The yellow manuscript is held in the Muriel Spark archive at the Department of Special Collections & University Archive Repository, McFarlin Library, University of Tulsa (UT), 1983.003.2.60. Referred to henceforth as YMS.
7. Harrison, 'Muriel Spark and *The New Yorker*', pp. 599–601.
8. Telegram from Rachel Mackenzie, cited in Harrison, 'Muriel Spark and *The New Yorker*', p. 600.
9. Quoted in Stephen Schiff, 'Muriel Spark Between the Lines', *New Yorker*, 24 May 1993, pp. 36–43 (p. 36).
10. Martin Stannard, *Muriel Spark: The Biography* (London: Weidenfeld and Nicolson, 2009), p. xxiii.
11. Stannard, op. cit., p. 161 and interview with Nan Robertson, 'The Prime Time of Muriel Spark', *New York Times*, 14 May 1979, A-16.
12. Stannard, *Muriel Spark: The Biography*, p. 176, also an early clash with William G. Smith, the editor of *Books & Bookmen* who 'updated' her text for the 1960 BBC radio talk 'How I became a Novelist' for publication the following year. Claiming she was 'passionate about principle and justice' she insisted that no one was therefore permitted 'to touch a punctuation mark' without her approval. Stannard reports that Spark forced Smith to make a charity payment to her local church organ fund when he defied this order (pp. 237–38).
13. 13 The following handwritten advice on the *dramatis personae* page: 'Note to the printer from the author:—The author thanks the printers for their queries on various points of style in her dialogue-prose, but respectfully requests them to cease from this practice when dealing with her work in future as she finds it more distracting than useful. The author suggests that the typographical sides stands in some need of attention & refuses to pass the proofs until satisfied in this respect.' (Muriel Spark, Manuscript, UT, 1983.003.3.16). This is the third and most polite version of this request, the two other drafts also being preserved in the archive.
14. Much later correspondence between Spark and Charles McGrath, a later editor at the *New Yorker*, however, reveals a more receptive Spark who responds positively to his request that she re-works and extends the ending of her short story, 'Going Up and Coming Down' (letter from Charles McGrath, 3 May 1994, NLS Spark archive (Acc. 11621/93)). But when Spark duly faxes a re-worked ending 5 days later with the expressed hope that 'you will find this version of GOING UP AND COMING DOWN

an improvement, as in fact I do' (Acc. 11621/93) he finally rejects the new version too (Letter from Charles McGrath, 30 June 1994, NLS, (Acc. 11621/93)), leaving Spark to publish the amended version of the story later in the year in the *Daily Telegraph*.
15 Stannard, *Muriel Spark: The Biography*, p. 275.
16 Ibid.
17 Loreto Todd, *Cassell's Guide to Punctuation* (London: Cassell & Co., 1995), p. 23.
18 'It's being aware of the value of words [...] in a very quick flash as one is going along. That I can do quite easily. That is a sort of poetic method' in Stephen Schiff, 'Muriel Spark Between the Lines', *New Yorker*, 24 May 1993, pp. 41–42.
19 Emma Hogan claims, 'Her Brevity often perplexed critics, but it let her strip away the flab. Leaving what Updike called a "sweet sting"' in *Economist* digital magazine, 11 March 2015. www.1843magazine.com/content/arts/emma-hogan/muriel-spark [accessed 24 November 2016].
20 Peter Kemp introduces her work as 'thrifty, frugal, economic' in *Muriel Spark* (London: Paul Elek, 1974), p. 7. Marilyn Reizbaum refers to the 'economy and compression' of her writing in 'The Stranger Spark' in *The Edinburgh Companion to Muriel Spark*, eds. Michael Gardiner and Willy Maley (Edinburgh: Edinburgh University Press, 2010), pp. 40–51 (p. 41).
21 Hope Howell Hodgkins refers to Spark and Barbara Pym's style as characteristic of the austerity of the post-war period, 'saying more for less through rhetorical minimalism' in 'Stylish Spinsters: Spark, Pym, and the Post-War Comedy of the Object', in *Modern Fiction Studies* 54.3 (Fall 2008), pp. 523–43 (p. 526).
22 'She was peerless, sparkling, inventive and intelligent [...]', Ian Rankin quoted on the cover of *Symposium* (London: Virago, 2006).
23 Evelyn Waugh describes *Brodie* as a 'tight little tale' in 'Love, Loyalty and Little Girls', *Cosmopolitan* 152, February 1962, p. 38.
24 A. L. Kennedy refers to the 'compression of her narratives and her 'sparse and simple vocabulary' in her introduction to *Memento Mori* [1959] (London: Virago, 2011), p. x.
25 In a review of *The Only Problem*, John Updike describes Spark's 'sudden, wilful largesse of image and wit, the cunning tautness of suspense, the beautifully firm modulations from passage to passage' in 'A Romp with Job', *New Yorker*, 23 July 1985, p. 104.
26 Sigmund Freud, 'Humour', in *Art and Literature: Pelican Freud Library*, trans. James Strachey, 15 vols (Harmondsworth: Penguin, 1985), XIV, pp. 427–33 (p. 429).
27 Muriel Spark, *The Prime of Miss Jean Brodie* (London: Penguin, 2000). All references are to this edition.
28 Muriel Spark, 'The Portobello Road', in *The Complete Short Stories* (Edinburgh: Canongate, 2011), p. 520.
29 For example, the capital 'M' has a longer mid-point on Spark's manuscript for the first edition. The numbers appear at the top and middle of the page in the yellow manuscript but the top right in Spark's first edition manuscript. The latter proceeds from 1–201, whereas the yellow manuscript starts at 01 and moves through 001, 0001 etc. for each chapter, with the final chapter having handwritten numbers at the top right of the page.
30 See Letters from MacKenzie to John Smith (19 September 1961) and Spark (12 September 1961), NLS Spark Archive (Acc. 11621/93), regarding the author's proof of *The Prime of Miss Jean Brodie*.
31 Ibid.

32 Theodor W. Adorno and Shierry Weber Nicholsen (trans.), 'Punctuation Marks', in *The Antioch Review* 48.3 (1990), pp. 300–305, www.jstor.org/stable/4612221 [accessed 5 May 2021]. As Lee Clark Mitchell points out in his analysis of the deployment of commas in the work of James Baldwin, however, commas are not deterministic in themselves and can 'alternatively weave together moods and unsettle ideas [...] to generate harmonious rhythms – or to disrupt them'. *Mark My Words: Profiles of Punctuation in Modern Literature* (London: Bloomsbury Publishing, 2020), p. 23.
33 Zadie Smith, 'Zadie Smith: dance lessons for writers', *Guardian* magazine, 29 October 2016. www.theguardian.com/books/2016/oct/29/zadie-smith-what-beyonce-taught-me [accessed 29 April 2021].

10. Already and Not Yet Written: Unfinished Acts of Writing in the Novels of Muriel Spark

MARK CURRIE

When Muriel Spark died in 2006, she had made a start on her twenty-third novel, which was to be titled *Destiny*. If only she had lived to complete it. On the other hand I am not sure that there is a better end to Spark's career than a novel on the topic of destiny which remained unwritten. This is because, as I will argue here, the images of and plots involving unwritten texts, not yet written novels, the images of blank pages and other representations of acts of writing that lie ahead are prominent throughout Spark's writings. These future acts of writing and unwritten futures operate in a kind of system with contrasting images, of scripts, novels or plots which are already written, of futures for which there already exists a complete and written version, but also with a whole spectrum of intermediate positions or texts which exist in a state between the already complete and the yet to be written, such as manuscripts, typescripts, drafts, copies, proofs and works in progress. It is not just that, as many of Spark's critics have noticed, the novels are full of books. There is something more specific at work in the relation between writing and destiny, which centres on the question of whether the future is already written, or perhaps more clearly, whether the future is an unalterable fact.

Destiny and chance may have been at the front of Spark's mind and in the foreground of her writing, but she also insistently linked these represented acts of writing to the question of facts. In most of Spark's novels there is a character, major or minor, who insists on facts. In her second novel, *Robinson* (1958), for example, that character is Robinson, the only inhabitant of the island of that name on which the protagonist January Marlow has been stranded by a plane crash. Robinson insists throughout the novel that January should stick to the facts, and record them in a journal, but the trouble with facts on Robinson is that everybody's name is also either a place or a time, and the recording of facts, of times, places and events, is a comic guddle of uncertain references.

Unfolding as it is throughout the narrative, the journal is one of those dramatised acts of writing that also plays its part as an object: over time January fills her blank notebook with facts, including the injunction to stick to them: 'I have these facts from Robinson. He has given me this notebook. He said, "Keep to the facts, that will be the healthiest course."'[1] When the book is full, January supplements it with loose pages that she tucks inside the cover. The whole written record also becomes a missing object, stolen from her drawer by Tom Wells because it has become a 'dossier' containing no direct proof but reflections on the murder that January suspects him to have committed. The journal, in other words, becomes an object which is lost and recovered, and it also charts the transition from factual record to speculation about events that may, or may not, have taken place. This is not the only pile of paper in the novel that has an uncertain relation to facts. Tom also makes a great fuss about documents that are missing from the briefcase that he has salvaged from the plane wreck, which are proofs of a magazine bearing the title *Your Future*. The joke here, that factuality or proof might attach to the future, is hard to miss, but just in case, the novel serves up a system of puns – proofs of *Your Future*, 'Show me Your Future', 'Give me Your Future', 'I want Your Future' – that take their place in a more general inversion that attaches uncertainty to the past, and factuality to the future. The missing proofs of *Your Future* are for the June edition, a written and as yet unpublished text that exemplifies Spark's interest in the intermediate stages between the already written and the not yet complete, and which relates directly to January's own past and future. Named after the month in which she was born, she is a person and an edition.

These two journals, January's journal and *Your Future*, work together to assault the proposition that facts are of the past, and that there are no facts about the future. *Not to Disturb* (1971) begins with a conversation amongst the staff of a grand house in Switzerland that disturbs both of these suppositions:

> 'When you say that a thing is not impossible, that isn't quite to say as if it's possible,' says Eleanor who, although younger than Lister, is

his aunt. She is taking off her outdoor clothes. 'Only technically is the not impossible, possible.'

'We are not discussing possibilities today,' Lister says. 'Today we speak of facts. This is not the time for inconsequential talk.'

'Of facts accomplished,' says Pablo the handyman.[2]

It appears, in this opening dialogue, that the topic of the future is being immediately overruled by Lister's insistence on facts, and therefore on what has already happened and can be known with certainty. 'Facts accomplished' are not, however, of the past; they are a bad, or perhaps merely literal, translation of the 'fait accompli', a phrase that refers either to events that have already happened or to future events that have a comparable degree of certainty. The accomplished facts referred to here are to take place the following morning, when the Baron and Baroness of the household are to be found dead, along with a secretary named Victor Passerat. That these events of tomorrow morning have already happened is a temporal absurdity that is readable in the hapless secretary's surname, which is a supine form in Swedish of the verb 'to pass', carrying the meaning of 'passed' or 'expired' and at the same time a homophone of the third-person singular future of the verb *passer* in French, meaning 'it will pass'. It breaks down into morphemes which might combine the English present of 'to pass' and Latin past of 'to be' – [pass][erat] – or references to both past and future in English and Italian – pas[sera]t. This is a joke that is extended by Ali Smith in *Hotel World*, whose main character Sara Wilby is named not once but twice after the future tense even though she is already dead, as a kind of echo of the song that her mother used to sing her as a child, with a lyric ('Que sera sera') that sits uncertainly between all four romance languages, while being grammatically incorrect in all of them.[3] The joke is clear, or clear only in that it obfuscates the distinction between what has been and what is to come, and therefore the distinction between the open future, figured as possibility, and the fated future, described as accomplished fact. The confusion of tenses is often acted out in dialogue that conveys uncertainty about the temporal position of actions, and sometimes made explicit as a topic: Heloise, for example, declares of the not-yet-deceased

Baron that 'He was a very fine man in his way. The whole of Geneva got a great surprise.' When Eleanor corrects her ('Will get a surprise') Lister intervenes with a formula for many of these strange convolutions of completion and uncertainty: 'Let us not split hairs', Lister says, 'between the past, present and future tenses'.[4] A few pages later, when counting the money that he has already, mysteriously received for the event that lies ahead, he links the language of 'fait accompli' with positions in the philosophy of time:

> 'Small change,' he says, 'compared with what is to come, or has already come, according as one's philosophy is temporal or eternal. To all intents and purposes, they're already dead although as a matter of banal fact, the night's business has still to accomplish itself'.[5]

It may be that Lister's conflation of the 'to come' with the 'already come' is just an expression of the 'eternal' philosophy. In her essay of 1953, 'The Religion of an Agnostic', Spark had outlined two basic philosophies of time in her analysis of Proust, which she called 'hierarchical' and 'evolutionary'. The first corresponds to the classical notion of *nunc stans*, the 'standing now', in which all moments are understood as co-present, as if time were a landscape apprehended as one vast synchronic stasis; the second is *nunc movens*, or the temporal succession of the 'moving now', in which one moment or state displaces another. Martin Stannard, Spark's biographer, sees this distinction as the basis on which she reconciled many of the dichotomies of her religion, between the commonplace and the eternal, body and spirit, and the presence and absence of God. It is also, for Spark, the basis of Proust's discussion of what is temporally absent, because it exists only in memory, and what is present:

> So, seeing life *sub specie aeternitatis*, Proust, like the Christian mystics, insists on the synchronic nature of Time. History is not, as Millais amusingly put it, 'one damn thing after another', but eternally 'present'. It is a Blakean notion, the eternal Now, developed by Eliot in *Four Quartets*, and by thinkers like Bergson and Jung.[6]

This ancient opposition of simultaneity and succession is adopted by Spark, in other words, as it has been adopted recurrently by writers and philosophers, as a way of understanding the collision between different conceptualisations of time, or the presence of things, moments and states that are absent. In the case of Proust, what is past is also present in the eternal now, and memory is the only access to this presence of absence for human consciousness. But the *eternal now* must also entail the presence of future moments, and these, as medieval theology tells us, are available only to God, or as modern phenomenology would have it, only in the form of contingent anticipations, expectations or predictions. Much of Spark's comedy, I suggest, derives from a kind of absurd collision between the divine and the human script, or from the projection of divine prescience onto human actors who must wait for the future to arrive. The vigil, the collective waiting for expected and known things to happen, has a philosophical, perhaps an existential, atmosphere which Spark inflects with the comic fatalism of people who are stuck in a book.

Not to Disturb is all about waiting and expecting, and yet the not-yet has already taken place. It begins with the household waiting for the Baron to come, and as soon as he arrives, the object of expectation shifts to the Baroness, who is 'late', even though she is still alive. At no point in the narrative do we feel as if we are waiting for confirmation of statements made by Lister and others, of what will happen, but at every point we are waiting for someone to arrive. The categories of expectation and arrival are shaped by the presence of a gatehouse, through which arriving guests, expected and even unexpected visitors must pass, announced by telephone to Lister, producing strange structures of delay and foreshadowing in which those whose arrivals have been announced arrive only after a delay, and those who are unexpected are nevertheless pre-announced. At times the dialogue is dense with the thematics of expectation expressed in a jumble of retrospective and prospective positions:

> 'Suppose the Baron wants his dinner?'
> 'Of course he expected his dinner,' Lister says, 'But as things turned out, he didn't live to eat it. He'll be arriving soon.'

'There might be an unexpected turn of events,' says Eleanor.

'There was sure to be something unexpected,' says Lister. 'But what's done is about to be done and the future has come to pass. My memoirs up to the funeral are, as a matter of fact more or less complete. At all events it's out of our hands. I place the event at about three a.m. so prepare to stay awake.'

'I would say six o'clock tomorrow morning. Right on the squeak of dawn,' says Heloise.

'You might well be right,' says Lister. 'Women in your condition are usually intuitive.'[7]

In the first place, the Baron is the object of an expectation, in the sense that he will arrive soon, but may also bring an expectation of dinner with him. Lister hastily translates this from a future prospect to a fact seen retrospectively, from a point which is, impossibly, both after his death (as things turned out) and before his arrival at the house. Lister's certainty – the *factivity* of his past-tensed statements about the future – is contested by Eleanor's modalised speculation that there might be an unexpected turn, but this is translated in turn into factive retrospect – the certainty that there would be something unexpected, despite the fact that, according to his own account, the future has already taken place. This statement ('There was sure to be something unexpected') is one of the places where Lister seems most clearly to be providing a commentary on the condition of being stuck in a novel, particularly a detective novel, where the unexpected twist is a generic expectation, referring us to the experience of readerly expectations in general. Heloise is expecting in a different sense, and this, according to Lister, gives her a kind of authority when it comes to the prediction of the only uncertain part of the future, which is the exact time of everyone's death. Perhaps most significant in the jumble is Lister's allusion to his own memoirs, an act of writing offered as an explanation of the fact that the future has come to pass: that their inscription, their completion in writing, confers necessity on these events, and places them 'out of our hands'. The death of the Baron, the Baroness and Passerat are necessary, Lister implies, because he has written them down, as if he were a God or an author. The events written in Lister's memoirs are, however, 'as a matter of fact more or less complete' to a point beyond their deaths, and this 'more or less' is one of Spark's representations of an ongoing act of writing: a script for the future, amendable, and as yet only complete up to a certain point. The manipulative agency[8] of Lister's memoir is limited by its incompletion, but it also reads like a strange kind of psychosis, or a species of agency that denies the contingency of future events. 'They have placed themselves', Lister says, 'unfortunately, within the realm of predestination'.[9]

Lister's memoir is not the only inscription of what is to come in *Not to Disturb*. At a level below predestination, a number of other written texts vie with each other to be the advance script of what is to come, many of which are similarly ongoing or incomplete. Some of these belong to Lister, who has already written the press handouts for reporters, who will arrive in the morning, and recorded his own press statement in advance. The novel's basic scenario, of those who will be found dead in the morning, and those who wait for it to transpire, is imagined repeatedly as a stage production, and latterly, as a film, the rights to which may have already been sold, and the script written, by Lister. Two of the narrative's arrivants, Mr Samuel and Mr McGuire, are in possession of a typescript and a soundtrack, the former being described by Mr Samuel as 'a first-rate film script' which 'only an authority on the subject' could have pieced together,[10] and yet which is amended by an assistant to make it correspond more exactly to events as they unfold. Bad photographic and filmic puns sometimes hint at the unreality of the events of this three-way shooting in the library, which may, after all, only be a film shoot, orchestrated around 'threats of exposure': 'Pablo says "He's gone to meet his Maker. He shoots the wife and secretary when they talk too fast. Then he shoots himself, according to the script."'[11] If there are authorial overtones in the concepts of maker and scriptwriter, they are blurred with the uncertainties that preside over authorship, in terms of the identity of the author, but also the degree and type of agency attached to authorial figures such as Lister. These puns point to a different interest in the insubstantiality of events and characters: that they are literalisations of linguistic idioms like 'exposure' and 'shooting', and that their being is insubstantial, papery and linguistic. A kind of counterfactual time projects the grammatical properties of the past, such as factivity, onto events in the future, and often seems to render characters and events insubstantial at the same time as it inverts chronological order: 'They haunt the house', Lister says, 'like insubstantial bodies while still alive'.[12]

The idea of literalisation – of presenting scenarios that are literalisations of linguistic idioms or metaphors – is certainly a plausible interpretative framework for *The Driver's Seat* (1970), the novel immediately before *Not to Disturb*. Martin Stannard tells us that both of these novels had papery beginnings, in the sense that they were inspired by 'factual' reports in newspapers:

> Muriel's obsessive reading [of newspapers] had concentrated on one story. A German woman, garishly dressed, had come to Rome and taken a stroll in the park. There she had been tied up, raped and stabbed to death. To Muriel, the compelling feature of this butchery was that the 'victim' appeared to have provoked it. Here was the germ of her next novel. Moreover, she had discovered a new source of inspiration. Three of her next four books – *The Driver's Seat* (1970), *Not to Disturb* (1971) and *The Abbess of Crewe* (1974) – derived from press reports.[13]

The genesis of *Not to Disturb*, Stannard also tells us, was 'a widely reported multiple Italian murder involving a Count, his wife, their mutual lover and voyeurism'.[14] As several critics have noted of *The Driver's Seat*, this first story gave Spark the scene on which to base a literalisation of the idiom 'she was asking for it', and the novel is therefore an elaborate account of just how insane the world would have to be for this idiom to make any kind of literal sense. Lise, the novel's apparently suicidal protagonist, is an example of the kind of insubstantial, papery being that Spark then developed in *Not to Disturb*: she is killed by a paper knife, and her body will be 'swept up' in the morning. Another foolish idiom, the idea of 'judging a book by its cover' is literalised in Lise's garish dress, which is linked at every step to the colour and style of book covers, and therefore to the way that she controls people's judgements, memories and expectations of her as a victim. Most prominently, though less discussed in critical commentary, Lise's search for a suitable murderer is a quest for her 'type', to be understood, ironically, as a romantic preference, and literally, as a movement towards the condition of a written mark. In *The Driver's Seat*, as in *Not to Disturb*, there are regular proleptic excursions that reveal not only the fact of a death to come, but also an act of writing that will follow, as journalists and investigators report the known facts of the crime. These are both counterfactual narratives, in the sense that they imagine a hidden story behind newspaper reports profoundly at odds with the official or public version, but the normal relation of the actual and the counterfactual, where the actual past is altered by the counterfactual, is inverted. In both of these narratives, the factual reports to come are hopelessly wrong in relation to the outlandish imagined events of the story, in which characters control and know the future: we are asked to believe in the actuality of the 'what if', and therefore of the counterfactuality of official facts. In both cases, the counterfactual is a hypothesis about an already inscribed future from which the past is misunderstood.

The pun of the 'type' is central to this effect, and it could be said that the pun itself reverses the logic of metaphor, which posits a secondary meaning in addition to a literal one. It feels at first as if the word 'type' works on the basis of resemblance – that a category of potential lovers is formed from some common denominator which is the basis of sexual and romantic attraction. The realisation that emerges for a reader of *The Driver's Seat* is that the resemblance unites potential killers, not lovers, and this displacement makes us realise that we have been misled by a conventional meaning from an unusual one. In relation to both of these categories 'type', understood as printed characters and letters, is not only a more literal meaning in the sense that it is not metaphorical, but literally literal because Lise only exists as letters on a page. Both of these ideas, of type as resemblance and type as printed letters, seem to fascinate Spark, and not only in these two novels. Resemblance, for example, plays a strange part in *The Prime of Miss Jean Brodie* (1961), where Teddy Lloyd's love for Miss Brodie expresses itself in the resemblance to her of any woman he paints, as if she were for him the common denominator. In *The Only Problem* (1984), a stranger resemblance is at work between two sisters, Effie and Ruth, who are the romantic partners of Harvey Gotham, stranger because they look alike and yet are entirely different: Ruth is the mothering type, and Effie is not; despite their striking resemblance Effie manages to be beautiful and Ruth the opposite; and, in an echo of the *Brodie* theme, both resemble the figure of Job's wife in *Job visite par sa femme,* a painting that stirs Harvey's appreciation of Effie's beauty. The plot, in which Effie turns to crime, is all about news, fake and factual, and turns on whether Effie can be identified from photos and identikit images in the press. *The Only Problem* is full of types, or sorts of people, and full of questions about physical resemblance; but it is also full of type and typing: the house is full of piles of paper, of notes and manuscripts, of business papers and typescripts, all related to a book that Harvey is writing about *The Book of Job*, a work that is to become, but is not yet, a monograph. When Harvey and Ruth take the nearby Château, they do so because of a woodpecker in the tree outside which 'makes a sound like a typewriter', reminding Ruth of her childhood, when she would fall asleep on summer evenings listening to the sound of her mother typing. Typing is a kind of soundtrack in *The Only Problem*, with newspaper reporters telling the story, Harvey writing his book, the woodpecker, and Ruth's memories, but the sounds also mix with Harvey's deep psyche:

> It was nine-fifteen when the telephone rang. This time it was from London. At the same time the doorbell rang. Harvey had been dreaming that his interrogator was one of those electric typewriters where the typeface can be changed by easy manipulation; the voice of the interrogator changed like the type, and in fact was one and the same, now roman, now elite, now italics. In the end, bells on the typewriter rang to wake him up to the phone and the doorbell.[15]

The idea of type as facial resemblance and type as print converge in this dream, in the image of interchangeable typefaces, just as the voice of the police interrogator and the appearance of the type become one. In *The Only Problem*, what seemed at first to be an arbitrary connection forced by the incongruous meanings of a pun begins to look more like a motivated enquiry into the way that printed letters can enter into relations of resemblance, copying and imitation, and the way that type, understood as graphic marks, can convey type, understood as fictional character.

These issues of writing and type are manifestly present from the start of Spark's career as a novelist, most obviously in her first novel, *The Comforters* (1957), in which the protagonist, Caroline, begins to hear the tap-tippity-tap of a typewriter:

> On the whole she did not think there would be any difficulty with Helena.
>
> Just then she heard the sound of a typewriter. It seemed to come through the wall on her left. It stopped, and was immediately followed by a voice remarking her own thoughts. It said: *On the whole she did not think there would be any difficulty with Helena.*[16]

Of all the complicated positions that Spark has offered us, of an act of writing to what it relates, or our own position in relation to an internally represented act of writing, this one is surely the most intriguing and difficult. If the words being typed are those that Caroline hears, it seems as if the act of writing is concurrent with the actions and thoughts being narrated, and the Typing Ghost is writing the novel that we are reading. Except that there is a delay between the sound of typing and the voicing of narrative sentences, and a gap too between the narrative sentence and its citation in italics. The novel that we are reading therefore includes the citation of its own words, and unless the typing ghost also inscribes those italicised words, there is a difference between the words we read and the words that Caroline hears. Thought of in terms of time, a gap of some kind is, in fact, necessary, since the act of writing cannot coincide with itself: if it did, it would have no content other than the act of writing itself. Thought of in terms of authorship, the Ghost Typist who writes Caroline in fact camouflages the real manipulative agent who writes both Caroline and the Ghost Typist. If the novel marks the difference between the narration and the narrated by switching typeface, the actual process of invention and factual act of authorial inscription, performed by Spark many years ago, is less visible, if not invisible. The gap between the tap-tippety-tap and the voice that follows immediately, for all that it truncates the conventional delay of narrative retrospect, nevertheless conforms to the definition of narrative as the recapitulation of past events, and yet it also poses a rather crucial question of which comes first, the action or the inscription: if the tapping of the typewriter is the sound of authorial invention, do these narrative sentences produce the events they purport to record? A lot is at stake in this puzzle, at least for Caroline, since it poses a threat to her freedom, and to the substance of her being. As Ali Smith puts in her introduction, 'Caroline is, understandably, a bit hurt to discover that her present-tense life is already a foregone conclusion, and that she isn't real.'[17] For us, the contingency of the story world is inseparable from these intricate questions of position – does the act of writing produce the novel's events, is it concurrent with them, or does it report after the fact?

The motif of 'type' does not accumulate, as most motifs do, over the course of a single work, but gradually and consistently over the course of twenty-two novels, and it makes friends with cognate words and phrases along the route. One example is the word 'frank', as for example when Heloise says to Lister and Pablo in *Not to Disturb*: 'You have to be frank with these types.'[18] I have been suggesting that the notion of type pulls together the notion of category or sort, and the notion of inscription, and that typing is an emblem of the literal fact, the written-ness, of fictional character. The word 'frank' has a comparable set of ambiguities, being on one hand an adjective attributing honesty and directness to an action, and on the other, a stamp or an act of imprinting – when something has been 'franked' it bears the mark of postage having been paid – so that Heloise's pun is doubled. Though the concept of frankness is openly linked with the issue of facticity – the Reverend, for example, declares to Lister 'You have to be frank about it. No point in concealing the facts'[19] – these are isolated moments, or glimpses of something that comes into view more clearly later in Spark's career. In *Loitering with Intent* (1981), for example, the role that I attributed earlier to Robinson (the person in a Spark novel who stickles for facts) falls to Sir Quentin, who also insists upon 'complete frankness'.[20] Both words of this phrase can be seen as a kind of reprise of the 'fait accompli', the first which puns on the grammar of the perfect mood, and the second which invokes the symbol or mark at the same time as it asks, on the surface, for candour. Variations on the phrase, such as 'perfectly frank',[21] seem also to make the link between the grammar of completed action and the graphic mark, and indeed the notion of 'type' which linked writing with fictional character in *The Driver's Seat* is repeated throughout this novel, mainly in relation to Fleur Talbot's observations of the English Rose:

> I thought often of Beryl Tims, a type of woman I had come to associate in my mind with the English Rose. Not that they resembled English roses, far from it; but they were English roses, I felt, in their own minds. The type sickened me and I was fascinated, such being the capacity of my imagination and my need to know the utmost.[22]

The interplay of resemblance and the graphic surface is implicit here, and the novel extends the contradiction it produces, between an observation about a type of living person and a reminder that they are paper beings, by dramatising it internally in Fleur's fictional creations. Fleur is writing a novel, *Warrender Chase*, in which her character Charlotte is her 'fictional English Rose',[23] and we are never in doubt that the people in this novel are typed, or rather that they are both true and typed. Fleur tells us that they are true in the sense that 'my sets of words should convey ideas of truth and wonder, as indeed they did to myself as I was composing them' and that she is 'sparing no relevant facts',[24] but also insists that both Warrender and Charlotte are pure surface:

> All these years since, the critics have been asking whether Warrender was in love with his nephew. How do I know? Warrender Chase never existed, he is only some hundreds of words, some punctuation, sentences, paragraphs, marks on the page. If I had conceived Warrender Chase's motives as a psychological study I would have said so. But I don't go in for motives, I never have.[25]

This dramatised (but plainly authorial) self-analysis describes the inaccessibility of a character's psychological motives not just as an artistic choice, but as an existential condition for the paper being. It describes the strange restrictions of the narrator of *The Driver's Seat* (who can know the future, but for whom Lise's thoughts are inaccessible) but it also reasserts the basis of this inaccessibility as writing itself.

As novels within novels go, *Warrender Chase* is a complicated example of the dynamics of completion and incompletion: Fleur has been working on it for years, but it is brought to completion, written in a flu-driven frenzy in Chapter 4 of *Loitering with Intent*. As an unfinished work, it takes its place alongside the ten unfinished narratives of the members of Sir Quentin's Autobiographical Association – stories which aim to 'place the facts on record for posterity' – and yet the interaction between these unfinished manuscripts, the causal relationships between Fleur's novel and the lives that the autobiographies purport to record, become confused. Employed as a kind of ghost writer by Sir Quentin, Fleur's job is to type the memoirs of the society's members: she is a ghost typist, like the figure behind the wall in *The Comforters*, whose job it is to bring the unfinished narratives to completion. But she is given some latitude beyond the typist's remit for invention:

> 'These works when completed,' said Sir Quentin, 'will be both valuable to the historian of the future and will set the Thames on fire. You should easily be able to rectify any lack or lapse in form, syntax, style, characterization, invention, local colour, description, dialogue, construction and other trivialities. You are to type these documents under conditions of extreme secrecy, and if you succeed in giving satisfaction you may later sit in at some of our sessions and take notes.'[26]

The basic ambiguity of the ghost writer, between typing and inventing, is deepened by the degree of their incompletion (none have 'yet got farther than Chapter One'), and multiplied by the relationship between these unwritten scripts and Fleur's novel, which draws new inventive energy from her involvement with the Society's 'characters'. As the novel and the autobiographies proceed towards completion, they become not only a prescription for actions and events, but a template for character types, most notably for Sir Quentin himself:

> Now the story of *Warrender Chase* was in reality already formed, and by no means influenced by the affairs of the Autobiographical Association. But the interesting thing was, it seemed rather the reverse to me at the time. At the time; but thinking it over now, how could that have been? And yet it was so. In my febrile state of creativity I saw before my eyes how Sir Quentin was revealing himself chapter by chapter to be a type and consummation of Warrender Chase, my character.[27]

'Type' and 'character' line up here on both sides of the pun, to designate the fictional person and the written letter, and remind us that both Sir Quentin and Warrender Chase are nothing but marks on a page. Fleur is not only a typing ghost, where the relation of writing to events is one of concurrence: jokes about types and characters, franks and stamps, place the act of writing in several different positions in time, as both the origin and the outcome of fictional writing, the template and the consummation of character. The difficulty of locating the act of writing in time is the central dynamic between *Loitering with Intent* and its readers and its humour derives, as here, from the protagonist's own uncertainty about the order of real and fictional events. The 'febrile state of creativity' is something like an *archive fever*, where the recording of events that are over is difficult to separate from the invention or creation of things that are still to come,[28] and Fleur's flu contributes to the uncertainty between the already and the not yet written. Like *Not to Disturb*, *Loitering with Intent* is full of scripts narrating events subsequently 'lived out' and 'acted out', and retrospect constantly changes places with foresight. 'One day I'll write about all this', Fleur declares towards the end of the novel, thinking of her beloved Cellini and his injunction that 'all men [...] should write the tale of their life with their own hand'; but the intention to write is immediately transposed into an act of writing that has already happened: '"You've already written it," Dottie said, clanking down her teacup.

"You know your *Warrender Chase* is all about us. You foresaw it all."'²⁹ Fleur is, in other words, a ghost typist, a writer of memoirs and a strange kind of prophet, and her acts of writing constantly transform concurrent narrations into acts of recollection and prediction.

Loitering with Intent pursues these questions of temporal order in a universe of paper and writing: of books on shelves, books lying around, manuscripts and typescripts, carbon copies, proof copies, pages torn out of diaries, notebooks and letters, pages torn up and stuck back together, typescripts and manuscripts that go missing, texts that are stolen or destroyed, and acts of rewriting and copying. The narrator knows, looking back on events in 1949 from 1979, that the existence of a photocopier – 'photocopy machines were not current in those days'³⁰ – would destroy the plot altogether, and this is because questions of temporal order are so often pursued, as they are in *The Only Problem*, as an enquiry into resemblance through the motif of the copy. This is not only, as it is discussed above, an issue of who is copying whom in the relation of art and life, but of a more literal, typographical kind of copy, of texts that lie somewhere between completion and incompletion in the process of production and publication. In the central section of the novel, for example, the plot turns on the theft of Fleur's manuscript of *Warrender Chase*. Having taken no carbon copy of the typescript on the grounds that it was a waste of paper, Fleur frantically searches for a copy – the manuscript written on foolscap pages, the typed copy that went to the publishers, the proof copy that came back from the publishers – from which to recover the novel. Because *Warrender Chase* 'bears the fault of most first novels, alas, it is too close to life', the publisher withdraws it in fear of libel action, from Sir Quentin in particular, and so 'the type has been distributed':

> Ignorant as I was then of printer's jargon I said, 'Distributed to whom?'
> 'Distributed – broken up. We are not printing the book, Miss Talbot.'
> 'And what happened to the proofs?'
> 'Oh, those have been destroyed, naturally.'³¹

The novel is distributed rather than distributed, and so the completed work is returned to its original state of pure possibility – of not existing yet:

> The possibility that all copies of *Warrender Chase* had been destroyed was one that I couldn't face clearly that night, but it hung around me nightmarishly – the possibility that nowhere, nowhere in the world, did my *Warrender Chase* exist any more.[32]

The state of not existing any more and not existing yet enter into a kind of exchange in this section of *Loitering with Intent*, as the completion of Fleur's novel is undone, and the type and template of the novel's characters and action is literally broken up. For Fleur, the permanence of writing is as fragile as paper itself, and it returns to where it came from, which is nowhere.

The origins of *Warrender Chase*, this novel that doesn't exist and which we have not read, are decisively *ex nihilo*: 'God knows where I got Warrender Chase from; he was based on no-one that I knew':

> I know only that the night I started writing *Warrender Chase* I had been alone at a table in a restaurant near Kensington High Street Underground eating my supper. I rarely ate out alone, but I must have found myself in funds that day. I was going about my proper business, eating my supper while listening in to the conversation at the next table. One of them said, 'There we were all gathered in the living room, waiting for him.'
>
> It was all I needed. That was the start of *Warrender Chase*, the first chapter. All the rest sprang from that phrase.[33]

The strangers in this restaurant are figures of pure potentiality before writing has taken place; they are, like the members of the Autobiographical Association, 'sheets of paper on which I could write short stories, poems, anything I cared'.[34] The scene, like those blank sheets of paper, gives us an image of contingency itself, as invention on a blank page, which is strikingly like an image that Giorgio Agamben finds in Aristotle's description of nous, or human intelligence: 'the nous is like a writing tablet on which nothing is actually written'.³⁵ For Agamben this image of contingency belongs to the same philosophical constellation as the notion of the divine script, established mainly in medieval theology, which links divine prescience to the image of already completed writing – that human lives follow the course of a script written by God in advance. The metaphor of the blank writing tablet, in other words, works as an image of contingency only because the already written divine script is an emblem of destiny.

This made-up novel begins, like *Not to Disturb*, with a household of people waiting for an arrival, gathered in a room waiting for Warrender Chase, but he is already dead, killed in a car accident before the novel starts. The suggestion that this is a necessity, a future which has already taken place, is redoubled by the fact that it is also Sir Quentin's future, so that the scene plays its part in the back-and-forth movement between reality and invention that hangs over Sir Quentin's relation to Warrender. The opening therefore combines elements of loitering and intent: loitering as an act of waiting for events to unfold, as if they existed already or were already written, and intent as an act of creative potentiality, as if events belonged to the realm of the artistic plan, or the not-yet-written. There are moments in the novel when this link, between the position of the act of writing and questions of destiny, step forward from the murk of suggestivity and become explicit:

> My thoughts went like this: Warrender Chase was killed in a car crash while everyone is assembled, waiting for him. Quentin Oliver's destiny, if he wants to enact Warrender Chase, would be the same. It was a frightening thought but at the same time external to me, as if I were watching a play I had no power to stop. It then came to me again, there in the taxi, what a wonderful thing it was to be a woman and an artist in the twentieth century. It was as if Sir Quentin was unreal and I had merely invented him, Warrender Chase being a man, a real man on whom I had partly based Sir Quentin. It is true that I felt tight-strung, but I remember those sensations very clearly.³⁶

The language of murder and psychosis is audible here, and not for the first time in the novel. Fleur is the manipulative authorial agent at two different levels of this story, but denies her agency in both: she is powerless to change the already written death of her Warrender, and also powerless to stop the play that ends in Sir Quentin's death, a destiny that he chooses to enact himself; as the real and the unreal swap places under the chilling hypothesis of the 'as if', her sensation of having invented the real is also an apprehension of destiny, or an unalterable future of which she is nevertheless the author. If manipulative causation in a novel normally hides the real manipulative agent, such as an author, under the proposed one, such as divine providence, Fleur seems to be hiding her own psychosis under the alibi that it is just art.

Literalisation reduces questions about art as an imitation of life into ordinary questions of copying such as plagiarism and transcription, but at the same time manages to amplify issues of contingency and necessity. A playful example of this comes at the beginning of Chapter 10, when Fleur sets out to tell

> how Sir Quentin Oliver tried to arrange for the destruction of *Warrender Chase* as a novel at the same time as he approved the spirit of my legend for his own use. I can show how he actually plagiarized my text. And so I am writing about the cause of an effect.[37]

'Legend' is another of those words, like 'stamp' and 'frank', that draw attention to the written imprint, meaning both a traditional (usually true but unauthenticated) story and an inscription, especially on a coin or medal. It works in the service of a very literal species of copying, the kind that Fleur remembers from childhood:

> I remember as a young child being obliged to write out in my copybook, Necessity is the Mother of Invention. The sample had already been effected in beautiful copperplate on the first line, and to improve our handwriting it was our task to copy out this maxim on the lines below, which I duly did, all unaware that I was not merely acquiring an improved calligraphy but imbibing at the same time a subliminal lesson in social ethics.[38]

The chapter begins with Fleur's declaration that 'it is not to be supposed that the stamp and feeling of a novel can be conveyed by an intellectual summary' and that she could not 'reproduce my *Warrender Chase* in a few words'; but this is exactly what this anecdote does for *Loitering with Intent*: it summarises its stamp and feeling.[39] The maxim itself speaks to the entanglement of necessity with invention, but it does so through an act of literal replication in a copy-book: the first line is already written, and it is the child's duty to rewrite what is already there. The maxim about necessity and contingency is therefore repeated in the action of writing whose location is somewhere between the already written line and the not yet written copy. The summary works as a kind of preamble to the novel's most witty and satisfying symbolic episode, in which Fleur finds the missing manuscript of *Warrender Chase*, and which develops these ideas, of the blank page and the copy in relation to both necessity and destiny. When Fleur finally finds her stolen novel in Dottie's flat, it is hidden in a black bag of knitting hanging on coat pegs behind the door, and whenever knitting is represented in a novel, we know we are in the presence of the Moirae, or hear the echo of Dante's gatekeepers, two figures who weave or knit the destinies of each human individually while a third waits to cut the wool at the designated time. In other words, two images of destiny are stuffed into the same black bag together, the knitting of the gatekeepers and the script which determines in advance how humans will act and what will eventuate, as *Warrender Chase* has done throughout *Loitering with Intent*. Part of the humour of this scene, in keeping with the high-brow wit of the knitting bag, is that the package containing the hidden script takes part in a literal exchange with an unopened pack of blank typing paper, so that the metaphors of the blank writing tablet and the orchestrating script enter a relationship of substitution:

> Out I whisked that package in a flash, and in another flash had opened it. My *Warrender Chase*, my novel, my Warrender, Warrender Chase; my foolscap pages with the first chapters I had once torn up and then stuck together; my *Warrender Chase*, mine. I hugged it. I kissed it. I went to Dottie's bedroom and put it in my own shopping bag. I

> snatched from Dottie's desk an unopened ream of typing paper. This I wedged at the bottom of Dottie's bag, and carefully arranged the knitting on top of it.[40]

As we go in and out of the italic font, the object of this rapturous reunion oscillates between a novel and a person, and the idea of a paper being is given one of its most comic and literal expressions, as Fleur hugs and kisses her manuscript. The novel has played with this throughout, not only with people presented as if they were bits of paper, nor only through her relationship with her beloved Newman and Cellini, who are books, but with a kind of interchangeability of Fleur's role as a writer and her role as a lover, of her prospects in love and her prospects as a novelist. This scene replays the basic ambiguity of 'type', between writing and romantic prospect, in a specific way, but it also replaces the divine script with the blank page, and so the governing image of necessity with that of pure potentiality, which is perhaps another way of saying pure nothingness. This is principally, in terms of its function in the plot, an act of reclamation: of reclaiming the text and the man, her novel and her Warrender, from another woman. The exchange of the manuscript and the blank paper is part of a more complex exchange of stolen objects, including the stealing of Dottie's husband Leslie by Fleur and her stealing of the 'biographies' of members of the Autobiographical Association, and in both cases Fleur's moral position is difficult to defend; but her position as a writer and an artist convey much clearer messages to the real world, such as 'write your own novel', or perhaps 'write your own life': in Cellini's words, that all men 'if so be they are men of truth and good repute, should write the tale of their life with their own hand'.[41] Similarly, if like 'Necessity is the Mother of Invention', this exchange is supposed to contain a coded, unconsciously imbibed lesson in social ethics, it is a comic lesson in ethical uncertainty, and certainly lacks the clarity of the episode's allegory about uncertainty itself: we cannot make sense of the climactic exchange in terms of good and evil, but on the interplay of contingency and necessity in writing, it has the kind of luminosity that Ali Smith calls 'glittering Sparkian ice'.[42]

In *The Fire and the Tale*, Giorgio Agamben describes Roland Barthes's interest, at the end of his life, in the 'poorly studied' period that precedes the drafting of a work. This period, which Agamben calls 'the before of the book', refers to 'all that precedes the finished book': 'to that limbo, that pre- or sub-world of fantasies, sketches, notes, copybooks, drafts, blotters to which our culture is not able to give a legitimate status nor an adequate graphic design.'[43] For Barthes, the interest of this period lies in the 'wanting-to-write', and more specifically, wanting to write in a new way; for Agamben, the before of the book is 'encumbered with the theological paradigm of divine creation': that 'incomparable *fiat*, which, according to the theologians, is not *facere de materia* but a *creare ex nihilo*'.[44] I am not convinced that the 'before of the book' is so little studied, nor that the theology of its images, of *ex nihilo* creation and scriptedness, are particularly obscure. But the conjunction of these two topics gives Agamben's formula for the relationship between the incomplete and the completed act of writing a Sparkian resonance:

> If we really want to comprehend that curious object that is a book, we need to complicate the relation between potentiality and actuality, possible and real, matter and form, and try to imagine a possible that takes place only in the real and a real that does not stop becoming possible.[45]

Spark's dramatisations of this formula, of this relation between contingency and writing, or between freedom and the graphic surface of a novel, belong to this species of curiosity about the book as an object. Did she also orchestrate the disappearance of those pages of her unwritten novel *Destiny* that were already written, as an expression of indistinction between the already and not yet written?

Endnotes

1. Muriel Spark, *Robinson* [1958] (Edinburgh: Birlinn, 2017), p. 12.
2. Muriel Spark, *Not to Disturb*, in *Spark's Europe: Not to Disturb: The Takeover: The Only Problem* (Edinburgh: Canongate, 2016), p. 3.
3. Spark's interest in saying the same thing in different languages, and in hybrid forms of language, can be found in several novels including *The Driver's Seat*, *The Prime of Miss Jean Brodie* and *The Only Problem*.
4. Spark, *Not to Disturb*, p. 4.
5. Ibid., p. 10.
6. Martin Stannard, *Muriel Spark: The Biography* (London: Weidenfeld & Nicolson, 2009), p. 149.
7. Spark, *Not to Disturb*, pp. 6–7.
8. 'Manipulative agency' is a phrase used by Hilary Dannenberg to name one of the forms of causation observable in the novel. Opposed to progenerative causation, which links events within a novel together in causal relations, manipulative causation relates to an authorial or divine presence. Dannenberg claims that divine forms of manipulative causation, such as Providence, function to camouflage the real, authorial manipulation at work in a novel, and so function as realistic devices. See Dannenberg, *Coincidence and Counterfactuality* (Lincoln, NE; London: University of Nebraska Press, 2008), p. 29.
9. Spark, *Not to Disturb*, p. 35.
10. Ibid., p. 55.
11. Ibid., p. 62.
12. Ibid., p. 20.
13. Stannard, *Muriel Spark: The Biography*, p. 364.
14. Ibid., p. 373.
15. Muriel Spark, *The Only Problem*, in *Spark's Europe*, p. 403.
16. Muriel Spark, *The Comforters* [1957] (London; New York, NY: Virago, 2009), pp. 34–35.
17. Ali Smith, 'Introduction', in *The Comforters*, p. x.
18. Spark, *Not to Disturb*, p. 62.
19. Ibid., p. 47.
20. Muriel Spark, *Loitering with Intent* [1981] (London; New York, NY: Virago, 2007), p. 77; p. 82.
21. Ibid., p. 88.
22. Ibid., pp. 15–16.
23. Ibid., p. 58.
24. Ibid., pp. 58–59.
25. Ibid., p. 61.
26. Ibid., pp. 13–14.
27. Ibid., p. 42.
28. Derrida's account of archive fever offers the archive as producer rather than recorder of events: 'the archive as printing, writing, prosthesis, or hypomnesic technique in general is not only the place for stocking and for conserving an archivable content of the past which would exist in any case, such as, without the archive, one still believes it was or will have been. No, the technical structure of the archiving archive also determines the structure of the archivable content even in its very coming into existence and in its relationship to the future. The archivization produces as much as it records the event'.

29 Jacques Derrida, *Archive Fever: A Freudian Impression*, trans. Eric Prenowitz (Chicago, IL: University of Chicago Press, 1996), p. 17.
29 Spark, *Loitering with Intent*, p. 153.
30 Ibid., p. 24.
31 Ibid., p. 103.
32 Ibid., p. 104.
33 Ibid., p. 60.
34 Ibid., p. 72.
35 Agamben's discussion of Aristotle's blank writing tablet identifies it as the origin of a fundamental figure of the philosophical tradition, which likens thought to an act of writing in the humble garb of the scribe. For Agamben this tradition explains Melville's Bartleby, the scribe who will not write, as an image of pure potentiality and freedom. See Giorgio Agamben, *Potentialities*, ed. and trans. Daniel Heller-Roazen (Stanford, CA: Stanford University Press, 1999), p. 255.
36 Spark, *Loitering with Intent*, p. 140.
37 Ibid., p. 114.
38 Ibid.
39 Ibid.
40 Ibid., pp. 128–29.
41 Ibid., p. 94.
42 Ali Smith, quoted on the cover of *The Finishing School* [2004] (Edinburgh: Canongate, 2016).
43 Giorgio Agamben, *The Fire and the Tale*, trans. Lorenzo Chiesa (Stanford, CA: Stanford University Press, 2017), p. 84.
44 Ibid.
45 Ibid., p. 94.

11. Muriel Spark's Windows and the Architecture of Surveillance

AMY WOODBURY TEASE

Muriel Spark is a self-proclaimed practitioner of surveillance. Early in her memoir *Curriculum Vitae* (1992) she confesses herself to be a vigilant observer of the world around her: 'I was fascinated from the earliest age I can remember by how people arranged themselves. I can't remember a time when I was not a person-watcher, a behaviourist. I was also an avid listener.'[1] Spark's penchant for eavesdropping emerges more acutely in the autobiographical essay 'The First Year of My Life' as she imagines herself an infant tapping into the wireless reports from the Western Front, an image that anticipates her future work with British Intelligence as a 'fly on the wall [...] in the dark field of Black Propaganda or Psychological Warfare' under the notorious Sefton Delmer.[2] While the notion of the writer as an observer is unremarkable in and of itself (one would be hard-pressed to find a writer who does not see themselves as such) the characterisation becomes more notable when considered alongside both Spark's wartime surveillance work and the carefully crafted post-war landscapes of her fiction, which are littered with detailed descriptions of bombed-out buildings, shattered windows, and empty lots, all physical reminders of the violence of war. These architectural elements that enter Spark's work through the eyes of both her narrators and her characters are proof of her rather ordinary habit of observation. Yet they also – perhaps more poignantly – produce a tension between inside and outside that underlies life during wartime, a tension that is also characteristic of surveillance culture.

In *The Culture of Surveillance* David Lyon explains that 'surveillance is an everyday fact of life that we not only encounter from outside, as it were, but also in which we engage, from within, in many contexts'.[3] This contemporary theory of surveillance is particular to the twenty-first century, but it is one that Spark anticipates and employs throughout her oeuvre in complex ways. To use our current example, in 'The First Year of My Life' Spark's exploration of the psychological impact of the war outside is experienced through an everyday act of surveillance on the inside: the infant sees herself at the dial, 'tuning in' to broadcasts from the warzone while remaining safely in her crib.[4] She writes:

> The Western Front on my frequency was sheer blood, mud, dismembered bodies, blistered crashes, hectic flashes of light in the night skies, explosions, total terror. Since it was plain I had been born into a bad moment in the history of the world, the future bothered me, unable as I was to raise my head from the pillow and as yet only twenty inches long.[5]

In the imagined context of her infancy, Spark positions herself as both inside and outside at once, physically contained in the domestic space of her Edinburgh home, yet radically open to violence from the outside through the incessant wireless reports that infiltrate it. Spark's confession in *Curriculum Vitae* about her 'fascination' with what she terms the 'arrangement' of people in time and space is explored here through an analysis of the synchronous movement between domestic and global spaces in 'The First Year of My Life'. This reading invites a more nuanced understanding of the writer as a 'master-builder'[6] of worlds, an architect whose interior *and* exterior landscapes reflect a pervasive anxiety about the future, a future informed by the rise of surveillance culture. This chapter explores how this anxiety resonates throughout Spark's work as symptomatic of post-war experience, tethered to what I will call Spark's architecture of surveillance.

I have argued elsewhere that Spark's engagement with surveillance technologies (the wireless, the telephone, the tape recorder, the camera) exposes the instability of modern life in a post-war world, a period that gives rise to the birth of surveillance society and the development of the more complex and multidirectional surveillance culture of the twenty-first century.[7] Lyon argues that surveillance culture 'depends deeply on the participation of those being surveilled'.[8] Spark can be read as an early architect of Lyon's surveillance culture, whose 'process of observation is always implicitly a project of construction'.[9] Michael Gardiner has identified Spark's 'fully-fledged fascination with surveillance'[10] as intermittent, popping up in novels that are motivated by surveillance plots such as the Watergate novel *The Abbess of Crewe* (1974), or through the exploration of the inner lives of spies that inhabit *The Hothouse by the East River* (1973), *Aiding and Abetting* (2000), and *Territorial Rights* (1979), among others. While acts of surveillance are explicitly engaged in the intrigue-filled landscapes of these popular novels, Spark's engagement with surveillance is much broader in scope; it informs and infiltrates her entire oeuvre, including the seemingly innocuous spaces of the hospital geriatric ward in *Memento Mori* (1959), the women's hostel in *The Girls of Slender Means* (1963), and the classrooms of *The Prime of Miss Jean Brodie* (1961) and *The Finishing School* (2004), to name just a few examples. Indeed, surveillance within Spark's novels is positioned as a fact of everyday life, an everyday occurrence that we participate in as both observers and the observed.

As an architect of surveillance, Spark constructs narrative spaces that examine how surveillance culture is cultivated even today, in a world where 'not only being watched but watching itself has become a way of life'.[11] In 'The House of Fiction: Interviews with Seven English Novelists', Frank Kermode considers the state of contemporary fiction through interviews with the most prominent writers of the post-war period, including fellow architect of surveillance and benefactor Graham Greene. The final paragraph of Kermode's seven-part piece, which concludes his interview with Muriel Spark, invokes the window as a metaphor to explore the changing state of the contemporary novel. Kermode writes:

> The house of fiction has many windows, but at any given period they may all be designed as variations on a few basic shapes. What you see from them varies more considerably within these limits: irreducibly complex personalities, a sadistic landscape, a gaunt country house full of secrets that cannot survive the preternatural explicitness of its inhabitants, a mountain of cheese. And for the most part the people at present standing at these windows are content to say 'My window is shaped thus and thus,' rather than 'all windows should be

myth-shaped or fact-shaped' – there may be above all a God-shaped window giving perfect all-round visibility, but theirs is in no case held to resemble it.[12]

Kermode's window metaphor resonates directly with my claim for Spark as an architect of surveillance. In his seminal work *Toward an Architecture*, modernist architect and theorist Le Corbusier defines the function of the window in the context of a house as such: 'Windows are for admitting light – a little, a lot, or none at all – and for looking outside.'[13] Le Corbusier's utilitarian view of the house as 'a machine for living in'[14] uses windows to create a specific atmosphere through the light and shadows they cast on the floors, walls, and ceilings. When opened, they also allow fresh air to circulate within the otherwise denaturalised space. In a broader context, windows also serve a protective function, offering security from the unpredictability of the external environment, which ranges from weather systems and wildlife to more sinister and situational ones such as vandals or, to bring it back to surveillance, a Peeping Tom. Likewise, Kermode's deployment of the window metaphor considers both its banal and extraordinary contexts as it privileges the writer as architect, a producer of houses with windows whose landscapes vary according to placement and perspective. He identifies the variability of the landscapes of the post-war writers he interviews in order to demonstrate that the stable framework of the more traditional pre-war novels of the nineteenth century is starting to shift, becoming more malleable. In the tumultuous post-war period in which Kermode's metaphor emerges, then, windows come to reflect the perspectives of their authors-as-architects, which are not static but panoramic in scope, allowing for new and more expansive visions of the world to take shape. Of course, this expansion of perspective comes at the cost of greater exposure to the outside, opening up a vulnerability that suddenly becomes visible when the glass begins to crack. Reading Spark's windows as agents of surveillance, this essay explores the role that windows play in two of Spark's post-war novels, *The Girls of Slender Means* and *The Hothouse by the East River*, and in Spark's relatively unknown children's story *The French Window*, a tale composed in the late 1960s, but left unpublished until 1993.

The windows in this triad of texts, while utilised in different ways, all produce a similar tension between inside and outside that permeates the post-war world and extends beyond it to inform our understanding of contemporary surveillance culture.

Spark's attention to the physical spaces that her characters inhabit is integral to her engagement with both architecture and surveillance. Her understanding of architecture in practice can be gauged by the impeccable precision with which she draws her plans, describing the worlds her characters live in with the detail of what Kelly M. Rich describes, in her reading of *The Girls of Slender Means*, as an 'architectural blueprint'.[15] Take, for example, the painstaking detail provided in the narrator's description of Lise's flat in *The Driver's Seat* (1970):

> The lines of the room are pure; space is used as a pattern in itself, circumscribed by the dexterous pinewood outlines that ensued from the designer's ingenuity and austere taste when he was young, unknown, studious and strict-principled. [...]. Lise moved in when the house was new, ten years ago. She has added very little to the room; very little is needed, for the furniture is all fixed, adaptable to various uses, and stackable. [...]. Unlike the other tenants she has not put unnecessary curtains in the window; her flat is not closely overlooked and in summer she keeps the venetian blinds down over the windows and slightly opened to let in the light. [...]. Lise keeps her flat as clean-lined and clear to return to after her work as if it were uninhabited. The swaying tall pines among the litter of cones on the forest floor have been subdued into silence and into obedient bulks.[16]

Lise's flat reflects a utilitarian design resonant of the 'machines for living in' championed by Le Corbusier: it is both 'fixed' and 'adaptable' for different kinds of living, stripped of a distinct personality in favour of functionality and versatility.[17] Through her description of the minimalist interior of Lise's flat, Spark engages with the commonplace notion of the home as a reflection of the subject that lives within it, which in the context of the narrative perpetuates the unknowability of what Vassiliki Kolocotroni has defined as Lise's uncontainable death drive, positioning her as an 'enigma' that produces 'estranging effects'.[18] Spark draws attention to how little Lise needs to furnish her home, casting curtains as unnecessary luxuries – add-ons like trinkets or wall hangings. Unadorned, Lise's windows fulfil their function as a source of light and air, controlled by nondescript venetian blinds that one might find in an office building. And if the lack of curtains triggers anxieties about potential intruders, Spark's narrator keeps them at bay, noting as a point of fact that 'her flat is not closely overlooked'. This observation also – and most significantly in the present context – recognises the window as an agent of surveillance, anticipating the question of Lise's safety from outside threats or intruders.

The inaccessibility of the motive that drives *The Driver's Seat* to its end is reinforced by the architecture of Lise's living space, characterised as unrevealingly neutral and 'uninhabited'. While Lise has escaped observation, curating her flat in anticipation of her own curated departure from the text, that order is progressively undone within the narrative which perpetually resists it. The contrast between the bland, utilitarian space of Lise's flat and the very bold and obscene appearance that Lise takes on in the outside world as she searches for the right 'type' to murder her demonstrates the unstable relationship between inside and outside that is quintessentially Sparkian, a relationship that is also central to the construction of surveillance culture. Lyon argues that

> [Surveillance] is sometimes welcomed as a means to greater security or convenience, sometimes queried or resisted as being inappropriate or excessive, and sometimes engaged as an enjoyable or reassuring possibility offered by systems or devices – there is a potential to observe and monitor others and ourselves as never before. [...]. Watching has become a way of life.[19]

For Lise, who has been read as both inappropriate and excessive in her manner and actions – 'a consumer in a materialist world of gloss and smoothness and plate glass windows'[20] – surveillance becomes a means to an end. Throughout the novel, she surveils the world around her, collecting information that eventually leads her to her killer, who executes her fatal plan. Lise's willingness to remain open to threats from the outside, alluded to in the description of her naked window, is realised through her violent death.

As an architectural element, the window is both inside and outside at once. It is two-faced and transparent. These characteristics nonetheless allow for interactions between inside and outside to occur, though preference is given to the subject on the inside as the controller of access or actions from the outside. In other words, the inside is often privileged as a safety zone with the window positioned as a barrier or protective force from the outside elements, from weather, to window-shoppers, to watchmen. The outside, then, is always a potential threat to the inside due to both its material vulnerability (glass shatters) and its transparency, indicated by the fact that most windows carry with them the added protection of curtains, blinds, shutters and, in extreme cases, bars.

According to Lyon, 'any discussion of surveillance culture also has to confront the issue of transparency'.[21] Spark would agree, as is clear from this frequently cited passage from *The Girls of Slender Means*:

> Windows were important in that year of final reckoning; they told at a glance whether a house was inhabited or not; and in the course of the past years they had accumulated much meaning, having been the main danger-zone between domestic life and the war going on outside: everyone had said, when the sirens sounded, 'Mind the windows. Keep away from the windows. Watch out for the glass'.[22]

The site – and physical *sight* – of a broken window in *The Girls of Slender Means* is marked as unstable territory, an indicator that the violence of the world outside has infiltrated the perceived safety-zone of the domestic space and shaken things up. For Le Corbusier, the window as an architectural element is a 'destroyer of form'; it is a 'hole' sealed up with glass.[23] This design-oriented vision of the window runs counter to its perceived 'social' function of providing security and protection from the outside. Kelly M. Rich also considers how, in the context of Britain's welfare state, the presence of the window invites an encounter with a wartime culture of violence that destabilises the subjects on the inside, compelling them to ask 'is it safe out (t)here?'.[24] Within the framework of this argument, in which windows play a leading role, Rich argues that Spark delivers 'a compelling account of how domestic architecture structures how we assume ourselves to be inside and outside wartime violence, staging the encounter between these two spheres'.[25] Breaking down barriers between inside and outside, the (threat of) shattered windows in *The Girls of Slender Means* serves as a forewarning that all claims of safety and security in the post-war world should be viewed with suspicion. As architect, Spark utilises the window to demonstrate the fragility of the post-war experience, creating a space for her characters literally to get stuck in the in-between, destroying the carefully manufactured barrier that sustains the comforting illusion of domestic safety that governs the May of Teck Club and protects its inhabitants from the outside.

The 'outside' in *The Girls of Slender Means,* set in 1945, is composed of the remnants of war and includes 'bomb-sites piled with stony rubble, houses like giant teeth in which decay had been drilled out', and shattered glass. These fixtures of the landscape create a sobering architecture that is juxtaposed with the interior perspectives of the 'eager-spirited' girls of the May of Teck Club, who spend their days musing on material matters, primping for gentlemen callers, and counting calories to maintain their delicate figures.[26] The hostel and, as it turns out, *hostile* community of the May of Teck Club remains temporarily sheltered from the realities of the war: as the girls 'glance out of the windows in the early mornings', their youthful eyes filled with expectation, they appear impervious to the 'brutal and disillusioning' space that surrounds them.[27] The May of Teck Club itself, the narrator reports, 'had been three times window-shattered since 1940, but never directly hit'; following the bombings, 'the shattered windows had been replaced with new glass rattling in loose frames'.[28] Windows secure the fantasy of stability and coherence for the girls of slender means as they are continuously replaced with new glass, supporting Rich's argument about the Club's resilience in these times of crisis. But the resilience of the Club's architecture is eventually tested and proven to fail when the explosion of a rogue bomb – a remnant of an attack on the city dating back to 1942 – reveals its inherent vulnerabilities and causes its complete collapse. As the building literally crumbles to the ground, crushing one of its boarders beneath it, the May of Teck Club becomes nothing more than 'a high heap of rubble', fading into the 'familiar ruins of the neighbourhood'.[29] Following its destruction, Joanna Childe's father comes to London to view the site of his daughter's death. After a few minutes, the rector says, 'There's really nothing to see. […] it's all gone, all elsewhere'.[30] The physical collapse of the building's façade signifies something remarkable about its insides; its collapse exposes the savagery of the girls within, a savagery revealed by Selina Redwood, whose slim figure allows her to slip back into the building through the 'slit window'[31] of the skylight to rescue a vintage Schiaparelli dress only to immediately escape with it, leaving Joanna, the 'largest'[32] of the girls, stuck inside and left to suffocate beneath its remains.[33]

Kelly M. Rich contends that the windows in Spark's *The Girls of Slender Means* have something to 'teach us about rebuilding Britain'[34] and are 'a way of understanding the changing relationship between domestic interiors, wartime events, and psychological interiority'.[35] Though Rich does not discuss it, Elsa's window in *The Hothouse by the East River* further illustrates her claim. Set in 1970s Manhattan, the novel, which is often considered a companion to *Girls* due to its post-war content, follows the lives of Paul and Elsa, a couple haunted by their experience doing spy-work for British Intelligence during the Second World War. As a reflection of Spark's personal wartime experience in the British Foreign Office, Elsa presents a haunting nostalgia for the past. Throughout the novel, she positions herself at the window, looking outside, as if searching for something beyond the glass. Paul is constantly wondering what Elsa is looking at and becomes increasingly agitated by the sight of her at the window. 'She is looking for something out there', he concludes, 'Yes, she is looking for it again. Silently, Paul says to himself: "It's not there." And again, "There's nothing there."[36] Paul's statement recalls Joanna's father's words in *Girls*, signalling that there may be something in the 'nothing to see' – the emptied-out landscape beyond the window – that is worth considering. That something is reflected in the strangeness felt about the shadow that Elsa's window casts. Paul observes that Elsa's shadow 'falls behind her. Behind her, and cast by what light? She is casting a shadow in the wrong direction.'[37] Elsa is a shadow of herself, a remnant in this post-war landscape. The windows of her upscale apartment overlooking the East River come to foreshadow the devastating impact of wartime experience which the novel finally exposes when it is revealed that in fact Elsa and Paul did not survive the war but died, like Joanna Childe, when a V-2 bomb hit the train they were riding in on their way home. As Victoria Stewart observes, 'the odd detail of Elsa's shadow is also a partial clue to the fact that the protagonists' New York existence is not really an existence at all'.[38] Unlike the windows in *Girls* that, before their collapse, maintain a sense of stability against the war-torn landscape that surrounds the girls, the windows in Paul and Elsa's apartment create an atmosphere of apprehension and suspicion that governs the novel from its beginning and speaks to the psychological damage of war that turns people into ghosts.[39] Elsa's signature activity of window-gazing positions her as always already elsewhere, suggesting that survival and recovery in the post-war era is nothing more than an hallucination.

Marina MacKay, in her examination of the meaning of treason in Spark's work, positions *The Hothouse by the East River* as 'a typical Spark novel in that it is set in an artificially closed community'.[40] But what makes the novel exceptional is the way that 'its wartime origins indicate most explicitly how Spark's microcommunities might be seen to intersect with and model the wider community of the nation-state' in its post-war context.[41] Here, as in the May of Teck Club, the insular spaces of Spark's post-war fiction reflect the more expansive and inherently violent landscapes of the world outside their respective windows.

A more playful, but quintessentially menacing tale, *The French Window* presents an explicit deployment of the window as a tool for surveillance and provides another lens through which to examine Spark's engagement with post-war surveillance societies and her anticipation of today's complex and multifaceted surveillance culture. Lyon explains that

> 'Surveillance society' was originally used to indicate ways in which surveillance was spilling over the rims of its previous containers – government departments, policing agencies, workplaces – to affect many aspects of daily life. But the emphasis was still on how surveillance was carried out in ways that increasingly touched the routines of social life, from outside, as it were.[42]

The French Window exhibits this understanding of the surveillance state as it informs more localised social and domestic spheres through its depiction of a surveillance system composed entirely of windows, placing the architecture of surveillance at its centre.

It was written in the early 1960s alongside two other stories for children, *The Small Telephone* (1993) and *The Very Fine Clock*, the latter garnering more publicity when it was published with illustrations by the well-known children's book writer and illustrator Edward Gorey in 1968.[43] Gerard Carruthers provides a brief reading of *The Very Fine Clock* on the University of Edinburgh's blog for Scotland's Early Literature for Children Initiative, where he cites it as Spark's only book for children,[44] demonstrating the obscurity of these stories among Spark's readers and critics. Even Martin Stannard mentions the children's stories only in passing in his extensive biography of Spark.[45] Given this lack of critical attention, one might position Spark's children's stories as misfits in her oeuvre, a characteristic validated by Spark herself who dismissed the stories as one-offs written on a whim to 'give [her secretary] something funny to type out'.[46] These stories have significance here because they embed characteristics of surveillance culture that we find in the post-war novels discussed above, inviting us to read them not as outliers, but as conspirators in Spark's house of fiction. All three children's stories feature commonplace objects as their protagonists who participate in surveillance in different ways: a Swiss clock named Ticky observes the daily routines of a Professor and the inner workings of his domestic space in *The Very Fine Clock*; a neglected telephone named Doctor Downey taps into a shared line in search of his perfect companion in *The Small Telephone*; and, most notably, in *The French Window*, a network of windows launch a surveillance operation that reveals tensions between the landowner of a hillside estate and his tenants in the community below.

The plot of *The French Window* centres around a wealthy man named Georgie who finds an antique French window in a junk shop and purchases her for his home, an estate he oversees called the Turrets that stands apart from a peasants' village over the hills. The window's name is Mademoiselle Marie-Louise Yvonne de Crespigny-Foulard, but Georgie calls her Lou. Lou comes to learn that the windows of Georgie's estate see and hear all that happens around them:

> They had a great deal to tell each other because they all looked out on different scenes and every window looked inward, too, on a different part of the house. So together they knew everything that was going on inside and outside the house from all sides.

The windows report their observations to Georgie but they also communicate over the hills with those in the peasants' cottages so that 'all the windows in the hillside villages where the peasants lived would know what Georgie was doing at all times and what guests were staying at the Turrets'.[47] In this way the windows operate as a surveillance system, communicating by 'secret signal' to report on what is happening on both sides of the hill. Surveillance is positioned as mutually beneficial in that Georgie can use the information gained about the peasants to respond to their needs before they lodge complaints, and the peasants, in turn, can use what they learn about Georgie to manipulate him into giving them what they want. At first glance, this surveillance arrangement appears to maintain the stability of the estate and the community it contains. Yet it quickly becomes a source of unrest as it comes to reveal the hostility underlying the relationship between Georgie and the chief peasant, Kasper, mirroring the tension between inside and outside that pervades Spark's post-war novels.

If windows appear in Spark's post-war fiction to expose the unstable boundaries between inside and outside in the aftermath of the Second World War, framing the windows as spies in *The French Window* makes this tension explicit, echoing Nicholas Farrington's assertion in *The Girls of Slender Means* that 'nowhere's safe'.[48] Georgie's purchase of Lou is the catalyst for this revelation as she causes a damaging glitch in the system that threatens its collapse.[49] Because of her decadent appearance and superior attitude, Lou is immediately positioned as an outsider. Her fancy ornamentation and coloured glass position her as an object that is not simply functional but 'made to be looked at', setting her apart from the more ordinary windows of the rest of the estate. Lou's self-proclaimed nobility sustains her alienation from the other windows, whom she sees as being below her in social status. These physical and cultural differences quickly become a problem for Lou as she feels quite 'discontented and scornful' in her new environment. She refuses to talk to the other windows or to participate in their daily communication about the goings-on around the estate.

Lou's insistence on her elevated status amongst the windows in the home is continuously refused by the others as the hierarchy established at the Turrets has nothing to do with origins: the windows are valued for their structural position as it allows them to conduct effective surveillance, to see beyond the estate and into the village below. For example, Edgar, the far-sighted window with the 'sharpest and clearest' eyesight of the house and Miss So-and-so, the clever attic window who 'could see over the crest of hills where the peasants lived' have the most clout within their community as they are the chief communicators of important information.[50] In an effort to improve her visibility within the surveillance network, Lou decides that she must become a valuable source of information as well. She reports the most 'interesting' news that Georgie and Betty, Kasper's wife, have been meeting in secret, alluding to a scandalous affair that she anticipates will be of interest to the other windows. In fact, Georgie and Betty did meet in secret, but it was to plan a surprise birthday party for Kasper, not to engage in an affair. Lou's unauthorised story quickly launches a surveillance operation and the gossip spreads to the peasants' cottages and to Kasper, who orders his people to storm Georgie's estate in rebellion against the landowner's despicable behaviour. The peasants descend on the estate armed with stones, intending to attack the windows and to infiltrate the house, breaking down the barriers between outside and inside, while unwittingly destroying the surveillance system that has worked to maintain the peace.

Unlike the windows in *The Driver's Seat*, *The Girls of Slender Means*, and *The Hothouse by the East River*, which are positioned as objects through which to project the unstable relationship between inside and outside, the windows in *The French Window* operate as the antagonists of the text: their surveillance tactics mobilise the plot and instigate a violent uprising that mimics the effect of a bomb, revealing the inevitable rupture between outside and inside that Spark has demonstrated, through her other novels, to be characteristic of the post-war experience. At the same time, the windows serve on the front lines of Kasper's charge, willing to sacrifice themselves to preserve the integrity and stability of their localised surveillance society. In the end, the peasant army is quieted by Miss So-and-so who 'rattle[s] her glass pane free of her frame' and lands on Kaspar's head, knocking him to the ground and allowing Betty to step in and clear up the misunderstanding.[51] Despite this final resolution, several windows remain damaged by the attack, most notably Lou, who requires more time for repairs due to her 'unusual' characteristics. Even when Lou's scar is no longer visible, the narrator notes that permanent damage has been done, for 'she was no longer as fine a window as she had been before'.[52] The narrator's suggestion that the disruption caused by the uprising has lingering effects speaks to the way in which Spark's windows signal that the threat of rupture or destabilisation is always present in the post-war world. Lou's scar remains, even when it is no longer visible. In this way, *The French Window* speaks to Rich's argument that Spark's domestic architecture in *The Girls of Slender Means* reveals 'Britain's postwar fantasy of repair, one that imagined that reconstruction – the gleaming schools, health centers, and housing flats of wartime propaganda – would result in new forms of social equality'.[53] In this light, Lou's projected rehabilitation reads as an act of reparation which reinstates a sense of order and stability and re-establishes a hierarchy of the windows within the Turrets estate which provides the closure of the happy ending that a young audience would expect. But readers familiar with Spark's work will see this conclusion a bit differently, because it is rare that she leaves us sitting comfortably as we were, in a state of blissful ignorance.

The final line of *The French Window* delivers the moral that one expects to find at the conclusion of a children's tale, operating as a stabilising force in the now destabilised narrative. The narrator states: '[Lou] gave no trouble after that, and settled down to be more friendly and agreeable towards the other windows in the house, because she had learned her lesson.'[54] Yet Lou's humble transformation and promise to be on her best behaviour resonates in the Sparkian universe as an instance of silencing, indicating that any repair she has undergone is superficial at best. What the story has to teach then, within the context of Spark's architecture of surveillance, is that a surveillance state cannot operate without compliance, and the lesson learned is that compliance comes at a price to the individuals and communities employed to sustain it. In the surveillance culture of *The French Window* Lou functions as the site through which judgement is rendered. Taken at face value, it is a didactic tale that demonstrates the consequences of spreading gossip – or the wielding of what might now be called 'fake news' – through the savagery that emerges in the peasant uprising and its subsequent damage.[55] The rupture of the rebellion at the climax of the story exposes the sinister side of surveillance society that makes Lou's complicity in the moral of the story unsettling and its closure suspect, echoing the chilling effect of the final reveal that turns *The Hothouse by the East River* into a ghost story.

Through the windows of this triad of works, all conceived within the period of tremendous change and uncertainty that launched Spark into her longstanding career as a novelist, an architecture of surveillance emerges. Within this architecture are windows that open up new spaces for inquiry and interrogation, as they simultaneously invite reflection on a past that is always already present. The windows that threaten to dissolve the boundaries between inside and outside also reveal a fluidity between the past, the present, and an uncertain future that cannot be circumvented or overlooked but must, as Benjamin's angel of history[56] suggests, be confronted, if only fleetingly.

But a final point of reference, one of Spark's earliest writings, a poem titled 'Omen', written circa 1949, is also relevant here. The poem returns to Spark's image of herself as an observer, opening with the line: 'Here is the time of watching birds.' The poem goes on to consider the fate of its speaker as it asks 'which window saw where I have been to-morrow?'.[57] One could ask this of all of Spark's windows as they possess, in their very design, a simultaneous relationship with the past and the future to come, a knowledge of the future that is inextricably tethered to the past but is withheld from the subject who seeks it. It is the window that observes, not the observer. This final example demonstrates how Spark's architecture of surveillance invites us into the space between past and present, present and future, to reflect on how the spaces *we* inhabit inform the world we live in and how we live in it. Spark's windows expose the dissolution of boundaries between inside and outside in her post-war fiction, but in doing so also show us something about our contemporary moment, where the boundaries have become even more malleable and the danger-zones less visible.

Lyon positions the culture of surveillance as a twenty-first-century development, aligning with the birth of social media, a product of what he calls 'digital modernity' and argues that 'surveillance is no longer merely something external that impinges on "our lives". It is also something that everyday citizens comply with – willingly and wittingly or not – negotiate, resist, engage with and, in novel ways, even initiate and desire'.[58] While Spark's windows exist before the digital age comes fully into being, they certainly foresee the future in which we now exist where surveillance is ubiquitous, taking on new forms while performing the same function. Our windows have become screens and the architecture is a code that offers us new frames of reference through which to observe ourselves and each other, and to make our own judgements about an unstable and ever-changing future.

Endnotes

1. Muriel Spark, *Curriculum Vitae: A Volume of Autobiography* (New York, NY: New Directions Publishing, 1992), p. 18.
2. Spark, *Curriculum Vitae*, p. 142. For a more detailed account of Spark's work with Delmer in the context of her life, see Martin Stannard, *Muriel Spark: The Biography* (New York, NY: W. W. Norton & Company, 2010), pp. 59–71. For recent critical work engaging Spark's post-war work for British Intelligence as it influenced her post-war novels, see Marina MacKay, 'Muriel Spark and the Meaning of Treason', in *Muriel Spark: Twenty-First-Century Perspectives*, ed. David Herman (Baltimore, MD: John Hopkins University Press, 2010), pp. 94–111; and Victoria Stewart, *The Second World War in Contemporary British Fiction: Secret Histories* (Edinburgh: Edinburgh University Press, 2011).
3. David Lyon, *The Culture of Surveillance: Watching as a Way of Life* (Medford, MA: Polity Press, 2018), pp. 10–11.
4. Muriel Spark, 'The First Year of My Life', in *All the Stories of Muriel Spark* (New York, NY: New Directions Publishing, 2001), p. 276.
5. Ibid.
6. 'Architect', *Oxford English Dictionary*, 2nd edn (London: Oxford University Press, 1989).
7. Amy Woodbury Tease, 'Call and Answer: Muriel Spark and Media Culture', in *Modern Fiction Studies* 62.1 (Spring 2016), pp. 70–91.
8. Lyon, *The Culture of Surveillance*, p. 9.
9. Lewis MacLeod, 'Matters of Care and Control: Surveillance, Omniscience, and Narrative Power in *The Abbess of Crewe* and *Loitering with Intent*', in *Muriel Spark: Twenty-First-Century Perspectives*, ed. David Herman, pp. 203–24 (p. 206). This quotation is taken out of context but resonates as well for Spark as it does for her villain of *The Abbess of Crewe*, Alexandra, who MacLeod positions on the side of controlled surveillance in a text governed by surveillance technologies.
10. Michael Gardiner, 'Body and State in Spark's Early Fiction', in *The Edinburgh Companion to Muriel Spark*, eds. Michael Gardiner and Willy Maley (Edinburgh: Edinburgh University Press, 2010), pp. 27–39 (p. 34).
11. Lyon, *The Culture of Surveillance*, p. 9. MacLeod also engages Lyon but in relation to surveillance society and its 'two faces' of surveillance: care and control.
12. Frank Kermode, 'The House of Fiction: Interviews with Seven English Novelists', in *Partisan Review* 30.1 (Spring 1963), pp. 61–82 (p. 82).
13. Le Corbusier, *Toward an Architecture*, trans. John Goodman (Los Angeles, CA: Getty Publications, 2007), p. 168.
14. Ibid., p. 151.
15. Kelly M. Rich, '"Nowhere's Safe": Ruinous Reconstruction in Muriel Spark's *The Girls of Slender Means*', in *ELH* 83 (2016), pp. 1185–1209 (p. 1194).
16. Muriel Spark, *The Driver's Seat* (New York, NY: New Directions Publishing, 1970), pp. 13–14.
17. Le Corbusier, *Toward an Architecture*, pp. 88–89.
18. Vassiliki Kolocotroni, 'The Driver's Seat: undoing character, becoming legend', in *Textual Practice* 32.9 (2018), pp. 1545–62 (p. 1549).
19. Lyon, *The Culture of Surveillance*, pp. 10–11.

20 Patricia Waugh, 'Muriel Spark and the Metaphysics of Modernity: Art, Secularization, and Psychosis', in *Muriel Spark: Twenty-First-Century Perspectives*, ed. David Herman, pp. 63–93 (p. 67).
21 Lyon, *The Culture of Surveillance*, p. 129.
22 Muriel Spark, *The Girls of Slender Means* (New York, NY: New Directions Publishing: 1963), p. 8.
23 Le Corbusier, *Toward an Architecture*, p. 111.
24 Spark, *Girls*, p. 125; Rich, 'Ruinous Reconstruction in Muriel Spark's *The Girls of Slender Means*', p. 1195.
25 Rich, 'Ruinous Reconstruction in Muriel Spark's *The Girls of Slender Means*', p. 1191.
26 Spark, *Girls*, pp. 7–8.
27 Patrick Parrinder, 'Muriel Spark and her Critics', in *Critical Essays on Muriel Spark*, ed. Joseph Hynes (New York, NY: G.K. Hall & Company, 1992), pp. 74–84.
28 Spark, *Girls*, p. 8.
29 Ibid., pp. 130–37. See also Woodbury Tease, 'Muriel Spark and Media Culture', p. 80.
30 Spark, *Girls*, p. 137.
31 Ibid., p. 120.
32 Ibid., p. 127.
33 This reading of *The Girls of Slender Means* was initially conceived in my doctoral dissertation: Amy Woodbury Tease, *Technical Difficulties: Modernism and the Machine* (unpublished doctoral dissertation, Tufts University, 2011), pp. 119–34. For recent additional discussions and interpretations of the 'savagery' of *The Girls of Slender Means*, see Rich and MacKay.
34 Rich, 'Ruinous Reconstruction in Muriel Spark's *The Girls of Slender Means*', p. 1187.
35 Ibid., p. 1192.
36 Muriel Spark, *The Hothouse by the East River* (London: New Directions Publishing, 1973), p. 10.
37 Spark, *Hothouse*, p. 15.
38 Stewart, *The Second World War in Contemporary British Fiction*, p. 44.
39 Patricia Waugh discusses Elsa's post-war experience in *Hothouse* in relation to metaphysics and mental illness, with attention to Elsa's shadow as it represents a 'splitting of the human relation to the world'. Waugh, 'Muriel Spark and the Metaphysics of Modernity', p. 79.
40 MacKay, 'Muriel Spark and the Meaning of Treason', p. 101.
41 Ibid.
42 Lyon, *The Culture of Surveillance*, pp. 16–17.
43 Muriel Spark, *The Very Fine Clock* (New York, NY: Alfred A. Knopf, 1968).
44 Gerard Carruthers, 'Muriel Spark: *The Very Fine Clock*'. www.blogs.hss.ed.ac.uk/selcie/2017/11/02/muriel-spark-the-very-fine-clock-london-1969/#comments [accessed 10 February 2020].
45 Stannard, *Muriel Spark: The Biography*, pp. 324–26.
46 R. Hosmer, 'An Interview with Dame Muriel Spark', in *Salmagundi* 146/47 (2005), pp. 127–58 (p. 140).
47 Muriel Spark, *The French Window and The Small Telephone* (London: Colophon Press, 1993), pp. 11–12.

48 Spark, *Girls*, p. 125.
49 Spark, *The French Window*, pp. 12–13.
50 Ibid., pp. 15–16.
51 Ibid., p. 29.
52 Ibid., p. 31.
53 Rich, 'Ruinous Reconstruction in Muriel Spark's *The Girls of Slender Means*', p. 1190.
54 Spark, *The French Window*, p. 32.
55 For another take on Muriel Spark's work in relation to fake news see Adam Piette, 'Muriel Spark and fake news', in *Textual Practice* 32.9 (2018), pp. 1577–91.
56 W. Benjamin, 'Theses on the Philosophy of History', in *Illuminations: Essays and Reflections* (New York, NY: Mariner Books, 2019), pp. 196–206.
57 Muriel Spark, 'Omen', in *All the Poems of Muriel Spark* (New York, NY: New Directions Publishing, 2004), p. 26.
58 Lyon, *The Culture of Surveillance*, pp. 14–15.

12. Art and Industry Must Walk Hand in Hand: Muriel Spark and Twentieth-Century Design Ideology

FIONA JARDINE

'One day in the middle of the twentieth century [...]' begins Muriel Spark in *Loitering with Intent* (1981). Fleur, Spark's alter ego in the novel, remarks on the bundles of letters she has kept: 'Why? They are all neatly bundled up in thin folders, tied with pink tape, 1949, 1950, 1951 and on and on.'[1] 1951 was a marquee year for Spark, 'the first real turning point',[2] as visions of a self-sustaining literary career slowly began to crystallise in her life. Living in London, she had been publishing regularly in poetry periodicals since 1947, becoming acquainted with luminaries and aspirants during her brief stint as Secretary at the Poetry Society. She won the *Observer* short story competition in 1951 with her first 'professional' short story, spending some of her prize money on a talismanic blue velvet dress.[3] She also saw her first independently authored book published. Commemorating the centenary of Mary Shelley's death in 1851, *Child of Light* was intended by Spark to constitute 'a definitive biography'.[4]

In the history of British design, 1951, the year of 'The Festival of Britain' – the very definition of 'mid-century' – is also a landmark. Ostensibly a commemoration of the centenary of 'The Great Exhibition of 1851', the Festival aspired to present a vision of the future – the future already here – as a 'tonic' to the beleaguered nation. Centred on events in London, twenty-two Festival pavilions on the South Bank aimed to tell the story of 'The Land and the People of Britain', past, present and imminent future. At the Crystal Palace in 1851, the glories of Victorian ingenuity had been exhibited as heavily ornamented technological and imperial triumphs, much to the aesthetic and political dismay of Design Reformers and, later, Arts & Crafts advocates. Over the next hundred years, the dissatisfactions of Design Reformers coalesced as principles strongly associated with the Bauhaus and European Modernism: 'Truth to Materials' and 'Form follows

Function' became recognised as tenets and directives. Progressive British designers and manufacturers looked to infuse their approach to production with reference to these ideas, attempting to produce 'industrial art' as 'good design' until the Second World War reprioritised manufacturing efforts. Associated with the Festival in 1951, a select group of designers, curators and critics were given the opportunity to return to Modernist ideas and try to develop them pedagogically for the British public-at-large, shaping post-war lifestyles and catalysing consumption. The Festival was intended to signal the end of austerity and promote the virtues of a brand new everyday life organised by experts.

Michael Frayn judged the Festival the last work of the publicly minded, left-leaning Herbivores:

> [...] gentle ruminants, who look out from the lush pastures which are their natural station in life with eyes full of sorrow for less fortunate creatures, guiltily conscious of their advantages though not usually ceasing to eat the grass. And in making the Festival they earned the contempt of the Carnivores – the readers of the *Daily Express*; the Evelyn Waughs; the cast of the Directory of Directors – the members of the upper- and middle-classes who believe that if God had not wished them to prey on smaller and weaker creatures without scruple he would not have made them as they are.[5]

Martin Stannard remarks that Spark 'seems not to have joined the crowds thronging the South Bank to visit the Skylon and the Festival Hall', suggesting that he half-expected to find some material trace of a visit in her archives.[6] His reading of Spark's papers from this period define the absence of comment for other significant political and cultural events too – 'the Coronation, the ascent of Everest, general elections, spy scandals, the Suez Crisis, the Hungarian uprising [...] [pass] her by as shadow play'.[7] In 1951, Stannard observes Spark was deeply engaged in producing a critical study of the Poet Laureate, John Masefield. Resident in Kensington, she was also 'writing speeches for industrialists based on very few data' at the public relations firm of Pearson Horder, contemplating conversion to Catholicism and teetering on the verge of a nervous breakdown.⁸ She continued to write poetry, including 'The Ballad of the Fanfarlo' and 'The Rout', a poem inspired by a report from Market Harborough of a battle between bees and wasps that played out in the eaves of an ancient church.⁹ As Frayn posits Herbivore against Carnivore in his assessment of the Festival, in 'The Rout', Spark posits 'the wealthy sweet', 'ancestral' Bees against 'upstart' Wasps, 'now eating the honey'. Frayn and Spark's binaries are reflected in the generational tensions between old, 'British', establishment industrialists and new, often 'European', design professionals that surface in inter- and post-war design literature: in his autobiographical treatise, *Eye for Colour*, Bernat Klein, a Jewish emigré and textile designer who worked in Scotland from 1951 until his death in 2014, explains:

> The post-war Years in British Industry [...] were not exactly peaceful. Two generations were confronting each other across the conference table: on the one side the old, old ones and the middle-aged old ones [...] filling the spaces or hanging on to power [...] because they wanted to make sure that things would continue to be done the way they had always done them; and on the other side, were the young ones who had no industrial achievements to boast of and had nothing to offer except vigour, enterprise and open minds.¹⁰

Even if Spark's frenetic schedule prevented a physical visit to the pleasure gardens and exhibition halls across the Thames, that Spark was more than merely conscious of the Festival, its rhetoric and political agenda, may be construed from her work dealing with the period, particularly some of the short stories published in *The Go-away Bird & Other Stories* (1958).

On one level, some of Spark's short stories in *The Go-away Bird* can be seen to deal directly with the objects and appearance of Festival style. 'Miss Pinkerton's Apocalypse' literalises a flying saucer, delivering the punchline 'It is not radioactive [...] it is Spode'.¹¹ The saucer's atypical behavior raises suspicion that it is a 'forgery' rather than genuine Spode. Harry Hopkins observes that the 'flying saucer' myth was given recurrent neurotic and popular expression in the decade following 1947, and Miss Pinkerton's hallucinatory saucer takes flight in an atmosphere of general anxiety punctuated with contemporary aesthetics designed to promote a new visual register populated with unusual geometeries and motifs derived from space and science.[12] While the alien presence of the Festival's hemispheric Dome of Discovery and 'floating' Skylon tower dominated the London skyline, in the Festival's pavilions, Wedgwood crockery decorated with illustrations derived from the atomic structure of beryl was on display.[13] Such crockery and similarly inspired domestic designs were realised through the activities of the Festival Pattern Group, which had been formed to demonstrate potential mutualities between crystallography and design across a range of household products.[14] According to Mary Schoeser, the Festival Pattern Group aimed, in part, to domesticate 'science', thereby diminishing the impact of its previously frightening nuclear representations – through a process of softer visual familiarisation, the public would, gently, intimately, obliquely, become inured to the rule of science in their lives.[15] In Spark's story, the collusion of the (supposedly) scientific and the domestic is suspect and intrusive, giving rise to a fantastical and comical paranoia.[16] 'Miss Pinkerton's Apocalpyse' is as trivial as Shelley's *Frankenstein* is epic, Spark having published *Child of Light* in 1951, and *My Best Mary: Selected Letters of Mary Shelley* with Derek Stanford in 1953.[17]

Spark's description of a Mayfair drawing room in her short story, 'Daisy Overend', plays with more immediately recognisable mid-century design tropes:

> [It] was furnished in a style that in many ways anticipated the Member's Room at the Institute of Contemporary Arts. Mrs Overend had recently got rid of her black and orange striped divans, cushions and sofas. In their place were curiously cut slabs, polygons and three-legged manifestations of Daisy Overend's personality, done in El Greco's colours. As Daisy kept on saying, no two pieces were alike, each was a Contemporary version of a traditional design.
>
> In her attempt to create a Contemporary interior, she was, I felt, successful, and I was quite dazzled by its period charm.[18]

Here, she undermines the essential, Modernist myth that 'good' design – exemplified by the Member's Room at the Institute for Contemporary Arts (ICA) – is timeless, defying 'fashion', uncorrupted by sentiment or personality, and in a seemingly casual inadvertence, she reveals the machismo that underpins it. 'Personality', an unthreatening quality assigned to women in this era (evident in, amongst other things, Spark's references to cosmetics in *The Comforters* from 1957) corrupts and commercialises that which is universal; but for Spark, control over the formation and perception of personality is a hermetic power. Hope Howell Hodgkins has discussed the pivotal symbolism of key garments in Spark's novels, remarking on the specific capacity of clothing to symbolise the trivial and the momentous in the same instance, to deploy as *non sequitur*.[19] What Hodgkins terms 'the postwar comedy of the object' capitalises on the life experience of female writers who, having been denied agency as women, were alert to the potential of using fashion as an unspoken tool for self-construction, for controlling the formation and perception of 'personality'. Hodgkins contends that the significance of dress as a rhetorical device has been overlooked in literary criticism, with the result that Spark's work has been marginalised:

> [T]he power of the approach lies in the frisson between serious and trivial, along with the decision to laugh [...] postwar women employed dress to humorously objectify the self: not in the free indirect discourse that privileged the modernist hero, but through a pared down grammar as wittily understated as any Movement poem, as chilly, and as funny.[20]

Appreciating Spark's sophisticated deployment of fashion requires an understanding of how fashion operates as a language to embody identities. Mention of a dress or a skirt allows Spark – a skilful dresser in her own life – to construct, almost in passing, a 'leveling aesthetic' that employs 'an ostensibly shallow surface over a deep structure of protest'.[21] The blindspot Hodgkins describes is, of course, a problem associated principally (and unevenly) with women's writing because of the gendered perception that clothes are more important to women as a cultural and creative negotiation in everyday life and can therefore be ignored or missed as the basis for general criticism: historically, fashion has been seen as a subject and language that is more appropriately 'female', a focus for women's writing but not for 'writing'. Hodgkins contrasts the use of dress in post-war fiction by Spark (and Barbara Pym) to that of Kingsley Amis. Whereas the former manipulate and undermine the objectification of women by interrupting the male gaze, using dress to give characters command or mastery over the process of objectifying and being objectified in order to alter the terms on which they may be read, the latter details dress to exemplify female instability and bad taste in a flat, one-dimensional manner:

> [I]n *Lucky Jim*, Dixon's hysterical girlfriend is characterised repeatedly by her hideous green Paisley frock in combination with the low-heeled, quasi-velvet shoes, whilst the dream-girl Christine is notable only for having blonde beauty and large breasts (the style of Dixon's ripped pants is never detailed).[22]

With specific reference to *Vogue*, Hodgkins considers the role that fashion magazines played in cultivating and shifting the behavioural boundaries for women during the Second World War: in post-war lifestyle journalism, 'personality' individuated women enough to generate traction for consumerism. Whereas the link between women's fiction, fashion and lifestyle magazines may be obvious in an off-the-cuff reference to a name like 'Schiaparelli', the proximity of female writers to the low-level language of these magazines, in editorials and advertising, positions them as important structural and social models. Spark, who trained in 'commercial and précis writing' at Heriot-Watt College, was perhaps more attuned than most to the sympathies between poetic expression and what Marshall McLuhan dubbed 'The Folklore of Industrial Man'.[23] There is evidence in her work of the direct appropriation of advertising slogans and metaphors – she uses the stem of an Edinburgh department store's slogan, 'Darlings of Edinburgh: Famous for Fashion', to preface descriptions of the qualities of each member of the set in *The Prime of Miss Jean Brodie* (1961); she opens her New York novel, *The Hothouse by the East River* (1973), with a casual exchange in a shoeshop – 'They fit like a glove' – a phrase which toys with the surrealist branding and narrative potential of 'Footgloves', a range of comfortable shoes widely advertised to women in the 1950s.[24] However, it is perhaps the formal and ideological properties of editorial and other non-literary language that asserts a more sustained presence in her work. The training she received at Heriot-Watt was practical rather than literary, designed to equip students to pursue clerical and secretarial work. The ability to condense and abbreviate was highlighted in the syllabus she followed:

> OUTWARD CORRESPONDENCE – (a) Commercial English; principles that make for good business style; solecisms; synonyms; business terms and phrases; abbreviations; reported speech; punctuation [...] INWARD CORRESPONDENCE – (a) Preservation of letters received; files; pigeon holes; the docket; inward letter book. (b) Indexing. (c) Principles of Précis Writing. (d) Indexing and Précis of commercial correspondence.[25]

Applied to fiction, do the skills she developed on this course (partly) explain her ability to construct concise, economic prose, or her attraction to short forms? In this respect, there is much to be gained from comparing Spark's vocabulary and literary style to texts found in magazines, advertisements and similar non-literary sources of the period.

For example, if Spark's story, 'The Black Madonna', is read through some of the texts produced to interpret Festival displays (Laurie Lee was chief caption writer), it can be seen to function as a critique of the 'contemporary' as the basis for the kind of ideal home and lifestyle promoted in the Festival.[26] In 'The Black Madonna', Raymond and Lou Parker befriend a couple of young Jamaican men who have been recently employed at the factory where Raymond works. When, after offering prayers to a 'miraculous' Madonna at the local church, Lou gives birth to a daughter, she is consternated to discover the baby is much darker than she or Raymond expect. Despite tests proving Raymond is the father, the Parkers arrange to have their longed-for child adopted. Spark is never explicit about the source of the baby's paternity, deliberately confusing the divine, adulterous and legitimate.

The Parkers live in a council flat, with three rooms and a kitchen, in the new town of Whitney Clay:

> Whitney Clay had swallowed up the old village. One or two cottages with double dormer windows, an inn called The Tyger, a Methodist chapel, and three small shops represented the village; the three shops were already threatened by the Council; the Methodists were fighting to keep their chapel. Only the double dormer cottages and inn were protected by the Nation and so had to be suffered by the Town Planning Committee.
>
> The town was laid out like geometry in squares, arcs (to allow for the by-pass), and isosceles triangles, breaking off, at one point, to skirt the old village which, from the aerial view, looked like a merry doodle on the page.[27]

Playing spatial order and disorder off against each other, Spark sarcastically sets the exposure of racial prejudices and religious hypocrisies against the controlled geometry of apparently civic-minded modernity, casting the willing embrace of post-war planned living as neurotic, snobbish and judgemental. The desire to secure better homes for all was a defining feature of the post-war British political and social imaginary, one that required the proposition of new models for living.[28] To this end, 'furnished rooms', captioned by Lee, were an important and popular attraction at the Festival. They were staged interiors, imagined theatrically, reliant on the characterisation of the 'types' supposed to inhabit them along lines of class and geography (urban or rural).[29] Promoting the notion of home as a place for leisure, relaxation and entertainment, furnished rooms presented open-plan, multi-purpose spaces and a range of goods – angle-poise lamps, sewing machines, record players – for hobbyists and hosts. Specific scenarios were set up – 'sitting room with dining recess for a farmer and his wife', 'day and night nursery for 4 years old girl', 'bed-sitting room for an elderly maiden lady' – and rooms were furnished accordingly, with these characters in mind.[30]

Furnished rooms were an established display form in British trade fairs and exhibitions, playing a central role in one of the Festival's immediate antecendants, 'Britain Can Make It!' in 1946. This hastily arranged exhibition of the best of British manufacturing involved the Design Research Unit (DRU) in a central planning role: Herbert Read, who co-founded the ICA in 1947, was involved with the DRU from 1943.[31] For 'Britain Can Make It!', John Betjeman, who had editorial roles at the *Architectural Review* during the 1930s, was commissioned to produce descriptions of the notional occupants of each room set according to their profession, family habits and cultural inclinations. Thus, for a 'dining room in a small suburban villa', Betjeman's label detailed an (absent) curate, 'keen naturalist and great reader; hard up. His wife; collects modern pottery. Their three children who do their homework in this room.' 'The living room in an old stone house in Scotland' is home to a 'Water engineer; strong Scots traditionalist; authority on local customs. His wife writes novels on Scottish Country life. Their son, an engineering student.'[32] It is tempting to scan Betjeman's treatments for the most 'Sparkian' set-up simply because her schematic approach to representation has so much affinity with the form: a single female journalist (aged thirty-five), 'widely travelled but now working in the Civil Service', occupies a bed-sitting room in a block of flats. It is furnished with a sheepskin hearth rug, a two-foot six-inch single divan, a colour print of the Roscommon Dragoon and a Good Companion portable typewriter: the occupant of this bed-sitting room could well be 'Caroline Rose'. Spark rehearses and extends the form of similar 'furnished rooms' demography in 'The Black Madonna':

> The Parkers were among the few tenants of Cripps House who owned a motor-car. They did not, like most of their neighbours, have a television receiver [...]. The Parkers went to the pictures only when *The Observer* had praised the film; they considered television not their sort of thing; they adhered to their religion; they voted Labour; they believed the twentieth century the best so far; they assented to the doctrine of original sin; they frequently applied the word 'Victorian' to ideas and people they did not like [...].[33]

In terms of post-war design ideology, 'Cripps House', the name of the Parkers' building, could hardly be less incidental. Sir Stafford Cripps held office in

Clement Atlee's post-war Labour government first as Chairman of the Board of Trade, then as Chancellor of the Exchequer. He was an enlightened supporter for the efforts of design's ideologues, initiating 'Britain Can Make It!' and advancing plans for the Festival of Britain until the brief passed to Herbert Morrison. Mention of Cripps effects a deliberate and disaffected 'levelling': it is a reference that would have been immediately appreciable by a British audience reading 'The Black Madonna' when it was first published. In Spark's hands, it is a perjorative aside that configures the story as a critique of culture, design and architecture as implemented through the policies of the Labour government: the Welfare State Madonna in Whitney Clay, crafted from bog-oak, '[l]ooks a bit like contemporary art' and cannot be despoiled with the addition of unnecessary frills, no matter how sincerely devotional.[34] Spark, voicing a popular British conservatism towards visual and material culture, is dismissive of new, 'contemporary' stuff and spaces, believing that when historical traces are removed from objects and the environment, the attendant loss of meaning and position is not properly compensated for by safety and order.[35] Safety, as Jean Brodie makes clear in *The Prime of Miss Jean Brodie*, is the enemy of Truth and Beauty.[36]

Alongside 'Daisy Overend' and 'You Should Have Seen the Mess', Derek Stanford viewed 'The Black Madonna' as a 'comedy of manners', commenting, in the terms popularised by Nancy Mitford, that the 'satire and observation in these pieces has no fixed social bias, but is dealt out freely to "U" and "non-U"'.[37] Stanford, whose place in Spark's life has, to date, been overlooked in terms of the extent of its potential 'soft' cultural influence, published a critical biography of Betjeman in 1961 (Spark and Stanford parted ways in 1959), and it is perhaps Betjemanian ideas, by way of Stanford, that inform Spark's consideration of the intermeshed issues of class and town planning:

> What [Betjeman] has to say about post-war 'progressive' thinking is couched with more acerbity. The 'Planster' with his 'Vision of the Future', with his 'workers' flats in fields of soya beans', with his 'microphones in communal canteens' proclaiming 'All's perfect

evermore' is only one version, one Left Wing symbol, of Mr Betjeman's distrust of the present. Brewers' combines, bent on converting the 'dear old inn' with its 'paraffin lamps' into uniform, neon-lit roadhouses, are duly and poetically black-listed by him.[38]

In her short stories and early novels, Spark maintains an ambivalence about class in order to construct the 'artistic' as a category apart, allowing certain characters to transcend their points of origin or maintain a fascinated, aestheticising distance from others. That said, Spark's construction of the 'artistic' belies her conservative, establishment leanings. She recalls her own accidental, reverent experience of Louis MacNeice's shabby, bohemian home, as a defining moment, effectively binding an aesthetic imbued with historical traces and casual privilege to the practice of being an artist.[39] The evidence of MacNeice's artistic life (prior and parallel to the work of art) is communicated as aura, through relics and remnants: essentially, an artistic life is a spiritual life and is thus removed from considerations of 'class'. Ironically, when Arthur Danto theorised this kind of auratic power within the idiom of conceptual art, he named his treatise *The Transfiguration of the Commonplace* after the one written by Sandy Stranger/Sister Helena in *The Prime of Miss Jean Brodie*:

> Hers was a title I admired and coveted, resolving to take it for my own should ever I write a book that might suit. As it happens, the events in the artworld which provoked the philosophical reflections in this book were just that: transfigurations of the common place, banalities made art. When it seemed I might then have a use for the title, I wrote to Muriel Spark of the takeover, curious to know what might have been the content of Sister Helena's book, which is not made manifest in the novel [...] she replied, to my delight, that it would have been about art, as she herself practiced it.[40]

Registers of practice between visual art, writing and design, are rarely seamless, and often contradictory. During the 1950s, Spark's position on art and design was undoubtedly informed by her close relationship with Stanford who, in addition to his demonstrable interest in Betjeman, had long venerated Herbert Read as an ideal anarchist-aesthete and was at least conversant with what was then fairly niche Modernist design ideology. Stanford notes that, during the 1930s, he was 'mightily taken' by Read's volumes on visual criticism, including his seminal work *Art & Industry*, and, in 1939, he had been in attendance at the opening of one of the first Surrealist exhibitions in Britain at the Whitechapel Gallery in order to hear Read speak. Read was, in effect, the main proselytiser for European Modernism in Britain, formulating his approach through ideas connected with, amongst others, the Bauhaus and Le Corbusier.[41] In 1950, Read provided the preface for *A Tribute to Wordsworth*, one of the books Stanford collaboratively authored with Spark.[42] That year, there appears to have been a shift in the way that Spark and Stanford viewed Read following an incident at the ICA which saw him rebuke the poet Emmanuel Litvinoff when he publically denounced T. S. Eliot on grounds of anti-Semitism.[43] Thereafter, Spark openly criticised Read's position on Mary Shelley's place in the life of her husband: 'Read's first faulty statement, however, occurs when he says that Mary "did nothing" but sentimentalize; for Mary did a great many things after Shelley's death besides bringing up a son and educating him well [...]'.[44] In 1952, she reviewed Read's recently published *The Philosophy of Modern Art* in tandem with a new selection of John Ruskin's writings. She calls into question Read's distance from Ruskin's 'Tory' ideals, finding Ruskin, who had been deeply opposed to industrial manufacture, 'too soft' and Read 'too hard', commenting further that Read, an archetypal Herbivore, 'addresses the sensibility of an artistic élite (rather than a wider public)', before qualifying that by stating he is 'a fundamental thinker who understands how far artistic expression had been separated from everyday life'.[45] Suffice to say that during the 1950s, Read is a significant presence in the shadow-land of both Spark and Stanford.

To return to 'The Black Madonna' with Read's influential design ideology and Betjeman's Middle England conservatism to hand deepens its appeal as a critique of Modernist design and architecture. When, in contrast to the

Parkers, Spark establishes Lou's fecund, feckless sister, Elizabeth, in a very downward quarter of Bethnal Green, Elizabeth's threadbare dirty rooms are evidence of both her poverty and moral turpitude, as well as her libidinous fertility. Lou trained as a nurse among white painted beds and white shining walls, and is secure enough to send Elizabeth a weekly postal order, imagining that the money will be spent on maintaining a well-scrubbed, spotless abode.[46] Disappointed that this is not the case, Lou reminisces:

> When she had first married, she had wanted all white-painted furniture that you could wash and liberate from germs; but Raymond had been for oak, he did not understand the pleasure of hygiene and new enamel paint, for his upbringing had been orderly, he had been accustomed to a lounge suite and autumn tints in the front room all his life. And now Lou stood and looked at the outside of Elizabeth's place and felt she had gone right back.[47]

Here Spark exploits the homophonic potential of 'Lou' as she deftly commutes Le Corbusier's austere 'Law of Ripolin' to a fetish for cleanliness that is the lot of the barren, house-proud woman, isolated from history (from relics and remnants), struggling with the first manifestations of a multicultural society and denied the comforts of true faith. Le Corbusier, the totemic Modernist architect, intended his 'Law of Ripolin' to obliterate the kind of nostalgic self-deception perpetuated by the accretion of dead things from the past:

> A COAT OF WHITEWASH [...] [is] a moral act [...]. Imagine the results of the Law of Ripolin. Every citizen is required to replace his hangings, his damasks, his wallpapers, his stencils with a plain white coat of Ripolin. His home is clean. There are no more dirty, dark corners. Everything is shown as it is. Then comes inner cleanness, for the course adopted leads to refusal to allow anything at all which is not correct, authorized, intended, desired, thought out [...]. Once you put Ripolin on the walls you will be master of yourself.[48]

Whether or not Spark's word play extends to Adolf Loos is a matter for conjecture, however his seminal polemic, 'Ornament & Crime', first delivered in 1910, sits in the background of Le Corbusier's 'Law of Ripolin':

> We have outgrown ornament; we have fought our way to freedom through ornament [...]. Soon the streets of the city will glisten like white walls. Like Zion, the holy city, the capital of heaven. Then fulfilment will be come.[49]

Boiled down and domesticated, 'Ornament & Crime' echoes, via Read, through Spark's casual descriptions of the interiors in 'The Black Madonna' – all that white-painted furniture. Loos, an Austrian architect, considered ornament to be degenerate and economically wasteful, a distraction from the pure, well-designed forms that would permit the full realisation of a healthy life. 'You Should Have Seen the Mess', a short story included in *The Go-away Bird*, can also be read in dialogue with the Modernist ideals of Loos and Le Corbusier. The narrative takes the form of a monologue delivered by Lorna, a young woman, educated at a 'light and airy', 'washable' secondary modern (in preference to a dusty grammar school). Lorna spurns the advances of her would-be suitor, Willy Morley, because he is unhygienic despite the fact that he is an artist with pots of money and she is attracted to him. Lorna's existential aspirations, which could have been artistic, are lampooned by the sad, controlled domesticity of their gendered materialisation. Loos viewed the propensity to decorate as indicative of regressive criminal, primitive and gendered tendencies, thus, it was out of step with properly evolved, twentieth-century imperatives:

> The rate of cultural development is held back by those that cannot cope with the present. I live in the year 1908, but my neighbor lives approximately in the year 1900, and one over there lives in the year 1880. It is a misfortune for any government, if the culture of its people is dominated by the past. The farmer from Kals lives in the twelfth century [...].[50]

Across her fiction, Spark's insinuations of temporal slippage bear comparison to such passages in 'Ornament & Crime'. For example, in her treatment of the public-facing and more rigourously private spaces in 'Daisy Overend', Spark, playing with the presentation of self, sets Mrs Overend's 'up-to-the-minute' drawing room against an ancestral, Edwardian bedroom. The bedroom's faded pink colour scheme hints at a colonial past, its frilly tulle despoiled, stained and burned:

> I did not solve the mystery of Daisy's taste in bedrooms, not then nor at anytime. For, whenever I provide a category of time and place for her, the evidence is default. A plant of the twenties, she is also the perpetrator of that vintage bedroom. A lingering limb of the old leisured class, she is also the author of that bedroom.[51]

Spark distrusts the emphasis of a Modernist like Loos on bringing objects, buildings, environments and, ultimately, people into line with a seamless, ideological present. In *The Prime of Miss Jean Brodie*, as Brodie leads her set through Edinburgh's Old Town, having witnessed the fascistic uniforms of the Girl Guides and sensitive to the risks inherent in subscribing to Brodie's cult of personality, Sandy becomes aware that 'there were other people's Edinburghs quite different from hers [...] other people's nineteen-thirties'.[52] Humorously, in *Loitering with Intent*, Fleur comments of her office job 'The wages he offered were of 1936 vintage, and this was 1949, modern times'.[53]

'The Black Madonna' and 'You Should Have Seen the Mess' anticipate *The Prime of Miss Jean Brodie* inasmuch as they deal with the risks of subjugating the self to ideology. At the Marcia Blaine School for Girls, the Modern curriculum, which Brodie dissuades her set from, is associated with domestic science, gymnastics and Guiding, developing team spirit as it curbs personal ambition. Pure science, of the experimental sort practiced by the thrilling, marvellous Miss Lockhart in her sexually charged science room, falls into the same artistic category as Brodie's wilfully idiosyncratic pedagogy which allows for the veneration of a charismatic leader like Mussolini at the same time as it dismisses unqualified adherence to authoritarianism: but that is a knife-edge. Miss Lockhart's Frankensteinian power to absolve stains from the tussore silk clothing of teenage girls is a literal fascination. Mediating the dialectics between chance and intention, embodiment and intangibility, permanence and transience, staining is a recurrent trope in Spark, exploited for all its metaphorical capacity in *The Driver's Seat* (1970). The connection with mortification of the flesh in Catholic theology is obvious, but in Spark's personal lexicon, staining is also bound up with the aesthetics and experience of being artistic, sexual and anti-Modern.

In *The Driver's Seat*, Spark returns to the interest she demonstrates in the rhetorical value of architecture and interiors in 'The Black Madonna' and 'Daisy Overend', though the notional period for the narrative has moved on a decade or so. Lise, Spark's anti-heroine, is established in a 'meticulously neat', uncompromisingly Modern and impersonal flat:

> Since it was put up the designer has won prizes for his interiors, he has become known throughout the country and far beyond and is now no longer to be obtained by landlords of moderate price. The lines of the room are pure; space is used as a pattern in itself, circumscribed by the dexterous pinewood outlines that ensued from the designer's ingenuity and austere taste when he was young, unknown, studious and strict-principled [...] She has added very little to the room; very little is needed, for the furniture is all fixed, adaptable to various uses, and stable. Stacked into a panel are six folding chairs, should the tenant decide to entertain six for dinner. The writing desk extends to a dining table, and when the desk is not in use it, too, disappears into the pinewood wall [...] everything is contrived to fold away into the dignity of unvarnished pinewood [...] nothing need be seen, nothing need be lying around.[54]

Multi-functional and modular living was heavily promoted in the Festival, and Lise's apartment is a rigorous demonstration of that. A smarter counterpart to Daisy Overend's living room, Lise's flat is expertly designed to be entirely simultaneous with itself, its desirable adaptability translates into a series of pre-determined functions that require the barest animation – an equivalent in interiors to the stain-resistant dress that Lise refuses to buy. In terms of its post-war context, stain-resistance, like wrinkle-proofing and colour-fastness, was promoted to women who constituted the principal market for clothes and domestic textiles (including those bought for others – husbands and children). Synthetic textiles that embodied these qualities had the capacity to perform some of the (female) labour associated with cleaning, maintaining and repairing clothing and household goods. They are co-extensive with the changing roles ascribed to women in the post-war years. Unlike textiles produced from natural materials, synthetic textiles incorporate values and performance capabilities that have been designed into fibres from the outset: their utility is in-built.[55] They directly encode twentieth-century capitalist drives for convenience, durability and the standards of mass production. Spark's strategic use of the stain-resistant dress symbolises the compromises that Lise has made – and cannot sustain – as a working woman who, aged twenty-nine or thirty-six, is (in the 1970s) no longer young, who is single and (still) self-creating. Lise's choice to self-determine is pitched against the absence of ordinary domestic chores in her life and facilitated by the conveniences offered by contemporary design: the housework required to maintain her meticulously neat, modular apartment is negligible, the clothes she rejects for purchase can look after themselves. She has time, but she is constricted. As well as performing labour, textiles which refuse signs of aging or wearing – fading, wrinkling, soiling, tearing – exist ideologically and phenomenologically in a permanent present, outwith expected chronologies: they embody and express the metaphysics of twentieth-century design. Subject to, and subjugated by, the male gaze, women were accustomed to negotiating a similar refusal to age physionomically. Cosmetic advertising at this time reiterates some of the promises made by, or for, stain-resistant, wrinkle-free clothing: 'The Time to be Lovely is – Always' declaims an advert for Boots No. 7.[56] The promotion of timelessness is therefore part of the ambient textscape that women inhabit, and again brings into focus the relevance of the language of fashion and lifestyle magazines as sources for the subjects and structures of Spark's fiction. Lise is a timeless woman with time to hand.

The cultural anxieties produced by the advent of synthetic textiles are dealt with in Alexander Mackendrick's film *The Man in the White Suit*, released in the Festival year of 1951. An Ealing production, it addresses the horrific implications of synthetic fabrics for a traditional firm of textile manufacturers whose patrician interests are threatened by the invention of a brilliant new material, a miracle fibre which does not deteriorate, nor does it stain. Sidney Stratton, the chemist responsible for inventing it, finds himself pilloried by mill-owners and workers alike. *The Man in the White Suit* sits most obviously in the hinterland of *The Ballad of Peckham Rye* (1960). The subject of textile manufacture and the drive to improve productivity surfaces casually when Dougal Douglas, Sidney Stratton's alliterative twin, finds employment in 'human research' at the textile firm of Meadows, Meade & Grindley, and at their more progressive rivals, Drover Willis. The mediation of labour relations in *The Man in the White Suit* reveals the acute tension between tradition and innovation in established manufacturing industries in the post-war period (recalling Bernat Klein's observations), though that is not Spark's main focus in *The Ballad of Peckham Rye*.[57] Spark's experience as a writer of 'speeches for industrialists' at Pearson Horder may have informed the novel, but the conversations that Dougal has with his employers reveal Read as an equally important influence.[58] At Meadows, Meade & Grindley, Read's theories appear to have found favour: 'At the interview Mr Druce said to Dougal, "We feel the time has come to take on an Arts man. Industry and Arts must walk hand in hand."'[59] Drover Willis appear to be driven by harder-nosed economies:

> Mr Willis smiled by turning down the sides of his mouth.
> 'Why do you want to come into Industry, Mr Dougal?'
> 'I think there's money in it,' Dougal said.
> Mr Willis smiled again, 'That's the correct answer. The last candidate answered, "Industry and the Arts must walk hand in hand," when I put that question to him. His answer was wrong [...].'[60]

Tasked with tackling absenteeism, Dougal, who is simultaneously 'ghosting' an autobiography for a Miss Cheesman, says he needs to conduct 'research' into the inner lives of employees at both firms. Whilst this might be read as a reference to the developing science of industrial psychology, and the role of time and motion surveys to improve productivity, the looseness of the term 'human research' also calls to mind the kind of 'research' conducted by Mass Observation. Mass Observation had been formed in 1937 on a very ad hoc and amateur basis by the poet Charles Madge, the filmmakers Humphrey Jennings and Stuart Legg, and the anthropologist Tom Harrison. At the time, Madge was married to the poet, Kathleen Raine, and was active in the Surrealist circles that Stanford recalls fondly in his memoirs. Raine described her husband's involvement with Mass Observation as 'less sociology than a kind of poetry akin to Surrealism', elucidating 'the hidden thoughts of the inarticulate masses'.[61]

Stanford recalls that when he went to hear Read speak at the opening of the Surrealist exhibition at the Whitechapel Gallery 'posters and leaflets proudly proclaimed that "the Exhibition will be opened by THE MAN IN THE STREET"', and it was with the hypothetical 'Man in the Street' in mind that Mass Observation came into being to observe.[62] Precipitated in part by the Abdication crisis of 1936, Madge, Jennings, Legg and Harrison felt that the government position on the monarchy was out of step with popular opinion and modern morals. They were driven to evidence 'real life' using a system of anonymous diarists and investigators: 'overheards', diaries, questionnaires and day surveys were some of their methods of data collection. Mass Observation, in a wide-ranging programme, studied subjects such as 'Dogs in Wartime', 'Anti-Semitism', 'Smoking' and 'Sundays' – an eclectic range of topics and voices. It was also commissioned to assess the popularity of the furnished rooms at 'Britain Can Make It!'. In *The Ballad of Peckham Rye*, Dougal's research and 'ghostwriting' parodies the data collection methods of Mass Observation. Allan Massie credits Spark with taking a quasi-anthropological approach in *The Ballad of Peckham Rye*: 'In turning to Peckham Rye, Muriel Spark was entering foreign territory: the London Suburb of the lower-middle-class, who work in offices or factories humbly; whose lives are humdrum and imaginations narrow.'[63] While it is true that Spark takes an anthropological delight in the absurdity of the division of labour expressed in the single-task specialisations of 'Dawn

Waghorn, cone-winder; Annette Wren, trainee seamer', her real interest is in the havoc that Dougal can wreck upon mundane, working lives. Evelyn Waugh labelled the activities of Mass Observation pseudo-scientific showmanship, and it is in this vein that Dougal's embedded 'pseudo' research operates. Immediately after Dougal's interview with Mr Druce at Meadows, Meade & Grindley, directly addressing the reader, Spark provides the following description of Peckham:

> If you look inexperienced or young and go shopping for food in the by-streets of Peckham it is as different from shopping in the main streets as it is from shopping in Kensington or the West End. In the little shops in the Peckham by-streets, the other customers take a deep interest in what you are buying. They concern themselves lest you are cheated. Sometimes they ask you questions of a civic nature, such as: Where do you work? Is it a good position? Where are you stopping? What rent do they take off you? And according to your answer they may comment that the money you get is good or the rent you have to pay is wicked, as the case may be.[64]

Peckham does not register as a 'foreign' territory as Massie has it, but as defiantly 'local', and the methods of Mass Observation are nothing more than those of a 'nosy neighbour'.

Spark treats Peckham in the same way as she treats her memory of Bruntsfield in *Curriculum Vitae* (1992). Warmly, she recalls the grocers dotted around her neighbourhood. Her descriptions of shopping convey a sense of the social nature of the transactions taking place – bread and butter enter her imagination through a taxonomy of forms and playfully associative thought. She enjoys the phatic discourse of shopkeepers, customers and habitués. Shops are not unlike people: the exchange of goods is not unlike conversation. There is a sense, in the passages Spark writes about these staple goods, that she co-locates local continuities, familiar objects and gossip – the revelatory power of an overheard comment. The methods of Mass Observation – diaries, autobiographies, reports – describe the overlap between documentary evidence, subjective interpretation and creative process, the impossible separation of which troubled and motivated Spark throughout her life. Characteristically, writing – as the prosthetic creation of other bodies – is her subject and her jealously protected craft.

> Why did I keep these letters? Why? They are all neatly bundled up in thin folders, tied with pink tape, 1949, 1950, 1951 and on and on. I was trained to be a secretary; maybe I felt that letters ought to be filed.[65]

Stannard reads Fleur's question parallel to the personal archive Spark sold to the National Library of Scotland: 'Like everyone else's material existence, it is clotted with tedium and discretion.'[66] Receipts, bank statements, appointment diaries, 'fan mail', business correspondence – these provided objective ballast in Spark's life, and now invite its reconstruction through mundane detail. Her drive to assimilate and preserve evidence of low-level, daily existence correlates to specific periods – it is not meticulous or habitual. However personally or idiosyncratically motivated in its existence, Spark's archive bears witness to the increasing importance of the 'documentary', a punishingly passive twentieth-century tendency which, in the approach of an organisation like Mass Observation, becomes active 'research'. Spark's practical training, desire to controvert and control the documentary evidence of her own life, the contexts she chose to write through, and the relevance of parallels to the methods of Mass Observation, place her within the ambit of what Kristin Bluemel recognises as 'intermodern': 'radically eccentric', non-canonical, popular literature which represents largely middle- and working-class themes and perspectives.[67] Reading Spark's short stories and early works through or adjunct to themes in twentieth-century British design history not only makes this clear, but reveals some of the contradictions in her cultural self-positioning. The dissociation and detachment experienced or represented by her protagonists is underwritten by a Romantic construction of what it means to be 'artistic'. For all Spark's radical form in writing, her appreciation of art and artistic personalities is a bulwark against progressive, planned design which sought to re-order everyday life safely, purposefully, rationally and, it would seem, impossibly.

Endnotes

1. Muriel Spark, *Loitering with Intent* [1981] (London: Virago, 2007), p. 3.
2. Muriel Spark, *Curriculum Vitae: A Volume of Autobiography* [1992] (London: Penguin, 1993), p. 198.
3. Alan Taylor, *Appointment in Arezzo: A friendship with Muriel Spark* (Edinburgh: Polygon, 2017), p. 68.
4. Muriel Spark, *Mary Shelley* [1987] (Manchester: Carcanet, 2013), p. xi.
5. Michael Frayn, 'Festival', in *Age of Austerity, 1945–1951*, eds. Michael Sissons and Philip French (Oxford: Oxford University Press, 1986), pp. 305–26 (p. 308).
6. Martin Stannard, *Muriel Spark: The Biography* (London: Phoenix, 2010), p. 121.
7. Ibid. p. 174.
8. Spark, *Curriculum Vitae*, p. 195.
9. Muriel Spark, *All the Poems of Muriel Spark* (New York, NY: New Directions, 2004).
10. Bernat Klein, *An Eye for Colour* (Galashiels; London: Bernat Klein; Collins, 1965), pp. 42–43.
11. Muriel Spark, *The Go-away Bird & Other Stories* [1958] (London: Penguin, 1963), p. 64.
12. Harry Hopkins, *The New Look: A Social History of the Forties and Fifties* (London: Secker & Warburg, 1964), pp. 383–98.
13. Pointedly, Spark uses the name 'Beryl Tims' in *Loitering with Intent*.
14. Christopher Breward and Ghislaine Wood (eds), *British Design from 1948: Innovation in the Modern Age* (London: V&A, 2015).
15. Mary Shoeser, 'Mary Schoser on Design and Science', Welcome Trust (2008), www.youtube.com/watch?v=8ZAF1u-EgHs [accessed 27 March 2020].
16. In *Loitering with Intent*, crystallography also provides Spark with a metaphor for the description of the artistic process: 'an infinitesimal particle of crystal, say sulphur, enlarged sixty times and photographed in colour so that it looked like an elaborate butterfly or exotic seaflower'. Spark, *Loitering with Intent*, p. 12.
17. Muriel Spark and Derek Stanford, *My Best Mary: Selected Letters of Mary Shelley* (London: Wingate, 1953).
18. Spark, 'Daisy Overend', in *The Go-away Bird*, p. 129.
19. Hope Howell Hodgkins, *Style and the Single Girl: How Modern Women Re-Dressed the Novel 1922–1977* (Columbus, OH: Ohio State University Press, 2016).
20. Ibid., p. 200.
21. Hope Howell Hodgkins, 'Stylish Spinsters: Spark, Pym, and the Postwar Comedy of the Object', in *Muriel Spark: Twenty-First-Century Perspectives*, ed. David Herman (Baltimore, MD: John Hopkins University Press, 2010), pp. 129–52 (p. 130).
22. Hodgkins, *Style and the Single Girl*, p. 221.
23. Marshall McLuhan, *The Mechanical Bride: Folklore of Industrial Man* (London: Duckworth Overlook, 2011).
24. See, for example, Darlings advert in British *Vogue*, December 1946, p. 14; McDonalds Ltd advert in *Vogue*, June 1950, p. 37; Muriel Spark, *The Hothouse by the East River* (London: Macmillan, 1973), p. 5.
25. Heriot Watt-College Calendar 1933–34, Heriot-Watt University Archive, HWC/2/12/48.
26. R. D. Russell and Robert Gooden, 'The Lion and Unicorn Pavilion', in *A Tonic to the Nation: The Festival of Britain 1951*, eds. Mary Bahman and Bevis Hillier (London: Thames & Hudson, 1976), pp. 96–101 (p. 98).

27 Spark, 'The Black Madonna', in *The Go-away Bird*, p. 12.
28 Harriet Atkinson, *The Festival of Britain: A Land and its People* (London: I. B. Taurus, 2012), p. 160.
29 'Type' is a keyword for Spark.
30 *South Bank Exhibition: Festival of Britain* (London: HMSO, 1951).
31 'Daisy Overend, small, imperious, smart was to my mind the flower and consummation of her kind, and this was not to discount the male of the species *Daisy Overend*, with his wee face, blue eyes, bad teeth and nerves. But if you have met Mrs Overend, you have as good as met him too, he is so unlike her, and yet so much her kind. I met her myself, in the prodigious and lovely summer of 1947.' Spark, 'Daisy Overend', p. 125.
32 *Britain Can Make It! Catalogue* (London: Council for Industrial Design, 1946), pp. 115–46.
33 Spark, 'The Black Madonna', p. 13.
34 Ibid., p. 11.
35 Stuart Laing, *Representations of Working-Class Life 1957–1964* (London: Macmillan, 1986).
36 Muriel Spark, *The Prime of Miss Jean Brodie* [1961] (London: Penguin, 1965), p. 10.
37 Derek Stanford, *Muriel Spark: A Biographical and Critical Study* (London: Centaur, 1963), p. 119.
38 Derek Stanford, *John Betjeman* (London: Neville Spearman, 1961), p. 61.
39 Muriel Spark, 'The Poet's House', in *The Golden Fleece: Essays*, ed. P. Jardine (Manchester: Carcanet, 2014), pp. 66–72.
40 Arthur C. Danto, *The Transfiguration of the Commonplace: A Philosophy of Art* (Cambridge, MA: Harvard University Press, 1981), p. v.
41 Robin Kinross, 'Herbert Read's *Art and Industry*: a history', in *Journal of Design History* 1.1 (1988), pp. 35–50.
42 Muriel Spark and Derek Stanford (eds), *Tribute to Wordsworth: A Miscellany of Opinion for the Centenary of the Poet's Death* (London: Wingate, 1950).
43 Litvinoff Incident.
44 Spark, *Mary Shelley*, p. 177.
45 Ibid.; Spark, 'Ruskin and Read', *The Golden Fleece*, p. 18.
46 Spark, 'The Black Madonna', p. 18.
47 Ibid., pp. 18–19.
48 Le Corbusier, 'Law of Ripolin', in *Colour*, ed. David Batchelor (London: Whitechapel/MIT, 2008), p. 82.
49 Adolf Loos, 'Ornament & Crime', in *Crime and Ornament: The Arts and Popular Culture in the Shadow of Adolf Loos*, eds. Bernie Miller and Melody Ward (San Luis Obispo, CA: XYZ Books, 2002), pp. 29–36 (p. 30).
50 Ibid., p. 32.
51 Ibid., p. 131.
52 Spark, *The Prime of Miss Jean Brodie*, p. 33.
53 Spark, *Loitering with Intent*, p. 4.
54 Muriel Spark, *The Driver's Seat* [1970] (London: Penguin, 1974), pp. 13–14.
55 Kaori O'Connor, 'The Other Half: The Material Culture of New Fibres', in *Clothing as Material Culture*, eds. S. Küchler and D. Miller (New York, NY: Berg, 2005), p. 46.
56 British *Vogue*, February 1954, p. 20.

57 Amy Sargeant, 'The Man in the White Suit: New Textiles and the Social Fabric', in *Visual Culture in Britain* 9.1 (June 2008), pp. 27–54.
58 Spark, *Curriculum Vitae*.
59 Muriel Spark, *The Ballad of Peckham Rye* [1960] (London: Penguin, 1963), p. 15.
60 Ibid., p. 68.
61 Tom Jeffery, 'Mass Observation Archive Occasional Paper No. 10 – Mass Observation: A Short History', *Mass Observation Online* (Brighton: University of Sussex Library, 1999), p. 24. www.massobservation.amdigital.co.uk/FurtherResources/Essays/MassObservationArchiveOccasionalPaper10 [accessed 17 November 2017].
62 Derek Stanford, *Inside the Forties: Literary Memoirs 1937–1957* (London: Sidgwick & Jackson, 1977), p. 26.
63 Alan Massie, *Muriel Spark* (Edinburgh: Ramsay Head Press, 1979), p. 30.
64 Spark, *The Ballad of Peckham Rye*, p. 18.
65 Spark, *Loitering with Intent*, p. 3.
66 Stannard, *Muriel Spark: The Biography*, p. xxii.
67 Kristin Bluemel, 'Introduction: What is Intermodernism?' in *Intermodernism: Literary Culture in Mid-Twentieth-Century Britain*, ed. Kristin Bluemel (Edinburgh: Edinburgh University Press, 2009), pp. 1–18.

13. The Publishing Scene in *A Far Cry from Kensington*

ERNEST SCHONFIELD

The 1980s were a good decade for Muriel Spark, in which she published *Loitering with Intent* (1981) and *A Far Cry from Kensington* (1988).[1] Both novels reflect on the publishing industry and the literary world 'in the early 1950s'.[2] Spark's association with Kensington began when she arrived in London in 1944, and stayed at the Helena Club in Lancaster Gate, the model for the setting of *The Girls of Slender Means* (1963).[3] Spark soon registered at the Kensington Public Library and took out a book by Ivy Compton-Burnett.[4] The woman at the Employment Bureau was so impressed by this that she found Spark a job with military intelligence.[5] *A Far Cry from Kensington* is set in a boarding house in South Kensington from 1954 to 1955.[6] The novel speaks to me in particular because I grew up in North Kensington, a centre for Caribbean, Irish, Spanish and Moroccan immigrants, where the Grenfell Tower fire took place on 14 June 2017, causing the deaths of seventy-two people. Spark's South Kensington is populated by Polish immigrants who attend the Polish mass at the Brompton Oratory in Chelsea. A couple of miles to the west you can find the Polish centre 'POSK' and café in Hammersmith. The borough of Kensington and Chelsea is a place where extremes of wealth and poverty have always rubbed up against each other. Growing up in the borough has helped me to appreciate a particular form of polite viciousness which I associate with that part of the world, exemplified brilliantly in *A Far Cry from Kensington*. As the narrator puts it: '"Cultured people are not necessarily nicer people", I told him. "Frequently, the reverse."'[7] *A Far Cry from Kensington* offers many insights into the publishing scene in the early 1950s as a nexus of poverty and polite cruelty. This argument deploys Pierre Bourdieu's theory of cultural discrimination to examine what is at stake in the way that Spark presents the inter-relationships of class privilege, publishing and cruelty in this novel.

The Rules of Art

Pierre Bourdieu is best known for his work *Distinction: A Social Critique of the Judgement of Taste*.[8] This ambitious study shows how 'taste' functions as a marker of class membership. The gatekeepers and guardians of 'high culture' help to regulate the consumption of high art and maintain its exclusivity, preserving the social privileges of the ruling class. These cultural barriers give the lie to the myth that European society after 1945 was characterised by social mobility and equal opportunity. Bourdieu's subsequent work extended and deepened this analysis. *The Rules of Art*, in particular, offers a route into Muriel Spark's depiction of the London publishing scene. He argues that the 'literary field' is effectively fenced off by measures of exclusion and discrimination. Those who lack the appropriate qualifications are, very often, effectively excluded. Entry to the 'literary field' is codified and has to pass through a series of tests (e.g. prizes, literary reviews, literary societies and sponsorship) which are carefully guarded by publishers and critics, who exert a decisive influence on cultural production within the literary sphere. Bourdieu thus widens the scope of literary enquiry to include the publishing industry itself, 'the ensemble of people who have their say on literary things'.[9] The 'literary field' comprises publishers, literary agents, editors, copy-editors, secretaries, booksellers, journalists, critics, academics and teachers.[10] As a result of their collective interaction there is a 'process of canonization which leads to the establishment of writers'.[11] Some writers are canonised by the established authorities – publishers, universities, schools, newspaper reviewers – while others are relegated to different levels of oblivion. This Spark centenary collection is an obvious sign of canonisation; but the process begins when a writer shows her work to friends, or submits a manuscript to a publisher. Having worked in the London publishing world of the late 1940s and early 1950s as an editor and sub-editor, Spark is well qualified to demystify the process of acceptance and rejection and *A Far Cry from Kensington* delivers a disillusioned and devastating behind-the-scenes look at the literary business. The novel is acutely aware of the gender and class hierarchies which prevail in this cultural field: all too frequently, this is a world of books commissioned, written by and about middle-class white men. Martin York, the 'gentleman publisher' who runs the Ullswater Press, has 'taken on a few "literary advisers", mostly young men of good family and no brains whose fathers had pleaded them a job. They were on the payroll.'[12] It is not what you know, it is who you know: these gatekeepers are selected from within a narrow echelon of society, ensuring that literary institutions remain an exclusive preserve. The decisive factor is class: 'Martin York had another, special illusion: he felt that men or women of upper-class background and education were bound to have advantages of talent over writers of modest origins. In 1954 quite a few bright publishers secretly believed this.'[13] The whole system is self-reproducing: 'He promised contracts to the most talkative, gossipy, amusing members of his own class, his old schoolfellows, their wives, his former army companions and their wives.'[14] This encapsulates an institutional bias similar to the one Pierre Bourdieu investigated in France. As one of Spark's practised literary operators comments: 'Nepotism I believe is still the order of the day.'[15] Given Spark's insights into how these social boundaries are effectively policed, Drew Milne's claim that Spark's fiction is 'profoundly unsociological' requires qualification.[16] In fact, the affinities between *A Far Cry from Kensington* and Bourdieu's literary sociology are striking. Bourdieu describes publishers and critics as having powers resembling those of the Catholic Church; they have the ability to canonise, absolve or even excommunicate. The fate of the narrator, Mrs Hawkins, exemplifies the workings of the system. She is fired from two publishing houses for committing heresy: that is, for calling the up-and-coming writer Hector Bartlett a *'pisseur de copie'*. Thus she is excommunicated for challenging the orthodoxy. Like the child in Hans Christian Andersen's fairy tale 'The Emperor's New Clothes', she is the only one who is bold (or naïve) enough to speak the truth. The element of coercion is clear: she is given to understand that if she persists, she 'will never work in this town again.'[17]

Meanwhile, the smooth running of the literary machine is facilitated by an army of women: secretaries, sub-editors, copy-editors, personal assistants. These nameless women work invisibly behind the scenes, meticulously copy-editing, administering and enabling the prominence of the (usually male) literary celebrities. Spark had professional secretarial qualifications. After leaving school, she took a course in précis-writing:

> I inscribed myself at Heriot-Watt College (now a university) to complete my education in English prose. I was particularly interested in précis-writing, and took a course in that. I love economical prose, and would always try to find the briefest way to express a meaning.[18]

This training informs the ethos of Mrs Nancy Hawkins, the narrator and protagonist of *A Far Cry from Kensington*, whose name echoes the beloved nanny in Evelyn Waugh's *Brideshead Revisited*, 'Nanny' Hawkins. Waugh's Hawkins is a children's nanny; Spark's Hawkins is a sort of literary midwife, who devotes herself to birthing the literary creations of others. The fact that she is usually referred to as 'Mrs Hawkins' is more suggestive of a servant or a hired help; the human being disappearing behind the professional role. She is, effectively, a dogsbody: 'I was, as usual, Mrs Hawkins, general do-all, proof-reader, literary adviser and secretarial stand-in when the respective secretaries of Mr York and Mr Ullswater left to get married and were never replaced.'[19] Thus, she finds herself doing the jobs of three people, although on a single salary.

Mrs Hawkins works for the Ullswater Press, based on the Falcon Press, where Spark worked in 1951. Martin York is modelled on Peter Baker, Spark's actual employer, who was sentenced to seven years for forgery.[20] In the novel, Martin York forges the signature of a top banker, Sir Arthur Cary. Then, York asks Mrs Hawkins to witness and sign the forged documents, trying to make her an accessory to fraud.[21] Unsurprisingly for a man who is deeply in debt, York explains to her that 'Credibility is everything'.[22] With York on the run from his creditors, it falls to Mrs Hawkins to act as deputy and keep the ship afloat. As she remarks:

> My advice to any woman who earns the reputation of being capable, is to not demonstrate her ability too much. You give advice; you say, do this, do that, I think I've got you a job, don't worry, leave it to me. All that, and in the end you feel spooky, empty, haunted.[23]

In other words, if a woman reveals herself as useful, she risks being completely used up by the men around her. Being capable means that you end up being exploited. Bertolt Brecht makes a similar point in his play *The Good Person of Szechwan*, where he calls it 'the suffering of the useful'.[24] No wonder Nancy Hawkins gets fed up with it and declares, 'I'm getting a bit tired of being capable'.[25]

After being fired from the Ullswater Press, Mrs Hawkins finds a job at 'the vast publishing firm of Mackintosh & Tooley',[26] a fictional firm which, according to Martin Stannard, draws loosely on Spark's experiences at Macmillan & Co.[27] Here, it is not long until the editor, Sir Alec Tooley, tells her 'we know you are a remarkably reliable woman'.[28] At once she becomes suspicious, and rightly so, since Sir Alec wants her to copy-edit Hector Bartlett's book and turn it into a viable publication:

> 'The manuscript', he said, 'needs putting into shape.'
> 'Do you mean rewriting?' I said.
> 'Well, of course, that, too. But there are facts to be verified and so on. Grammar and syntax and so forth. Dates.'
> [...]
> 'The book,' said Sir Alec, 'is entitled *The Eternal Quest, a study of the Romantic-Humanist Position*. Somewhat deep. It is a comparative study of *The Pilgrim's Progress*, *Wilhelm Meister* and *Peer Gynt*, or at least, purports to be. I know very little of the subject.'[29]

Nancy intuits at once that she is being asked to rewrite the book. Even the title sets alarm bells ringing: it commits 'that mortal sin of art, pomposity'.[30] The ponderous title contrasts with Spark's own aesthetic position, which, as Paddy Lyons points out, was to steer clear of 'Romanticism's liking for endowing art with the aura of the sacred and the tones of religiosity'.[31] Sir Alec's response speaks volumes: he knows 'very little of the subject', and wishes to stay out of it. The book is, effectively, a total mess. The grammar will need surgery, and the claims will need to be 'verified', in other words, the book is wildly inaccurate, even mendacious. Sir Alec Tooley would rather not get his hands dirty, so he leaves it to the woman to clear up the mess. Nancy shows the manuscript to her neighbour, the medical student William Todd, who is not impressed: '"A lot of balls", he said. "Completely phoney. On every page Nietzsche, Aristotle, Goethe, Ibsen, Freud, Jung, Huxley, Kierkegaard, and no grasp whatsoever of any of them. Send it back."'[32] Bartlett, it seems, is a shameless name-dropper. Nancy wisely decides to tell her employer that she is not up to such a task. She sends a carefully worded note to Sir Alec: 'I consider that it cannot be improved upon'.[33] Through this deliberately ambiguous formulation, she refuses to martyr herself on the altar of Bartlett's incompetence.

Although 'the vast publishing firm of Mackintosh & Tooley' is successful, Mrs Hawkins soon discovers that they, too, are adept at manipulation: 'Principles were the last thing that anybody bothered about'.[34] Her new manager Ian Tooley – the name alone proclaims a kind of mechanised factory production – is an expert on radionics, a pseudoscience which claims to treat conditions using radio waves. Tooley's obsession with horoscopes and radionics allows him to appear as a harmless crackpot and is thus 'his own alibi'.[35] As for his employees, Mrs Hawkins soon discovers that most of them are 'in some way handicapped and vulnerable, either physically or in some other of their circumstances'.[36] She soon realises that Mackintosh & Tooley employ such people because they provide a useful façade: authors and agents are likely to feel so sorry or embarrassed when dealing with such figures that they are less likely to complain about the conditions on offer. When Hugh Lederer says he would like his daughter Isobel to get a job in publishing, Nancy tells him: 'I don't recommend publishing for your daughter. The secretaries are underpaid; everyone's underpaid.'[37]

The publishing industry then, like most industries, is actually a bit of a meat-grinder. In Spark's earlier novel, *Loitering with Intent*, the publisher Revisson Doe echoes this directly in his advice to the aspiring author Fleur Talbot: 'You must remember [...] that an author is a publisher's raw material'.[38] *Loitering with Intent* also features a sinister figure called Sir Quentin Oliver, a kind of glorified literary agent who treats his circle of aspiring autobiographers as 'raw material' to be blackmailed and bullied. Living authors can be recalcitrant; often publishers are forced to use coercion in order to make them toe the line. Colin Shoe, one of Nancy Hawkins's colleagues at Mackintosh & Tooley, puts it bluntly: 'The best author is a dead author'.[39] Nancy Hawkins is 'quite aware of this feeling', but at the same time wants 'human contact in [her] work'.[40]

In this way, Spark's novels of the 1980s depict a publishing scene characterised by snobbery, sexism and endemic exploitation. After experiencing the manipulative behaviour of various employers, Mrs Hawkins is almost relieved to find herself unemployed, as she reflects:

> [T]here was a residue of uneasiness in my mind about the publishing scene, a weariness of authors, agents, books, printers, binders, critics, editors [...] I was tired of the whole scene and longed to be able to go into a bookshop as in former times and choose a book without being aware of all that went into its making.[41]

Despite its apparent gentility, then, the publishing world is portrayed as a particularly cut-throat environment. And yet Nancy Hawkins successfully rises above such things. She eventually finds a better class of employer: two gay American men, Howard Send and Fred Tucher, the editors of the *Highgate Review*.[42] Here, finally, she is treated with a measure of respect and appreciation. Her new colleague, Abigail, says that she finds it 'easier to work for homosexuals than for straight men' because there are 'no personal complications'.[43] But Send and Tucher are also extremely courteous: 'We were impressed by the way the Boys generally got up when we came into the room'; Abigail wonders: 'Is that American or is it homosexual?'.[44] The question remains unanswered, but these two gay American men are a welcome breath of fresh air, lifting the tone of the narrative after the stifling stuffiness of their English predecessors.

The Art of Sub-Editing

While *A Far Cry from Kensington* lifts the lid on mechanisms of exclusion in the publishing world, it also pays tribute to the neglected art of sub-editing. The sub-editor's job is to correct and check texts before they are printed – a vital role in the publication process. But sub-editors are not simply error checkers. They are also cosmetic surgeons. A skilled sub-editor can look at a piece of writing, see what it is about, and knock out a third of it. Almost everything that people write can be cut down again and again.[45] Mrs Hawkins is such a professional sub-editor that we do not even learn her first name until more than halfway through the novel, when she finds a new boyfriend, the medical student William Todd. He asks her: 'were you christened "Mrs Hawkins", Mrs Hawkins?' She replies: 'No, I was christened Agnes. But I'm called Nancy.'[46] The absence of the first name underlines the professionalism of her ethos. And indeed, despite her misadventures, Mrs Hawkins shows that she has no hard feelings about the publishing world by seasoning her narrative with valuable advice for aspiring authors. Her experience as a sub-editor gives her valuable insights into every aspect of the creative process. The masterclass begins on the first page of the book: 'You can sit peacefully in front of a blank television set, just watching nothing; and sooner or later you can make your own programme better than the mass product. It's fun, you should try it.'[47] This wisdom on how writers can begin the process of writing is provided in addition to the plot: 'I offer this advice without fee; it is included in the price of the book.'[48]

The literary advice in *A Far Cry from Kensington* is a distillation of Spark's own professional experiences. From 1946 to 1947 she had worked as a researcher and sub-editor for *Argentor*, a quarterly magazine which specialised in the applied arts and crafts of jewellers and goldsmiths. Here she performed corrective surgery on the articles of experts and art historians:

> Quite a lot of articles by specialists had to be touched up from the stylistic point of view, and we spent long hours recasting the articles that had been commissioned. [...] The essays written by experts which needed some form of recasting were mainly passed on to me. I learned how to copy-edit tactfully. I recall that I took out a great many adjectives.[49]

By improving other people's articles, Spark honed her own craft. 'Recasting' is, of course, a polite euphemism for 'rewriting'. As she explains, her operation on the text was largely a slimming operation, taking out adjectives and eliminating unnecessary verbiage. In this way, Mrs Hawkins's physical transformation from fat to thin is a physical equivalent of the cosmetic surgery that she performs on other people's texts. Just as she reduces her weight by sheer force of will, so she removes the excess padding in other people's writing until it is as elegant and graceful as she is.

After working on *Argentor*, in 1947 Spark became the editor of the *Poetry Review*, the journal of the Poetry Society. Improving the quality of the review required her to decline a number of poor-quality submissions from members of the society. While the sub-editor's job involves rejecting unnecessary phrases, editors must be prepared to reject entire books, entire concepts. As Mrs Hawkins puts it:

> A large part of an editor's job is rejection. Perhaps nine-tenths. In those days at least, it was not only rejection of manuscripts but of those ideas that seemed to come walking into my office every day in the shape of pensive men and women talking [...] about such mutilated concepts as optimist/pessimist, fascist/communist, extrovert/introvert, highbrow/middlebrow/lowbrow; and this claptrap they applied to art, literature and life, to the effect that all joy, wit and the pleasures of curiosity were quite squeezed out.[50]

This passage expresses the narrator's suspicion of certain ideological concepts, and it rejects them in the name of 'joy, wit and the pleasures of curiosity'. These are the values which guide Mrs Hawkins in her work as an editor. Ideology has a dangerous tendency to stifle 'wit' and 'curiosity'. A text will be selected if it gives 'joy'; rejected if it does not.[51] Nine-tenths of the submissions she received are, it seems, unpleasant and even suffocating, oppressive. She will not be browbeaten. In order to produce a book which is slim, charming and attractive, the editor and the sub-editor must have the ability to say 'no'. There is a sense that Spark is setting out her own artistic manifesto here: what matters is the ability to grasp the essentials and to reject unnecessary verbiage. Drew Milne terms this Spark's 'neoclassical perspective'.[52] A literary work should be graceful, playful, teasing and charming. It should be enticing, not hectoring or strident. Here, the narrator reflects on the business of writing itself, and on what distinguishes good writing from bad. Bartlett's prose is rejected not only because it is morally evasive, but because it is showy, obscure and unpleasant to read. Mrs Hawkins trims and whittles away at literary productions and rejects leaden ideological tracts. A literary work must excite the imagination; it must be capable of flight.

Mrs Hawkins's pearls of wisdom should be brought to the attention of staff and students on any creative writing course:[53]

> 'You are writing a letter to a friend,' was the sort of thing I used to say. 'And this is a dear and close friend, real – or better – invented in your mind like a fixation. Write privately, not publicly; without fear or timidity, right to the end of the letter, as if it was never going to be published, so that your true friend will read it over and over, and then want more enchanting letters from you.'[54]

In other words, the literary work should be a labour of love, a letter from the heart. A Brigadier General who plans to write his war memoirs is lucky enough to get 'some very good advice' from Mrs Hawkins:

> If you want to concentrate deeply on some problem, and especially some piece of writing or paper-work, you should acquire a cat. [...] And the tranquillity of the cat will gradually come to affect you, sitting there at your desk, so that all the excitable qualities that impede your concentration compose themselves and give your mind back the self-command it has lost.[55]

This implies that many people have little 'self-control' and would therefore benefit from purchasing a cat to restore their moral equilibrium. Indeed, Nancy Hawkins is so fluent at giving literary advice, that she also offers counsel for life and love: 'It is my advice to any woman getting married to start, not as you mean to go on, but worse, tougher, than you mean to go on. Then you can slowly relax and it comes as a pleasant surprise.'[56] If necessary, Mrs Hawkins can also dispense some punchy one-liners. At her job interview with the editor of the *Highgate Review*, she is fully prepared:

'"When you are editing copy, Mrs Hawkins, what sort of things do you look for?" said Howard Send. "Exclamation marks and italics used for emphasis," I said. "And I take them out."'⁵⁷ No wonder she gets the job. Her response is beautifully concise; it embodies the elegance of the sub-editor's trade.

The Crime Scene

We have seen that *A Far Cry from Kensington* shows that the publishing world is both sordid and exclusive. Sometimes this tips over into crime, in the case of Martin York's fraudulent activities. As Drew Milne puts it, Spark's work is 'figured so as to question literary fiction's similarity to the work of con artists and professional blackmailers'.⁵⁸ The literary world she depicts thrives on exploitation, and this appears in its most vicious form in the relationship between the *pisseur de copie*, Hector Bartlett, and Wanda Podolak, 'the Polish dressmaker whose capacity for suffering verged on rapacity'.⁵⁹ Thus we learn from the outset that Wanda is a budding martyr, a victim waiting for a perpetrator. Bartlett's abusive relationship with Wanda Podolak is at the core of the book.

Hector Bartlett is a composite figure. The first name expresses his hectoring tone; the surname comes from Miss Alice Hunt Bartlett of New York, who tried to bribe Spark with a cheque for twenty-five dollars when she was the editor of *Poetry Review*.⁶⁰ There are points of comparison between Bartlett and Derek Stanford, Spark's former lover and collaborator.⁶¹ For example, Bartlett exploits Emma Loy's literary connections, and then later writes a poisonous hatchet job on her which could be an allusion to Stanford's book *Muriel Spark: A Biographical and Critical Study*, which contained a number of claims about Spark which she dismissed in her autobiography as inaccurate.⁶² But the name Emma Loy is an obvious reference to the English modernist Mina Loy (1882–1966), so the figure of Bartlett also draws on Mina Loy's husband, the painter Stephen Haweis, who she later described as 'parasitic'.⁶³ Bartlett may be a *parvenu*, a chancer riding on the coat-tails of Emma Loy, but he knows the rules of the publishing scene and how to use them to his advantage.

Bartlett's victim, Wanda Podolak, is, in contrast, a Polish woman whose immigrant status means that her social position is vulnerable and precarious.

She utterly lacks Bartlett's social connections and cultural capital: her only support is her church community. Wanda, who lives in the same boarding house as Mrs Hawkins, starts to receive threatening anonymous letters from 'the Organisers', accusing her of 'not declaring your income to the Authorities'.[64] She is terrified and tells Mrs Hawkins: 'this is the end of me. They will put me in prison. They will deport me.'[65] But Bartlett poses as a student priest and begins a sexual relationship with her. His impersonation of a priest echoes the religious posturing of his book *The Eternal Quest* – it is a 'blatant pose'.[66] The religious view of the artist derives from the Romantic movement, for example W. H. Wackenroder's *Outpourings of an Art-Loving Friar*. A century later, the dramatist Gerhart Hauptmann admired the monastic life to such an extent that he asked to be buried in a monk's habit. Spark's first novel, *The Comforters* (1957), acknowledges the attractions of the monastic life, but opts instead for a strategy of 'deconsecration'.[67]

Bartlett's religious airs are pure hypocrisy. He is, of course, the author of the letters to Wanda. He initiates her into radionics experiments and encourages her to place a telepathic curse on Mrs Hawkins. Unfortunately, Wanda attributes Mrs Hawkins's radical loss of weight to the radionics experiments and blames herself. Bartlett even fakes a newspaper article claiming that the police are investigating Wanda's radionics experiment on Mrs Hawkins.[68] Terrified that the police are after her and tormented by her guilt for having participated in witchcraft, Wanda commits suicide by jumping into Regent's Canal.[69] This is horrible enough, but there is a further cruel twist when Bartlett writes up Wanda's story in the form of a scientific case study entitled *Radionics, A Power Against Evil*. Innocent Wanda is reduced to a guinea pig, and driven to her death, by a sadistic would-be author, who exploits her as raw material for his own literary production. This is much more than a sub-plot. Wanda's death probes the difficult moral core of artistry itself, asking what it means when artists write about other people and use them as material for their work: 'You plot, Mrs Hawkins', Wanda accuses her.[70] Of course, the real plotter, the real 'cannibal', is not Mrs Hawkins, but Hector Bartlett. However, Mrs Hawkins feels a pang of conscience. Looking at Wanda's possessions with Wanda's sister Greta and Milly, the landlady, Mrs Hawkins is suddenly reminded of Mary Shelley's *Frankenstein*:

> Watching them for a moment it struck me they were trying to reconstruct Wanda, and I thought of a passage in *Frankenstein* where the scientist-narrator dabbles in the grave for material to construct his monster. I have looked up this passage. Here it is precisely:
>
> > Who shall conceive the horrors of my secret toil, as I dabbled among the unhallowed damps of the grave, or tortured the living animal to animate that lifeless clay?[71]

As Wanda's housemates examine her possessions and try to piece together the events which led to her demise, they are suddenly placed in the position of narrators. But this narrator-position is itself uncanny, resembling that of the scientist-demigod Victor Frankenstein, who put together a monster from body parts. The comparison between storytelling and the creation of Frankenstein's monster figures authorship itself as something dubious and immoral. Are authors' experiments with their material legitimate, or not? What happens when they take other people's lives as their material? Mrs Hawkins says: 'I enjoy a puritanical and moralistic nature,'[72] and it is hard to escape the suspicion that her 'sweet insomnia'[73] is linked to her role as a narrator, and the fact that, thirty years later, she is still haunted by what happened to Wanda. Mrs Hawkins has a sense of creative unease that will not let her rest as she lies in bed in the 1980s and thinks about the 1950s.

Unlike Nancy Hawkins, though, Bartlett is a liar and a manipulator; he is 'gratuitously vicious'.[74] Nancy has, of course, recognised Bartlett for what he is early on in the novel. Because she stands up to him, he uses Emma Loy's influence to get Nancy fired. Later on, Emma Loy confronts her about this, and asks: 'Mrs Hawkins, why do you hate Hector Bartlett?' Her reply is precise: 'He only wants to use people.'[75] But while Nancy sees through him, Wanda does not. Unwittingly, she becomes a human experiment: she serves as the raw material for Bartlett's most haunting and disturbing literary creation.

In conclusion, *A Far Cry from Kensington* gives the game away about the London publishing industry of the 1950s, showing how the rules of that game are rigged in favour of middle-class and upper-class white men, who ruthlessly defend their privileges and sense of entitlement. Spark's class analysis is razor-sharp and resonates with Pierre Bourdieu's observation that 'The educated are powerful in virtue of the official legitimacy of their (educated) culture and they use their power to maintain and defend its legitimacy'.[76] This codified cultural sphere serves to reinforce existing hierarchies. It is significant that, in *A Far Cry from Kensington*, the frauds and exploiters are all middle-class males. Ironically, although Bartlett claims 'at every opportunity, both directly and by implication, to be upper class', he is not.[77] His invocation of 'higher values' is designed to appeal to the cultural arbiters of taste who regard themselves as a spiritual elite, what Bourdieu would call 'distinction'. But Bartlett's reliance on name-dropping and pretentious clichés is anything but distinctive. It is cheap and it shows how easily 'cultural capital' can be used instrumentally for career purposes. Bartlett is an 'operator' who is going through the motions. The only truly distinctive things about him are his cruelty and his 'short staccato laugh like a typewriter'; the machine-like embodiment of an anti-human system, or, as Bourdieu would have it, a codified cultural field in which class privileges and gender privileges are deeply entrenched.[78] It is highly significant that the only genuine love interest in the novel is provided by the working-class medical student, William Todd. Plain-speaking Todd is the one who sees through Bartlett's flannel, and his verdict on the manuscript is 'a lot of balls'. Honesty is the defining and unifying feature of both Nancy Hawkins and William Todd.[79] As Nancy puts it in one of the most memorable lines of the book, 'no life can be carried on satisfactorily unless people are honest'.[80] Yet she works in a publishing 'field' in which dishonesty is an essential career requirement.

A Far Cry from Kensington shows us an elitist publishing scene with a strong structural resemblance to Bourdieu's Parisian cultural eminences. Spark depicts a crew of 'gentleman publishers' who claim to recognise good writing, but who systematically exclude unwanted interlopers. This is a world of rigid orthodoxy, peopled by self-serving hacks, users and plagiarists.

It encourages the formation of a literary canon reliant on the exclusion of other voices who are 'outside the narrative',[81] and rarely acknowledges the vital labours of (often female) sub-editors who help to make literary works more readable and pleasurable.

Endnotes

1. I would like to thank Willy Maley for his helpful comments on the first draft of this essay. I would also like to thank Helen Stoddart and Gerard Carruthers for their insightful critical editorial comments on the second draft.
2. Muriel Spark, *A Far Cry from Kensington* [1988], with an Introduction by Ali Smith (London: Virago Press, 2009), p. 2.
3. Martin Stannard, *Muriel Spark: The Biography* (New York, NY; London: Norton, 2009), p. 66.
4. The Kensington Library was in Holland House, Holland Park. The house was destroyed by bombs in 1940 but the library was largely undamaged. It was rehoused in the new Kensington Central Library, opened in 1960.
5. Muriel Spark, *Curriculum Vitae* [1992] (Manchester: Carcanet, 2009), pp. 145–48.
6. The house is loosely based on Tiny Lazzari's boarding house in Camberwell, where Spark stayed in the late 1950s.
7. Spark, *A Far Cry from Kensington*, p. 57.
8. Pierre Bourdieu, *Distinction: A Social Critique of the Judgement of Taste* [1979], trans. Richard Nice (Abingdon: Routledge, 2010).
9. Pierre Bourdieu, *The Rules of Art* [1992], trans. Susan Emanuel (Cambridge: Polity Press, 1996), p. 224.
10. See John Sutherland, 'Publishing History: A Hole at the Centre of Literary Sociology', in *Critical Inquiry* 14.3 (1988), pp. 574–89.
11. Bourdieu, *The Rules of Art*, p. 225.
12. Spark, *A Far Cry from Kensington*, p. 41.
13. Ibid., p. 42.
14. Ibid.
15. Ibid., p. 47.
16. Drew Milne, 'Muriel Spark's Crimes of Wit', in *The Edinburgh Companion to Muriel Spark*, eds. Michael Gardiner and Willy Maley (Edinburgh: Edinburgh University Press, 2010), pp. 110–21 (p. 117).
17. This recalls the title of Julia Phillips's exposé of Hollywood in the 1970s and 1980s: *You'll Never Eat Lunch in This Town Again* (New York, NY: Random House, 1991).
18. Spark, *Curriculum Vitae*, p. 102.
19. Spark, *A Far Cry from Kensington*. p. 12.
20. Spark, *Curriculum Vitae*, p. 198.

21 Spark, *A Far Cry from Kensington*, pp. 40–41.
22 Ibid., p. 113.
23 Ibid., p. 131.
24 Bertolt Brecht, *Der gute Mensch von Sezuan* (Frankfurt am Main: Suhrkamp, 1963), p. 93: 'das Leiden der Brauchbarkeit'. John Willett translates this inaccurately as 'the price of utility' in Brecht, *The Good Person of Szechwan*, trans. John Willett (London: Bloomsbury Methuen Drama, 2014), p. 70.
25 Spark, *A Far Cry from Kensington*, p. 134.
26 Ibid., p. 68.
27 Stannard, *Muriel Spark*, p. 483.
28 Spark, *A Far Cry from Kensington*, p. 102.
29 Ibid., p. 102–03.
30 Spark, *Curriculum Vitae*, p. 180.
31 Paddy Lyons, 'Muriel Spark's Break with Romanticism', in *The Edinburgh Companion to Muriel Spark*, eds. Michael Gardiner and Willy Maley, pp. 85–97 (p. 87).
32 Spark, *A Far Cry from Kensington*, p. 104.
33 Ibid., p. 105.
34 Ibid., p. 77.
35 Ibid., p. 76.
36 Ibid., p. 74.
37 Ibid., p. 57.
38 Muriel Spark, *Loitering with Intent* [1981] (London: Virago, 2007), p. 103.
39 Spark, *A Far Cry from Kensington*, p. 81.
40 Ibid.
41 Ibid., p. 108.
42 The name 'Tucher' may be a discreet reference to the Yiddish word 'tuches', meaning 'buttocks'. Of course, 'Tuch' also means 'cloth' or 'fabric', so perhaps Fred Tucher is simply descended from tailors.
43 Spark, *A Far Cry from Kensington*, p. 178.
44 Ibid.
45 I am grateful to Val Wilmer for explaining the role of a sub-editor, in conversation on 3 October 2020.
46 Spark, *A Far Cry from Kensington*, p. 130.
47 Ibid., p. 3.
48 Ibid., p. 7.
49 Spark, *Curriculum Vitae*, pp. 164–65.
50 Spark, *A Far Cry from Kensington*, p. 98.
51 Compare Spark, *Curriculum Vitae*, p. 155: 'I wanted to give pleasure through my writings.'
52 Milne, 'Muriel Spark's Crimes of Wit', p. 115.
53 Spark's final novel, *The Finishing School* (2004), also explores creative writing and publishing. See Willy Maley, 'Workshopping and Fiction: Laboratory, Factory, or Finishing School?', in *Does the Writing Workshop Still Work? (New Writing Viewpoints)* 5, ed. Dianne Donnelly (Bristol; New York, NY; Ontario: Multilingual Matters & Channel View Publications, 2010), pp. 78–93.
54 Spark, *A Far Cry from Kensington*, p. 84.

55 Ibid., p. 94.
56 Ibid., p. 119.
57 Ibid., p. 157.
58 Milne, 'Muriel Spark's Crimes of Wit', p. 115.
59 Spark, *A Far Cry from Kensington*, p. 3.
60 Spark, *Curriculum Vitae*, pp. 169–70.
61 Stannard, *Muriel Spark*, p. 484.
62 Spark, *Curriculum Vitae*, p. 190.
63 Carolyn Burke, *Becoming Modern: The Life of Mina Loy* (Berkeley, CA: University of California Press, 1996), p. 81.
64 Spark, *A Far Cry from Kensington*, p. 25.
65 Ibid., p. 26. This resonates uncomfortably with British politics today, as EU migrants living in the UK are required to apply for 'settled status'.
66 Spark, *A Far Cry from Kensington*, p. 43.
67 Lyons, 'Muriel Spark's Break with Romanticism', p. 87.
68 Spark, *A Far Cry from Kensington*, p. 172.
69 Ibid., p. 143.
70 Ibid., p. 128.
71 Ibid., p. 161.
72 Ibid., p. 51.
73 Ibid., p. 2.
74 Ibid., p. 40.
75 Ibid., p. 136.
76 Nick Crossley, 'Social Class', in *Pierre Bourdieu: Key Concepts*, ed. Michael Grenfell, 2nd edn (Durham: Acumen, 2012), pp. 85–97 (p. 94).
77 Spark, *A Far Cry from Kensington*, p. 43.
78 Ibid., p. 194.
79 Honesty is also Milly's chief characteristic: 'she never exaggerated'. Spark, *A Far Cry from Kensington*, p. 9.
80 Spark, *A Far Cry from Kensington*, p. 51.
81 Tom Leonard, *Outside the narrative: Poems 1965–2009* (Edinburgh: Word Power Books; Exbourne: Etruscan Books, 2011). See also his anthology, Tom Leonard (ed.), *Radical Renfrew: Poetry from the French Revolution to the First World War* (Edinburgh: Polygon, 1990).

14. Dramatic Contexts and Metatheatricality in Muriel Spark's Writing for Performance

IAN BROWN

On 26 February 1957, Rayner Heppenstall, novelist and BBC radio producer, wrote to Muriel Spark, wondering if she 'were predisposed [...] to writing in a dramatical form for broadcasting'.[1] At this stage, she was known as a poet and for her critical biographies, but her first novel, *The Comforters* (1957), was still to make its full effect. The approach arose, it would appear, from her involvement in literary circles rather than any published evidence of 'dramatical' skills or even, at this stage, of the undoubted gift for dialogue seen in her novels, though her short stories were having impact. Her response was *The Party Through the Wall* (1957). This was followed between 1958 and 1961 by three more radio plays: *The Interview* (1958), *The Dry River Bed* (1959) and *The Danger Zone* (1961).[2] All are contemporary in setting, the first two London-based. Spark then attracted the support of the leading London play agent of the late twentieth century, Peggy Ramsay. Ramsay's clients already included such playwrights as James Bridie, Robert Bolt and Eugene Ionesco, while she was then developing her creative three-decade relationship with the remarkable West End producer Michael Codron: she was 'perhaps the most crucial of all [his] mentor figures'.[3] Although he had produced successful West End revues such as *Pieces of Eight*, Codron's primary interest in often-challenging, edgy new writing saw him produce Pinter's ground-breaking *The Caretaker* at the Arts Theatre before transferring to a larger West End theatre – the Duchess – in 1962, a pattern he sought to repeat with Muriel Spark's stage play *Doctors of Philosophy* (1962), premiered on 2 October 1962. With Ramsay and the energetic Codron behind the production, all seemed set fair for the successful addition of the 'dramatical form' to her repertoire like other novelist-playwrights on Ramsay's books including John Mortimer, Iris Murdoch and J. B. Priestley. This chapter explores the nature and context of Spark's dramatic work and concludes by suggesting possible reasons that *Doctors of Philosophy* was, in fact, to become her only original stage play.

Her first radio play, *The Party Through the Wall*, explores the developing relationship of the Narrator, a Dr Fell, and Miss Ethel Carson who has moved into accommodation at 10 Romney Terrace, Kensington, next door to Dr Fell on a bomb-damaged street. Fell is a 'specialist' of some kind in 'exceptionally interesting cases' (p. 177). Spark plays dramaturgically with his interweaving narration and participation in dialogue: at times he chides Miss Carson for interrupting his narration in which they participate. She, a member of the 'Astral-Radiation Trance Club', seeks quiet for her paranormal investigations: Spark gently sends up her earnest mysticism. Fell's sister is confined to her room next door, through the wall from Ethel's. After some months in her new accommodation, Ethel hears in the middle of the night loud music and noisy voices through the wall, including that of a Countess. When Ethel complains to Fell, he brings her to his sister who turns out to be the Countess, but denies her brother is called Dr Fell. Rather, she says he is locked in a room, while the Countess has not entertained for fifty years, her room full of dust and she a shadowy presence. At three the next morning a dialogue disturbs Ethel again, the Countess rebuking her brother for not being in his room attended by his keeper. Saying he has cut his keeper's throat, he refuses to let his sister leave: 'Stop screaming, my dear, stop screaming. Stop, stop, stop. That's better. Now you've stopped screaming, haven't you? [*Laughing.*]' (p. 187). Nonetheless, next morning Ethel visits Fell. Entering his house, she cannot see him. He speaks to her while invisible. Ethel calls out that she is haunted. Fell agrees. After a pause, the play concludes with his informing us that Miss Carson has left: 'Just as well, she was getting frightfully on my nerves, she gave me the creeps.' (p. 188). The play's atmosphere is spookily mysterious, even creepily grand guignol. One remains uncertain whose version of reality to believe. Ethel's neurasthenia raises doubts about her sanity, while the elusive relationship of Fell, the Countess and Ethel carries a Hitchcock-like sense of menace.

Spark's next radio play, *The Interview*, a three-hander, is not about an interview in any everyday sense. Its characters convey a sense of surrealism, even absurdism, in a species of lacerating banter, a minuet of minds frequently comic, often irritable: it opens with Dame Lettice asking 'Why don't you get your teeth seen to, Tiggy? They look terrible.' (p. 129). The fretful relationship of Dame Lettice – '*who was well known in political circles during the "twenties"*' – and her companion-secretary, Miss 'Tiggy' Bone recalls the interaction of Beckett's Hamm and Clov in *Endgame*, if one can imagine that apocalyptic piece set in up-market Knightsbridge. Lettice throughout tries to dictate her memoirs to Tiggy, while Tiggy interrupts her own flow and others' conversation with random facts she is memorising to win a 'Quiz' offering sufficient prize money to leave Lettice's service. We hear the third character, Lettice's nephew Roy, a theological student, is going over to Rome at which Lettice asserts, as she does at every shift in his spiritual/political direction, 'Not another penny would he get from me, Tiggy.' (p. 137). Roy claims to have been hunting witches in St John's Wood where human blood is drunk in 'a Sabbath once a month' (p. 134). Later he claims to be a communist fleeing from MI5, Lettice remarking, 'If Roy has become a Communist, Tiggy, I think I shall go mad.' Tiggy responds tartly, 'Well, you won't have to go far.' (p. 142). Later Roy presents as a self-interested smuggler in France, the play concluding with his return when it becomes clear he has returned as a ghost, having died in a plane crash ten minutes before entering the final scene. As with her first radio play, Spark's bleakly comic tone explores issues of social status, the other-worlds of people's imagination, and elusive reality and 'realities' in miscommunication and misperception.

The Dry River Bed is set in a tobacco-growing 'Colony' clearly based on Southern Rhodesia (now Zimbabwe) where she lived for several years after marriage in 1937. It opens with a tea party of expatriate women, the hostess, Sarah, patronising the others on the grounds she has been there for twenty-five years, so understands Colony life better than them. A young woman, Peggy Whitehead, has vanished and Sarah's daughter Marjorie, who has had only one driving lesson, has been seen driving very fast on her own, when she was supposed to be being taught by her fiancé Borden Reeves. We hear that lesson: Marjorie is confused, accelerates too fast, crashes into a dry riverbed and is hospitalised. There, she talks of Borden's having attacked her after the crash. Meantime, at the crash site the body of Peggy, her bridesmaid-to-be, is discovered. Despite the scenes where we have heard Borden teaching Marjorie, we discover he had by then fled to Mombasa, where police seek him for Peggy's murder. Before any arrest, he shoots himself. His motive appears to be Peggy's intention to reveal to Marjorie his being mixed-race. During the hunt for him different witnesses see him as entirely either white or black. The play ends with the sound of a dust devil, a sign earlier referred to as an ill omen. Spark's play again satirises snobbery, here with added racism, while she develops her interest in uncannily disorientating mystery. Earlier plays each represented ghost stories; this subverts mundane murder mystery with deployment of inexplicable differences in perceptions of everyday 'realities' and such improbabilities as Marjorie's reckless twenty-mile drive during her first driving lesson with an instructor actually in Mombasa.

Such exploration of the seeming-inexplicable continues in Spark's last radio play. *The Danger Zone*, scheduled for broadcast in February 1961,[4] set in Welsh borderlands, concerns a community fearing invasion by younger people from over the mountain. These, with their own songs and a different eye-shape from the valley-dwellers, threaten mysterious alien intrusion. The play, roughly twice the length of each of Spark's first three, involves a complicated plot in which somewhat caricatured Welsh adults face rebellion among their own young and must offer a hostage to the intruders, led by 'Danger-Boy'. Spark establishes various social conflicts centring on tensions: familiar/alien; young/old. The atmosphere is of science-fiction mystery, eerie otherworldliness in the midst of mundane rural life. It concludes with Danger-Boy and his fellows settled among the adults, their eyes slowly ceasing to appear different, while the community's children, led by the apparently illegitimate son of village leader Richard Jones, have withdrawn, living near the top of the hill. The play concludes with their mountain-top song.

When Spark was writing these plays, she wrote *Robinson* (1958), *Memento Mori* (1959), *The Ballad of Peckham Rye* (1960), *The Bachelors* (1960) and *The Prime of Miss Jean Brodie* (1961). Obvious parallels in these to her radio plays include witty language use, but also interest in the uncanny, the apparently supernatural and 'reality', identity and the nature of 'truth'. In terms specifically of dramatic craft, these years see clear development in her radio playwriting's range and confidence: Spark moves from three-handers with constrained dialogue – *The Party* (though it includes the brief part of a Housekeeper and the party's general hubbub) and *The Interview* – to more complex cast interaction and plot development. *The Dry River Bed* with its cast of eight and *The Danger Zone* its fourteen characters embody an often complex flow of dialogue. While the first two plays unfold in essentially single sets, both later ones vary their locations considerably.

Oddly, Spark appears to consider her radio plays as generically compatible with her short stories. She included them with six short stories in *Voices at Play* (1961). Her 'Author's Note' to that collection claims, 'The excuse for both sorts [of writing] being put together is that all were written on the same creative wavelength. The plays were written for the outward, and the stories for the inward, ear.'[5] She adds:

> The plays were written at the suggestion of Mr Rayner Heppenstall for the Third Programme. By definition they were supposed to be 'features' rather than proper plays. I never quite grasped the distinction between dramatic features and plays except to discern what was in my favour, namely the freedom to do as I pleased with characters and voices without thought of conforming to a settled category. [...]
> And so if the plays have turned out to be plays, that is by accident; and if it comes to that, in many ways the same could be said of the stories.

This is oddly disingenuous. Heppenstall specifically invited work 'in a dramatical form for broadcasting'. It is hard to see this as commissioning radio features, rather than 'proper plays'. Indeed, Spark clearly produced 'proper' plays, fitting happily the 'settled category' of radio drama, not 'features'. Far from appearing plays turned out 'by accident', they show a dramatist developing in confidence and expertise in radio drama. As Michael Codron and Alan Strachan observe, 'It is easy to overlook the importance of radio in shaping some of post-war British theatre's major playwrights.'[6] Spark was on the pathway to theatrical success followed by contemporaries like Harold Pinter, John Mortimer, Joe Orton, Giles Cooper, Tom Stoppard and Alan Ayckbourn. Moreover, around the time Spark was writing her 'Note', she had, like Mortimer, Orton, Cooper and Ayckbourn, become a client of London's leading 'proper' play agent of the day, Peggy Ramsay.

Spark's 'Note' suggests an odd ambivalence about her playwriting, reluctance to define herself as a dramatist, preferring to conflate short story writing and playwriting as if their difference were simply that they are written for differently orientated ears. Certainly, it is axiomatic that radio drama is absorbed by the ear, stimulating the visual imagination in the absence of a play-set, but equally it has none of the prose dimensions of the short story, while the forms of dialogue found in fiction are often formally distinct from stage dialogue's quasi-colloquial structures. Given the dramaturgical skills Spark's broadcast plays demonstrate, it is hard to explain her apparent ambivalence about her 'proper plays', whose achievement drew the attention of as acute an observer as Ramsay, who, having received the draft of *Doctors of Philosophy*, sent it to Michael Codron, whose (auto)biography comments:

> The search for new work sometimes produced plays from unexpected sources. Peggy Ramsay represented one of the modern novelists Michael most admired – Muriel Spark – and when her play *Doctors of Philosophy* (1962) arrived he was struck by its unusual dialogue and keen to programme it for the Arts, although he sensed it might divide opinion.[7]

The significance then of the Arts Theatre in Great Newport Street may be deduced from the fact that here in 1955 Peter Hall directed the first English production of Beckett's *Waiting for Godot*, and, as we have seen, Codron had used it as a launch pad before transferring *The Caretaker* to a larger playhouse. Its location within the West End theatre district – but with an audience capacity at 350 seats substantially smaller than other West End theatres – made it attractive for testing plays which might either move up in scale if box office successes or be in themselves a *succès d'estime*. In 1962, Codron, on Ramsay's advice, had taken over as Managing Director of the theatre, which had been newly refurbished.⁸ She predicted 'that he would make his reputation there, but [...] not much money either'.⁹ The Arts then was a 'proper' play venue for the rising new play producer mentored by Ramsay. In approach to new plays under their aegis, both were interventionist and complementary: Ramsay fiery, flamboyant, fierce and forthright; Codron courteous, stoic and steely; both skilled West End dramaturgs.¹⁰ Committed to *Doctors of Philosophy*, Codron gave it prominence by opening his season at the 'New' Arts with it.

Codron's production process shows every sign of an intention to make the play a West End success. He engaged Donald McWhinnie, experienced in radio, television and film, who had directed work for Peter Hall at the Shakespeare Memorial Theatre in 1960 and again in 1961 when it became the Royal Shakespeare Company (RSC). He had already worked with Codron earlier in 1962 when he directed Giles Cooper's play, *Everything in the Garden*, which opened on 13 March at the Arts in an RSC production and transferred – on the pattern already identified – to the Duke of York's. Martin Stannard observes that 'Muriel had a high reputation, particularly as a master of dialogue, and Codron and McWhinnie were delighted to have secured her first stage play. She took their advice, confident of success'.¹¹ Nonetheless, it would have been difficult to recruit recognised stars to a first stage play by a novelist, however well-known, not being presented in a larger, prestigious West End theatre. Casting in the West End was, and is, critical to a play's prospects for success and what the production team could do was recruit a cast of recognised West End 'names', actors not 'stars', but often seen on Shaftesbury Avenue whose reputation was high, capable of drawing audiences that would trust their ability. They cast, for example, in the major parts Gwen Cherrell (1926–2019) as Catherine, the leading female role; Laurence Hardy (1911–1982) as Charlie Delfont, her husband; Ursula Howells (1922–2005) as her cousin, Leonora; Hazel Hughes (1913–1974) as Mrs S, their daily help; and Fenella Fielding (1927–2018) as Annie Wood, another cousin. Not all these names resonate now, although Fielding, then well-known for her work in intimate revue, including Codron's production, *Pieces of Eight*, with Kenneth Williams and scripts by, *inter alia*, Harold Pinter and Peter Cook, and in plays by Ibsen, Shakespeare, Henry James,

Sheridan and Chekhov, may be remembered, more relevantly to our current topic, for her extravagant vowels and thespian overstatement, not least as the vampish Valeria in *Carry On Screaming!*, a performance style exactly right for playing Annie. Each actor had a steady 'line', a specific strength in characterisation that suited them to a series of similar roles. In choosing such a cast, Codron, McWhinnie and, no doubt, Ramsay were buttressing Spark's play for West End production.

However new Spark was to the stage, she was now no neophyte. Her radio scripts showed a developing facility and complexity, while the structure of *Doctors of Philosophy* shows understanding of theatrical conventions, both historic and contemporary. The character of the daily help Mrs S represents, for example, Spark's take on a millennia-old theatrical convention, the impertinent servant, wiser and more sophisticated than the master. First found in western theatre in Graeco-Roman drama, in the twentieth-century theatre, the figure is found in plays by Shaw – for example, in the chauffeur Straker in *Man and Superman* – by Barrie in the title role in *The Admirable Crichton* and in several of Coward's plays. A female manifestation, popular in the 1950s, Aggie – the pert Scottish housekeeper, played by Molly Weir – featured in the radio situation comedy *Life with the Lyons* while Hazel Hughes had previously played similar parts as a Londoner in film and on stage. Spark brings to this tradition, as she must have been well aware, her own version of subversive servant power: in an academic household Mrs S's expertise includes Yeats editions. Yet, she also embodies common sense: when in Act Two Scene 2, Leonora observes, 'Reality is very alarming at first, and then it becomes interesting. Are you interested in the nature of reality, Mrs S?', she replies, manoeuvring a floor-polisher, 'Very, I'm trying to give it a polish as you can see' (p. 47). As Joe Farrell observes, this reply

> is comic but not [one might add 'just'] because of the waspish common sense of the down-to-earth Englishwoman who will not stand airy-fairy intellectual nonsense. Mrs. S. is a striking comic creation because she overturns what is expected of her class, and can be as intellectual as her upper-crust employers.[12]

Farrell also observes that Charlie Delfont,

> an economist who churns out articles which will remain unread and unappreciated outside his own circle but which are sufficiently highly esteemed inside it to guarantee his promotion [...] is also a miser of a type recognizable from traditions of comedy in any language.[13]

Not only is Spark engaging with long-established theatrical traditions, she is specifically subverting then-contemporary versions of it: when daily helps were seen as irrepressible 'lovably cheery cockneys [given to] malapropism and apparent dimness',[14] her daily is literate, bright and witty.

There are other signs that Spark was alert to current theatrical conventions and could follow them. Otherwise, it is improbable that Ramsay, let alone Codron or McWhinnie, would have picked up her play, however prominent she was becoming as a novelist. Her theatrical nous is seen in several ways. She constructs a three-act play, each act of two scenes, on the then West End model – even radical plays like John Osborne's *Look Back in Anger* or Arnold Wesker's trilogy employed the three-act form, contrary to more progressive structural experiments found in different ways in Brecht's or Beckett's plays. Further, despite the more radical themes and settings then emerging in, among others, Royal Court plays, Spark sets her comedy in a bourgeois home reflecting the sets of successful period boulevard plays. As Farrell characterises it,

> The setting is precise. The stage directions inform us that 'the Delfonts live in a house overlooking the Regent's Canal', and further that 'the whole play takes place in the living room and on the adjoining terrace'. Nothing seemingly challenging, uncomfortable, exotic or avant-garde there. The audience can relax in the expectation of an undemanding comedy of manners, for this seems quintessentially bourgeois territory.[15]

Though Regent's Canal was still used commercially in the early 1960s, the house is in a still-fashionable part of London, near to Regent's Park.

Spark was toying with expectations, like another Scottish playwright, William Douglas Home, then enjoying great commercial success with fashionable comedies of manners. Though his plays are in no sense as intellectually challenging as *Doctors of Philosophy*, the prominent *Sunday Times* critic of the time, Harold Hobson, argued consistently that to see Douglas Home as simply a writer of light comedy missed the dark undercurrents of his scripts. Adam Benedick, however, summarises a more general view:

> What Douglas-Home was undeniably skilled at, however, was the composition of light-hearted lounge-hall comedies for actors who knew their way about lounge-halls and how to behave in them. This breed of player has almost vanished but the art of men like A. E. Matthews, Rex Harrison, Wilfrid Hyde White and Kenneth More was bound to prosper in his plays because he let his upper-class types revel in their eccentricities.[16]

While Douglas Home is now largely forgotten, Alan Ayckbourn, a younger contemporary, was, from 1959 onwards, developing his playwriting under the Ramsay-Codron aegis. His early work was initially regarded as insubstantial, like Douglas Home's, but increasingly his masterly comic exploration of abysses underlying apparently secure bourgeois life has been recognised. Drew Milne observes that descriptions 'of Spark's writing invariably recognise that her narrative textures are playful, ironic or satirical, as if the pleasures of levity might afford some dance of the intellect over dark matter'.[17] Her use of comic theatre conventions for a serious underlying exploration of societal and familial relations accorded with Douglas Home's and Ayckbourn's contemporary West End practice.

While dialogue in *Doctors of Philosophy* has all the snip and snap of her prose fiction and the opening scene opens a plotline where Charlie's cousin-in-law Leonora outrageously demands he give her a child, a challenge later comically denied, re-asserted and tape-recorded, Spark shows, as one might expect given her interest in fashion discussed elsewhere in this volume, acute awareness of the potential of costume and staging for characterisation and humorous impact. The most obvious example lies in Annie Wood's costumes. We first see Catherine's flirty, socialising cousin in Act Two Scene 1 in 'an opulent dressing-gown' (p. 39). In the next scene she is 'dressed "for boating on the Canal"' (p. 51), an improbable activity, given the canal's navigation by commercial barges, but allowing for a spectacular ending to the scene when Annie, having capsized, is carried in dripping wet, exclaiming with relish in Fenella Fielding's plummy accents, 'What a crowd I drew! It's just as well I was suitably dressed.' (p. 69). In Act Three Scene 1, she enters dressed 'for lunch at the Ritz' (p. 73); we learn after she leaves for lunch she has 'laid out her scarlet velvet to wear tonight. [...] The one with the enormous skirt' (p. 77). When in the final scene she enters in that evening gown, Catherine scolds: 'You can't wear that tonight. And why are you dressed so early? It's only five', Annie responds, 'I thought this would be a suitable dress to be asked to change out of' (p. 87). Young Charlie has impregnated Catherine's daughter, Daphne, a participant in CND demonstrations, who refuses to marry him, since he is a nuclear scientist. His mother, having come to resolve this situation, compliments Annie on the dress. Catherine responds, 'Annie's going to change into something less formal. We want to give the right impression of the family as a whole, and so Annie has kindly agreed to give the wrong impression of herself.' (p. 90). Annie's final costume reverses the hitherto glamorous impression of her costumes: she enters *'dressed in black skirt, black stockings, white blouse with floppy black tie and heavy-rimmed glasses'* (p. 93). The visual gag's comic impact is highly theatrical: Annie, who has been resolutely anti-intellectual throughout the play, is costumed as a conventional version of a serious scholar. Her entry, so dressed, is a veritable *coup de théâtre* surely drawing audience laughter.

Spark's employment of such theatrical effects and indeed the theatricality of the character of Annie, played we remember by one of the more exaggeratedly flamboyant of late twentieth-century West End actresses, reflects a metatheatrical quality Spark employs throughout the play. In the first lines, Charlie comments 'Leonora ought to look at reality' in the vacation when she is not distracted by 'geographical and historical and sociological' ideas (p. 1). While such dialogue recurs and reflects Spark's typical concern with the elusive relationship of 'truth' and 'reality', as the play proceeds she uses theatrical devices to remind us we are watching a play onstage. There are several examples of lines like those in Act Two Scene 2 when Leonora talks of 'A definite sense of being observed and listened to by an audience [...] Looking at all of us and waiting to see what's going to happen' (p. 63). Indeed, the recurrent joke of reminding an audience that it is watching 'characters' acting for its benefit was reflected in the physical opening Spark sought for that scene. While Act One and Act Two Scene 1 stage directions establish the kind of setting for the play Farrell outlines, Spark opens Act Two Scene 2 with the stage direction *'The stage is empty and without scenery except for various pulleys and switches to adjust stage scenery and lighting, but with various coloured lights upon it'* (p. 46). Mrs S is polishing the stage floor with an electric polisher at this point, giving rise to the exchange noted above which leads to her talk of polishing reality. Not only is Spark drawing on the 'wise servant' tradition, she seeks a mid-act metatheatrical phenomenon, the audience witnessing the stripped back 'reality' of the stage from which in the time-shift between Scenes 1 and 2 behind the curtain the 'reality' of the set and its furniture have been removed. One page of dialogue later, Charlie Brown is to enter with pieces of scenery and he and Mrs S are to adjust the scenery within the abbreviated playing time of nine lines – improbably tight in practical terms – until 'The room is now normal' (p. 49), as Mrs S puts final touches to it.

As the scene develops, Annie suggests Leonora stick to the safely mundane – bricks and mortar – a position Leonora questions: 'Look. (*Takes hold of a tall pillar. It moves.*) It doesn't look very safe to me.' Leonora proceeds to shake the terrace wall and Annie trills: 'It's thrilling! It gives me a horrible feeling. Do it again, Leonora.' After this quasi-orgasmic response, dialogue continues:

> LEONORA (*shaking pillar*)   I blow all your theories to hell and you tell me it's thrilling.
> ANNIE   I think it's a brilliant discovery of yours, Leonora.
> LEONORA   Some people have known it all their lives. The scenery is unreliable, Annie. Some people know that by instinct, they take it for granted. (p. 67)

The blowing of 'all your theories to hell' addressed to the least theoretical of the three cousins, the only one without a doctorate, echoes a phrase used by Annie when at the end of Act One she reveals to Leonora a newspaper report that shows how the result of two years of her research has been undermined by a recent discovery. The trope of the unreliability of life's ideas, research and scenery recurs. In Act Three Scene 2 Young Charlie's mother Mrs Weston remarks 'You scholars are not realists, that's my theory'. Annie responds, 'Show her realism, Leonora. Go on! Blow all her theories to hell' and Leonora, according to Spark's stage direction, *'reaches out and gives the wall a push. The ceiling rises, while the wall recedes. Everything then settles back into place.'* (p. 97). The idea that 'reality' is variable and deceptive pervading Spark's writing is here intended to assume a 'real' physical expression.

Alan Bold has argued that in Spark's novels appearance 'was not to be accepted empirically but penetrated by the artist's vision'[18] and that the 'straightforward rendering of so-called reality is not challenging enough for Mrs. Spark, so her work confronts realistic detail with surrealistic tension, invests natural incidents with supernatural overtones'.[19] Talking of Iris Murdoch's and Spark's fiction, Randall Stevenson talks of 'strong components of realism, even while challenging, at a level of parable or metaphor, the reliability of art's representation and ordering of reality'.[20] Clearly, Bold's and Stevenson's insights read across to Spark's drama: as Charlotte Higgins put it, discussing a reading of the play at the 2018 Edinburgh International Book Festival, Spark reveals 'the literal, material reality of the machinery behind the illusionistic set [while the] work also shows her dealing in ideas about surveillance, eavesdropping and blackmail'.[21] Famously, Spark told Frank Kermode, 'I don't pretend that what I'm writing is more than an imaginative extension of the truth – something inventive.'[22] In *Doctors of Philosophy*, she seeks scenographic inventiveness. Just as David Goldie has spoken of 'characteristic Sparkian metafictional experiment',[23] we are here faced with Sparkian metatheatrical experiment at the service of her satire and sense of the mysterious and numinous in the context of the everyday. The ways in which Spark ties her surreal exploration to the mundane is reflected in the resolution of her nuclear-crossed lovers' conflict. Daphne agrees to marry Young Charlie after he appears to have attempted to drown himself in the canal, a tragi-farcical version of Annie's comedic capsize at the end of Act Two. Daphne relents: 'I told him to disappear out of my life. But I didn't say out of his.' (p. 106). Mrs S, however, has just spotted that the suicide may not be all it seems: she identifies the notepaper of the suicide note as Queen's Velvet, not Basildon Bond; the latter would be appropriate to a younger person's price- and quality-range; the more expensive notepaper suggests involvement of better-off plotters, choreographing a scene. Spark's attention to social detail underpins her escalating comic denouement.

The question arises with regard to the premiere production of *Doctors of Philosophy*, however, of how far Spark's metatheatricality was sustainable in the face of practical theatricality. Here we must return to the question of the disappearance of the set and furniture between the two scenes of Act Two, not least since, as we shall see later, it appears to have caused problems not only for the technical staff at the time, but later for relations between Spark and her producer, Codron. As already noted, questions arise with regard to the theatrical feasibility of this effect in actual, as opposed to fictional, reality. John Faulkner[24] points out that at the time, such a set would have been set up by a stage crew using flats tied together using cleats and supported by props and heavy stage weights.[25] The stripping back of this, let alone removal of furniture and furnishings would have required – even for a skilled and expanded crew – more than the normal time-lapse between scenes. Further, the idea all might be restored and re-erected by two actors within the time provided by the playing of less than one page of dialogue is hard to countenance, even with a stage crew remaining out of sight. Flying equipment might help solve the problem, but the Arts does not have high flies and the directions do not allow for this solution.

In fact, an 'Author's Note' – dated New York, November 1962 – makes it clear that her stage directions at this point were not followed:

> I thought it right to give a general permission to the contractual management for constructional changes to be made to the play, as the Arts Theatre was not equipped for the full scenic effects I wished to obtain. [...] I believe the scenic effects in question were omitted. But as these scenic effects are directly related to my original meaning

and intention throughout the play, they remain, for better or worse, in the published text which I can properly call my own.²⁶

One review makes it clear that on the play's opening the solution to the technical problem was not just to ignore Spark's emphatically specific stage direction, but to move the scene-change forward to between Acts One and Two, thereby nullifying the actual effect Spark sought between Act Two's first and second scenes. David Nathan of the *Daily Herald* (4 October 1962) is clear: 'the second act curtain rose on a drawing-room in which the walls had been pushed aside and where, through the window that had once disclosed a view of the Regent's Canal, there was – nothing.'²⁷ The evidence is that the effects within Act Two that Spark sought, their theatrical demands and metatheatrical significations, were not achieved, nor apparently even attempted, in the Arts Theatre production. What appears to have happened is that the upstage flat containing the window was left in place, while the image of the canal perhaps painted on a stage-cloth was out of sight, perhaps rolled up, and the side flats were not removed, but, rather, pushed towards the wings of the stage, but still in view. The implications of this beyond the play will be discussed later, but what the critics saw was not the expression of (meta)theatrical meanings that Spark wanted and intended, even if – perhaps because – that intention was in theatrical terms very difficult to achieve. The effects Spark sought were not, after all, trivial nor tangential to her meaning. *Doctors of Philosophy* has a zany quality, which, with its prominent female characters (all men reduced to being called 'Charlie') combines elements of comedy of manners, West End boulevard theatre, absurdist philosophy and the Marx Brothers. As Higgins commented in 2018,

> Two things are certain: first, the play is killingly funny, full of stiletto-sharp lines. And second, in its deep interest in the roles women play and how they are expected to perform them, it is a work of our time. In this, as in so many of her concerns, she was utterly prescient.²⁸

Nonetheless, the play received mixed reviews on its opening in 1962. Harold Hobson described it positively: 'It all goes on with the quiet confidence of a proposition of Euclid, only more entertainingly'.[29] T. C. Worsley of the *Financial Times* relished 'the sharp dialogue and sense of the bizarre'.[30] Others were less positive: the panel on *The Critics* on the BBC Third Programme

> acknowledged amusing lines and situations, then savaged the piece: 'manufactured feyness and clumsy obscurantism'; 'half-converted stereotypes, or unfinished enigmas'. Its wit and intelligence, they thought, failed to disguise a flawed dramatic structure. 'In fact, it's rather a shambles. But it's not a *boring* shambles.'[31]

Tom Stoppard, then a critic, concluded the play had 'undoubtedly failed', but was 'a thoroughly entertaining failure'.[32] Indeed, Higgins headlined her article, echoing Stoppard, '"A thoroughly entertaining failure": the return of Muriel Spark's mega-flop'. She quoted David Greig's characterisation of the play as an 'almost Wildean thing' which suddenly 'takes an unexpectedly Pirandello-esque turn', Greig continuing, 'sentence after sentence is perfectly weighted [and] "need[s] to be heard on the stage"'.[33] Greig's response to the play, however, citing its 'almost Wildean' qualities and its 'unexpectedly Pirandello-esque turn', may highlight the very aspects of the play that on its premiere disturbed the critics of the time. J. C. Trewin in the *Birmingham Post* (4 October 1962) is quite clear, substituting Shaw and Coward for Greig's reference to Wilde:

> I rather wish Muriel Spark has decided whether she was going to write a realistic comedy, or a fantasy with a bit of Pirandello, a touch of Shaw, and perhaps a 'flicker' of Coward. (Or are all these names outmoded?)
>
> As it is, *Doctors of Philosophy* [...] has what I can say unhesitatingly is the wittiest first act I can remember in more or less straight modern comedy.[34]

Trewin's review suggests that the play's playfulness and erosion of the boundaries between realism and magic realism, its generic border-crossing (a feature, one might add, of much specifically Scottish literature),[35] transgression and toying with theatrical possibility (however beyond the technical potential of the Arts Theatre) threw the critics. The response on the BBC Third Programme *The Critics*, a wonderfully definite article before their programme title – 'a flawed dramatic structure' and 'rather a shambles' – can be seen as their failure to grasp the nature of the theatrical experiment and exploration of varieties of reality with which Spark was engaged. Though Stoppard concluded the play had 'undoubtedly failed', surely part of what made it, in his words, 'a thoroughly entertaining failure', was just this capacity for working across expectation – especially those settled generic expectations of the critics – combined, of course, with the typically Sparkian wit addressed by Trewin and, more recently, Higgins. As if to make the point explicit, David Nathan headlined his *Daily Herald* review, 'When the laughter died away'. His analysis suggests the 'failure' in critical response (and as we shall discuss in a moment producer reaction) derived from the 'experimental' nature of the play:

> There had to be some reason why *Doctors of Philosophy* was staged at the Arts Theatre. Here was a first play by novelist Muriel Spark and a cast whose names are usually seen in Shaftesbury Avenue.
>
> And here was a first act so funny, so swift, so sparkling that it creased the audience into continuous laughter.
>
> There had to be a catch, an experimental angle to justify producer Michal Codron's caution in not going straight to the West End.
>
> It came as the second act curtain rose on a drawing-room in which the walls had been pushed aside and where, through the window that had once disclosed a view of the Regent's Canal, there was – nothing.
>
> [...]
>
> There is even a reference to the feeling of being watched by an unseen audience at which point the audience became noticeably less obtrusive in their demonstrations of laughter.[36]

Nathan concludes 'this is a comedy that makes most comedies look not funny, but silly. Despite the odd abstractions.'[37] But the 'odd abstractions' were the point. It is, of course, debateable how far initial criticism alone can affect a play's long-term commercial, or even critical, success: another Codron production, Pinter's *The Birthday Party*, was famously attacked on its opening at the Lyric Hammersmith to the extent it was being taken off within one week, before Hobson's adulatory review appeared on the Sunday. Certainly, there was no rave review of Spark's play, but mixed reviews do not in themselves create a 'mega-flop' and it was emphatically not taken off. Indeed, its run was extended by a week. The play was seen, even by those who disliked it, as having real strengths and, beyond critical responses which carry some weight, it had the strength of the Codron-Ramsay axis behind it.

Arguably, other circumstances prevented the play's being a West End success of the kind Spark clearly desired. Stannard notes that the play 'meant a lot to her'[38] and summarises the impasse that arose: 'Although she had left the play (kept on for an extra week) pleasing audiences well enough, Michael Codron exasperated her.'[39] Codron sought rewrites, but as Stannard notes, 'This was how commercial theatre worked. It was not, however, how Muriel worked.'[40] Codron specifically suggested rewrites to Act Two in a letter which she stuffed in a drawer. 'And there it would stay, she said, until he found a West End theatre. As he could not find one without a revised script, the project soon collapsed.'[41] Spark's correspondence at the time makes the position even clearer.[42] Writing to her US agent Ivan von Auw on 3 November, while the play is still in performance, she said:

> I don't think the question of my present commitments is relevant to any discussion with Michael Codron, because even if I had no other work to do I wouldn't touch the play until he decides to move it to a West End Theatre for a definite date. [...] I would now like to call a halt to any further alterations to the text and construction that they might want to do in my absence. I hope you will feel that the above is reasonable. I've spent a whole year on the writing and re-writing of the play on a speculative basis, and now wait for something concrete on the management side of things.[43]

On 16 November 1962 Spark wrote to her literary agent, John Smith, 'On *Doctors of Philosophy* in general, I will just say that I have not looked at Michael Codron's changes, but do not feel that he could possibly improve on my work by them'.[44]

Yet, Codron had invested in an extra week's run. Despite his sense that some plot lines were 'stuck on'[45] to the main plot, which he saw as the relationship between the Delfonts and Leonora, there appears to have been no lack of goodwill on his part, nor, given the extra week, a sense of no audience for the play, despite a 'fairly tepid' (as Codron put it) critical reception.[46] Though he hoped 'Spark would write another original play (and continued to read all her novels as published), he never received one'.[47] Colin Chambers, Peggy Ramsay's biographer, comments 'Codron and Peggy were exasperated by Spark but in the end realised she wasn't that interested in the theatre, and what that entailed'. He continues, reflecting on the English theatre aesthetic of the time,

> James Saunders, who featured in that opening season, had a hit with *Next Time I'll Sing to You* but didn't make the impact his talent merited, possibly because of his absurdism. [...] Perhaps there was something in the English theatre-goers' taste that resisted what Spark had to offer, though her stubbornness didn't give us a chance to test that.[48]

If Chambers is right in his comment on prevailing taste, Drew Milne is surely off-target when he suggests of *Doctors of Philosophy* that 'the dramatic form makes the satire appear clumsily populist'.[49] While such a barb might be aimed at the contemporaneous farces of Brian Rix at the Whitehall Theatre (though how 'clumsy' those highly successful popular hits were is a matter for debate), it is hard to see Spark's play as populist at all. In any case, populism would not have been a drawback in seeking West End transfer and success. A variety of practical factors seem to have stymied the progress of the play and its future potential, at least for the English-language stage. The technically difficult scene-shift in the middle of Act Two has already been commented on: such a shift might be entirely feasible in the imaginative world of a radio play, but, given the actuality of a stage and scenery, the playing with 'reality' Spark was exploring would come, in the actual context of a theatre, hard against the actuality of scenery, furniture and stagehands. Stoppard, in his review, pointed out that Spark's prose fiction dealt with 'a world of everyday reality made brittle by the admission of the unreal'.[50] Theatrical unreality has a different relationship to 'reality' or, indeed, 'unreality', to that of fiction or, for that matter, radio drama.

Spark also clearly rejected the advice of the nurturing Codron-Ramsay partnership with its formidable growing record of helping playwrights develop their work to achieve lasting success: Orton, Ayckbourn, Christopher Hampton, David Hare, Caryl Churchill are only a few who benefitted from it. Clearly, Spark was not interested in the kind of imaginative and collaborative co-operation commonplace in the theatre. Two distinguished creative people were in irreconcilable conflict: she demanded, somewhat unrealistically, Codron find a West End main house for a play that he, an expert in the field, believed needed adjustment to be ready for that exposure. When Spark remarked that she had a contract for a West End production, she did not seem to accept, as Pinter had with *The Caretaker* in 1960 or James Saunders with *Next Time I'll Sing to You* later in the 1962 Arts Theatre season, that there might be, as part of that contractual process, a developmental phase at the Arts. Indeed, the question of how far the Arts counts as a West End theatre was then open to debate. One would give much to have been present at discussions between the formidable Spark and her equally formidable play agent, Peggy Ramsay, around such issues.

When Vassiliki Kolocotroni and Willy Maley ask of *Doctors of Philosophy*, 'How did a play by one of our greatest modern writers get lost?',[51] one is tempted to answer, 'Because she was not prepared to make her play theatrically practicable on the advice of two of our greatest modern theatrical mentors'. In many respects, the potentially positive circumstances of the premiere of *Doctors of Philosophy* would have been hard to exceed, but willingness to undertake the rewrites that might have allowed the play to achieve success in English-language theatre of the time did not exist. Nonetheless, in 1964, *Doctors of Philosophy* was produced in Stockholm, directed by Mimi Pollak of the Swedish Royal Dramatic Theatre, ran successfully and was further produced to full houses in Norway and Denmark. The success of that production suggests that there were aspects of English-language theatre of the early 1960s inimical, as Chambers suggests, to the kind of theatrical experiment Spark was undertaking not found in other contemporary theatres; that ways round the technical issues identified above were found; or that somehow in translation rewrites were allowed. If the prompt books and cue sheets of the Arts production could be found and compared with those of the Swedish premiere and Codron's proposed rewrites, fruitful insights would surely emerge.

However that may be, despite Codron and Ramsay's welcome, Spark never again wrote a play, 'proper' or not. Her great theatrical success was an adaptation not written by her but by the experienced screenwriter and dramatist Jay Presson Allen. When *The Prime of Miss Jean Brodie* opened in London in 1966, Codron was not its producer. That must say something about the relationship of Spark and Codron, but, according to Chambers, Ramsay 'was very much behind it'.[52] After Ramsay's death in 1991, her firm merged to create the leading play agency Casarotto Ramsay. Its client list still includes Dame Muriel Spark.

Endnotes

1. Martin Stannard, *Muriel Spark: The Biography* (London: Weidenfeld and Nicolson, 2009), p. 180.
2. All are published in *Voices at Play* (Harmondsworth: Penguin, 1961). Page references are to this edition.
3. Michael Codron and Alan Strachan, *Putting It On: The West End Theatre of Michael Codron* (London: Duckworth, 2010), p. 128.
4. Stannard, p. 233.
5. Muriel Spark, 'Author's Note', *Voices at Play* [1961] (Harmondsworth: Penguin, 1966), p. 7.
6. Codron and Strachan, p. 87.
7. Ibid., p. 133.
8. Ibid., p. 137.
9. Ibid., p. 153.
10. I make these observations from personal knowledge: Ramsay was my play agent from 1973 until her death in 1991; Codron was a member of London's National Theatre Board which, as Arts Council Drama Director (1986–94), I attended as assessor. An acute and lively insight into Ramsay and her methods is found in Colin Chambers, *Peggy: The Life of Margaret Ramsay, Play Agent* (London: Nick Hern Books, 1997).
11. Stannard, p. 265.
12. Joseph Farrell, 'Doctors of Philosophy', in *Scottish Review of Books* 13.1 (February 2018). www.scottishreviewofbooks.org/2018/02/doctors-of-philosophy/ [accessed 12 March 2020].
13. Ibid.
14. Codron and Strachan, p. 154.
15. Farrell, op. cit.
16. Adam Benedick, 'Obituary: William Douglas-Home', *Independent*, 30 September 1992. www.independent.co.uk/news/people/obituary-william-douglas-home-1554492.html [accessed 13 March 2020].
17. Drew Milne, 'Muriel Spark's Crimes of Wit', in *The Edinburgh Companion to Muriel Spark*, eds. Michael Gardiner and Willy Maley (Edinburgh: Edinburgh University Press, 2010), pp. 110–21 (p. 120).
18. Alan Bold, 'Introduction', in *Muriel Spark: An Odd Capacity for Vision*, ed. Alan Bold (London: Vision Press, 1984), p. 8.
19. Ibid., p. 9.
20. Randall Stevenson, 'The Post-war Contexts of Spark's Writing', in *The Edinburgh Companion to Muriel Spark*, eds. Gardiner and Maley, pp. 98–109 (p. 108).
21. Charlotte Higgins, '"A thoroughly entertaining failure": the return of Muriel Spark's mega-flop', *Guardian*, 8 August 2018. www.theguardian.com/stage/2018/aug/08/a-thoroughly-entertaining-failure-return-muriel-spark-flop-doctors-of-philosophy-edinburgh-festival [accessed 12 March 2020].
22. Frank Kermode, 'The House of Fiction: Interviews with Seven English Novelists', in *Partisan Review* 30.1 (Spring 1963), pp. 61–82 (p. 80).
23. David Goldie, 'Muriel Spark and the Problems of Biography', in *The Edinburgh Companion to Muriel Spark*, eds. Gardiner and Maley, pp. 5–15 (p. 12).

24 John Faulkner was Prospect Theatre Company Production Manager and occasional Company Manager (1964–72); later, amid many other theatre technical and management roles, Chairman (1988–94) and Fellow (2017) of the Association of British Theatre Technicians.
25 John Faulkner, Email to author, 6 April 2020.
26 Muriel Spark, Author's note, November 1962. The Muriel Spark archive, National Library of Scotland (NLS), Acc. 10607, File 16.
27 David Nathan, *Daily Herald*, 'When the laughter died away', 4 October 1962.
28 Higgins, op. cit.
29 Harold Hobson cited by Stannard, p. 266.
30 Ibid.
31 Ibid.
32 Tom Stoppard cited by Higgins, op. cit.
33 Higgins, op. cit.
34 John C. Trewin, 'Doctors of Philosophy', *Birmingham Daily Post*, 4 October 1962, p. 10.
35 For discussion of this factor see, for example, Aileen Christianson, 'Gender and Nation: Debatable Lands and Passable Boundaries', in *Across the Margins: Cultural Identity and Change in the Atlantic Archipelago*, eds. Glenda Norquay and Gerry Smyth (Manchester: Manchester University Press, 2002), pp. 67–82; Ian Brown and Colin Nicholson, 'The Border Crossers and Reconfiguration the Possible: Poet-Playwright-Novelists from the Mid-Twentieth Century on', in *The Edinburgh History of Scottish Literature*, eds. Ian Brown et al., vol 3 (Edinburgh: Edinburgh University Press, 2007), pp. 262–72; and Ian Brown, 'Imagined Borders, Subverted Centres and Hybridity', in Brown, *Performing Scottishness: Enactment and National Identities*, (London: Palgrave Macmillan, 2020), pp. 123–40.
36 Nathan, op. cit.
37 Ibid.
38 Stannard, p. 309.
39 Ibid., p. 282.
40 Ibid.
41 Ibid., p. 283.
42 Held in the Spark archive in the NLS. I am grateful to Dr Colin McIlroy, Curator of Modern Scottish Literary Manuscripts and Collections after 1832 at the NLS, for assisting me with suggestions and access and to Steven Harvie, NLS and University of Glasgow doctoral candidate under the AHRC Doctoral Training Partnership scheme, who is working on a PhD on the Muriel Spark archives in the NLS and provided me with the relevant texts.
43 Muriel Spark, Letter to Ivan von Auw, 3 November 1962. Spark archive, NLS, Acc. 10607, File 17.
44 Muriel Spark, Letter to John Smith, 16 November 1962. Spark archive, NLS, Acc. 10607, File 17.
45 Codron and Strachan, p. 133.
46 Ibid., p. 134.
47 Ibid.
48 Colin Chambers, Email to the author, 30 March 2020.

49 Drew Milne, 'Muriel Spark's Crimes of Wit', in *The Edinburgh Companion to Muriel Spark*, eds. Gardiner and Maley, pp. 110–21 (p. 118).
50 Tom Stoppard cited by Higgins, op. cit.
51 Willy Maley, Vassiliki Kolocotroni and David Greig, 'Spark at Play: A Dialogue with Vassiliki Kolocotroni and Willy Maley', in *Textual Practice* 32.9 (2018), pp. 1677–80 (p. 1677).
52 Colin Chambers, Email to the author, 31 March 2020.

Notes on Contributors

Ian Brown is Honorary Senior Research Fellow in Scottish Literature at Glasgow University and Professor Emeritus in Drama at Kingston University, London. Widely published on aspects of theatre, literature and cultural policy, he has edited a wide range of volumes. A playwright and poet, his most recent monograph is *Performing Scottishness: Enactment and National Identities* (Palgrave Macmillan, 2020).

Gerard Carruthers is Francis Hutcheson Professor of Scottish Literature at the University of Glasgow. He is the author of ten essays on Muriel Spark and is co-editor of *The Cambridge Companion to Scottish Literature* (2012). Currently, among other projects, he is editing *The Blackwell Companion to Scottish Literature*.

Mark Currie has been professor of Contemporary Literature at Queen Mary University London since 2010. He currently focuses on the theory of narrative and contemporary fiction, working on questions about time in philosophy, fiction, and narrative more generally. His publications include *About Time* (Cambridge University Press, 2007, 2011) and *The Unexpected* (Cambridge University Press, 2013). He is currently completing a book on the topic of uncertainty.

Monica Germanà is Reader in Gothic and Contemporary Studies at the University of Westminster. Her research concentrates on Gothic and popular culture, with a specific emphasis on Scottish Gothic and gender. Her publications include *Bond Girls: Body, Fashion, Gender* (Bloomsbury, 2019). She is currently collaborating with Scottish and Icelandic academics and practitioners on a collaborative research project under the title of *The North and the Scottish Imagination: Arctic Pasts and Futures*.

Cairns Craig is Glucksman Professor of Irish and Scottish Studies at the University of Aberdeen, having been, previously, Professor of Modern and Scottish Literature at the University of Edinburgh. He has written extensively on the history of ideas, and on Scottish, Irish and American literature. His most recent books are *The Wealth of the Nation: Scotland, Culture and Independence* (Edinburgh University Press 2018) and *Muriel Spark, Existentialism and the Art of Death* (Edinburgh University Press, 2019).

Fiona Jardine teaches Design History & Theory in the School of Design, Glasgow School of Art. Her PhD research at the University of Wolverhampton focused on the materiality of artists' signatory practices. Her research is concerned with histories of production and promotion in Scottish textile industries and with life-writing through fashion. It takes form as exhibitions, films and drawings as well as essays and other written texts.

Carole Jones is Senior Lecturer in English and Scottish literature at the University of Edinburgh where she teaches twentieth-century and contemporary fiction. Her research is focused on representations of gender and sexuality in contemporary Scottish writing. She has published widely on the Scottish context including the monograph *Disappearing Men: Gender Disorientation in Scottish Fiction 1979–1999* (Brill, 2009).

Colin Kidd is Wardlaw Professor of Modern History at the University of St Andrews. He is the co-editor, with Gerard Carruthers, of both the *International Companion to John Galt* (Scottish Literature International, 2017) and *Literature and Union: Scottish Texts, British Contexts* (Oxford University Press, 2018). He has had a longstanding fascination with the Watergate scandal – Spark's subject matter in *The Abbess of Crewe* – since his boyhood in the 1970s.

Catriona M. M. Macdonald is Reader in Late Modern Scottish History at the University of Glasgow, a former editor of the *Scottish Historical Review* and the current president of the Scottish History Society. Her publications include *The Radical Thread* (Tuckwell, 2001) and *Whaur Extremes Meet* (John Donald, 2009). She is currently working on a major history of the evolution of Scottish historiography since 1832.

Colin McIlroy is Curator of Modern Literary Manuscripts at the National Library of Scotland. He completed his doctorate at the University of Glasgow in 2015, focusing on aspects of romanticism in the novels of Muriel Spark.

Willy Maley is Professor of English Literature at the University of Glasgow. He is author of *Muriel Spark for Starters* (Capercaillie, 2008), and co-editor, with Michael Gardiner, of *The Edinburgh Companion to Muriel Spark* (Edinburgh University Press, 2010).

Dini Power is a writer, artist and photographer based in Glasgow. She is a graduate of the University of Strathclyde, a former teacher of English, and has a particular interest in Scottish art and literature.

Ernest Schonfield is Lecturer in German at the University of Glasgow. His research is on German literature from 1800 to the present day, although he has also published essays on James Joyce and Edwin Morgan. His most recent book is *Business Rhetoric in German Novels: From Buddenbrooks to the Global Corporation* (Boydell & Brewer, 2018). He edits a website: **www.germanlit.org**.

Helen Stoddart is Senior Lecturer in Modern and Contemporary Literature in the School of Critical Studies at the University of Glasgow. She is the author of *Rings of Desire: Circus, History, Representation* (Manchester University Press, 2000) and *Angela Carter's Nights at the Circus* (Routledge, 2007) as well as a number of articles and book chapters on circus, film and contemporary literature.

Amy Woodbury Tease is Associate Professor of English at Norwich University in Vermont where she teaches courses on modernism, contemporary British fiction, world literatures, and film. Her current research explores the relationship between art, politics, and the rise of surveillance societies in the post-war period.

Susannah Thompson is an art historian, writer and art critic and Professor of Contemporary Art and Criticism and Head of Doctoral Studies at the Glasgow School of Art. Her research focuses on twentieth-century and contemporary art in Scotland, particularly the work of women artists, and on feminist approaches to art and visual culture. Forthcoming projects include essays and events related to the painter Joan Eardley, essays on the sculptor Edmonia Lewis and the artist and critic Cordelia Oliver, and a range of activities on the theme of Scotland and Surrealism.

Index

Abraham, Pearl, 8
Acker, Kathy, 27
Adorno, Theodor W., 175
Agamben, Giorgio, 196
   The Fire and the Tale, 201
Ahmed, Sara, 30, 31, 39
   The Promise of Happiness, 31
Allen, Jay Presson, 145, 284, xvii
Amis, Kingsley, 32, 228
Annan, Gabriele, 140
Arditti, Michael, 8
Aristotle, 196, 252
Atlee, Clement, 232
Atwood, Margaret, 59
Auden, W. H., xxvi
Austen, Jane, 52
Ayckbourn, Alan, 269
Bailey, James, 25
Bainbridge, Beryl, 8, 17
Baldwin, Stanley, 147
Banks, Lynne Reid, 51
Barrie, J. M., xvi, xxv, 103–14, 116, 119–123
   The Admirable Crichton, 116, 271
   The Little Minister, 116, 117–18
   The Little White Bird, 114–115
   Mary Rose, 103, 109, 112
   Peter Pan, xvi, xxv, 103, 105–07, 109–10
   Tommy and Grizel, 108, 119, 120
   Walker, London, 111–13
Barth, John, 32
Barthes, Roland, 201
Bauhaus, 223, 234
Beauvoir, Simone de, 64
Beckett, Samuel, 272
   Endgame, 266
   Waiting for Godot, 269
Bellow, Saul, 1–2, 17
Bennett, Arnold, 59
Bernstein, Carl, 128
Betjeman, John, 231
Bluemel, Kristin, 243
Bold, Alan, 146, 276
Boswell, James, xxii
Bourdieu, Pierre, 248–49
   Distinction: A Social Critique of the Judgement of Taste, 248
Braine, John, 176

Brecht, Bertolt, 251, 272
Brooke-Rose, Christine, 8
Brontë, Charlotte, 58, 67
Brontë, Emily, x, 67
Brown, George Mackay, 17
Burns, Robert, 146
Butler, Judith, 27, 40–41
Calvinism, xviii
Carter, Angela
   Wayward Girls and Wicked Woman, 26
Carruthers, Gerard, 49, 56, 65, 149, 214
Catholicism, ix, xv–xvi, xviii, xxiv, 13, 67, 77, 97, 109–10, 114, 118, 126, 134–35, 138–39, 140–41, 224, 238, 249
Cavallaro, Dani, 63, 65, 75
Cellini, Benvenuto, 194, 200
Cheyette, Brian, 32
Church-Gibson, Pamela, 79, 81
Codron, Michael, 264, 268–73, 277, 280–84
Compton-Burnett, Ivy, xvii, 247
Comyns, Barbara, 59
Cook, Peter, 270
Cooper, Giles, 269
Craig, Cairns, xix
Cripps, Stafford, Sir, 231
Dante, 199
Danto, Arthur
   The Transfiguration of the Commonplace, 233
Davis, Fred, 64
Delany, Paul, 58
Delmer, Sefton, 204
Dickens, Charles, 52
Doan, Laura, 52, 59
Drabble, Margaret, 51, 53
Dunant, Sarah, 59
Dundy, Elaine, 59
Edinburgh, xiii, xxii, 1, 14–15, 48, 65, 104, 144–51, 173, 205, 228, 237
   International Book Festival, 276
   Univeristy of, 112, 214
Eliot, George, 67
Eliot, T. S., xxvi, 3, 17, 183, 234
Fagan, Jenni, 28
The Festival of Britain, 223, 232
First World War, 104
Frank, Anne, 16
Frayn, Michael, 224–25

INDEX

Frazer, J. G.
  The Golden Bough, 117
Freud, Sigmund, 166, 252
Galloway, Janice, 25
Gardiner, Michael, 206
Gibb, Andrew Dewar, 148
Ginsberg, Allen, 91
Gissing, George, 58
Gorey, Edward, 214
Greene, Graham, xvii, xviii, 2, 6, 9, 17, 139, 206
Gregson, Ian, 25
Grieg, Edvard, 16
The Guardian, 127
Guinness, Alec, 17
Gun, Nell, 53
Gutkin, Len, 25
Halberstam, Jack (formerly Judith), 28, 32, 35, 38
Hall, Stuart, 29
Hamilton, Patrick, 44
Harrison, Tom, 241
Hartland, Beryl, 66
Harvey, Melinda, 45
Heller, Zoe, 52
Heppenstall, Rayner, 264
Herman, David, 32
Hodgkins, Hope Howell, 50, 54, 75, 227–28
Hoffman, Dustin, 75
Hogg, James, xvi, 146
Holden, Katherine, 44, 52
Holtby, Winifred, 58–59
Honeyman, Gail, 52
Hosmer, Robert E., xxvi, 16, 65
Hume, David, xxii, xxiii
Ibsen, Henrik, 270
Jack, R. D. S., 103
Jacob, Violet, 32
James, Henry, 16, 270
Jardine, Penelope, vii, 2, 14, 22, 85
Jenkins, Robin, xv
Jennings, Humphrey, 241
Johnson, Pamela Hansford, 8–9
Kemp, Jonathan, 25, 72
Kermode, Frank, xvi, 21, 69, 72, 206–07, 276
Kerouac, Jack, 91, 100
Kesson, Jessie, 28, 32
Khrushchev, Nikita, 132
Kipling, Rudyard, 53
Kissinger, Henry, 129, 132, 134–37
Klein, Bernat, 240
  An Eye for Colour, 225

Kolocotroni, Vassiliki, 74, 78–79, 209, 283
Lane, Harriet, 52
Lang, Theo
  Edinburgh and the Lothians, 147
Le Corbusier, 208, 210, 234–36
  Towards an Architecture, 207
Lee, Joori Joyce, 71
Legg, Stuart, 241
Lessing, Doris, 2, 17, 22, 54–55, 58–59
Little, Judy, 44, 52
Lodge, David, 139–40, 145, 155, 157
Loos, Adolf, 236–37
Lyon, David, 205, 209–10, 214, 219
  The Culture of Surveillance, 204
Lyons, Paddy, 251
MacDiarmid, Hugh, xv, xvi
Macdonald, Kate, 55
MacKay, Marina, 213
Mackay, Shena, 53
MacKendrick, Alexander
  The Man in the White Suit, 240
MacKenzie, Rachel, xvi, 162–63, 164, 166–67, 169–70, 172–74, 175
MacKintosh, Elizabeth, 55
Maclean, Alan, 99, 163
Macmillan, Harold, 17–18, 132
MacNeice, Louis, 233, 241
Madge, Charles, 241
Manning, Olivia, 53
Manzù, Giacomo, 4
Margolyes, Miriam, 18
Marvell, Andrew
  'His Coy Mistress', 89
Masefield, John, x, 17, 224
Massie, Allan, xxvii, 138, 241–242
Masson, David, 112
Maupin, Armistead, 54
Maxwell-Scott, Mairi, Lady, 148
Maxwell-Scott, Walter, Sir General, 148
McEwan, Geraldine, xvii
McFarlin Library, 3
McGovern, George, 130, 132–33
McLuhan, Marshall, 228
McQuillan, Martin, 25
Meaney, Gerardine, 33, 36
Messud, Claire, 52
Metafiction, 32, 86, 276
Modernism, 12, 32, 123, 207, 223–24, 227, 234–37, 257
Moore, Brian, 54

INDEX

Mortimer, John, 269
Moshfegh, Otessa, 52
Moten, Fred, 29–30, 34
Mowat, C. L.
   Britain Between the Wars, 146–147
Muir, Willa, 32
Mullholland, Terri, 47
Mulvey, Laura, 73
Muños, José Esteban, 29
Murata, Sayaka, 52
Murdoch, Iris, xvii, 2, 17–18, 264, 276
Nash, Andrew, 103
National Library of Scotland, 175
Newman, John Henry, Cardinal, xv, 12–13, 200
   Apologia Pro Vita Sua, xv, 12–13
The New Yorker, 140, 145, 161–62, 165–71, 173–76
Nicholson, Jack, 128
Nietzsche, Friedrich, 252
   The Birth of Tragedy, 108–109
Niven, Frances, 14, 103
Nixon, Richard, xxiv, 126–27, 129–33, 135–38, 140
Nouveau roman, ix, 32
Oates, Joyce Carol, 58
The Observer, 10, 12, 66, 97, 140, 223
O'Hagan, Andrew, 67, 72
Onassis, Jackie, 17
Orbach, Susie
   Fat is a Feminist Issue, 80–81
Orton, Joe, 269
Orwell, George, 54, 126, 139
   Animal Farm, 126, 139
Osborne, John, 272
Outposts, 88, 94, 97
Piette, Adam, 71
Pinter, Harold, 269–70
   The Birthday Party, 281
   The Caretaker, 264, 283
Pitchford, Nicola, 27
Platt, William, 53
Poetry Commonwealth, 94
Poetry Quarterly, 88, 93
Poetry Society, xi, 3, 11, 56, 96, 223, 255
   Poetry Review, xi, 11–12, 56, 89–90, 255, 257
Postmodernism, xix, 25, 32
Prolepsis, xiii, 15, 33
Proust, Marcel, 66, 183–184
Pym, Barbara, 44, 56, 59, 228
Raine, Kathleen, 241
Ramsay, Peggy, 264, 269–73, 281–84
Rankin, Ian, xxiv, 74, 79, 86

Ray, Philip E., 146
Read, Herbert, 231, 234, 236, 240–41
Redgrave, Vanessa, xvii, 17–18
Reizbaum, Marilyn, 25, 149, 157, 178
Rhys, Jean, 46
Rich, Kelly M., 208, 211–11, 217
Robbe-Grillet, Alain, 32
Roberts, Alasdair, 148
Roof, Judith, 33
Rossetti, Dante Gabriel, 16, 146
Rousseau, Jean-Jacques, 16
Royle, Trevor, 146–148
Ruskin, John, 234
Sackville-West, Vita, 59
Sage, Lorna, 140
Said, Edward, 107
Scott, Walter, Sir, 146
Second World War, xii–xiii, xvi, 35, 104–05, 108, 212, 216, 224, 228
Sellers, Susan, 37, 78
Sergeant, Howard, 88, 90, 92, 95–98, 99
Shakespeare, William, 112, 128, 170, 270
Shawn, William, 164, 174
Shelley, Mary, x, 83, 223, 234
   Frankenstein, x, 83, 226, 259
Shepherd, Nan, 28, 32
Sillitoe, Alan, 176
Simmel, Georg, 75–76
Smith, Ali, 28, 182, 191, 200
Smith, Dodie, 55
Smith, John, vii, 173, 282
Smith, Maggie, Dame, xvii, xxviii, 17–18, 22, 145
Smith, Stevie, 59
Spacks, Patricia Mayer, 140
Spark, Muriel, Dame
   The Abbess of Crewe, xxiv, 5, 48, 126–41, 187, 206
   Aiding and Abetting, 113–14, 138, 206
   'Anniversary', 88, 90–91, 93–95
   The Bachelors, xviii, 7, 103, 112, 267
   'The Ballad of the Fanfarlo', 101, 225
   The Ballad of Peckham Rye, xvi, xxviii, 8, 49, 119, 162, 240–42, 267
   'Bang-bang You're Dead', 48
   'The Black Madonna', xxviii, 229, 230–232, 234–38
   Child of Light, x, 223, 226
   The Comforters, x, xvi, xviii, 3, 7, 9, 45, 47, 50, 55, 97, 109, 110–13, 123, 162–63, 190–91, 193, 227, 258, 264

Spark, Muriel, Dame (*cont.*)
  'Created and Abandoned', 20
  Curriculum Vitae, xi, xii, 2, 4–5, 14, 16–17, 47, 63, 85, 88, 92, 95, 97, 103, 148, 160, 204–05, 242
  'The Curtain Blown by the Breeze', 48
  'Daisy Overend', 226, 232, 237–38, 245
  'The Desegregation of Art', 25, 40
  Doctors of Philosophy, xxi, 163, 264, 265, 269–84
  The Driver's Seat, xiv, xxiv, 15–17, 26, 29–30, 32–36, 48, 53, 63, 72–75, 187–188, 192–93, 202, 208–10, 217, 238–39
  The Dry River Bed, 264, 266, 268
  Emily Brontë: Her Life and Work, x
  'The Executor', 1, 17, 20–21
  A Far Cry From Kensington, xi, xii, 9, 47, 49, 51, 53, 56, 63, 80–83, 89, 247–60
  The Finishing School, 4, 9, 14, 48, 206, 262
  'The First Year of My Life', 204–05
  'Flower into Animal', 99
  The French Window, 207, 213–18
  The Girls of Slender Means, xiii, xxiii, 18, 47–49, 51, 56–57, 63, 65, 68–71, 75, 81, 206–08, 210–13, 216–17, 221, 247
  'Going Up to Sotheby's', 20
  The Golden Fleece: Essays, 4
  'Harper and Wilton', 20
  The Hothouse by the East River, xvi, xx, xxv, 26, 29, 32, 35–37, 39, 103–04, 105–06, 108, 114, 206–07, 212–13, 217–18, 228
  The Interview, 264–65, 268
  'A Letter to Howard', 88, 93
  'Like Africa', 88, 93
  Loitering with Intent, xi, 3, 5, 9, 19–20, 47, 50–52, 54, 56–57, 89, 97–99, 138, 191, 193–200, 223, 237, 247, 252
  'Lost Lover', 88, 94, 96
  'Love', 98
  The Mandelbaum Gate, xiv, 9, 89
  Memento Mori, xviii, xxviii, 9, 48–49, 162, 206, 267
  'Miss Pinkerton's Apocalypse', 225–26
  My Best Mary: Selected Letters of Mary Shelley, 226
  Not to Disturb, x, xix, xxv, 15, 48, 181–88, 191, 194, 197
  'Omen', 219
  The Only Problem, 188–189
  'Open to the Public', 20–21
  The Party Through the Wall, 264–65
  'The Portobello Road', 169
  The Prime of Miss Jean Brodie, x, xiii, xvi–xvii, xxi, 3, 15, 17–18, 47, 50, 55–56, 63, 65, 74–77, 117, 119, 122, 144–59, 161–62, 166–72, 174–76, 188, 202, 206, 228, 232, 233, 237–38, 267, 284
  The Public Image, xx, 26, 29, 32, 37–39, 40, 63, 77–80, 82
  Reality and Dreams, 48
  'The Religion of an Agnostic', 183
  Robinson, 267, 114–16, 180–81
  'The Rout', 225
  'She Wore his Luck on Her Breast', 88, 94
  The Small Telephone, 214–15
  'Song of the Divided Lover', 94
  'Standing in Dusk', 92
  Symposium, xvi, 116, 119
  The Takeover, 117–18, 127
  Territorial Rights, 206
  A Tribute to Wordsworth, 234
  The Very Fine Clock, xviii, 214–15
  'The Voice of One Lost Sings Its Gain', 98
  'What Images Return', 26
  'You Should Have Seen the Mess', 232, 236–37
Spark, Robin, 11
Sproxton, Judy, xxiii
Stanford, Derek, x–xi, 9, 11, 84–85, 88, 90, 99, 101, 226, 232, 257
Stannard, Martin, x–xi, 52, 56, 66, 90, 251
  Muriel Spark: the Biography, 66, 90, 93–94, 96, 99, 163, 183, 187, 214, 224, 270
Stevenson, Randall, 276, 152
Stevenson, Robert Louis, 145–46
Stewart, Victoria, 213
Stopes, Marie, xi, xxii, 11, 17
Stoppard, Tom, 269
Storey, David, 176
Strachan, Zoë, 25
Swift, Jonathan, 126
  Gulliver's Travels, 126, 140
Taylor, Alan, 10, 57, 66
Taylor, Mary, 58
Tennant, Emma, 141
Tey, Josephine, 44, 55
Thomas, Dylan, x
Townsend, Sylvia, 58
Turner, Jenny, 50, 56
Updike, John, vii, 17, 50, 137, 140, 161–62, 164–65, 171, 173–75, 178
Variegation, 19, 91–92, 100

Vidal, Gore, 17
Vogue, 66, 69, 70, 228
Voltaire
   Candide, 134
Walker, Michael, 73
Waugh, Evelyn, vii, xvii, 6–7, 17, 139, 141, 242
   Brideshead Revisited, 250
Waugh, Patricia, 25, 221
Warwick, Alexandra, 63, 65, 75

The Washington Post, 128
Watergate, xxiv, 5, 126–33, 135–41, 206
Wesker, Arnold, 272
Whittaker, Ruth, 137
   The Faith and Fiction of Muriel Spark, xix
Wilde, Oscar, xii, 279
Wilson, Angus, xvii, 1, 32
Woolf, Virginia
   'A Room of One's Own', 45–46

www.ingramcontent.com/pod-product-compliance
Lightning Source LLC
Chambersburg PA
CBHW052052230426
43671CB00011B/1877